INTERNATIONAL ECONOMIC LAW SERIES

General Editor: John H. Jackson

THE FUTURE OF INTERNATIONAL ECONOMIC LAW

The Future of International Economic Law

Edited by
WILLIAM J. DAVEY
and
JOHN JACKSON

OXFORD
UNIVERSITY PRESS

OXFORD
UNIVERSITY PRESS

Great Clarendon Street, Oxford OX2 6DP

Oxford University Press is a department of the University of Oxford.
It furthers the University's objective of excellence in research, scholarship,
and education by publishing worldwide in

Oxford New York

Auckland Cape Town Dar es Salaam Hong Kong Karachi
Kuala Lumpur Madrid Melbourne Mexico City Nairobi
New Delhi Shanghai Taipei Toronto

With offices in

Argentina Austria Brazil Chile Czech Republic France Greece
Guatemala Hungary Italy Japan Poland Portugal Singapore
South Korea Switzerland Thailand Turkey Ukraine Vietnam

Oxford is a registered trade mark of Oxford University Press
in the UK and in certain other countries

Published in the United States
by Oxford University Press Inc., New York

First published 2008

British Library Cataloguing in Publication Data
Data available

Library of Congress Cataloging in Publication Data
Data available

Typeset by Newgen Imaging Systems (P) Ltd., Chennai, India
Printed in Great Britain
on acid-free paper by
Ashford Colour Press Ltd, Gosport, Hampshire

ISBN 978-0-19-955113-2

1 3 5 7 9 10 8 6 4 2

General Editor's Preface

When the editors of the Journal of International Economic Law (JIEL) began working on the volume for the year 2007, we realized that this would be the tenth volume of the JIEL, and consequently deserved some special attention. After various consultations, the editors agreed that it would be interesting and appropriate to devote one issue of volume ten to a set of essays which would be 'forward-looking' concerning the very broad subject matter of international economic law. Consequently it was decided to devote the third issue of volume ten to a set of essays relating to the title selected for this book, namely, *The Future of International Economic Law*, understanding that so broad a title would enable authors maximum scope for their creative efforts to produce relatively short but very penetratingly worthwhile manuscripts. As Editor-in-Chief of JIEL, I asked one of our associate editors, Professor William Davey, to be the special editor for this issue, based on planning that he and others of the Board worked out. We invited a number of authors, many (but not all) of whom are JIEL editors, to choose a subject and agree to undertake a contribution to this project.

Much credit must go not only to the authors who have produced this group of essays, but also to Professor Davey, who coordinated and oversaw the work, and Ms Michelle Grando, who is the current editorial assistant for the JIEL, whose work has been outstanding throughout her two-year tenure in that position. These two worked closely together, with some input from other editors including myself, to assure that the manuscripts were handled in a timely manner and the issue was produced correctly.

The result, we believe, is a spectacular issue, which has gained much praise. In fact, the result was impressive enough for us to put forward to Oxford University Press the idea of also publishing this issue as a separate book to provide a wider audience for this remarkable group of essays at a time of considerable world difficulty concerning the subject matter. As the outstanding introductory chapter to the volume by Professor Davey demonstrates, the book presents the insights and reflected experience of an impressive list of distinguished scholars, covering fifteen specific approaches and subjects designed to assist readers to think deeply about a number of fundamental questions which are interlaced into world economic activities. Oxford University Press undertook the usual peer review, which resulted in considerable praise for the substance and form of the volume, particularly noting the advantage of having a volume moderately priced to maximize potential use for classroom and other academic purposes.

The editors of JIEL, including those who are not represented in the list of essays for this book, invite readers to take advantage of this effort, and hope that such readers will agree with our judgements reflected in the paragraphs above.

JOHN H. JACKSON
Editor-in-Chief
Journal of International Economic Law

Contents

THE FUTURE OF INTERNATIONAL ECONOMIC LAW

William J. Davey

In celebration of the tenth anniversary of the *Journal*, the Editors felt that it would be particularly useful and interesting to request members of our Editorial Board to contemplate the future of international economic law. Thus, this third issue of Volume 10 contains a wide-ranging discussion of key issues facing the international economic system in the coming years.

As one contemplates the current scene in international economic relations, there seems to be one over-arching concern that is repeatedly stressed: Are the institutions now in place—and I refer, in particular, to the International Monetary Fund (Fund), the World Bank (Bank), and the World Trade Organization (WTO)—suitable for the 21st century? Certainly, the three institutions have been going through a trying period. The Fund's borrowers have been paying off their loans at a rate such that it cannot currently support itself on the profits of its lending activities. The Bank has recently been in turmoil over its leadership and alleged conflicts of interest at the very top, a particular embarrassment in light of its recent emphasis on rooting out corruption in developing country governments. The WTO's first wide-ranging negotiation—the Doha Development Agenda—was launched only with great difficulty (recall the protests at its failed Seattle ministerial meeting) and little has been accomplished in six years of formal negotiations, despite regular upbeat appraisals emanating from the Secretariat and periodic reports that the four key players (Brazil, the EU, India, and the US) are about to make unspecified progress in bridging their differences over agriculture and market access issues. As this issue goes to press in late June, optimism seems to be in short supply.

Some of the questions raised about these organizations go to the very essence of their existence. For example, are they still needed? As noted above, the Fund seems to be running out of borrowers and alternative official sources of assistance seem to be coming into existence. Even if the institutions are still needed, questions have been raised as to whether they now focus their main efforts on the appropriate activities. Should the Bank, for example, give greater emphasis to concessional lending or outright grants? In the case of each of the institutions, there are difficult and controversial issues involved in integrating the developing world, and particularly such major and fast-growing countries as Brazil, China, India, and Russia, into the governance of the institutions.

The importance of these fundamental issues is reflected in the papers included in this issue. Indeed, the first six papers focus in particular on these issues. In the first paper, Hector Torres analyzes what the Fund must do to regain its legitimacy *vis à vis* its developing country membership. That is followed by Frank Garcia's paper, in which he relies on the thinking of philosopher John Rawls to establish a framework that allows one to analyze whether the activities of the Fund and the Bank are appropriate—in particular in light of the interests of the developing countries and the least developed among them. The following four articles deal specifically with the WTO. Debra Steger notes that the culture of the WTO stems from that of GATT and catalogs a number of problems that it now faces that require changes. She reviews in that regard several proposals for reform—from Russian President Putin's recent call for a new international trade organization to the more detailed analyses on reform contained in the WTO's Sutherland Report and the Atlantic Council's report on transatlantic leadership in the new global economy. In his paper, Thomas Cottier comprehensively sets out a list of the structural issues now facing the WTO and suggests the creation of new fora for consideration of those issues. In particular, he suggests the creation of (i) a consultative committee on structural reform that would consider questions referred to it by the WTO organs and would have non-governmental members (especially from academia) as well as governmental members and (ii) a new standing committee on legal affairs. Dan Esty's paper lays out a framework for assessing good governance in the WTO. He reviews what the critical elements of good governance are, how the WTO rates in respect of those elements and considers what could be done to improve good governance at the WTO. Ernst-Ulrich Petersmann rounds out this group of papers by examining what he characterizes as 'judicial governance'. In his view, international economic law has increasingly recognized the role of such judicial governance in providing citizens with judicial remedies at various levels for defending their rights and interests as participants in international trade. This trend is one that he argues should be encouraged. All in all, these six papers offer a comprehensive overview of the institutional issues facing the international economic institutions.

The next six papers focus on current problems facing the WTO, which for the most part have arisen in the Doha negotiations or as a result of the limited progress that has been made in those negotiations. The first paper—by Seung-Wha Chang—grapples with the difficult issue of special and differential treatment. The Doha negotiations have been billed from the beginning as a 'development round'. Yet, given the diverse needs and attributes of developing countries, it may be necessary to re-think how special and differential treatment should be incorporated into WTO agreements. Chang reviews the possible alternatives. As the Doha negotiations have faltered, there seems to be increased interest in bilateral or plurilateral preferential trade agreements, even in those areas of the world where they have not been so common in the past (e.g. East Asia). Two papers consider this trend. Fred Abbott's paper suggests that PTAs have become the primary focus of trade negotiators. He finds the way in which the United States and the European Union are able to impose their views on their weaker negotiating partners to be troubling. While he does not find PTAs to be all that threatening to the WTO multilateral system for the time being, he notes that the situation bears watching. Matthew Schaefer argues that perhaps the most effective way to ensure that these new agreements comply with WTO rules is for the United States (and perhaps others) to use their negotiating leverage to promote such compliance—in particular in the areas where compliance with WTO rules is often problematic: coverage of agricultural products, rules of origin and trade remedies. Gary Hufbauer and Sherry Stephenson examine trade in services and how successful the WTO has been to date in liberalizing such trade—both through the commitments undertaken in GATS and in dispute settlement. They also examine the record on services trade liberalization in regional agreements, as well as the difficulties that have been encountered in the ongoing Doha negotiations on services. They also note the relative successes in services liberalization that have been achieved in PTAs.

One of the more controversial types of cases faced by the WTO dispute settlement system is that where the discretion of a member government to regulate within its borders is challenged. Joel Trachtman explores this question by examining three particularly controversial cases—*Helms Burton, Shrimp* and *Gambling*—as background for examining theoretical bases for allocating regulatory jurisdiction in the WTO. In WTO dispute settlement, one of the vexing questions concerns remedies. Currently, the basic remedy is the possibility of 'retaliation' by the prevailing party if the defaulting party fails to conform to WTO rules. Whether this is the best remedy, or even an effective remedy or usable at all by smaller WTO members are some of the issues that will have to be addressed in the long run. Andrew Green and Michael Trebilcock explore this issue in the context of considering what is the best remedy for a violation of WTO export subsidy rules. While their analysis focuses on that narrow question, their approach and discussion is of great interest to the more general issue as well, since it lays out a framework for systematically considering the remedy issue.

The third group of papers include three that explore issues that are treated to some limited degree in WTO agreements, but which are generally dealt with by other international organizations or agreements. First, Steve Charnovitz reviews the WTO's experience in dealing with environmental issues, particularly in dispute settlement where the WTO Appellate Body has played a major role in reshaping the perceived relationships between

WTO rules and member government discretion to act to protect environmental interests. The last two papers deal with issues that were tentatively agreed to be the subject of negotiations in the Doha talks, but which were ultimately not included because of developing country opposition. In respect of competition rules, David Gerber takes a skeptical view of whether the WTO is an appropriate locus for such rules in the near term, citing both the WTO's institutional shortcomings and the difficult substantive question of exactly what might be the basis for agreeing on such rules in light of the diverse approaches taken by various countries for their internal markets. Finally, Won-Mog Choi explores the world of individual-state dispute settlement under investment agreements and what that experience suggests for the WTO.

While not every issue facing the WTO and the international economic regime more generally has been treated in this anniversary issue, these 15 papers cover most of the key issues. Of particular note is the concern raised in many of the papers over institutional issues and questions of legitimacy. Certainly that is one area where the international economic organizations and the WTO in particular will have to devote considerable attention in the coming years.

REFORMING THE INTERNATIONAL MONETARY FUND—WHY ITS LEGITIMACY IS AT STAKE

*Hector R. Torres**

ABSTRACT

The International Monetary Fund was designed to promote international monetary cooperation and foreign exchange stability, so as to facilitate international trade, high levels of employment and real income, and the development of the productive resources of all its members. However, the Fund's capacity to influence its key members' policies through its advice, and to give confidence to potential borrowers by offering opportune and meaningful financial assistance in case of trouble, has been seriously put into question. Its governance structure is inconsistent with its multilateral nature and is dysfunctional to its purposes. There is also an ideological bias in its policy advice that prevents the Fund from being responsive to citizens' concerns and challenges posed by globalization. The ongoing reform process is tinkering on the margins and if not redressed will fail to bring additional credibility and effectiveness to the Fund.

INTRODUCTION

The International Monetary Fund ('the Fund' or 'the IMF') serves its purposes by exercising surveillance on its members' economies, giving them policy advice and if necessary assisting those facing balance of payment (BoP) problems with short-term 'lending'.[1]

* Alternate Executive Director at the International Monetary Fund, Washington, D.C. 20431, USA. Opinions are those of the author (E-mail: htorres@imf.org). The author is indebted to María Flores-Isch and Luan Aggersberg for their support and patience.

[1] The Fund does not technically or legally 'lend' money to its members, although its financial support is normally described as such. The borrower 'purchases' reserve assets from the Fund with its own currency and the repayment is made by 'repurchasing' its currency from the Fund at a determined exchange rate. As this financial support from the Fund is not technically nor legally a loan, this could have relevance if the Fund's preferred creditor status is legally challenged (as it was) by other 'creditors' to a sovereign in arrears, claiming *pari-passu* treatment. For further understanding of the Fund's financing mechanism, please consult IMF General Department http://www.imf.org/external/pubs/ft/pam/pam45/pdf/chap2.pdf (visited 5 May 2007).

However, the Fund has lost its effectiveness. Its capacity to influence its key members' policies through its advice, and to 'give confidence'[2] to potential borrowers by offering opportune and meaningful financial assistance in case of trouble, has been seriously put into question. On the one hand, 'global imbalances'[3] indicate that the Fund has not been capable of persuading large members to follow its policy advice; whereas on the other hand, more and more emerging economies (precisely those that face higher capital volatility and that are therefore the Fund's potential borrowers), rather than relying on the Fund's 'multilateral insurance', prefer to self-insure by accumulating massive amounts of foreign reserves.[4] This is a costly option[5] which, among other causes, is explained by their lack of confidence in the capacity of the Fund to assist them financially. Moreover, many of these countries are also pooling their reserves in regional agreements[6] that may end side-lining the Fund.[7]

This is, in short, what we could categorize as the 'effectiveness deficit' of the Fund, which is in turn compounded and interlinked with a

[2] IMF, Article I (v) of the 'Articles of Agreement'.

[3] The US is running a current account deficit of approximately 6% of its national income (i.e. it spends far more than it saves). This requires a massive annual lending to the US, much of it coming from developing countries that run current account surpluses (i.e. save more than they spend) and who, rather than using these savings to invest in their own development, buy financial assets mostly valued in US dollars. This massive transfer of capital from the poor to the rich raises the fear of a correction that could, in turn, require raising US dollar interest rates and which could result in economic recession.

[4] Martin, Redrado et al, find that in the past ten years there has been 'an explosive growth at global level of international reserves' mainly driven by emerging economies and estimate the current level of reserves at 'a record (...) of 3.8 trillion dollars', Central Bank of Argentina, 'The Economic Policy of Foreign Reserve Accumulation: New International Evidence', Working Paper 2006/13 (September 2006), at 5.

[5] Setting aside reserves that normally give a very low return has a clear opportunity cost as savings could be better used to serve development needs. Joseph Stiglitz estimates the cost to developing countries is in excess of US$ 300 billion per year. Joseph Stiglitz, *Making Globalization Work*, (1st edn, New York: W.W. Norton & Company, Inc., 2006) 249.

[6] The most challenging for the Fund is the Chiang Main Initiative, which includes all ASEAN countries (Brunei, Cambodia, Indonesia, Laos, Malaysia, Myanmar, the Philippines, Singapore, Thailand and Vietnam) plus China, Japan and Korea. It was launched in the aftermath of the Asian Crisis, and the volume of reserves accumulated by its most important members (2201 USD billions, circa) could enable them to turn it into an Asian Monetary Fund. Latin America also has a regional Fund, the FLAR (*Fondo Latino Americano de Reservas*); albeit so far much smaller and limited to a subset of Latin American countries (Bolivia, Colombia, Costa Rica, Ecuador, Peru and Venezuela). The appeal of these pooling arrangements appears to be related to governments' dissatisfaction with Fund lending decisions and the burden of conditionality.

[7] Mervin King, Governor of the Bank of England, argues that '[...] the growth of private capital flows *and the build-up of massive foreign exchange reserves by many Asian economies* have made redundant the idea that the primary function of the Fund is to be an international lender of last resort' (emphasis added). Mervin King, 'Reform of the International Monetary Fund' (speech delivered at the Indian Council for Research on International Economic Relations, New Delhi, 20 February 2006).

second deficit, one that has to do with failures in its governance structure, a 'legitimacy deficit'.

As I will argue, the Fund's governance structure, beyond considerations of fairness, is dysfunctional to the Fund's purposes of ensuring financial and monetary stability, by providing uncompromised policy advice and by offering short-term financing to countries facing BoP problems.

One of the key problems is 'quota' distribution among members. 'Quotas' to the Fund, namely contributions made by members, determine their capacity to participate in the Fund's decision-making process, and borrow from the Fund's resources. However, quotas are distributed according to an obscure method that gives wealthier members the right to contribute more capital to the Fund. This grants them more votes (and, therefore, more capacity to condition the Fund's policy advice) and, ironically, also more capacity to borrow from the Fund. As a consequence, advanced economies (i.e. those with no need to borrow from the Fund) have more access to its resources and virtually run the institution.

On the other hand, developing countries, i.e. potential borrowers, have little influence and relatively low (and expensive, as we will see) access to the Fund's resources. Not surprisingly, they feel sidelined from its decision-making process and have little or no ownership of the Fund policies (the legitimacy deficit).

These two 'deficits' are interlinked in a vicious circle as ultimately '[t]he Fund's credibility depends on its perceived legitimacy as an international organization representative of its members and [its] effectiveness suffers if countries of growing economic importance are not adequately represented'.[8]

In this article, I will focus on the Fund's 'legitimacy deficit' and suggest possible solutions that could help recover the Fund's credibility as a truly multilateral institution.[9]

I. THE EGALITARIAN FOSSIL

In every decision-making process there is tension between formal power and real power. Whereas formal power normally reflects, in some way or another, the egalitarian paradigm, real power reflects the fact that actual equality is only an idealization but hardly ever a reality in itself. Citizens are all equal in rights and obligations but do not have equal skills, assets or opportunities.

In other international organizations, such as the World Trade Organization (WTO), this tension is somehow resolved by using consensus to make decisions. All countries are deemed to be equal and, theoretically, any one of

[8] Rodrigo de Rato y Figaredo, Managing Director of the IMF, Remarks at the Banco de Mexico, Mexico city, 'The IMF's Medium-Term Strategy: Meeting the needs of emerging market members' (23 March 2006).

[9] Joseph Stiglitz prefers to categorize this as a 'democratic deficit' that has contributed to the Fund's 'lack of legitimacy, which has undermined [its] efficacy'. Above, n 5, at 19.

them could block consensus if strongly determined. However, countries with small markets can only actually do it if they join together in significant numbers. Consensus may be disappointingly slow but arguably it is a good compromise between a paradigm (every country is equal in rights and obligations) and a reality (only big markets count for trade concessions).

The Fund's decision-making process gives prominence (almost absolute prominence) to 'real power' and even this – the calculation of 'real power' – is obscure and deficient. The egalitarian paradigm found some place in the original design of the Fund when 'basic votes' were distributed to all members regardless of their quotas.[10] In 1944, basic votes represented 11.3% of the aggregate voting power. Now they only represent 2.1%. Why? Because quotas have expanded significantly over the decades in the context of general and ad hoc quota increases (e.g. due to the addition of new members),[11] but basic votes remained unchanged[12].

In sum, at the Fund, the egalitarian paradigm is no more than a fossil; votes are distributed according to quotas and quotas are meant to reflect wealth. G7 countries[13] alone have 41.72% of votes[14] and advanced economies (28 countries which represent somewhat less than 14% of world population[15]) hold over 61% of the voting power both at the Fund and at the World Bank. Not surprisingly, decisions are made quite expeditiously (*vis-à-vis* a consensual decision-making process).

Ironically, the Fund is keen to say that its decisions are mostly taken by consensus. This is because the Executive Board rarely votes; however, not voting and taking the trouble to build up consensus are quite different things. In lieu of taking a formal vote, the Chair of the Executive Board, either the Managing Director or one of his deputies, is responsible for identifying the 'sense of the meeting', which in plain language is to ascertain whether there would be a qualified majority of votes if there were to be a vote on the issue under consideration.

Putting it in a nutshell, members buy their votes and rich countries run the Fund. Ruthless as it may sound; what is wrong with this? The Fund is borrowing money from the rich and lending it to the poor. Is it not then just

[10] Article XII, Section 5(a) of the Articles of Agreement states: 'Each member shall have two-hundred fifty votes plus one additional vote for each part of its quota equivalent to one hundred thousand special drawing rights'. This article was never amended.

[11] Quotas were increased approximately 37-fold.

[12] The basic votes for original members represent 0.5% of current total aggregate voting power. The 2.1 percent figure includes basic votes allocated to members that were incorporated after 1944.

[13] Canada, France, Germany, Italy, Japan, United Kingdom and the United States.

[14] This does not include the aggregate voting power of the constituencies led by Canada and Italy.

[15] USA, Japan, Germany, UK, France, Italy, Canada, Netherlands, Belgium, Switzerland, Australia, Spain, Sweden, Austria, Norway, Denmark, Finland, New Zealand, Portugal, Singapore, Ireland, Greece, Luxembourg, Iceland, San Marino, Israel, Korea and Cyprus (ordered according to voting power).

logical that the rich should have a major saying in determining when, where and how to lend it? The answer is not as simple as it may appear.

II. VOTES FOR MONEY: IS THIS A GOOD IDEA?

Perhaps before answering this question I should clarify that potential borrowers cannot chose to integrate more capital into the Fund. Countries are allotted with certain quotas and cannot unilaterally decide to integrate more money into the Fund in order to be able to count on a larger access to financing in case of need.

I turn now to the question of whether it makes sense to let the wealthy run the Fund. The short answer is 'no', and I will offer five reasons why.

First, because even if it made sense to allocate quotas exclusively according to relative wealth, this would be shortly outdated without a mechanism to revise and adjust quotas to changes in relative weight in the global economy. There is no such mechanism and as a consequence 'it is not even today's dollars that count'.[16]

The Fund's quotas are calculated in an obscure way using five formulas that are almost impossible for the average person to understand, including policy makers.[17] They are far from reflecting the relative economic importance of members in the world economy, let alone their potential need to borrow.[18] A few examples may help to illustrate this; the Netherlands's quota is only 36% smaller than China's; India's is smaller than Belgium's; Switzerland's quota is bigger than Brazil's and Austria's is bigger than Nigeria's. Moreover, when quotas were allotted to original members they were not established to reflect relative weight in the global economy but predetermined political objectives.[19] The same thing happened for acceding members.[20]

[16] Joseph Stiglitz, above, n 5, at 12.

[17] The quotas are calculated using five different formulas. The original Bretton Woods formula was supplemented with four additional formulas and the calculated quota of a member is the higher of the Bretton Woods calculation and the average of the lowest two of the remaining four calculations. All formulas use four variables: GDP at current market prices, Reserves [foreign exchange, special drawing rights (SDRs) and gold], Openness (of current account) and Variability (of current receipts).

[18] Abbas Mirakhor and Zaidi Iqbal, walk us along the labyrinth of how quotas are calculated and what variables are used; see IMF, 'Rethinking the Governance of the International Monetary Fund', IMF, Working Paper, WP/06/273 (December 2006).

[19] This was explicitly recognized in his memories by Raymond Mikesell, the economist from the US Treasury to whom Mr White (then Secretary of the Treasury) instructed to prepare a formula that would give the US a quota twice as big as that of the UK, a bit more than twice that of the USSR, and more than a bit more than twice that of China. See Mikesell R., 'The Bretton Woods Debates: a Memoir', Essays in International Finance, Department of Economics, Princeton University Intl Economics, N.192 (March 1994).

[20] Germany and Japan were allotted closely similar quotas despite that Japan's economy was much bigger.

Second, the Fund has a regulatory capacity as its money comes together with conditionality. When the Fund lends money, it ties this financial support to conditions that, more often than not, have effects on income distribution for the borrower's population.[21] When a country gets into financial trouble it may call on the Fund; the Fund then evaluates its needs and 'negotiates' (actually lays down) a set of conditions[22] (purportedly) meant to help the country regain access to voluntary private financing, which ultimately ensures that the Fund will be repaid. These conditions go from macroeconomic objectives (e.g. limiting the size of the fiscal deficit or setting a target for reserves) to structural reforms (e.g. requiring changes to taxes, tariffs and the privatization of state-owned enterprises or reforms in labour rights). In the 80s, as the Fund stopped lending to industrial countries, structural conditionality stepped up[23] and with it the fear that requiring financial support from the Fund comes at the cost of accepting intrusive conditions 'possibly motivated by the ideology of powerful members or their need to secure a political or competitive advantage'.[24]

In democracies, citizens have a legitimate expectation to participate in decisions that have direct consequences on their incomes and assets. But at the Fund, their only voice is that of the Executive Director who supposedly represents their interests. However, if you happen to be a citizen living in a developing country 'your' Executive Director (beyond not having been elected and not being accountable), normally has very little capacity to influence decisions at the Board. Naturally, conditionality is normally perceived as sympathetic to the interests in the borrowing country's economy of those Fund members with bigger quotas and, not surprisingly, there is a high degree of resistance to comply with conditionality.[25] As Joseph Stiglitz accurately notes, conditionality undermines confidence in democracy and breeds radical political opposition as '[t]he electorate sees its government

[21] Joseph P. Joyce, 'The adoption, implementation of IMF programs: A review of the issues and evidence', Wellesley College, Department of Economics (December 2003), at 12, '[...] Fund programs [have] important distributional effects that depend on a country's pre-income situation, with negative consequences for countries in the worst circumstances'.

[22] Theoretically, it is the authorities' responsibility to lead the process of designing a program and therefore choose which conditionality should be included in it (see IMF, 'Operational Guidance on the 2002 Conditionality Guidelines'; revised 9 January 2006 - SM/06/14). Unfortunately, things are quite the opposite, as the Fund uses its financial leverage to virtually impose the conditions to which the financial support is contingent [see Ariel Buira, 'An Analysis of IMF Conditionality', Challenges to the World Bank and IMF, Buira (ed.) for the G24 Research Program (Washington: Anthem Press, 2003)].

[23] At the peak of abusive use of financial leverage, Indonesia had to accept 140 conditions in its program with the Fund in 1998.

[24] Raghuram Rajan, Economic Counselor and Director of Research at the Fund, 'The IMF in A Changing World', keynote address at the International Conference on Global Asset Allocation at the Arison School of business in Israel (17 May 2006).

[25] Joseph P. Joyce quotes studies that indicate that only 47% of the programs were successfully complied with, Above, n 21, at 7.

bending before foreigners or giving into international institutions that it believes to be run by the United States'.[26]

Conditionality is included in the 'Letters of Intent'[27] signed by finance ministers of borrowing countries. Beyond requiring action from the executive branch of the government, it frequently requires the approval of legislation by a certain date[28] and sometimes even rulings by courts![29] It is no wonder then why the Fund is so unpopular and why self-insurance (despite its economic cost) makes so much political sense.

Third, members are legally obliged to collaborate with the Fund (and other members) 'to assure orderly exchange arrangements and to promote a stable system of exchange rates'.[30] Consequently the Fund, as part of its regulatory capacity, exercises surveillance on members' economies, monitoring compliance with obligations contained in the Articles of Agreement and provides them with policy advice.

This oversight function came into being in 1978 when the present Article IV of the IMF's Articles of Agreement was adopted. The Fund's initial 'surveillance' responsibility was rather simple, limited to safeguard the Bretton Woods system of fixed exchange rates. When this system collapsed, the Fund had to find 'new means [...] to insure against the risk that countries might run their policies in blind pursuit of their own short-term interests',[31] disregarding the effects this could have on global welfare. The Fund was then entrusted with its more complex and discretional current surveillance function but, alas, the additional discretion needed to discharge its regulatory function did not entail any adjustment to its governance structure. Indeed, the distribution of votes remained linked to the logic of its 'lending function' (the more contributions to the multilateral pooling of reserves, the more capacity to condition its decision-making process).

As a consequence, 'creditor' countries, namely those whose domestic policies can potentially have more damaging consequences on its neighbours, are those with greater capacity to condition the Fund's oversight function

[26] Above, n 5, at 12.

[27] Governments have to sign 'Letters of Intent' before borrowing from the Fund. Ironically, when the Board reviews compliance with the conditionality there included, the government's 'intent' is read as commitment to deliver.

[28] Joseph P. Joyce quotes studies that, not surprisingly, indicate that '[d]emocracies with fractionalized legislatures perform poorly in IMF programs and are more likely to be sanctioned'. Above, n 21, *at* 10.

[29] In its latest program with Argentina, the Fund wanted the Supreme Court to stop '*amparos*' against banks (legal actions of depositors requesting banks to return their assets in US dollars). The government refused to accept this condition. For further information, Hector Torres, '*Argentina and the IMF: Learning Lessons from our Experience*', Initiative for Policy Dialogue, Columbia University, New York (December 2005) (visited 5 May 2007)

[30] Article IV, Section 1 of the 'Articles of Agreement'.

[31] IMF, The Framework for IMF Surveillance: Enhancing the Effectiveness of Surveillance in a Globalized World, background document prepared by Fund Staff for a 'Dialogue with High-Level Officials', Santiago de Chile (11 December 2006).

(despite their lip-service to the 'independence' of staff). In any event, if the staff's criticism ever gets too candid, they can always use the Board to water-down the public communiqués that normally follow the Fund's Article IV consultations.

Beyond this, members that issue currencies of international reserve or those that have accumulated massive amounts of them (e.g. China), feel insulated from the Fund's criticism, normally politely worded, conveniently encrypted or reduced to its minimal possible expression.[32] Developing countries do not have this advantage, as the Fund's seal of approval counts in volatile economies. If the Fund gives a low mark to a developing country's government, this would normally entail more basic points of interest payments when borrowing from the markets, which in turn means either more taxes or less money for the government to distribute, or most likely both.[33] In short, the governance structure pushes the Fund to exercise pressure where it can and not where it should.

The fourth reason why it makes very little sense to allot higher quotas, and, therefore, higher access to the Fund resources to wealthy countries is that they do not need to borrow from the Fund. Advanced economies are able to borrow on their own currency and with little or no premium for default or exchange risk. The last instances where the Fund had to provide financial support to a developed country were in 1977 (to Italy and the UK), and in 1978 (to Spain).

However, as quotas are used to calculate access to Fund resources (and of course also votes), the result is that those countries that are less likely to need the Fund's support are those with more access to its credit (and more capacity to shape conditionality imposed on others to their national interests), whereas the potential borrowers see their access limited to a percentage of their meagre quotas.

This forces developing countries in need of financial support to apply for 'exceptional' access, namely to borrow beyond the established annual limit of 100% of quota or beyond a cumulative limit of 300% of their quota.[34]

[32] There was only one paragraph, out of 54, addressing the Common Agricultural Policy in the 2005 report on the EU economy.

[33] At this point, it is worth making a digression. In delivering a positive or a negative signalling with its seal of approval, the Fund's responsibility goes beyond markets. As countries are obliged to provide information to the Fund and hold regular consultations with its staff, the Fund has an informational advantage. Naturally, common citizens give credibility to its approval or disapproval seal. This was evident during the 90s in Argentina when the country was 'touted as a model for other developing countries to follow' (Paul Blustein, *And the Money Kept Rolling In (and Out)*, Public Affairs, New York, 2005), 147. Common citizens in Argentina, guided by their past experience and conventional wisdom mistrusted the sustainability of the fixed peg of the Argentinean Peso to the US dollar. However, the repeated and enthusiastic support given by the Fund to the government of former President Menem (unfortunately) did not go unnoticed when voters had to decide on whether his economic policies were sustainable.

[34] Net of scheduled 'repurchases'—reimbursements of credit.

Naturally, exceptional access comes at 'exceptional' costs, both financial[35] and political.[36]

Needless to say, as 'normal access' (under 300% of meagre quotas) usually falls short of what is needed to help a country overcome the consequences of a balance of payments crisis, exceptional access is anything but usual business.[37] Indeed, total new resource commitments by the Fund during 2003–04 (arguably the last period in which the Fund had to provide meaningful assistance to members in balance of payments crisis) amounted to approximately SDR 19.6 billion; of these SDR 15.7 billion was committed in arrangements involving exceptional access.[38]

Last but not least, the Fund lives mostly on borrowing countries. As there are less and less borrowers,[39] the Fund's financial situation has worsened and it is currently running a deficit close to 17% of its administrative expenses.[40] Ironically, the Fund has preferred to draw from its reserves rather than living up to the draconian budget adjustments that it has so often 'recommended' to its borrowers.

[35] There is a surcharge of 200 basis points for borrowing over 300% of quota. The cost of borrowing over 300% of quota (first trimester of 2007) is of 7.38% in SDR. Repayment is normally expected within 2.25 to 4 years (the bulk of the IMF lending is provided under short-term 'Stand-By' Arrangements). This can be compared with the cost of borrowing in private capital markets (Uruguay issued a bond in November 2006 at a cost of 7.525% in US dollars and with a 30 years maturity period and, of course, with no 'conditionality' attached).

[36] A country requesting exceptional access has to comply with four criteria: (i) it has to be undergoing 'balance of payments pressures on the capital account, resulting in a need for Fund financing that cannot be met within the limits'; (ii) it has to have a 'high probability that debt will remain sustainable established on the basis of a rigorous and systematic analysis'; (iii) it has to have 'good prospects... to regain access to private capital markets within the time Fund resources would be outstanding and (iv) it has to implement a '*strong adjustment program*... [with] a reasonably strong prospect of success, *including not only the member's adjustment plans but also its institutional and political capacity to deliver that adjustment*' (emphasis added). On top of this, before entering in negotiations with a Member requesting exceptional access, the Fund's management has to consult the Board, giving the Executive Directors representing the main creditors the opportunity to set 'prior actions' that the potential borrower should undertake. IMF 'Review of Access Policy in the Credit Tranches, the Extended Fund Facility and the Poverty Reduction and Growth Facility and Exceptional Access Policy' (14 March 2005) Box 1, Summary of Access Policies.

[37] In 1995, Mexico had to request borrowing 688% of its quota. In 1997, Thailand had to request borrowing 505% of its quota; Indonesia 490% of its quota (augmented in 1998 to 557%); Korea 1938% of its quota. In 1998, Russia borrowed over 350% of its quota; Brazil 600% (augmented by 2002 to 752%). In 1999, Turkey requested to borrow 300% of its quota and this had to be augmented in 2001 to 1560% of its quota. By 2001, Argentina had to request to borrow 800% of its quota and in 2002, Uruguay had to request to borrow equivalent to 694% of its quota. Ibid, Table 10.

[38] Ibid, para 21.

[39] The Fund's outstanding credit peaked at 70 billion SDR in 2002 and by the end of 2006 it had fallen to approximately 15.5 million SDR.

[40] The Fund's projected income shortfall for FY2007 is equivalent to approximately 17% of its Net Administrative Budget (not counting depreciation for capital assets and IT equipment) and projections for the period 2008–10 bring the red up to 41%!

There are proposals under consideration which would allow the Fund to live from an investment account that could be fed by selling part of its gold reserves and members' quotas;[41] however, their approval will require a qualified majority at the Board that so far has been elusive and its implementation would require amendments to the Articles of Agreement (which should be approved by parliaments). So the reality is that for the time being, and possibly for still a quite long period, the Fund's income will continue to come from the differential between its borrowing cost and what it charges for its financial support (the 'rate of charge'[42]). In short, it is taxpayers from borrowing countries (i.e. poor countries) who are called to shoulder most of the expenses of an institution in which salaries are annually indexed and benefits are first class, but does not give them much of a say in its decisions (taxation without representation). I find this pathetic.

As Woods and Lombardi correctly note, 'the costs of most of the "public goods" functions undertaken by the IMF fall mostly on the shoulders of borrowing members'[43] and a breakdown of costs of financing the Fund's 'administrative expenses and precautionary balances shows that, in the period from 1980 to 2000, borrowers have raised their relative contribution from 28 to 71 percent [whereas] creditors have decreased their contributions from 72 to 29 percent'.[44]

In sum, and beyond fairness considerations,[45] it does not seem functional for the Fund's purposes that the rich should have the right to integrate bigger quotas and, therefore, have greater access to the Fund's financing and the privilege of running the institution by themselves.

III. THE 'STRATEGIC' REFORM: MORE NOISE THAN NUTS

In implicit recognition that the Fund either changes or fades away into irrelevance,[46] Mr Rodrigo de Rato launched a 'strategic' reform that delivered

[41] Final Report of the 'Committee to Study Sustainable Long-Term Financing of the IMF', chaired by Andrew Crockett (31 January 2007) http://www.imf.org/external/np/oth/2007/013107.pdf (visited 5 May 2007).

[42] In December 2006, the margin for calculating the rate of charge is of 108 basis points over the SDR (Special Drawing Rights) interest rate.

[43] Ngaire Woods and Domenico Lombardi, 'Uneven patterns of governance: how developing countries are represented in the IMF', 499; Review of International Political Economy 13:3 August 2006: 480–515. Global Economic Governance Programme, University College, Oxford, UK.

[44] Ibid, at 498.

[45] For more on fairness see, Abbas Mirakhor and Iqbal Zaidi, who assess the IMF's governance structure using John Rawls' concept of justice. Above, n 18.

[46] The International Monetary and Financial Committee of the Board of Governors of the IMF candidly acknowledged that the effectiveness and credibility of the Fund needed to be 'safeguarded and its governance further enhanced, emphasizing the importance of fair voice and representation for all members'. IMF, Communiqué of the International Monetary and Financial Committee issued in Washington, D.C. (22 April 2006) http://www.imf.org/external/np/cm/2006/042206.htm (visited 20 May 2007).

a first result on 'quotas and voice' at its 2006 Annual Meetings in Singapore. On that occasion, the Governors of the Fund adopted the decision to grant four countries, namely China, Korea, Turkey and Mexico, the right to modestly increase their quotas (an overall 1.8% increase in the capital of the Fund).[47] These countries appeared to be the most underrepresented using the current (flawed) quota calculation method, so arguably the start has not been bright and many developing countries voted against the reform[48] or supported it only after strong lobbying from the Fund's management.[49]

As for basic votes, it was decided to 'at a minimum' double them and thereby, the 'existing voting share of low-income countries (LICs) as a group' [50] should be protected. The actual amount of increase in basic votes is yet to be decided since in Singapore it was agreed that the amount of increase in basic votes will be defined together with a second round of quota increases, no later than by the Annual Meetings of 2008. The actual implementation of both the increase in basic votes and the aforementioned second round of quota increases will, however, take some time.

Indeed, increasing basic votes will require an amendment to the Articles of Agreement of the Fund[51] and a second stage of more meaningful quota increases will only come after the adoption of a new quota formula. The Fund's Executive Board is requested to 'reach agreement on a new quota formula'[52] no later than by the 2008 Spring Meeting of the IMFC. Then, by the Annual Meetings of 2008 (normally taking place in the northern hemisphere's fall) the Board of Governors should consider new quota increases for those members who appear as underrepresented. However, this will not be the end of the saga, since the aforementioned 'at a minimum' doubling of basic votes requires an amendment of Article XII, Section 5(a) of the Fund's Articles of Agreement and the foreseen next increase in quotas shall not become effective until the basic votes amendment enters into force. In sum, parliaments will have the last word and, most probably, the US Congress.[53]

The reservations that several developing countries had with the decision approved in Singapore were two-fold. First, the reform foreshadowed in that

[47] Resolution No. 61-5 on 'Quota and Voice Reform in the International Monetary Fund', adopted at the Sixty-First Annual Meeting, September 2006, Singapore.

[48] Argentina, Bolivia, Brazil, Chile, Colombia, Comoros, Dominican Republic, Ecuador, Egypt, Haiti, India, Iran, Maldives, Oman, Panama, Paraguay, Peru, Qatar, Sri Lanka, Trinidad and Tobago, Uruguay, Venezuela and Yemen.

[49] This was confirmed to the author by several colleagues that found that, against their own advice, their governors had been lobbied to vote in favor of the Resolution.

[50] Above, n 47, para 4.

[51] Above, n 10.

[52] Above, n 47, para 3.

[53] Such an amendment of the Fund's Articles of Agreement can only enter into force for all of its members if it is accepted by three-fifths of the Fund's members having 85% of the total voting power. As the US holds more than 15% of the total voting power, this means that ultimately the US Congress holds the key of the reform initiated at Singapore.

Decision may result in more, not less, quotas and voting power for the most advanced economies. The discussion of a new quota formula had not yet started when the aforementioned Decision was adopted, but GDP[54] and 'openness'[55] were already put as the two variables that should bear more weight. This was a bad start, as including reference to other variables which better capture likeliness to borrow would have presented a more promising reform for the majority of developing countries.[56] However, front-running GDP and openness is made even worse by the insistence of the most advanced economies in using market exchange rates to calculate GDP (rather than Purchasing Power Parity[57]) and that of EU members of factoring their intra-Euro trade as part of their 'openness' to the world.[58]

Admittedly, the US manifested that it was only looking forward to restoring the voting power that it had before the implementation of the aforementioned token quota increase approved in Singapore.[59] The Europeans did not join the US in its pledge, but decided to put forward an alternative proposal, that of using a 'compression factor'[60] to reduce the disparities between large and small economies to which a new formula could lead. The Japanese have neither joined the US in its pledge of self-restriction, nor the Europeans in their proposal to mend the problem by compressing the disparities; far from that, they have made it clear that they are not ready to forego any increase in quotas/voting power to which they could result entitled with a new quota formula.

Naturally, a reform on quotas and voice that would further deteriorate the already minority position that developing economies hold in the Fund's aggregate voting, would be clearly at odds with the objective of giving additional legitimacy to the Fund and reinforcing multilateralism.

But there is a second and perhaps more powerful reason behind the square opposition or the very reluctant support of many developing countries to the Singapore Decision. The drafting of that Decision creates a very high risk

54 Gross Domestic Product.

55 The sum of total receipts of current account.

56 Ariel Buira shows how combining GDP calculated at Purchasing Power Parity with volatility of movements in commodity prices and capital movements would increase developing countries' participation in aggregate voting. 'The Bretton Woods Institutions: Governance without Legitimacy?' table 4, in: *Reforming the Governance of the IMF and the World Bank*, G-24 research program, (Anthem Press, Washington: 2005), 23.

57 It should be noted that measured at market exchange rates, developing economies' share of global output is roughly 26% [in 2005] whereas measured at PPP, it is over 50%. The Economist (21 January 2006), 69.

58 Trade within a same currency unit could not bring BoP problems and, therefore, no need for Fund financial support.

59 The US has also hinted that it may be ready to accept a 'blended' measurement of GDP, however, giving PPP a very small weight.

60 The end result of a linear formula which, on its own, would increase the quotas and votes for large economies would be multiplied by a negative number (the 'compression factor') so as to partially smooth-out the resulting disparities. This would be to the benefit of most developing countries and small European countries as well.

that, even if advanced economies were not to increase their current share in quotas and votes, the end result of the reform could allow for the increase of the quotas of a handful of successful emerging economies at the expense of middle-income developing countries. As the increase in quotas for the most dynamic emerging markets could not come at the expense of advanced economies because they have the voting power necessary to prevent it, and it could neither come at the expense of LICs, to which the Singapore Decision guarantees no further erosion in their quota share, it would necessarily come at the expense of middle-income developing countries. The irony is that whereas emerging markets such as China or Korea or some ASEAN countries, seem to be 'graduating' from potential use of Fund support (thanks to their persistent current account surpluses), middle-income countries remain to be Fund potential borrowers. Thus, it would be self-defeating for the Fund to reduce their quotas' relative weight. Indeed, this would encourage this large group of countries to step up their policies of self-insurance, shoot for depressed exchange rates that allow them to accumulate more reserves, and build up new (or reinforce existing) regional reserve pooling arrangements.[61]

I am not, of course, against prudential policies, or against the pooling of reserves amongst neighbours, but I am wary of a world that resorts to bilateralism or regionalism as an alternative to inefficient and unreliable multilateral institutions.

IV. FAT CATS COME FIRST

The questioning of the Fund's legitimacy goes way beyond the quota issue and its consequences on its decision making process. The independence and objectivity of its policy advice and conditionality are also questionable and doubts are raised on the 'difficulty [of Fund officials in] resisting the temptation to lavish praise on countries that are implementing orthodox economic policies'.[62]

The Fund is basically an organization designed to foster monetary and financial stability; it is, therefore, natural that it is keener to give priority to financial interests over the overall interests of society. However, governments have to take care of a multiplicity of interests, financial amongst them. It is not uncommon to perceive that financial interests are disguised behind the Fund's policy advice and conditionality, for instance, by giving a *de facto* preferred creditor status to financial liabilities.

Governments have a variety of liabilities to attend to and any unbiased observer would agree that, unless otherwise determined, public liabilities are to be honoured *pari pasu*, namely, regardless of who holds the claim.

[61] We are already seeing some of this in South America with the '*Banco del Sur*' initiative.
[62] Paul Blustein, Above, n 33, at 212.

Alas, the Fund does not seem to agree. When it comes to financial liabilities no budgetary effort has to be spared and the 'sanctity of contracts' has to be respected at any rate.[63] But if claim-holders are pensioners or public employees, then public liabilities are recategorized as 'budgetary rigidities' that need to be removed.[64]

Unfortunately, the Fund does not limit its advice and conditionality to financial issues. In exercising surveillance over national economies and in 'proposing' conditionality before lending, it covers a variety of policies such as trade, fiscal and labour. Promoting coherence between the different international agencies and UN bodies seems to be a very sensible thing to do. Therefore, it would only be reasonable for the Fund to consult with the International Labour Organization (ILO) before putting forward advice on labour policies, an area in which it has no particular expertise. Alas, the Fund feels appropriate to give policy advice on labour without consulting the ILO. I have personally requested repeatedly—and so far hopelessly—that reports on national economies put forward for the consideration of the Executive Board should include the opinion of the ILO every time they touch on labour policies.

Asking these two organizations to consult each other on topics that overlap is elementary good governance as ultimately it is tax-payers who shoulder the cost of running both the ILO and the Fund. This was, precisely, one of the key recommendations included in the report of the World Commission on the Social Dimension of Globalization;[65] to increase coherence between the Fund, the World Bank, the WTO, the ILO and other relevant UN bodies.

[63] In 2002–03, Argentina arguably lived through its deepest social and economic crisis. More than half of its population was suddenly sent below the poverty line, social unrest was rampant and the country was in political chaos. In that socially volatile context, the transitional government gave fiscal priority to its 'social debt' (rather than to its financial debt). The influential Fund's driven 'Capital Markets Consultative Group' disagreed: 'The rule of law need[s] to be firmly established and the sanctity of contracts honored [in Argentina]', otherwise it viewed a 'risk of "wider" contagion of weakening policies to other countries in the region and elsewhere'. Report from management on the seventh meeting of the Capital Markets Consultative Group, 8 September 2003 http://www.imf.org/external/np/cmcg/2003/eng/091803.HTM (visited 5 May 2007).

[64] For example 'To reduce budget rigidities, it would be crucial to control the growth of the wage bill, including through a renewed effort at civil service reform [...] It would also be essential to substantially reduce [...] government contributions to pensions'. Ecuador, 2005 Article IV Consultation-Staff Report, para. 17 www.imf.org/external/pubs/cat/longres.cfm?sk=19009.0 (visited 5 May 2007). 'The pattern of [public] health spending reflects [...] budget rigidities' Republic of Slovenia (July 2006), IMF Country Report No. 06/250, para. 21 www.imf.org/external/pubs/cat/longres.cfm?sk=19422.0 (visited 5 May 2007).

[65] The report was issued on February 2004. The Commission was created by the ILO. It was co-chaired by H.E. Ms Tarja Halonen, President of the Republic of Finland and H.E. Mr Benjamin Mkapa, President of the United Republic of Tanzania. Commissioners included former Prime Minister of Italy Guliano Amato, Former President of Uruguay, Julio M Sanguinetti and Nobel Prize Winner Joseph Stiglitz. http://www.ilo.org/public/english/fair-globalization/report/index.htm (visited 5 May 2007).

Labour policies are crucial to avoid globalization deepening social inequities among countries and also within countries themselves. The asymmetry of mobility between capital and labour puts the latter in a bargaining disadvantage which is compounded by the lack of enforcement of Core Labour Standards (CLS).[66] Needless to say, the approaches that the ILO and the Fund take to labour matters are quite different. Whereas the ILO has made it a priority to promote respect for CLS, at the Fund, labour regulations are mostly perceived as obstacles to hiring and firing workers and its policy advice normally includes additional 'flexibility', code word that at the Fund translates as further reducing labour rights[67] (and, therefore, not respecting contractual terms which, in this case, seem to have a lesser 'sanctity' status than financial contracts).

It is well documented that globalization, together with technological innovation, are pushing 'labour's share of GDP [down] to historic lows, while profits are soaring'.[68] Labour's participation in national income is at its lowest level for decades.[69] This preoccupying deepening of inequality appears to be correlated with the reduction in labour protection and the decrease in the bargaining power of unions; which is compounded by capital mobility, a key feature of globalization.[70] Political consequences are quite obvious and the protectionist sentiment is on the rise.[71] This should concern the Fund, as one of its purposes is 'to facilitate the expansion and balanced growth of international trade'.[72]

Unfortunately, an ideological bias prevents the Fund from taking a more balanced approach to labour matters. For instance, it has

[66] 'Core Labour Standards' are internationally agreed fundamental human rights recognized for all workers, irrespective of whether they toil in developed or developing countries. They are defined by the ILO conventions that cover freedom of association and the right to collective bargaining (ILO Conventions 87 and 98); the elimination of discrimination in respect of employment and occupation (ILO conventions 100 and 111); the elimination of all forms of forced or compulsory labour (ILO conventions 29 and 105); the elimination of all forms of forced or compulsory labour (ILO Conventions 29 and 105); and the effective abolition of child labour (ILO Conventions 138 and 182).

[67] Joseph P. Joyce quotes studies that indicate 'that labor's share of income is lower in countries with IMF programs'. Above, n 21, at 12.

[68] 'Rich Man, Poor Man', The Economist, 20 January 2007, 15.

[69] 'A Survey of the World Economy, The New Titans', The Economist, 16 September 2006, 6.

[70] Guscina, Anastasia, 'Effects of Globalization on Labor's Share in National Income', IMF Working Paper, WP/06/294, December 2006; in researching on the reasons that made labour's share of national income in industrial countries steadily decline in recent decades, finds that 'by making capital more mobile, globalization may have decreased the bargaining power of the less mobile factor—labor' (ibid, at 5). Moreover, she also finds what should be pretty obvious for the Fund, that 'a higher degree of employment protection benefits labor more than capital, resulting in higher compensation and labor share' (13).

[71] According to the Financial Times (12 January 2007), 3, 'Wages gap "undermines support for free trade"') Tim Geithner, the president of the Federal Reserve Bank of New York, stated that sustaining support for further global integration 'may be the most important economic challenge of our time' and warned that rising inequality and economic insecurity (of workers) was undermining support for open markets.

[72] IMF, Articles of Agreement, Article I, (ii).

consistently opposed minimum wage settings, disregarding the social and political benefits that such a floor of protection for low-skilled workers could have.[73] Just to illustrate the point, it is worth referring to Germany's economy, where unemployment 'has dropped sharply in the last two years', 'business confidence remains close to a 15-year high' and '[d]eclining real wages and a modest upswing in productivity have together produced a sustained drop in unit labour costs'.[74] Despite this 'good news', consumer confidence (which depends on household's perception of their future income) 'failed to take off convincingly'[75] and the EU enlargement is bringing uneasiness on the consequences that the immigration of workers ready to work for lower wages could bring. This should not surprise us since consumer confidence and openness to immigrants are clearly related to job stability and wages. The government was, therefore, considering the introduction of 'minimum wages to "protect" against competition from immigrants from low-wage countries (and to limit potential fiscal costs of wage subsidies)'.[76] The Fund staff was quick to categorize this as a 'serious policy error',[77] without taking the trouble to consider whether the government, by introducing minimum wages, was aiming at making it easier for German workers to assimilate legal immigrants who would otherwise be pushing salaries down and nationalist sentiments up. Introducing minimum wages may come at a cost, but in assessing its convenience, the Fund should take a more balanced and less dogmatic approach.

Admittedly, the Fund is making some progress. Albeit timidly, it is progressively taking the good practice of consulting with civil society representatives, including trade unions, before presenting Article IV reports to the Board. However, I do not recall ever having read a report in which the Fund touches on labour matters and recommends members to respect core labour standards and other ILO conventions ratified by the country or, perhaps even more evident, to duly enforce their own labour legislation!

Our concern goes beyond questioning the fairness of the Fund's advice. I also believe that its pro-profits advice may not be functional to the purpose of preserving global economic stability, let alone political stability. If productivity grows at the expense of labour retribution, it will eventually

[73] Just to cite a few of the latest examples; in 2006 it opposed increase in Chile's minimum wages (IMF, 'Chile-Staff Report for the 2006 Article IV consultation', SM/06/245) and 'high' minimum wages in France (IMF, 'France- Staff Report for the 2006 Article IV consultation', SM/06/329) and the 'excessively rigid' collective wage bargaining system in Spain (IMF, 'Spain-Staff Report for the 2006 Article IV consultation'SM/06/174). It also opposed the introduction of minimum wages in Germany, as we will see next.

[74] 'Beggar Thy Neighbour', The Economist 27 January 2007, 73.

[75] Ibid.

[76] IMF, 'Germany—Staff Report for the 2006 Article IV Consultation' (13 November 2006), SM/06/370, para 16.

[77] Ibid, para 17.

affect consumer confidence, and this is particularly dysfunctional at a time the world needs to rely less on US consumers' spending. We should be doing more to integrate into the market those who currently feel sidelined from the benefits of globalization. Needless to say, most of these would-be-consumers are living in countries that are currently running huge current account surpluses.

V. CONCLUSION

The Fund has two well-differentiated roles. First, a regulatory role, which comes from its capacity to design conditionality, exercise surveillance on the economy of its members and oversee compliance with members' obligation to collaborate with the Fund to assure 'orderly exchange arrangements and to promote a stable system of exchange rates'.[78]

Second, a lending role, which comes from its capacity to serve as a multilateral pool of reserves meant to 'give confidence to members by making the general resources of the Fund temporarily available',[79] so as to help them correct their BOP problems while promoting 'high levels of employment and real income'[80] and 'without resorting to measures destructive of national or international prosperity'.[81]

The current governance structure of the Fund, beyond being inconsistent with its multilateral nature, is dysfunctional to both these roles. A promoter of international monetary and financial stability requires the capacity to perform and put forward uncompromised arms-length assessments of the economies of its members and blow the whistle (loud and clear) when domestic policies are systemically disruptive. The fact that its decision-making process is dominated by its largest and most powerful members, precisely those whose domestic policies have systemic implications, attempts against the independence of the Fund's assessment and its capacity to police compliance with its obligations. This handicap is compounded by the fact that two of its members, the US[82] and the EU,[83] can veto its most important decisions.[84]

As regards its 'lending role', it makes very little sense that those countries that will not need to borrow have the right to integrate higher quotas, and, therefore, have more access to Fund resources (and weight in its decisions). Not surprisingly, potential borrowers are keen to accumulate reserves and design regional pooling agreements.

[78] IMF, Articles of Agreement, Article IV, Section 1, General obligations of members.
[79] Article I, (v), Purposes. Above, n 2.
[80] Article I, (ii), Ibid.
[81] Ibid.
[82] The US holds 16.83% of the votes.
[83] The European Union countries act individually, but coordinately. As Woods and Lombardi note the EU countries form a coalition with a Brussels permanent Sub-committee on the IMF. Above, n 43. Together they hold 32.18% of the votes.
[84] The most important decisions require a qualified majority of 85% of votes.

The reform process launched in Singapore in September 2006 is not likely to help the Fund, neither recover credibility nor improve efficiency. At the Board, we are just tinkering with the variables used in the current flawed quota formula and preparing ourselves to horse-trade on the weight that should be given to those that better accommodate narrow national interests. At most, it will result in giving some more votes to a few successful emerging economies, already weaned off the Fund's financial support, at the expense of other less successful developing countries that remain to be potential borrowers. This will not bring additional effectiveness or credibility to the Fund.

Other international organizations (e.g. the EU Council, the Council of the Global Environment Facility, the International Seabed Authority and the African Development Bank) have also been confronted with the need to find a compromise between regulatory capacities that call for an even distribution of votes among members with the need to accommodate the reality of members with very unequal economic weight. They have resolved the dilemma by establishing a double majority system in which an economically-weighted majority is complemented by a one-country one-vote majority. This combines the recognition for differences in relative economic weight with the equality of rights and obligations for all members. The Fund is much more than a club of creditors; a double majority system could help bring both additional sense of ownership for its policies and effectiveness.

The redressing of its ideological bias will require more than 'just' reaching agreement on a fairer and more functional distribution of votes and quotas (and access to its financial resources). It will require making the Fund more accountable and responsive to citizens' concerns, as its policy advice and conditionality has direct implications on their income. We should start by recognizing that policies recommended or 'conditioned' (i.e imposed) in Fund programs are not technically neutral but imply trade-offs in terms of social justice and should, therefore, be subject to democratic accountability. As Joseph Stiglitz rightly points out, '[n]o economic issue affects people more than the macroeconomic performance of the economy. Increasing the unemployment rate makes workers worse off, but the resulting lower inflation makes bondholders happy. Balancing these interests is a quintessentially political activity'.[85] There is no way to depoliticize these decisions and those involved in taking them, namely those that have the privilege of sitting at the Fund's Executive Board, should be accountable to Congresses.[86]

[85] Above, n 5, at 279.

[86] Ngaire Woods, and Domenico Lombardi (above, n 43) find it astonishing that there are virtually no mechanisms to hold accountable elected Directors (those representing 'constituencies' of countries that gather to have a seat at the Board). The situation for appointed Directors (those appointed by countries that enjoy their own seat at the Board, i.e. US, Japan, Germany, France, the UK, China, Russia and Saudi Arabia) is somewhat different, as in some cases (e.g. the US) their appointment has to be approved by the legislature.

GLOBAL JUSTICE AND THE BRETTON WOODS INSTITUTIONS

*Frank J. Garcia**

ABSTRACT

Together with the WTO, the Bretton Woods Institutions are the pre-eminent international institutions devoted to managing international economic relations. This mandate puts them squarely in the center of the debate concerning development, inequality and global justice. This essay explores how justice criteria might apply to the ideology and operations of the World Bank and the International Monetary Fund. Using the Rawlsian model of egalitarian justice adapted to international institutions by the author in connection with the WTO, this essay asks what difference it would make for the Bank and Fund if an explicit justice framework informed their international lending activities.

INTRODUCTION

Global social policy is currently managed through a variety of institutions including in particular the WTO and what are popularly called the Bretton Woods Institutions (BWIs): the International Monetary Fund (IMF or the Fund) and the World Bank (Bank).[1] In this essay, I propose to use the normative analysis I developed for the WTO[2] as a model for exploring

* Professor, Boston College Law School, 885 Centre St, Newton, Mass.02459 USA. E-mail: frank.garcia.1@bc.edu, garciafr@bc.edu. Thanks to Jefffrey Dunoff for his insightful comments, and to Matthew Hoisington, Daniel Blanchard and Michael Garcia for exceptional research assistance.

[1] By global social policy, I mean (broadly speaking) policies designed and/or implemented at the trans-national level which affect the creation and allocation of social primary goods (such as wealth, income rights, opportunities, privileges, status, legal standing, etc.), and the elaboration of secondary social goods (such as education, employment, health care, sustenance, security, etc.). In this essay I am focusing on social primary goods and the institutions which influence their allocation through their policy decisions. Such policies are obviously formulated and affected by domestic institutions, but also, increasingly, by global institutions as well. For a comprehensive and insightful overview of the institutions which manage global social policy, see Bob Deacon, 'Social Policy in a Global Context', in Andrew Hurrell & Ngaire Woods (eds), *Inequality, Globalization and World Politics* (Oxford, UK:Oxford University Press, 1999) 211–47.

[2] Frank J. Garcia, *Trade, Inequality and Justice: Toward a Liberal Theory of Just Trade* (Transnational Publishers, Ardsley, N.Y. 2003); Frank J. Garcia, *Trade and Inequality: Economic Justice and the Developing World*, 21 Michigan Journal of International Law 925

the relationship between justice and the work of the BWIs. Insofar as the Bank and Fund are social institutions, charged with making decisions involving the allocation of social resources, their activities are the direct subject of justice theory. The fact that the Bank and Fund are international organizations does not alter this fundamental point. In particular, I want to consider the role of the Bank and Fund as institutions which form part of the 'basic structure', those institutions which discharge a fundamental allocative role in society and are therefore part of the larger inquiry into justice.[3]

The Bank began when one of its two primary lending organs, the International Bank for Reconstruction and Development (IBRD), was created in 1945 to help finance European reconstruction. Its mission soon broadened into supporting development investment on a global scale, and the IBRD continues to carry out what is often considered the Bank's core activity, development lending at preferential (but near-commercial) rates. The Bank's second lending institution, the International Development Association (IDA), was created in 1960 to assist the Bank's poorest clients through concessional (zero-interest) lending and outright grants.[4]

The IMF was created to bring stability to the exchange rate system and facilitate cooperation on international monetary matters in the aftermath of the Great Depression.[5] Following the demise in the 1970s of the so-called Bretton Woods system of gold-pegged exchange rates, the Fund's role has shifted more towards that of an international financial institution.[6] The IMF engages in short- and medium-term lending of hard or 'trade' currencies[7] in response to balance of payments difficulties, with accompanying IMF 'conditions' involving domestic policy reforms.[8] The IMF carries out

---

(2000); reprinted in *International Law Today* (Anthony D'Amato and Jennifer Abbassi, eds) (West, 2006); *Heights of Justice*, Lawrence A and Cunningham (eds), (Carolina Academic Press, Durham, N.C. 2006).

[3] Both the Bank and the Fund were conceived at the Bretton Woods Conference to serve complementary roles in the post-war economy. *Bahram Ghazi, The IMF, the World Bank and the Question of Human Rights* (Ardsley, NY, Transnational Publishers, 2005) at 19–37. For an overview of the concept of a global basic structure and its role in the global justice debate, see Simon Caney, *The Global Basic Structure: Its Nature and Moral Relevance* (Paper presented at the annual meeting of the American Political Science Association, 2 September 2004, http://www.allacademic.com/meta/p58933_index.html).

[4] See Ghazi, above n 3, at 19–37.

[5] See generally Ghazi, above n 3, at 1–17.

[6] See R.M. Lastra, 'The International Monetary Fund in Historical Perspective', 3 Journal of International Economic Law 507 (2000) at 512 (upon demise of exchange rate system, Fund shifted to broader international financial role).

[7] See ibid.

[8] The IMF also continues to monitor and investigate member states' exchange rate policies, and work to encourage members to remove any exchange controls, though I will not focus on those activities here. See generally Remarks by Sean Hagan, IMF General Counsel, *Proceedings of the 93rd Annual Meeting, American Society of International Law (ASIL)*, 24–27 March 1999, 115–116.

this lending through a variety of distinct lending programs or 'facilities', each with different terms and conditions suited to different categories of borrowers in different types of need.[9]

In this essay I seek to be 'normative' without being 'prescriptive'. In other words, my primary aim is to employ a normative framework drawn from domestic political theory and first adapted to international trade, to suggest one approach to analyzing the work of the Bank and Fund with respect to global distributive justice.[10] The theoretical challenge is to articulate for the Bank and Fund specific normative criteria that should inform their policy choices and operational decisions. In this essay I employ a version of Rawls' Difference Principle, which I call the International Difference Principle, to derive initial versions of such normative criteria for the Bank and for the Fund. I conclude by illustrating the application of such criteria in one area of Bank and Fund operations, their involvement with the domestic policy of borrowing states. By doing so, I hope to suggest how introducing justice explicitly into the ongoing conversation concerning Bank and Fund reform, alters the nature of the questions asked and offers some guidance as to where appropriate solutions might lie.

I. INTERNATIONAL JUSTICE AND INTERNATIONAL ECONOMIC INSTITUTIONS

Elsewhere I have summarized my approach to the generation of an international normative application of domestic political theory,[11] based on my work applying Rawls' theory of Justice as Fairness to international trade law.[12] Here I will only outline the minimum necessary in order to explain how this approach forms the basis for the specific application of the theory to the Bank and Fund in the sections which follow.

[9] See Ghazi above n 3, at 10–11.

[10] I have initially couched this discussion in terms of global justice, although I believe a true theory of global justice requires either cosmopolitan or communitarian grounding, or both, and I offer neither here, relying instead on a more traditional international law/'society of states' model of justice. See Frank J. Garcia, 'Globalization and the Theory of International Law', 11 International Legal Theory 9 (2005) (surveying arguments regarding normative basis of global justice in globalizing social relations). Thus what I am actually engaging in here is more properly an international justice argument, or justice between states and with their citizens, although I believe the substantive conclusions would be quite similar either way.

[11] Frank J. Garcia, *Developing a Normative Critique of International Trade Law: Special & Differential Treatment*, Working Paper Series No, University of Bremen Transformations of the State Research Centre, http://www.sfb597.uni-bremen.de/pages/pubAp.php?SPRACHE=en (forthcoming).

[12] Garcia, above n 2.

A. International justice as fairness

The initial task is to choose a particular body of normative political theory through which to develop the analysis of the obligations of justice as they apply to the BWIs. For a variety of substantive and rhetorical reasons I think liberalism is the best normative language for modern secular international law.[13] Within liberalism, I have chosen Rawls' 'Justice as Fairness', despite its complex relationship to international justice,[14] because of its approach to the problem of inequality.

Rawls is particularly concerned with inequalities that arise in the distribution of social primary goods. The fundamental problem of distributive justice is that inequalities in natural primary goods (such as intelligence, health and imagination) often lead, through the operation of social institutions, to inequalities in the social distribution of social primary goods, such as rights, privileges, wealth, income, status, opportunities, etc. Such inequalities in social primary goods are not deserved, since they are deeply influenced by an underlying natural inequality which is morally arbitrary.

Rawls argues that as a result, the basic structure of society must be arranged 'so that these contingencies work for the good of the least fortunate'.[15] Rawls develops this view into the theory of Justice as Fairness, in particular the 'Difference Principle', which states that inequalities in the distribution of social primary goods are justifiable only to the extent they benefit the least advantaged. Satisfying this criterion at the domestic level could entail a variety of social measures, ranging from altering the structure of incentives to reward actions which benefit the least advantaged, such as the charitable gifts deduction of the tax code, to the outright redistribution of private wealth through progressive tax and welfare legislation.[16]

There are many ways to catalogue similar inequalities in international economic relations, although the natural inequalities in this case are not

[13] Liberalism is the normative tradition of many of the most wealthy and powerful states which control the BWIs, which are primarily western or western-style liberal democracies. This is important on topics of international justice, since if you develop arguments for justice in this language, it is harder for such states to ignore them. Moreover, the BWIs themselves have roots in the same tradition of liberalism, in particular liberal internationalism. On the intertwined roots of political liberalism, liberal internationalism, international law and the modern state system, *see* Anne Marie Slaughter, 'International Law in a World of Liberal States', 6 European Journal of International Law 1 (1995) at 5–10; Deacon, above n 1, at 223 (acknowledging liberal internationalist roots of IMF).

[14] In *A Theory of Justice* Rawls limits his theoretical enterprize to principles of justice for what he assumes to be a closed domestic society, which by 1979 was already a questionable assumption. See Charles Beitz, *Political Theory and International Relations* (Princeton, NJ: Princeton University Press, 1979) 143–49. Globalization, and other developments in international relations generally and in international economic relations in particular, have rendered such assumptions untenable today. See Thomas Franck, *Fairness in International law and Institutions* (New York, USA, NY: Oxford University Press, 1995) 12–13 (the requisite level of community has emerged at the international level to sustain a fairness analysis).

[15] See John Rawls, A Theory of Justice (Belknap Press: Cambridge, 1971) at 102.

[16] Ibid at 179.

individual attributes such as intelligence but national 'attributes' such as geography and climate. With respect to trade, contemporary analyses usually adopt economic 'size' as the most relevant concept by which to evaluate and measure the impact of inequality on trade liberalization.[17] The central insight from the literature on smaller economies and trade is that smaller economies share certain characteristics that make their participation in the international trading system problematic.[18] Small size is also an additional complicating factor affecting a country's growth, policy options and development potential.[19]

These contingencies form the essential context in which any normative international political theory must operate. Translated into Rawlsian terms, the characteristics of smaller economies are a complex blend of both natural and social inequalities. Natural inequalities are strongly reflected in smaller economy characteristics such as smallness in population, smallness in territory, and heavy reliance upon commodities exports. Social inequalities are essentially connected to social institutions, including the smaller economy's political and economic systems, prior geopolitical arrangements, and international economic law and diplomacy, all of which together establish patterns of distribution of social goods such as wealth, knowledge, rights and privileges within and between states, which 'define men's [sic] rights and duties and influence their life prospects'.[20] Smaller economy characteristics that reflect social inequalities include their limited human and technological resources, which reflect both small populations and the effects of social allocations resulting in inadequate educational and research institutions. Such allocations are heavily influenced by underlying natural inequalities, and by non-economic factors such as racial, religious or nationalistic prejudice.

The key normative assumption underlying a Rawlsian account of inequality is that differences in natural endowments, and consequent differences in the allocation of social goods, are unmerited. In Rawls'

[17] The smallness of an economy will always be determined in comparison with other economies, usually in terms of per capita GDP, supplemented by population and land size, as rough indicators of an economy's human, land and capital resources.

[18] Smaller economies are vulnerable when they participate in trade for two reasons: the relative openness of smaller economies, and the asymmetry between larger and smaller economies in resources and economic strength. Overall, smaller economies face the risk that the distribution of benefits and burdens within the trading system will be skewed in favor of the dominant party. See, e.g. Dermot McCann, 'Small States in Globalizing Markets: The End of National Economic Sovereignty', 34 New York University Journal of International Law & Policy 281 (2001) (citing broad consensus as to factors leading to smaller economies' overdependence on exports, and consequent vulnerability).

[19] Overcoming Obstacles and Maximizing Opportunities: A Report by the Independent Group of Experts on Smaller Economies and Western Hemispheric Integration, March 1998, at 2; see ibid (intensity of pressures facing smaller economies raises question as to their continued effective sovereignty); Richard L. Bernal, 'The Integration of Small Economies in the Free Trade Area of the Americas 9 (Ctr. for Strategic and International Studies, Policy Papers on the Americas, vol. IX no. 1, 6–10, 1998).

[20] *Theory of Justice*, above n 15, at 7.

terms, they are morally arbitrary.[21] The fact that a particular state should be favorably situated with respect to natural resources, and that this fact results in advantages in the acquisition of social goods through the operation of domestic and international social institutions, does not by itself justify that state's claim to the benefits arising from that happy fact of geography. To accept the status quo without further justification, would be to endorse a system of natural liberty as one's principle of justice, which Rawls rejects as unjust precisely because it allows arbitrary advantages too much sway in determining life prospects.

Together, these natural inequalities, the arbitrariness of their distribution, and their social consequences, form the subject of international justice. The task of international justice is to furnish principles that will serve both as a standard for evaluating the social response to natural inequalities, and as a guide to social institutions for making distributive allocations that will justify social inequalities.

In a Rawlsian approach to international justice, those principles are to be chosen in the original position.[22] Rawls argues in *A Theory of Justice* that the representatives would choose principles of justice which maximize the minimum bundle of social goods they are likely to receive in the face of life's inequalities.[23] In the domestic original position, the representatives chose two principles, a principle of equal liberty and a principle of distributive justice. In Rawls' account of the second international choice problem, representatives of states do not in fact choose a principle of distributive justice.[24] However, as has been argued by Beitz, Barry and others, 'there is no reason to think that the content of the principles would change as a result of enlarging the scope of the original position'.[25]

1. An international difference principle

I therefore follow these theorists and suggest an international difference principle drawn directly from Rawls' own domestic elaboration:

> (I). International social and economic inequalities are just only if they result in compensating benefits for all states, and in particular for the least advantaged states.

[21] Ibid at 72.

[22] For Rawls, the problem of choice of principles is articulated in terms of the original position, in which representative individuals must choose principles that will govern their future social relations under conditions of limited knowledge of the general human condition, and ignorance as to their particular future socioeconomic situation. Ibid at 152–57.

[23] Ibid.

[24] Rawls has been criticized for bifurcating the original position into a second, separate choice problem for interstate principles of cooperation, and for failing to take into account the evolution of contemporary international law to recognize non-state actors, including individuals. See Lea Brilmayer, 'What Use is Rawls' Theory of Justice to Public International Law? 6 International Legal Theory 36 (2000); Fernando Tesón, *A Philosophy of International Law*, Ch. 4. (Boulder, CO: Westview Press, 1998).

[25] Garcia, above n 2, at 134 note 8 and sources cited therein (quoting Christopher Stone).

Parties to this international original position would view the distribution of resources in the same manner that parties in the domestic original position viewed the distribution of natural talents: as morally arbitrary.[26] Therefore, Rawls' argument should lead to the same conclusion: international social inequalities are justifiable only if they satisfy the difference principle.

B. International economic institutions and international justice as fairness

Once the basic principles of justice have been identified, the next step according to Rawls is 'to choose a constitution and a legislature to enact laws, and so on, all in accordance with the principles of justice initially agreed upon'.[27] In the case of international trade, we already have the equivalent of a constitution and a legislature, though imperfect ones, in the GATT/WTO system and its attendant rounds of international economic negotiation and diplomacy.[28]

1. Operationalizing international justice as fairness: the example of trade law

The difference principle requires that inequalities in the distribution of social primary goods be justified by their contribution to the well-being of the least advantaged. At the international level, the doctrine of free trade is key to the justification of such inequalities. By allowing the principle of comparative advantage to operate, liberalized trade moves the trading system in the direction of operating to the benefit of the least advantaged, by affording them the opportunity for welfare increases through specialization.

However, merely liberalizing trade, which establishes a libertarian system of equality of opportunity (reciprocal free trade rules), is not adequate to make the system work to the benefit of the least advantaged, since the reality of gross inequalities in international endowments undercuts the possibility of effective equality of rights among states (sovereignty).[29] For this reason, the difference principle suggests that just trade cannot consist only of free trade. Trade law needs justification according to the difference principle: it should make inequalities work to benefit least advantaged.

For trade, the key lies in understanding the way many of the natural and social inequalities among states translate into the relative strength of

[26] This conclusion is consistent with the positions taken by the leading proponents of a Rawlsian theory of international distributive justice. See ibid, at 134 note 6 and sources cited therein.

[27] Theory of Justice, above n 15, at 13.

[28] On the constitutional and law-making function of trade institutions, and their shortcomings in this regard, see Ernst-Ulrich Petersmann, 'Constitutionalism and International Organizations', 17 Northwestern Journal of International Law & Business 398 (1997); but see Jeffrey L. Dunoff, 'Constitutional Conceits: The WTO's "Constitution" and the Discipline of InternationalLaw', 17 European Journal of International Law. 647 (2005) (arguing that Petersmann's account is descriptively inaccurate and normatively undesirable).

[29] *Accord* Beitz, above n 14, at 163 (objections to justice of a domestic system of natural liberty apply with equal force to an international version as well).

consumer markets and producer groups. States that are rich in natural resources and have developed significant social resources such as wealth, industrial capacity and technology, will generally have as a result a strong consumer market, as manifested in per capita income, and a strong production base, as manifested in per capita GDP. States that are poor in resources will generally have a weak consumer market, manifested in low per capita income, and a weak production base, manifested in low per capita GDP.

This means that market access becomes a key variable in any attempt to address inequalities through trade law. The International Difference Principle applied to trade requires that states organize market access in such a way that it benefits the least advantaged. This can be stated in normative terms as follows:

> (II). In order to justify inequalities in the size of markets, states must ensure that market access is structured so as to benefit the least advantaged.

Free trade is a principle of market access, but it is reciprocal market access: you open yours, and I will open mine. Something more than reciprocal trade liberalization is needed in order to ensure that market access benefit the least advantaged.

Trade law offers that something more in the form of special and differential treatment. At the core of special and differential treatment is the practice of asymmetric trade liberalization, to secure the benefit of developed country wealth and resources for the least advantaged states through non-reciprocal market access. It is this asymmetry which enables special and differential treatment to play a key role in justifying inequalities in the international allocation of social goods. By opening their markets to developing country exports on a preferential basis, developed countries in effect place the consumption power of their larger, richer consumer market at the service of the developing country, which can increase its exports and thereby strengthen its economic base. Such preferential access for developing countries allows the inequalities that manifest themselves in the form of wealthy consumer markets to work to the benefit of the least advantaged, thereby meeting the central criteria for distributive justice.

This conclusion can be restated in normative terms as follows:

> (III). In order to justify inequalities in the size of markets, states must offer preferential market access structured so as to benefit the least advantaged.

This can be understood as an obligation upon states with respect to how they structure trade law as a distributive mechanism, in particular how they structure special and differential treatment, as a condition of the difference principle.

In order to more fully determine the necessary contours of such a policy in practice, we must examine how in fact special and differential treatment operates in contemporary international trade relations. I will give only an abridged summary of this process here, in order to illustrate the approach before turning to the proper objects of inquiry here, the Bank and the Fund.[30]

Current applications of the market access aspects of S&D have been subject to a variety of political constraints and conditions: they are unilateral, they exclude the most competitive goods, and they impose non-trade related conditions.[31] The difference principle as applied to international trade suggests that these conditions are not normatively justifiable.[32] First, as a matter of basic justice the unilateralism of existing trade preference programs must be reconsidered, since justice is not optional and unilateralism favors the more advantaged.[33] Second, the exclusion of the goods most competitive with the manufactured goods of developed states is truly perverse: instead of structuring the trading relationship for the benefit of the least advantaged partner, the import sensitivity exclusion deliberately structures the relationship in favor of the less-competitive domestic industry of the granting state. Third, by subjecting the actual availability of the preferences to conditions clearly related to the domestic and foreign policy agendas of the granting state, GSP programs again turn the normative justification of market inequalities on its head, benefitting the granting state and not the beneficiary.[34]

By examining current special and differential treatment practice in view of the normative guideline developed above, I further distill policy-specific criteria with respect to market access programs:

> (IV). In order to benefit the least advantaged, preferential market access (special & differential treatment) must be binding, non-exclusionary, and unconditional.

These criteria should be observed in the implementation of special and differential treatment today, if the goal is to implement it in a form that will reflect justice as fairness and contribute to the justification of the international trade system.

II. JUSTICE AND THE BRETTON WOODS INSTITUTIONS

In the foregoing section, I have outlined one approach to developing a normative theory of international economic law, in the area of trade.

[30] For a fuller treatment, see above n 2 and n 14 and sources cited therein.
[31] See generally Garcia, above n 2, at 155–68.
[32] Ibid.
[33] Ibid.
[34] Ibid.

To recap, it involves four steps: first mapping the domestic theory onto the international subject and generating an international form of the relevant normative principles, in this case the International Difference Principle; second, examining the specific nexus between the policy context and the normative system (i.e. what is the institution allocating?), which was market access and the terms of market access in the case of trade; third, formulating at the constitutional level the core distributive principle, derived from the International Difference Principle, that should guide the institution's allocative activity; and fourth, developing specific criteria for policy development at the operational levels by applying the international normative criteria to the specific allocative policies of the relevant institution, which are special and differential treatment in the case of trade.

What remains is to perform this same exercise for the Bank and Fund. As allocative social institutions created by states, the Bank and Fund make decisions which influence the distribution of social primary goods, in this case development capital and hard currencies.[35] Therefore, the appropriate policy nexus, is lending – development capital lending in the case of the Bank, and balance of payments lending in the case of the Fund. Generating a normative theory for the BWIs will involve analyzing the lending activities, terms and policies of the Bank and Fund with reference to distributive justice criteria stemming from states' obligation to implement justice in how they set up the basic structure.

This will involve application of the methodology of the previous section to the Bank and Fund.[36] The first step, derivation of an international normative principle, has already been taken, resulting in the International Difference Principle:

> (I). International social and economic inequalities are just only if they result in compensating benefits for all states, and in particular for the least advantaged states.

[35] As mentioned above, (see above n 1), there are other important social primary goods subject to institutional allocation; and there are many public and private entities and institutions at both the national and international levels which make decisions influencing the allocation of these two specific examples of social primary goods, development capital and hard currencies. The Bank and the Fund stand at the confluence of these two factors, as the principal international institutions allocating these two kinds of social primary goods; hence my focus on them here.

[36] This is of course a large undertaking—my aim in this essay is to offer a preliminary analysis and overview of what such an undertaking might involve and reveal. A more extensive but still preliminary discussion can be found in Frank J. Garcia, *Justice, Bretton Woods Institutions and the Problem of Inequality*, 'Developing Countries in the WTO Legal System' Conference, University of Minnesota Law School, May 25, 2007 (on file with author); a definitive discussion of these issues will involve a book-length treatment, in process.

Steps two through four will involve identifying the core implications of the International Difference Principle for Bank and Fund activity.[37] I will carry out this process in sections A and B, respectively.

A. International development lending: the bank and global inequality

1. The bank's role in international justice

The Bank is a social institution created and managed by states, whose core activity is to allocate primary social goods: development capital, and the terms of access to such capital, which are themselves a social good. Development capital is a socially produced resource. A country's supply of development capital reflects a complex blend of natural and social factors. It reflects the country's natural resource endowment, and the complex blend of its history, policies, and trade relations, all of which affect the capacity of the system to generate surplus capital for development, and the amounts of such capital.

Since the Bank's core function with respect to these resources is to influence their allocation among states through its lending decisions and policies, this intimately involves the Bank in distributive justice concerns: by what principles and rules are these social goods allocated, and to whose benefit? To normatively evaluate this, we need a theory of Just International Development Lending.

a. Toward a theory of just international development lending

As with trade law we looked at the function of market access, here we look to the Bank's role as a lender, specifically a development lender, which suggests we focus on access to development capital.[38] The key normative implication of Justice as Fairness for development lending is that states do not in a significant sense deserve their relative supply of development capital, insofar as it is a product, in part, of natural inequalities which are morally arbitrary, compounded by social inequalities.[39] This means that states cannot be

[37] I want to emphasize that in this analysis, I am taking as given that these two institutions exist, and arguing that given their allocative roles, their operations are subject to the International Difference Principle. I am not arguing that the International Difference Principle *requires* the existence of these two institutions, nor am I arguing that these institutions are the only, or even best, mechanism through which to address the inequality in distribution of development capital and hard currencies. Rather, given that states have created [for rational reasons, as I suggest elsewhere (see above n 36)] global markets for development capital and currency exchange, and these institutions in particular, the next question is how justice might influence their operations.

[38] Hockett suggests a further theoretical link between justice and lending, or as he puts it between justice theory and finance theory, on an insurance model, namely, that both involve risk allocation under conditions of uncertainty. See Robert Hockett, From '"Mission Creep" to Gestalt Switch: Justice, Finance, the IFIs, and Globalization's Intended Beneficiaries', 37 George Washington International Law Review. 167 (2005) at 179–81.

[39] In this respect, we do face the problem of how to account for the fact that good social policies contribute to an abundance of development capital, or the problem of the degree of ambition-sensitivity of a particular distributive theory. See Garcia, above n 2 at 61. Hockett, for

presumed to be entitled to their particular supply of development capital, and that resulting inequalities in the distribution of development capital must be justified. This has implications for how states structure the Bank's role as development capital lender. We can formulate the following, as an application of the International Difference Principle to the work of the Bank:

> (II). In order to justify inequalities in the distribution of development capital, states must ensure that access to development capital is structured so as to benefit the least advantaged.

How does this apply to the work of the Bank?

As an initial matter, access to development capital is a function of the private capital markets. Whenever there is a general or country-specific economic crisis, however, it is much harder for certain states to borrow needed development capital on the private market. Moreover, their demand for development capital exceeds capital-poor states' ability to pay commercial rates, so if the only access to development capital was through private banks at commercial rates, their development capital needs would go under-supplied.[40] Therefore, by putting surplus capital to work on near-commercial terms in the economies of states without adequate indigenous supplies of capital, the Bank is conferring a benefit on less advantaged states.

This brings us to the issue of the *terms* on which the Bank makes development capital available. The terms of access to this development capital are themselves a social resource. In other words, the terms on which the IBRD makes its development capital available (preferential rates), and the terms on which the IDA makes its credits and grants available (concessionary rates) are themselves a further socially produced, and socially allocated, resource.

In this sense, the Bank's IBRD lending is similar to the principle of free trade in WTO—helping to equalize opportunity of access to development capital in a manner consistent with the basic requirements of Justice as Fairness. However, in the same manner that with respect to trade, a system of purely free trade was not enough due to the facts of inequality, I want to suggest that in development lending a system of pure private market commercial lending, or even a blended system of private bank commercial lending and Bank preferential lending, would not be enough. Because the least advantaged states have limited domestic capital formation capabilities and limited resources to borrow capital, they cannot get enough through these avenues, meaning that the overall inequality in capital will not work to

---

example, suggests in this regard that global distributive justice by BWIs should focus on what he calls 'ethically exogenous' benefits and burdens only. See. Hockett, above n 38, at 193.

[40] This was one reason for the formation of the IDA. See Ghazi above n 3, at 24.

their advantage. Continuing the analogy to free trade from the previous section, IBRD-style lending is necessary, but not sufficient, for international justice. It is not enough that capital is made available, even at below-commercial terms – the International Difference Principle asks much more. It asks that capital be made available under such terms and in such a manner, that it benefits the *least* advantaged.

In terms of the International Difference Principle, this suggests the following corollary:

> (IIA). In order that access to development capital benefit the least advantaged, states must offer concessional access to development capital.

In this sense, the IDA's policies and programs are the structural analog in lending to the WTO's Special and Differential Treatment policies reviewed in the trade justice analysis set forth above—concessional access to capital as a tool for justifying inequality. It is this specific aspect of the Bank's activities which most directly addresses the inequality in development capital from the perspective of the least advantaged.

This brings us to the third step in the process, which can be restated in normative terms as follows:

> (III) In order to justify inequalities in the distribution of development capital, states must offer concessional access to development capital that is structured so as to benefit the least advantaged.

In order to fully reflect the International Difference Principle in its mission and operations, the Bank must ensure that its concessional lending programs will *actually* benefit the least advantaged.

2. Operational implications of a theory of just international development lending

How can this normative agenda be carried out at the operational level? In this essay, I will focus on only one area of inquiry: how the Bank determines the nature and extent of its involvement in the domestic policies of borrowing state.[41]

a. The bank's role in domestic social policy

Consistent with its prudential obligations, the Bank has a role in evaluating the degree to which the domestic social policies of borrowing states are themselves part of the problem of inadequate capital, and the degree to which such policies help or hinder the project goals and risk squandering development capital, which is after all an exhaustible social resource.[42]

[41] Other fruitful areas of inquiry include the Bank's mission and priorities, how the Bank selects and evaluates ongoing projects, and how the Bank determines success. See Garcia, above n 36.

[42] Hockett refers to this as the 'stick' aspect of Bank operations, or the ways in which the Bank and other BWI's implement their policies. See Hockett above n 38, at 195.

This has been one of the most controversial aspects of the Bank's operations, particularly with respect to its participation in Structural Adjustment Programs or SAPs, through which the Bank seeks in concert with the IMF to 'improve resource allocation, increase economic efficiency, expand growth potential and increase resilience to shocks'.[43] This criticism is largely due to two factors: the Bank's leverage to insist on domestic policy reforms, and the controversy surrounding the soundness of the Bank's approach to domestic policy.[44] The former is essential to the Bank's proper stewardship. However, the latter is, and should be, a constant source of inquiry and criticism both within and without the Bank, as its experts search for the appropriate blend of policies for each borrowing state.[45]

In order to be consistent with the International Difference Principle, the Bank's domestic involvement should focus on the degree to which such policies affect the welfare of the poorest segments of a borrower's society.[46] This can be restated affirmatively as follows:

> (IV). The Bank must ensure that its involvement in the domestic policy of borrowers operates to the benefit of the least advantaged.

Current Bank practices have been criticized for failing to take into account the redistributive effects of Bank policies.[47] Inequalities in wealth distribution affect economic stability, levels of education, life expectancy, levels of health care, job training, etc., in short, the factors which are already the subject of Bank activities. To look at the way in which a country's social

[43] The SAPs themselves have been actually been replaced first by the Enhanced SAPs and most recently by the Poverty Reduction and Growth Facilities, although following Ghazi I will refer to all such programs collectively as SAPs. See Ghazi above n 3, at 47–9.

[44] I am referring here most recently to the Bank's neoliberal approach, which has been the subject of much criticism. See ibid; see generally John W. Head, *The Future of the Global Economic Organizations* (Ardsley, NY: Transnational Publishers, 2005) at 11.

[45] Naturally, the more demonstrably sound and ideologically minimal the Bank's policies are seen to be, the less its leverage will be resented.

[46] I believe this approach is consistent with the Bank's own responsibilities and Articles and with the 'political prohibition'. The purpose of the prohibition is to ensure the Bank acts impartially: to prevent discrimination based on politics, and the application of leverage through the Bank by one Member against another. See Jonathon Bradlow, 'Should the IFIs play a Role in the Implementation and Enforcement of International Humanitarian Law? 50 University of Kansas Law Review 695 (2002) at 728 (citing legislative history of the political prohibition); Garcia, above n 36 at 45–8.

[47] Although the Bank has moved away from its traditional approach to SAPs, by creating Poverty Reduction and Growth Facilities based on each borrowing country's Poverty Reduction Strategy Paper, and began together with the Fund in 2001 a program of 'social impact analysis' (SIA) through which to 'assess the consequences of policy interventions. . .on the well-being of different social groups, with a special focus on the vulnerable and the poor', the Bank continues to be criticized on this front. See Ghazi above n 4, at 72. Hockett, for example, argues that BWIs need to take a stronger public position on the normative justification of such social insurance programs. See Hockett above n 38, at 198.

resources are distributed internally among its members is not to act with partiality. Internal inequalities in wealth are matters of economic policy that are squarely within the Bank's mandate.

B. International currency lending: the fund and global inequality

1. The fund's role in international justice

The starting point is to recall that the Fund is a social institution, whose core activity is to allocate primary social goods: access to currency reserves, and the cost of such access. Trade currencies are an exhaustible social resource.[48] As with market size in the case of trade and capital supply in the case of development, the socioeconomic factors which influence the market's determination of which currencies are hard and which are soft, reflect a complex blend of natural and social inequalities, including the arbitrary distribution of natural resources and good or bad luck, and contingent social factors such as sound or unsound policy choices, colonialism, etc.

The fact that certain currencies are considered hard and others are not, necessarily creates inequalities in the distribution of trade currencies. This inequality is in part a function of the fact that currencies are national in nature, and those countries' whose economic policies and performance support the hardness of their currency have a built-in advantage in the supply of that currency, and in part a function of the larger operation, inequality and colonial legacy of the global economic system, which contribute to the hard-currency attributes of some economies, and undercuts such attributes of others.

Those states whose currencies are hard have an abundance and a capacity to self generate, whereas those states whose currencies are soft are always at risk of scarcity and cannot create this resource indigenously.[49]

Since states have established the Fund to play a central role in allocating these resources in view of such inequality, this intimately involves the Fund in distributive justice concerns: by what principles and rules are these social goods allocated, and to whose benefit? To determine this, we need a theory of Just International Monetary Policy.

2. Toward a theory of just international monetary policy

As with trade law we looked at the function of market access, here we look to the Fund's role as a lender, specifically a balance of payments lender,

[48] *Accord* Lastra, above n 6, at 516 (Fund resources are finite hence their use is subject to oversight). While it is true that countries whose currencies are hard could in theory print more money, it is in the very nature of hard currency countries that they not pursue such policies or risk the tradability of their currency. Therefore, hard currency is in essence exhaustible even for hard currency countries.

[49] I am setting aside for the moment the issue of whether by making better policy choices they could harden their currency. This would not in any case deal with natural inequalities or historical contingencies.

which suggests we focus on access to hard currencies.[50] As an initial matter, access to hard currencies is a function of the private currency market. The Fund exists to make these currencies available to states which for one reason or another cannot meet their needs through the export operations of their private sector, their own central bank reserves, and through the private currency market.[51]

The key normative implication of Justice as Fairness for hard currency lending is that states do not in a significant sense deserve their relative supply of hard currency, insofar as it is a product, in part, of natural inequalities which are morally arbitrary, compounded by social inequalities.[52] This means that states cannot be presumed to be entitled to their particular supply of hard currency, and that resulting inequalities in the distribution of hard currency must be justified.

This has implications for how states structure the Fund's operations. Applying this principle to the Fund's role as manager of international currency reserves, we can derive the following as an application of our basic principle of global distributive justice to the work of the Fund:

> (II). In order to justify inequalities in the distribution of trade currencies, states must ensure that access to trade currencies is structured so as to benefit the least advantaged.

How does the Fund look from this perspective?

The very existence and mission of the Fund suggest that the Fund plays a normatively justifiable role, making wealthy states' abundance of trade currencies available to states with less access to trade currency. By putting hard currency to work on near-commercial terms in the economies of states without adequate indigenous supplies of such currencies, the Fund is conferring a benefit on less advantaged states.[53]

However, the facts of inequality mean that, just as in trade it is the case that reciprocal market access could not in all cases benefit the least advantaged, so in the case of hard currencies a private market would not be equally beneficial to all states. Whenever there is a general economic crisis or a country-specific crisis, it is much harder for certain states to generate or borrow needed hard currencies. Moreover, the demand for hard currency

[50] Hockett suggests a further theoretical link between justice and lending, or as he puts it between justice theory and finance theory, or an insurance model, namely, that both involve risk allocation under conditions of uncertainty. See Hockett, above n 38, at 179–181.

[51] See ibid., at 194 (existing necessity of both markets, and justice, to the possibility for international financial institutions to deliver on their social promise).

[52] As with development capital supplies, we face the problem of ambition-sensitivity, namely how to account for the fact that good social policies contribute to an abundance of development capital. See above n 38 and sources cited therein.

[53] Head, above n 44, at 95–6 (documenting the considerable wealth transfers which IMF facilities have affected for the benefit of the least developed members).

exceeds currency-poor states' ability to pay commercial rates, so if the only access to hard currency was through private banks at commercial rates, economic opportunities would go unrealized.[54]

This brings us to the issue of the *terms* on which the Fund makes hard currency available. The Fund offers two basic types of facilities: 'regular' or non-concessional facilities, which are not in fact loans but purchase and repurchase agreements;[55] and concessional facilities, which are truly trade currency loans to developing countries.[56] The Fund's regular facilities consist of five main lending programs: Stand-By Arrangements, the Extended Fund Facility, the Supplemental Reserve Facility, Contingent Credit Lines, and the Compensatory Financing Facility.[57] All have varying eligibility criteria and repayment terms, and charge interest that is slightly below, but keyed to, market rates.[58] The Fund's concessional facilities consist of the Poverty Reduction and Growth Facilities (PRGF), which replaced the earlier SAPs and Enhanced SAPs, and charges only 0.5% interest per year.[59]

The terms of access to such currencies through each facility are themselves a social resource. In other words, the terms on which the Fund makes its currencies available through regular facilities (preferential rates), and the terms on which the Fund makes its currencies available through concessional facilities (concessional rates) are themselves a further socially produced, and socially allocated, resource.

In this sense, the Fund's regular facilities lending is similar to the principle of free trade in WTO and the Bank's preferential lending through the IBRD – helping to equalize opportunity to hard currencies in a manner consistent with the basic requirements of Justice as Fairness. However, in the same manner that with respect to trade, a system of purely free trade was not enough due to the facts of inequality; so in hard currency lending a system of pure private market currency transactions, or even a blended system of private bank commercial currency transactions and Fund preferential lending, would not be enough. Because developing countries have limited domestically generated supplies of hard currency and limited resources to

[54] Exporting states would lose sales, importing states much-needed goods and services, and less advantaged states would be tempted to employ currency controls, devaluations, etc., destabilizing the international monetary system to the detriment of all.

[55] See Head, above n 44, at 24 (describing operation of SBA and EFF purchase/repurchase obligations).

[56] See Lastra, above n 6, at 517–518.

[57] See generally Head, above n 44, at 24–5 (reviewing types of facilities).

[58] See Ghazi, above n 3, at 13.

[59] See Ibid. One commentator suggests that the category of concessional facilities also includes special facilities such as the oil facility, accelerated procedures such as the emergency financing mechanism, and exceptional facilities such as the supplemental reserve facility and contingent credit line for sudden and disruptive events. See Lastra above n 6 at 519–20. I will follow the narrower approach and restrict my attention to the PRGF since the rest charge higher, near-market rates.

borrow such currencies, they cannot satisfy their need for hard currency through these avenues, meaning that the overall inequality in currency supplies will not work to their advantage.

Continuing the analogy to free trade from the previous section, regular Fund facility lending is necessary, but not sufficient, for international justice. It is not enough that hard currencies be made available, even at below-commercial terms. The International Difference Principle asks that hard currencies be made available under such terms and in such a manner, that it benefits the *least* advantaged.

In terms of the International Difference Principle, this suggests the following corollary:

> (IIA). In order that access to trade currencies benefit the least advantaged, states must offer concessional access to development capital.

The PRGFs are in the balance-of-payments lending context the structural analog to the WTO's Special and Differential Treatment policies in trade and the Bank's IDA lending – concessional access to hard currencies as a tool for justifying inequality. They represent that specific aspect of the Fund which directly addresses the inequality in the distribution of hard currencies from the perspective of the least advantaged.

This leads to the third step in the process, which can be restated as follows:

> (III) In order to justify inequalities in the distribution of trade currencies, states must offer concessional access to trade currencies that is structured so as to benefit the least advantaged.

It is the Fund's responsibility to see that this most valuable social good—concessional access to trade currencies—is in fact structured so as to benefit the least advantaged. How can this be carried out at the operational level?

C. Operational implications of a theory of just monetary policy

There are many aspects of the Fund's operations which would seem to meet the basic thrust of the International Difference Principle, at least at a general level. To begin with, there is the Fund's very existence and basic mission. Moreover, there is the fact that the Fund operates through all of its facilities almost exclusively with countries that are in some stage of development. Finally, there is the fact that the Fund does indeed offer concessional hard currency lending through its PRGF.

However, a thorough evaluation of the justice of the Fund's operations, and the full development of a theory of just international monetary policy, would require taking this general principle, and deepening the analysis through a program by program evaluation of the Fund's operation: are they in fact structured to benefit the least advantaged, and do they in fact operate this way? And what does the way the Fund actually works, suggest about principles of just monetary policy in the real world?

As with the Bank, I am going to focus in this essay on one area: the Fund's involvement in the domestic policies of borrowing states.[60]

1. Conditionality

Consistent with its prudential obligations, the Fund has a role in evaluating the degree to which the domestic social policies of borrowing states are themselves part of the balance of payments problem, and the degree to which such policies risk squandering Fund currency reserves, which are an exhaustible social resource.[61] The Fund exercises this role through what it calls 'conditionality', which it defines as the link between 'the approval or continuation of the Fund's financing and the implementation of specified elements of economic policy by the country receiving this financing'.[62]

Conditionality functions in IMF lending as a substitute for collateral, through the imposition of policy restrictions on borrowing states as a condition of releasing credit tranches.[63] When a Fund member needs to draw on the Fund for hard currencies in excess of its own reserve account, such draws are subject to conditions negotiated between the Fund and the drawing country. Such conditions can include such sensitive domestic issues as wage rates, levels of public expenditures, budget deficits and export levels.[64] Similar conditions are also imposed as a function of a borrower's participation in the Bank's HIPC program, through the link between HIPC and participation in the Fund's PRGF.[65]

Conditionality has been one of the most controversial aspects of the Fund's operations. The conditions the Fund imposes as a cost of its intervention, have a tremendous impact on the domestic policies and development strategies of recipient countries.[66] Criticism has been particularly strong with respect to the Fund's Structural Adjustment Programs or

[60] Other promising areas include the Fund's mission and priorities, its system for allocating SDRs, its decision making structure, and its system for choosing and evaluating projects. See Garcia, above n 36; see generally Head above n 44 (summarizing critiques).

[61] This is the 'coercive' aspect of Fund operations. See Ghazi, above n 3, at 5; Hockett, above n 38, at 195.

[62] IMF, 'Conditionality in Fund-Supported Programs—Overview', http://www.imf.org/external/np/pdr/cond/2001/eng/overview/index.htm (last visited 8 June, 2007).

[63] Lastra, above n 6, at 517.

[64] See generally Ghazi, above n 3, at 16–7.

[65] *Charles Abugre, SAPping the Poor: Structural Adjustment—the Forgotten Issue*, www.wdm.org.uk/resources/reports/debt/sapping the poor01061999.pdf (June 1999) (citing link between HIPC participation and PRGF).

[66] See generally Ngaire Woods, *Order, Globalization, and Inequality in World Politics*, in Andrew Hurrell and Ngaire Woods (eds), *Inequality, Globalization and World Politics* (Oxford, U.K.: Oxford University Press, 1999) 30–33 (surveying impact of IMF).

SAPs, and the successor Enhanced Structural Adjustment Facility.[67] As with the Bank, such criticism is largely due to two factors: the leverage the Fund has by virtue of its role to insist on domestic policy reforms,[68] and the controversy surrounding the soundness and ideological basis of the Fund's approach to domestic policy.[69]

Although the Fund has begun to acknowledge shortcomings in its conditionality and structural adjustment programs,[70] Justice as Fairness requires more than a recognition of problems in the implementation of the Fund's policies—it requires a radical re-examination of the Fund's conditionality program.

What principles or criteria should guide this re-evaluation? According to this analysis, it should be the International Difference Principle, restated as follows:

> (IV). The Fund must ensure that its involvement in the domestic policy of borrowers operates to the benefit of the least advantaged.

Current Fund practices have been criticized for failing to adequately take into account the redistributive effects of Fund policies.[71] While the Fund has begun to publicly note the distributive impact of its policies,[72] and develop new approaches to conditionality,[73] such policies continue to be criticized,[74] and require a sustained normative reevaluation according to the international difference principle, so that the inequality in international

[67] See Ghazi, above n 3, at 47 (1990 Bank paper).

[68] But see Head, above n 44, at 75 (downplaying the leverage aspects of conditionality in view of borrowing countries' formal right to say no).

[69] I am referring here to the Fund's ideological approach, which has been called 'unrepentant neoliberalism'. Deacon, above n 1, at 220; see generally Joseph Stiglitz, *Globalization and its Discontents* (New York, NY: W.W. Norton, 2003). But see Head, above n 44, at 61–63, 69–75 (summarizing and rejecting the ideology, or what he calls the 'bad medicine', critique).

[70] See Head, above n 44, at 72–73 (discussing 2002 reforms to Fund conditionality policies).

[71] See, e.g. Head, above n 44, at 81–84 (summarizing and largely endorsing the distributive critique of Fund policies). Hockett, for example, argues that BWIs need to take a stronger public position on the normative justification of social insurance programs. Hockett, above n 38, at 198.

[72] Hockett, above n 38, at 223.

[73] The Fund now guides its PRGF lending through Poverty Strategy Reduction Papers, designed in consultation with borrowing states, and supplemented since 2001 by the 'social impact analysis' (SIA) program, through which the Fund attempts to assess the consequences of its conditionality policies on the well-being of different social groups, with a special focus on the vulnerable and the poor. IMF Annual Report 2003 at 44. However, these reforms do not specifically address the most critical issue highlighted by the International Difference Principle, namely that conditionality policies be specifically tailored to benefit the least advantaged. Even the SIA is intended more to mitigate adverse effects rather than to make the benefit of the least advantaged a policy priority.

[74] See, e.g. Ghazi above n 3, at 72; Abugre, above n 65; but see Head, above n 44, at 82 (equity criticisms understate Fund efforts in this area).

currency resources can be effectively put in the service of the least advantaged.[75]

III. CONCLUSION

Justice as Fairness presents a very basic question to states in their international economic relations: given the facts of inequality, their arbitrary nature, and their adverse effects on the least advantaged, how can the international economic system be re-structured to ensure that such inequalities work to the benefit of the least advantaged? In general the Bank and Fund are in fact doing much that is consistent with international egalitarian justice, but they can and should do more. In this respect, the International Difference Principle can offer normative guidance as to precisely what more the Bank and Fund should do. I have sought in this essay to illustrate in one area of Bank and Fund activity – their involvement in borrowers' domestic policies – the sort of normative guidance which such an analysis can offer, as the Bank and Fund seek to reform their policies in this area. Using the normative framework of justice is itself a subtle but significant change in emphasis – one commentator has likened it to a 'Gestalt shift'[76]—that offers valuable substantive and political benefits. The states which set Bank and Fund policy should more explicitly embrace and articulate the redistributive aspect of the BWIs and couch their efforts in the language of justice. To refuse to do so is to court the danger that Bank and Fund policies will serve a particular hidden theory of justice, not, as claimed, to avoid entangling the Bank and Fund in such issues at all. If justice means ensuring that inequalities in the international distribution of social goods work to the benefit of the least advantaged, then states must ensure, among other things, that the Bank and Fund delve far enough into domestic social policy and with appropriate criteria, to reach and affect those structures that actually determine whether capital and currency inequalities will or will not work to the benefit of the least advantaged.

[75] See also, e.g. Namita Wahi, 'Human Rights Accountability of the IMF and the World Bank: A Critique of Existing Mechanisms and Articulation of a Theory of Horizontal Accountability', 12 U.C. Davis Journal of International Law & Policy 331 (2006) (critical of conditionality from a human rights perspective); Ofer Eldar, 'Reform of IMF Conditionality: A Proposal for Self-imposed Conditionality', 8 Journal of International Economic Law. 509 (2005) (proposing that conditionality be entirely borrower-driven, with Fund approval).

[76] See Hockett, above n 38 at 169.

THE CULTURE OF THE WTO: WHY IT NEEDS TO CHANGE

*Debra P. Steger**

ABSTRACT

The WTO is an international organization with its own distinctive culture, which is derived from the practice and experience of the GATT. The WTO, however, is not the old GATT. The multilateral trading system was transformed into an international organization in 1995, and today, the WTO also administers a host of agreements that contain detailed rules regulating international economic activity. The membership of the WTO has grown to 150, the vast majority of which are developing countries. Most importantly, the trading system, which was once bi-polar, driven by the United States and the European Union, has changed dramatically to become multi-polar, with the large emerging economies, such as China, India and Brazil, becoming major economic powers in their own right. The WTO needs major surgery in order to respond effectively to the new political realities in the international economic system. The current impasse in the Doha Round is in large part due to the great transformation in geopolitical power relationships taking place in the world today. If the Round fails, it will not be the end of the WTO. On the contrary, it might provide a useful 'time out' for the multilateral system to find its new stride. A related problem is that the mandate of the WTO is no longer clear. This article suggests that WTO Members work together to define the new purpose and mandate of the WTO to make it relevant to governments, companies and people in the 21st century. Institutional reform of the WTO is needed to provide it with the architecture and decision making machinery that will allow it to become a vibrant, responsive and accountable organization.

INTRODUCTION

Like the countries which form its membership, the World Trade Organization (WTO) has a culture. Its culture or theology is not derived from the Uruguay Round agreements, but rather from the culture and practice of the General Agreement on Tariffs and Trade (GATT). Moreover, the culture of the WTO does not reflect the present geo-political realities and

* Professor and Director, Emerging Dynamic Global Economies (EDGE) Network, Faculty of Law, University of Ottawa.

power relationships among its members. It was developed in a very different time by a small group of countries—the original contracting parties of the GATT 1947—for a very different purpose.

A major institutional negotiation took place in the Uruguay Round that attempted to set out a new 'constitution' for the multilateral trading system.[1] The results of this negotiation are reflected in the *Marrakesh Agreement Establishing the WTO* (the *Marrakesh Agreement*) and the *Understanding on Rules and Procedures Governing the Settlement of Disputes* (the DSU). The dispute settlement system of the WTO has been used very actively by members, and is viewed as being strong and effective by its members and commentators. In contrast, the political institutions of the WTO do not function much differently than they did in the previous GATT system—which is not very effectively. Despite the fact that the institutional rules have been changed, allowing WTO Members more flexibility in how they take decisions and amend agreements, the experience of members since 1995 has been to follow the old GATT procedures and practice rather than using the flexibilities provided in the *Marrakesh Agreement.*

Thus, even though the rules in the *Marrakesh Agreement* provide members with flexibilities and options for taking decisions and making new rules, such as amending existing provisions or adding new agreements, it is the culture of the WTO (which is a carryover of the culture of the old GATT) that inhibits progress. The rules are there, but the members do not use them. Rather, they rely on the old GATT practice with which they are familiar.

The problem is that the WTO is not the old GATT. Its membership has changed from the original 23 contracting parties in 1948, to 128 contracting parties of the GATT in 1994,[2] to 150 Members of the WTO today. The overwhelming majority of WTO members are developing countries, including the major emerging economic powers of China, India, and Brazil. Although the developing countries are not a homogeneous group, they hold the balance of power in the WTO. The major developed powers, United States and European Union, cannot drive the system as they could in the old days. Sylvia Ostry has characterized the old GATT system as a 'bicycle built for two' with the United States in the front seat and the European Communities in the back.[3] The current WTO is more like a bus careening down a hill with many drivers, none of whom are certain about where they want to go. In the past, the United States always drove the

[1] For an insider's perspective on that negotiation, see: Debra Steger, 'The World Trade Organization: A New Constitution for the Trading System', in Debra P. Steger (ed.), *Peace Through Trade: Building the WTO* (London: Cameron May, 2004) 25–46.

[2] BISD, 42S/95, at ix.

[3] Sylvia Ostry, 'The Uruguay Round North-South Grand Bargain: Implications for future negotiations', in Daniel L. M. Kennedy and James D. Southwick (eds), *The Political Economy of International Trade Law, Essays in Honor of Robert E. Hudec* (Cambridge: Cambridge University Press, 2002) 285–300, at 299–300.

negotiations – from the original negotiation in 1947 through the Tokyo Round in the 1970s and the Uruguay Round in the 1980s and 1990s. Today, even if the United States and European Union did try to demonstrate some leadership in the Doha Round, the developing countries would not let them set the agenda and drive the negotiations. Those days are over.

Some of the major new economic powers in the WTO, in particular, China, are not market economies. This poses enormous challenges for the multilateral trading system which is based on market principles and principles of non-discrimination and transparency. Vietnam has recently become a member of the WTO, and Russia remains in the process of accession. The accession of these new members raises obvious difficulties for the implementation and administration of WTO obligations.

The culture of the WTO needs to change to reflect the new political realities in the international economic system. President Vladimir Putin of Russia recently emphasized:

> The new architecture of economic relations implies a principally new approach to the work of international organisations. It has become increasingly apparent of late that the existing organisations are not always up to the measure in regulating global international relations and the global market. Organisations originally designed with only a small number of active players in mind sometimes look archaic, undemocratic and unwieldy in today's conditions. They are far from taking into consideration the balance of force that has emerged in the world today. This means that the old decision-making methods do not always work. The World Trade Organisation and the Doha round of trade negotiations, which are proceeding with great difficulty, to put it mildly, provide a clear example in this respect.[4]

He also highlighted that the rapid growth in regionalism has emerged for a reason:

> It is not coincidence that a parallel system of regional alliances and agreements is taking shape, essentially giving the global market a new structure. And the trade liberalisation process is now taking place more and more through these new agreements. It is worth thinking about creating regional Eurasian free trade institutions in order to encourage trade and investment. These institutions could of course draw on and use the positive experience of the World Trade Organisation.[5]

The mandate and purpose of the WTO is no longer clear. The mandate of the GATT system was continuing the process of trade

[4] President of Russia, 'Meetings with Representatives of Various Communities', Speech presented at the XI Saint Petersburg International Economic Forum, June 10, 2007, Saint Petersburg, Russia, http://www.kremlin.ru/eng/speeches/2007/06/10/1823_type84779_133685.shtml (visited 14 June 2007).

[5] Ibid.

liberalization—reducing barriers to trade in order to encourage economic growth that would bring greater wealth and prosperity. The preamble to the GATT 1947 reflected these goals. The preamble of the WTO Agreement is broader—it includes the goals of environmental sustainability and development. These new goals have been recognized by the Appellate Body and the dispute settlement bodies, but they have not become part of the accepted theology or culture of the WTO as perceived by its members. So, there is a difference between what the preamble of the WTO says the purpose of the organization is and what its members perceive it to be. And, there is a difference between the actual procedures of the WTO for decision making and rule making, and the practice of the members in taking decisions.

Why is there the current paralysis in the Doha Round? The short answer is that the world has changed, and the WTO, because of the cultural attitudes of its members, is mired in the old GATT theology of the past. Until the members of the WTO wake up and face the new realities, and develop decision making and rule making procedures that reflect the new geo-political power relationships, there will continue to be paralysis in the system.

Unlike other international organizations which have Secretaries-General and/or Executive Boards and Secretariats with real power, the WTO is driven solely by its members acting collectively (like the old GATT CONTRACTING PARTIES). The members will not allow the Director-General to have any real power, nor will they delegate any significant policy setting or even administrative or budgetary responsibilities to the Director-General or the Secretariat. There is no Executive Committee or Management Board that sets overall administrative or substantive policy or direction for the WTO.

Who and what is the WTO? It is the governments who are its members, nothing more, nothing less. That is why their perceptions of what the WTO is, and how it should function, are critical. There is no institutional counterbalance to the collectivity of the members, except for the dispute settlement system. Rather than weakening the dispute settlement system, the political institutions—including the decision making and rulemaking procedures—of the WTO need to be strengthened.

The current impasse in the Doha Round has occurred because of the rapid transformation in the global economy, in particular, as a result of the recent tremendous growth of the emerging economies—China and India. The geopolitical power relationships have changed—China is recognized by the United States as a major economic power—but the new 'clubs' in international relations have not yet been formed. The Doha Round, while important, is fundamentally about market access—in agriculture, on manufactured goods, and on services. In many ways, this is an old agenda from a different era. The international trading system has moved from a bi-polar system driven by the United States and Europe—to a multi-polar one, but most members have not yet figured out what is in their interest in this negotiation. The dispute settlement system continues to work effectively, but the WTO decision making and rule making machinery needs a major overhaul in order to equip the organization for the challenges of the new economic order.

One of the real challenges for the WTO, as well as for other international organizations such as World Intellectual Property Organization, the World Bank, and the International Monetary Fund, is to develop new institutional structures and models that will allow these organizations to collectively determine their new mandates, set priorities, and develop plans for the future.

I. THE 'MANTRAS'

Professor John Jackson, the 'father of international trade law', has identified seven 'mantras' that WTO Members faithfully chant, mostly he says, to avoid having to think issues through.[6] The 'mantras' provide a theology or an explanation for the way things are done and decisions are taken in the WTO which prevents members from dealing with the really difficult and challenging issues, such as the proper mandate of the WTO, its relationship to the outside world, the role of development in the organization, and how the proliferation of regional trade and investment agreements affect the multilateral system. As a result, developing countries feel disenfranchised in the system and representatives of civil society believe that the WTO is a closed, unaccountable organization run by faceless bureaucrats. That is not how the WTO works in practice, but it is clear that the perceptions do not accord with the realities.

Professor Jackson's list of 'mantras' includes:

- *The WTO is a government to government organization.*

Increasingly, the stakeholders in international trade—companies and interest groups—are global. The issues and problems are global. Understandably, the stakeholders would like to influence the international institutions in order to resolve global problems.

- *The WTO is a member-driven organization.*

WTO Members are opposed to the Director-General and Secretariat having any real power or authority. There is a lack of formal management or governance structures in the WTO. All members of the WTO can participate in every Council and Committee meeting.

[6] John H. Jackson, 'The WTO 'Constitution' and Proposed Reforms: Seven 'Mantras' Revisited', 4 Journal of International Economic Law 67 (2001), at 71.

- *Decisions are taken in the WTO by consensus.*

The GATT 1947, Article XXV provided that decisions of the CONTRACTING PARTIES were to be taken by majority vote. Consensus decision making is a practice that developed in the 1960s. Decision making rules became more complex as a result of the institutional negotiations in the Uruguay Round. The United States, supported by Japan, insisted upon the practice of consensus decision making being enshrined as a rule. And so, in Article IX of the *Marrakesh Agreement*, the practice of consensus decision making became recognized as the rule. However, for every type of decision contemplated by Article IX (decision making) and Article X (amendments), there is a fallback to different types of majority voting if consensus cannot be reached after a specified time. Although the rules provide for flexibility in methods of decision making, WTO Members have only resorted to voting once in the history of the WTO.[7] Why? The culture of the WTO forbids even thinking about voting.

- *Nation state sovereignty must be preserved at all costs.*

By engaging in international cooperation and entering into treaty obligations, governments necessarily cede some sovereignty. Europeans have a wonderful concept, rather than worrying incessantly about losing sovereignty, they speak about the benefits that come from 'pooling' sovereignty. The WTO is often criticized because its rules reach behind the border and affect the regulatory autonomy of states in a range of areas. Article III of the GATT, the national treatment principle, has in fact limited domestic regulatory autonomy since 1948. This is not new. However, it is true that the scope of the *Agreement on Technical Barriers to Trade*, the *Agreement on Sanitary and Phytosanitary Measures* and the *General Agreement on Trade in Services* (GATS) go far beyond traditional GATT rules. The GATS Article VI negotiations on 'domestic regulation' could extend that reach even deeper into national autonomy. And, of course, the dispute settlement cases continue to clarify exactly how deep and how far those intrusions are.

- *Single undertaking.*

The Uruguay Round agreements were negotiated, agreed and accepted as part of a 'single undertaking'—an 'all or nothing' package. The idea of the 'single undertaking' was developed in order to repair the serious fragmentation in the GATT 1947 system that resulted from the Tokyo Round of multilateral trade negotiations. In the old GATT system, there were different levels of obligations because of the Tokyo Round 'Codes' each of which had

[7] The General Council decision approving the accession of Ecuador to the WTO was taken by a majority vote in 1995. Since then, accessions and waivers have been approved by consensus in the General Council. See Steger, above n 1.

different memberships. Some commentators, including Professor Jackson, have queried whether the 'single undertaking' is too strict a rule and have suggested that there should be some flexibility in adding new plurilateral agreements. Both the Report of the Consultative Board to Director-General Supachai Panitchpakdi on 'The Future of the WTO: Addressing Institutional Challenges in the New Millenium' (the Sutherland Report), published in 2004, and the recent Report of the Atlantic Council, 'Transatlantic Leadership for a New Global Economy' recommended that the idea of 'variable geometry' be explored.[8] Article X of the *Marrakesh Agreement* makes it difficult to incorporate new plurilateral agreements into the *WTO Agreement*. To add new agreements, a consensus decision of the General Council is required.

The argument could be made, however, that the WTO has moved away from the single undertaking in several key decisions that have been taken since 1995. Indeed, the obligations and commitments of recently acceded countries, such as China and Vietnam, with their lengthy protocols of accession, are in many significant aspects greater than those of the original members of the WTO. The information technology understanding and commitments agreed in 1998 and the telecommunications reference paper agreed in 1997 were, in effect, plurilateral understandings that were implemented by means of commitments in certain WTO Members' Schedules. The principle of the 'single undertaking' has already been deviated from, especially in the protocols of accession of many members that have been approved since 1995 as well as in some of the understandings and agreements concluded since that time.

- *MFN is a sacrosanct principle, no reservations.*

This is a myth. The WTO Agreement is replete with exceptions, including Article XXIV which allows regional trade agreements to be established and the Enabling Clause which came into effect in 1979 allows developed countries to provide preferences for developing countries. The recent protocols of accession for members, such as China, that have acceded to the WTO in the past few years also have many provisions which derogate from the Most-Favoured-Nation (MFN) Principle.

Regionalism is on the rise, and with it, comes a whittling away of respect for and adherence to the principle of MFN. The Sutherland Report sounded a clarion call about the potential dangers of the rapid increase in the number of regional trade agreements (RTAs).[9] They bring with them the potential for restrictive rules of origin which can create trade diversion and raise

[8] Report of the Consultative Board to the Director-General Supachai Panitchpakdi, *The Future of the WTO: Addressing Institutional Challenges in the New Millennium* (Geneva: World Trade Organization, 2004); Stuart E. Eizenstat and Grant D. Aldonas, Co-chairs, *Transatlantic Leadership for a New Global Economy*, The Atlantic Council of the United States, Policy Paper April 2007 (Washington DC: The Atlantic Council of the United States, 2007).

[9] The Sutherland Report, above n 8, Chapter II.

barriers to trade. There will be an increasing focus on regionalism, especially in Asia and Africa where, until recently, there were not many RTAs. That is the political reality. The real question is whether the WTO can develop appropriate surveillance mechanisms to review and supervise the administration of these agreements to reduce their potential negative impacts on the multilateral system.

The sheer number of regional agreements with restrictive rules of origin is indeed hampering the Doha Round negotiations on market access both with respect to agricultural products as well as non-agricultural products. Because of the complicated rules of origin in the over 300 RTAs around the world, it has become overwhelmingly difficult for negotiators to agree on formulae for reduction of tariffs. This is one of many reasons why the Doha Round negotiations have been so challenging and complex.

- *In any Round or multilateral negotiation, there must be early deliverables.*

Given the length of time that Rounds usually take, government negotiators sometimes set unrealistic goals to conclude certain aspects of the Round early so as to appear to be making progress. The problem with this strategy is that deadlines are established that cannot be met, and then they are repeatedly amended. This gives the general public the perception that the Round and/or the WTO is continually failing to meet its objectives. In the Tokyo Round, there was an 'early harvest' on some improvements to the GATT dispute settlement system at the 1988 Montreal Ministerial Meeting to assuage the impression that the Round had failed. Often it is the dispute settlement system that is tinkered with to create an illusion of progress. In the Doha Round, the Doha Declaration provided that the dispute settlement negotiations would be independent of the more general negotiations, but after a number of missed deadlines for completing them, it now seems that they are effectively viewed as part of the overall negotiations.

The real problem is the conviction of WTO Members that changes to the agreements can only be made through major multilateral, multi-issue Rounds. The *Marrakesh Agreement* explicitly allows for modifications to be made to the existing agreements and new agreements to be negotiated whenever and however the membership wishes. In fact, the Uruguay Round legal texts of the *WTO Agreement* specifically contemplate and mandate 'built-in' negotiations in many agreements, including the *General Agreement on Trade in Services*, the *Agreement on Agriculture*, the *Agreement on Rules of Origin*, among others.

II. MYTHS AND MISUNDERSTANDINGS

I would add the following four myths and misunderstandings to Professor Jackson's list:

- *The WTO is a 'contract' that countries can withdraw from at any time.*

While it is true that countries acceded to the GATT 1947 through a legal instrument called, the *Protocol of Provisional Application*, and the original GATT allowed contracting parties to withdraw on 60 days notice,[10] no country has formally withdrawn from the GATT 1947 or from the more recent *WTO Agreement*.[11] The WTO now has 150 members, with another 29 in the process of accession clamoring to join.[12] The *Marrakesh Agreement* provides that a member can withdraw from the WTO Agreement six months after it has provided notice of withdrawal to the WTO.[13] Withdrawal, however, is subject to the 'single undertaking' requirement, which means that a country cannot withdraw from only one part of the WTO treaty, it must withdraw from the *WTO Agreement* as a whole.[14]

The *WTO Agreement* is a treaty, an international agreement, with rules and obligations that are binding in international law. It is not a commercial contract that countries can cancel whenever it suits them, nor is it 'soft law' that is not binding on Members. The myth that it is simply a 'contract' is related to the common perception that it is nothing more than a collection of reciprocal exchanges of concessions.[15]

- *The WTO, like the GATT, is about reciprocal exchanges of concessions – the goal is to balance concessions—it is not about rules.*

Another carry-over from the old GATT is the belief that the *WTO Agreement* is comprised of a collection of bilateral, reciprocal exchanges of concessions.[16] On the contrary, the Uruguay Round legal texts comprising the *WTO Agreement* contain hundreds of pages of treaty rules, many of which are not under negotiation in the Doha Round. Many of these agreements do not have Schedules of access commitments attached to them, and consist only of substantive rules. In fact, only the GATT 1994, the GATS, and the

[10] *Protocol of Provisional Application*, Article 5.

[11] China was a contracting party to the GATT 1947, and did not formally withdraw but was not recognized by the GATT CONTRACTING PARTIES during the Maoist Regime.

[12] WTO Secretariat, 'Understanding the WTO: The Organization, Members and Observers, 150 Members of 11 January 2007', http://www.wto.org/english/thewto_e/whatis_e/tif_e/org6_e.htm (visited 14 June 2007); 'Accessions: Ongoing Accessions, Summary Table of Ongoing Accessions (Updated January 2007)', http://www.wto.org/english/thewto_e/acc_e/status_e.htm (visited 14 June 2007). The countries in the process of accession are: Afghanistan, Algeria, Andorra, Azerbaijan, Bahamas, Belarus, Bhutan, Bosnia and Herzegovina, Cap Verde, Ethiopia, Iran, Iraq, Kazakhstan, Lao People's Democratic Republic, Lebanese Republic, Libyan Arab Jamahiriya, Montenegro, Russian Federation, Samoa, Sao Tome and Principe, Serbia, Seychelles, Sudan, Tajikistan, Tonga, Ukraine, Uzbekistan, Vanuatu and Yemen.

[13] *Marrakesh Agreement*, Article XV.

[14] Except, of course, for the plurilateral agreements contained in Annex IV of the *WTO Agreement*, which have their own provisions on withdrawal.

[15] Joost Pauwelyn, 'A Typology of Multilateral Treaty Obligations: Are WTO Obligations Bilateral or Collective in Nature?', 14 European Journal of International Law (2003), at 907–51; Kyle Bagwell, Petros C. Mavroidis and Robert W. Staiger, 'It's a Question of Market Access', 96 American Journal of International Law (2002), at 56–76.

[16] See Pauwelyn, above n 15, at 925–45.

Agreement on Agriculture have market access schedules that relate to them. Other major agreements, such as the *Agreement on Technical Barriers to Trade*, the *Agreement on Trade-Related Intellectual Property Rights*, and the *Agreement on Sanitary and Phytosanitary Measures*, do not have schedules attached to them and are not fundamentally about market access. Rather, they establish international rules that limit countries from regulating in ways that unduly restrict or burden commerce.

- *The purpose of the WTO is exclusively trade liberalization.*

The mandate of the WTO is no longer clear. This is a major problem in the Doha Round that is contributing to its current impasse. The old analogy used by trade policy 'insiders' was that trade liberalization within the GATT was like a bicycle – you had to keep pedaling, or you would fall off. Sylvia Ostry observed some years ago that it would be more appropriate to describe the post-Uruguay Round WTO as a bus with many drivers, and no one knows where it is going.[17]

While especially developed country negotiators would describe the purpose of the WTO as solely dedicated to trade liberalization, it is clear that the developing country members of the WTO (which now form the vast majority of its membership) also view development as a key goal of the organization. There is presently, it is fair to say, no common understanding on what the mandate of the WTO is. However, if one takes into account the views of two-thirds of its membership, it is clear that the WTO serves the development agenda, and is no longer solely concerned with the goal of accelerating trade liberalization.

The preamble to the *Marrakesh Agreement* differs in some respects from the preamble to the GATT 1947. It includes the goals of 'optimal use of the world's resources in accordance with the objective of sustainable development, seeking both to protect and preserve the environment' and recognizes that WTO Members are at 'different levels of economic development'.

Taking into consideration the broad scope of many of the WTO agreements, and the topics being discussed in WTO committees and councils as well as in the Doha Round negotiations, the rules clearly affect regulation of the environment, public health, services, investment, and intellectual property as well as trade.

- *Rule change can only take place through negotiating Rounds.*

The *Marrakesh Agreement* provides that the WTO is a forum for negotiations among its members about any matters relating to the agreements and also for negotiations about other matters related to the multilateral trading system. Indeed, Article II of that *Agreement* does not expressly contemplate major negotiating rounds, it allows the members

[17] Ostry, above n 3, at 299–300.

to negotiate, for example, an entirely new agreement outside of the context of a round. Also, the amendment procedures for the WTO agreements set out in Article X of the *Marrakesh Agreement* explicitly provide for changes to be made to specific agreements without the necessity of a round. The preference of WTO members for negotiating rounds is a long standing practice, but it is not required by the rules.

These mantras and myths are interlinked. The perception that trade negotiations should be conducted in mercantilist fashion, based on reciprocal exchanges of concessions, also contributes to the belief that the only way to make changes to the existing agreements is through reciprocal exchanges of concessions which can only be negotiated in a major round in which everything is up for negotiation.

III. A LOOK TOWARD THE FUTURE

We live in an interdependent, globalized world. Problems, like companies, do not know borders. Issues cannot be resolved by nation states acting alone. Strong, effective institutions are needed to manage global interdependence. Unlike the situation in the 1980s when the Uruguay Round was launched, the multilateral trading system is not in disarray today. The Doha Round deals with only some of the agreements administered by the WTO. The WTO is a strong, effective, rules-based organization. Nation states cannot, by themselves, regulate effectively to deal with global problems – they need a strong multilateral institution to do this.

However, new regional 'clubs' and arrangements are being formed. The developed countries must take President Putin's warnings seriously. The rise of the new emerging economies, such as China, India, and Brazil, as major economic powers has transformed the geopolitical alignments. There is no longer one hegemon, the world is rapidly becoming multi-polar. The new economic powerhouses may decide that the best course of action is to work within and reform the existing international economic architecture, or they could opt to create their own regional organizations and alliances.

The Doha Round is in its current state, in large part because the geopolitical power relationships have changed and the WTO has not as yet responded to these new realities. If this Round does indeed fail, it will not be the end of the WTO, nor of the multilateral trading system. The first failure of a major trade negotiating round in GATT/WTO history may provide a useful 'time out' for the multilateral system to find its new stride, with the new relationships that are currently being forged.

A 'time out' can be put to good use if we seize the opportunity to search for a new culture and mandate for the WTO – a culture and a mandate that meets the needs of all the global players in this multi-polar, interdependent world. New models for global economic governance need to be forged, with the active participation of researchers and negotiators from the emerging economies and the developing world. These models cannot be based on Western values and traditions, but must be developed by a new consensus among the emerging economic powers, the industrialized world, and the developing countries. A 'time out' could also be useful as a period of much-needed reflection about how to improve the institutional mechanisms of the WTO to make them more accountable, more effective, and more responsive to the needs of the developing country members but also to civil society and the outside world.

What will the new mandate of the WTO be? The WTO should be recognized for what it is – an international organization that regulates trade as well as international economic relations generally. What does this mean? It means that all aspects of economic regulation come within the ambit of the WTO.

If the WTO is to become truly representative of all of its members, the developed world will have to accept that development is a major part of its purpose and mandate. Protection of the environment and sustainable human development are also important, but harmonization of labor standards is not likely to become a common concern in the foreseeable future. Movement of persons and the role and responsibilities of multinational corporations in the trading system are issues that clearly must become part of the new negotiating agenda. While it is not part of the Doha Round negotiations, reform of international intellectual property rules will have to be contemplated within the very near future. Not only are there real problems with patent protection and public health, but technology is moving at such a remarkable pace that traditional concepts of copyright and intellectual property are being seriously challenged by needs to expand access to knowledge to aid development. Protection of indigenous knowledge also will have to be taken seriously by the developed world. Moreover, investment and competition policy cannot remain forever outside of the multilateral rules-based system. They are simply too important to the way that firms operate in the global economy.

What are the major issues for institutional reform of the WTO? The Sutherland Report highlighted a number of key topics and made some modest recommendations that would not require amendment of existing agreements.[18] However, that Report has yet to be taken seriously by the WTO Membership. The following areas of institutional reform should be explored: decision making in the WTO, the internal management structure, external relations, transparency, and the role of RTAs within the multilateral system. WTO Members have discussed many of these issues in the past. However, they have not demonstrated an appetite for significant reform of the WTO institutional machinery.

[18] Above n 8.

The current impasse in the Doha Round should signify to all WTO Members that there is a problem with the architecture of the multilateral trading system. It is almost impossible to take decisions in the WTO, largely because of the practice of decision making by consensus. The current practices and procedures are not serving the WTO or its members very well. There is a general paralysis in the system because of the cumbersome institutional machinery. As a consequence, governments are increasingly turning to regional agreements to manage their trade relations.

The WTO needs major surgery in order to respond effectively to the new political realities in the international economic system. The WTO is not the old GATT, and members should abandon the mantras, myths and misunderstandings that are no longer relevant. They hinder rather than promote progress in the Doha Round and hamper the effective functioning of the WTO. Instead, members should recognize that the mandate of the WTO is not exclusively confined to the liberalization of trade; it includes development as well as a host of other topics that relate to international economic regulation generally. Institutional reform of the WTO is needed to provide it with the architecture and decision making machinery to make it a vibrant, responsive and accountable international organization, relevant to governments, companies and people in the twenty-first century.

We are at a turning point in history. We have a unique opportunity to reform the WTO so that it reflects present day realities. However, that window of opportunity will close if the industrialized world does not take the needs and demands of the large emerging economies and the developing countries seriously.

PREPARING FOR STRUCTURAL REFORM IN THE WTO

*Thomas Cottier**

ABSTRACT

The structure and operation of the WTO have not been at the forefront of attention of negotiations ever since the General Agreement on Tariffs and Trade was introduced in 1947. The modus operandi of negotiations has essentially remained unchanged despite the turn towards non-tariff barriers in complex operations of treaty-making ever since the Kennedy Round. The note argues that the evolution and introduction of the two-tier system of dispute settlement in 1995 marks the most profound structural change, but is not able on its own to deal with all of the challenges of tackling non-tariff barriers in the WTO. Today, the Organization forms part of a complex system of multilayered governance, both horizontally and vertically. It calls for more appropriate structure–substance pairings. The note addresses the need to review negotiating processes in the field of non-tariff barriers. It suggests establishing a proper balance with dispute settlement and case law, and rendering the function and role of the Secretariat of the WTO more transparent. The creation of a two-tier system is suggested, with a Consultative Committee and a Standing Committee on Legal Affairs within the WTO in order to support and initiate a long overdue structural debate in the WTO.

INTRODUCTION

Ever since the inception of the Journal of International Economic Law ten years ago, editors and authors have attempted to contribute to the long-term evolution of the World Trade Organization (WTO) and its body of law, interacting with domestic legal systems and other international organizations. Systemic issues rank among its main concerns. This note offers a tribute to the Journal and these efforts, and it certainly is timely to address the issue and the prospects of long-term institutional reform of the WTO. Since 1947 the GATT and subsequently the WTO have operated under the same principles in negotiations based upon consensus diplomacy: multilateralizing bilateral tariff reductions within defined trade rounds, gradually addressing non-tariff barriers in increasingly complex agreements, and expanding membership on the basis of negotiated and agreed terms in

* World Trade Institute, Berne. E-mail: t.cottier@rw.unibe.ch

protocols of accession. Dispute settlement has emerged and developed from diplomatic modes to become a fully-fledged legal dispute settlement system which, since 1995, has no longer depended upon consensus, but operates on a very successful two-tier system with reverse consensus and the possibility of majority opinions in panels and the Appellate Body. The two pillars—negotiations and dispute settlement—moved the WTO to the centre stage in international economic law and—finally—placed international trade regulation firmly within public international law, which had tended to ignore the subject until then. The WTO, combined with the retaliatory powers granted to its Members upon multilateral clearance, emerged as one of the most powerful international institutions at the end of the 20th century. The procedural principles upon which it relies have been successful from a long-term perspective. Indeed, the WTO system, with its 22,000 pages of treaty text, works every day of the year: millions of transactions are continuously taking place based upon the regulatory system which greatly contributes to presently flourishing and ever-expanding international trade. Dispute settlement works and shows high levels of compliance. The efforts of the WTO have significantly enhanced transparency, and access to documents has been greatly improved thanks to modern information technology. Far more than before has it become possible to follow the work of the WTO from the outside.

The need for structural change is not obvious, even if the current difficulties in concluding the 1991 Doha Development Agenda are considered. Indeed, the problems faced today have mainly arisen because international trade in agriculture was belatedly placed on the agenda of trade liberalization. It faces fifty years of arrears, and the pace of regulatory change is constrained by difficulties in bringing about structural changes in the agricultural systems of industrialized countries. Likewise, the reluctance of developing countries to engage in enhanced market access commitments in industrial goods and services may partly be explained by fundamental changes induced with the entry into force of WTO law for the People's Republic of China in 2001. It may thus be argued that the current difficulties are quite normal from a long-term perspective and that they cannot and should not be attributed to the operating principles of the WTO. It may also be argued that Members have been able to adjust processes over the years by means of diplomatic practices, convention, and perhaps even customary law. Thus, the procedures set forth in article XXVIII GATT for trade liberalization have been superseded by ad hoc structures and processes adopted for subsequent trade rounds, reflecting the agenda and the needs of the agenda adopted. Dispute settlement emerged on the basis of customary state practice. It was codified only in 1979 and formed the platform from which to negotiate the Dispute Settlement Understanding with its innovations in due course. While other organizations may operate on the basis of blueprints and constitutions set out in advance, the GATT and the WTO have followed an inductive approach, developing practices and law from the bottom up, and subsequently refining them in treaty law. As a corollary, the WTO does not have particular bodies focusing on procedural and constitutional issues in a comprehensive way. These issues are dealt with wherever they may come up in practical terms. Apart from the trade policy review mechanism, it is mainly in the field of dispute settlement that fundamental procedural changes—the principles of reverse consensus and a two-tier system—were introduced ex ante with great success. Overall, it may be concluded that contemporary WTO procedures are a combination of customary practices and blueprint reform in dispute settlement. The question arises as to whether the same combination may also apply in the field of diplomacy and negotiations. Is there a need for changes, and if yes, should they be introduced gradually in diplomatic practices, or by way of explicit reform? Answers, of course, will primarily depend on an assessment of needs as to long-term structural reform.

I. THE CALL FOR APPROPRIATE STRUCTURE–SUBSTANCE PAIRINGS

The structure of GATT was primarily conceived as a forum for international tariff negotiations, essentially driven by Members in a process of claims and responses. The same tradition essentially applies to the WTO, and it is still perceived as a member-driven organization with little attention paid to the role of the organization itself in driving the process. Members are interested in outcomes, less so in structures. Nevertheless, the structure and operation of the WTO is not without impact. The ways in which decisions are prepared and made do affect outcomes and results. This is common to all law, domestic and international. Process and substance are inextricably intertwined. I call this substance–structure pairing. The modus operandi of the GATT and the WTO were coined for, and shaped by, the process of progressive liberalization of tariff barriers. The unique concept of trade rounds is based upon the logic of multilateralizing tariff reductions under the principle of most-favoured nation (MFN). It has been highly successful over decades, reducing industrial tariffs from 40 to 4% on average. It has made a substantial contribution to opening up markets and to economic growth. The same modus operandi was applied in due course to negotiations on non-tariff barriers, as both areas were dealt with in parallel in subsequent trade rounds ever since the Kennedy Round. It has remained unchanged ever since.

With an increasing emphasis on non-tariff barriers, however, the nature of GATT and WTO negotiations gradually changed. Even more than tariffs, non-tariff barriers entail a host of complex relations to domestic law and to other areas of international law, often dealt with in other international organizations. It entails complex operations of treaty-making, and it is not limited to negotiating schedules of concessions. Addressing non-tariff barriers, such as TBT, SPS, subsidies, services, intellectual property, anti-trust issues and government procurement inherently placed the WTO in a complex web of multilayered governance vertically in relation to domestic law, as well as horizontally, in relation to the jurisdictions of other international bodies and organizations. The substance of WTO law thus evolved not only in terms of coverage and quantity, but also in terms of complexity and interface with other jurisdictions. These matters all need to be dealt with within the structures and time constraints of trade rounds. Ongoing negotiations in between rounds have remained the exception, essentially addressing important left-over issues, such as financial services or telecommunication after conclusion of the Uruguay Round. Activities of the Organization independently of the cycle of rounds relate to the administration of agreements, dispute settlement, surveillance (Trade Policy Review), training and capacity building. Moreover, complex issues of interfacing WTO and domestic law, and other fields of international law have proved to be very difficult in negotiations, to the extent that they have been addressed at all during trade rounds. It is not a coincidence that these issues are primarily shaped by case law in dispute settlement. This may be considered the appropriate answer and branch of the WTO to deal with the complexities of these issues and to develop the law on a case-by-case basis. Indeed, dispute settlement and case law may be seen as the prime response for dealing with complex interfaces. Progress in dispute settlement, however, created an imbalance with the political process. The advent and role of binding dispute settlement does require rethinking the modes of negotiations in the vast field of non-tariff barriers. It cannot simply be addressed by adjusting dispute settlement to traditional and no longer adequate modes of negotiations, since these very negotiations fail to address the intricacies of a complex web of different bodies of law, both within and outside the WTO. To the contrary, structure–substance pairings need to be improved in the political process and equation in order to bring about a proper balance. Finally, questions as to the legitimacy of the WTO processes have been raised in relation to issues having a strong impact on domestic law and other areas of international law. While other areas are affected by trade regulations, it is argued that they are not sufficiently included in the process of policy formulation and law-making. Although the responsibilities for remedying the situation lie primarily with national governments, debate and cooperation with other international organizations and non-governmental organizations with global outreach, and addressing global concerns, remains a challenge.

While I agree that the current stalemate in trade negotiations primarily relates to traditional issues within given agreements and to structural adjustment at home, and can be partly dealt with by the traditional structures of trade rounds, the political and diplomatic modus operandi of the WTO no longer adequately responds to the current and future issues of complex non-tariff barrier regulation. For example, negotiations on environmental goods and services call for new structures which allow combining negotiations on goods, services and technical barriers and intellectual property (transfer of knowledge and technology) in a meaningful manner. The structure–substance pairing, to this effect, needs review and efforts to address procedural devices with a view to addressing the complex interfaces among different areas of WTO law, domestic law, international law, including the protection of human rights, and legitimacy of outcomes need to be made in the coming years. It cannot all be left to dispute settlement and case law.

II. ISSUES FOR THE STRUCTURAL DEBATE

Commensurate with traditional perceptions of the GATT and the WTO, relatively little attention is paid to structural issues of the organization by governments in the process of negotiations. They do come up in various fora. Yet there is no committee explicitly mandated to address such issues of the organization in a comprehensive manner. Except for the General Council and the Ministerial Conference, no body is mandated and authorized to address procedural issues in a horizontal manner, coming forward with new ideas and informed proposals. Overall, the WTO not only suffers from the complex clashes of interests of Members, but equally from a lack of attention paid to procedural issues. A general debate on structural reform therefore is essential with a view to reinforcing the multilateral trading system and establishing a proper balance with unilateral, bilateral and regional trade policy and regulation. There is no shortage of issues for discussion. I recall the following issues randomly. Some are fundamental in nature, others may allow for adjustment in diplomatic practices of the Organization:

(i) *The relationship of trade rounds and ongoing work*: How to bring about a proper mix of trade rounds and a process of continuous treaty-making in its many regulatory fields. How to combine established principles of trade rounds, useful for tariff reductions, with the virtues of ongoing negotiations in complex areas of non-tariff barriers. How to establish the necessary momentum in ongoing negotiations. Could trade rounds increasingly conclude with a mandatory programme for negotiations in complex areas which require complex interfacing with other international organizations? Do we need criteria for secondary legislation which could be enacted on the basis of existing treaties?

(ii) *The balance of negotiations and dispute settlement*: How to bring about the possibility of an effective means of legislative response which does not depend on trade rounds and thus takes a very long time. How to make better use of the possibility of interpretative statements by Members. Can this be brought about without reviewing consensus-based diplomacy in law-making? The debate should address underlying principles of checks and balances in the system.

(iii) *The role of the Secretariat in negotiations and dispute settlement*: Under the auspices of a Member-driven organization, the Secretariat is conceived as a purely supportive instrument. This perception does not adequately reflect the real functions and position of the Secretariat in terms of institutional memory, policy advice and policy-making. How to bring about more transparency on the influence and role of the Secretariat in the process of negotiations and dispute settlement. What should be done in order to enhance and develop the Secretariat into a warden of multilateral disciplines? Could the Director-General obtain powers to submit motions of his or her own? Should the Secretariat be represented by its own counsel in dispute settlement?

(iv) *The structure and process of decision-making in the WTO*: Is consensus-based diplomacy the best way to proceed with 150 Members in the complex areas of non-tariff barriers and law-making? Does consensus truly reflect the principle of equality of Members? In reality, some are clearly more equal than others, and blocking consensus is, in substance, not available to all in the same way. It is submitted that the WTO in fact operates under a system of de facto preponderance, reflecting political clout and market size. Is this a necessary precondition for a functioning multilateral system? Large powers having a significant stake in the system need appropriate representation and influence. The issue arises as to whether this should not be rendered more transparent and be part of a more sophisticated system of checks and balances. What are the viable alternatives to consensus diplomacy, in particular in the field of non-tariff barriers? Is it possible to contemplate a system of weighted voting, taking into account shares of world trade, openness of markets and size of population? How can blocking powers be dealt with? Should they be retained, or should the system be aligned to a reverse consensus rule? How can the negotiation processes be rendered transparent and open to all those interested in participating?

(v) *Single undertaking or variable geometry:* What are the criteria by which basic decisions should be made on package deals or plurilateral agreements? What are the long-term implications of variable geometry for developing countries?

(vi) *Alternatives to special and differential treatment (S&D)*: How can the current and ineffective models of S&D be replaced? In-depth thought is required on alternative approaches. How could graduation be defined? Is it possible to bring about progressive regulation, commensurate with levels of development of competitiveness within a particular uniform set of rules? How could economic indicators be employed to this effect?

(vii) *The structure and operation of WTO in the field of technical assistance and capacity building:* What are the structural implications of enhanced technical cooperation in aid for trade? Should the WTO develop regional offices? How should cooperation with other international and regional organizations be managed? How should cooperation with universities be managed?

(viii) *The legal relationship of WTO law and other international agreements*: Efforts to clarify this relationship in specialized committees have failed, since the matter is one of horizontal importance and impact. What is the proper body to deal with this issue beyond dispute settlement in general terms?

(ix) *The legal relationship of WTO Agreements and preferential trade agreements:* How can a proper legal balance be struck between multilateralism and preferential trade? How to develop hierarchies of rules and enhance enforcement of multilateral disciplines in the field. How to go beyond disciplines of enhanced transparency adopted in the Doha Development Agenda. How to bring about a hierarchy of rules in defining the relationship of multilateral and preferential rules.

(x) *The relationship of WTO and other international organizations*: Given the interdependence of subject matter, the relationship needs clarification beyond observer status. What should be the proper role in negotiations and in dispute settlement of other organizations? To what extent can they be employed in the process of impact assessments of proposals tabled? What are the pros and cons for limiting the rights and obligations of other organizations in interacting with the WTO?

(xi) *The relationship of WTO law and domestic law; the role of WTO law in domestic courts and proceedings*: Should this issue be entirely left to domestic constitutional law or should it be part of WTO disciplines and thus of multilateralism? How can we translate direct effect and thus effectiveness in terms of market access concessions? What can be done to achieve a more nuanced approach to direct effect and the doctrine of justiciability of WTO law?

(xii) *The relationship of WTO to civil society and business (non-governmental organizations)*: How can operational relations with NGOs in the process of negotiations and dispute settlement be shaped? To what extent can they support impact assessment of tabled proposals? To what extent can they assist in enhancing the legitimacy of WTO rules and acceptance around the world?

(xiii) *The relationship of WTO to national parliaments:* What can be done to foster inclusiveness of democratic legislators in the process, thus enhancing information, awareness and understanding of the multilateral system? What can be done to provide independent information and mutual exchange among legislators, if they so wish?

(xiv) *The role of academia*: What, in particular, should be the relationship of WTO to the academic community? How can its work be better integrated in the process? What can be done to forge better links between discussions in trade diplomacy and in academia? What can the WTO do to foster academic training in the field, still largely lacking around the world?

The Sutherland Report ('The Future of the WTO')[1] made a number of structural recommendations which may well serve as a starting point for the debate. The Report recommends a limited role for other international organizations and restricted observer status. It suggests defining clear objectives for dialogue with civil society organizations and the public at large. It submits that dispute settlement reports should be reviewed by an independent group of experts. It supports enhanced technical assistance with a view to strengthening implementation and rule-orientation of national trade policies. It submits a Luxembourg-type compromise on consensus: blocking consensus should be limited to declared national interests, in writing and with reasons stated. It recommends reviewing the plurilateral approach, as opposed to single undertakings, and seeks enhanced recourse to scheduling. It recommends having annual Ministerial Conferences. It suggests the creation of a consultative body of senior officials from capitals to meet quarterly or biannually with the Director-General, with limited membership and partly on a rotating basis. Finally, it recommends clarifying the key role of the Director-General in the process of negotiations.

These topics, and perhaps others, support the view that the WTO needs a debate on how it functions and on structural reform with a view to establishing appropriate structure–substance pairings able to deal with complex issues of non-tariff barrier regulations and a Membership of widely diverse levels of development. While some of the proposals are technical in nature, most of them address the basic structure of the WTO and its operation and thus require anchorage in a political agenda and process. This calls for the creation of appropriate fora.

[1] Report of the Consultative Board to the Director-General Supachai Panitchpakdi, *The Future of the WTO: Addressing Institutional Challenges in the New Millennium* (Geneva: World Trade Organization, 2004)

III. CREATING FORA FOR DEBATE AND STRUCTURAL NEGOTIATIONS

It was noted that there is currently no official standing body within the WTO (except for the Secretariat) mandated to prepare and discuss these controversial horizontal matters in a comprehensive and systemic manner. To some degree, such issues are dealt with in specialized committees and in an isolated manner. For example, the Committee on Trade and Environment dealt with the relationship of WTO law and multilateral environmental agreements (MEAs); a problem, however, which equally exists in other areas of law, for example in the fields of trade and investment, trade and human rights, or trade and culture. A Negotiating Group deals with reform of the dispute settlement system, but cannot sufficiently address the relationship to, and the interconnection with, the process of negotiations. Special and differential treatment is dealt with in the Committee on Trade and Development, but affects all areas and Committees of the WTO alike. Pledges for technical cooperation are made by Members, but remain outside discussions as to how the WTO should be structured to effectively employ the funds. There is no committee dealing in a comprehensive manner with relations with other international organizations. The Committee on Budget, Finance and Administration is limited to financial issues and does not assess the overall operation and functioning of the WTO.

The International Law Association, in its 2006 Report,[2] recommends establishing a legal or institutional committee in the WTO which would be mandated to deal with structural and horizontal issues of the type indicated above. It is necessary to create structures which allow a comprehensive discussion of proposals relating to the improvement of the functioning of the WTO. During the Uruguay Round, such a Committee existed (Functioning of the GATT system: FOGS), but was discontinued under the new Organization. FOGS was neither appropriate nor sufficient to discuss innovation. This was a serious shortcoming and partly explains the difficulties in taking up structural issues in subsequent negotiations under the Doha Development Agenda. More than that is needed in the future. The design of a two-tier structure which allows the influx of outside ideas has been suggested. The first tier would operate as a think tank, a forum of expertise, information-exchange and non-hierarchical deliberation between government and academia. The second tier would be mandated to negotiate and prepare political decisions in the field. It is important to distinguish these functions and define their relationship.

A. Consultative committee

A body should be designed and mandated to develop conceptual ideas and proposals on horizontal systemic issues such as those indicated in the

[2] Published at: http://www.ila-hq.org

extensive list above. Over the last decade, a true and international academic community dealing with institutional and structural issues of global governance, the role of international organizations and constitutionalisation of international law has emerged; much of its work is reflected in this Journal. Problems are discussed from a detached point of view and are not interest-driven in the same way as governmental processes. Scholarly findings and discussions, however, often remain academic. They do not reach policy-makers. There is an insufficient linkage between academic discussions, the WTO Secretariat and Members. The results of academic work and conferences do not find their way into negotiations other than by accident. It is submitted that this community could strongly support long-term thinking on structural issues and should be included in the process. This can only be successful if academics work closely with senior government officials and representatives of the WTO Secretariat from the very beginning.

(a) The Consultative Committee should be structured in such a manner as to allow discussion and proposals made both from capitals and from academia. It would be beneficial to create a body composed of constitutional international lawyers, political scientists, economists and representatives of governments dealing with systemic issues of international governance in capitals or Geneva-based missions. The Committee could consist of a core group and work with flexible membership and working groups, depending on the subject matter being dealt with. A special interface mechanism (e.g. exchange forum) with national parliaments and non-governmental actors should also be an important design feature of such a Committee.

(b) The mixed think tank would operate under a broad mandate. Ideally, it would decide upon the initiatives to be taken. Alternatively, more restrictive mandates would need to entail a decision-making process. Different models are possible, ranging from mandates by the Ministerial Conference or the General Council to those granting powers to the Director-General.

(c) A discussion will be necessary to decide to whom the Committee reports. Again, different options could be considered and should be explored. The Committee could report to the Director-General who would obtain the right to make proposals of his or her own to the General Council and the Ministerial Conference on institutional matters relating to the functioning of the Organization. The idea expressed in the Report of the Consultative Group of creating a senior officials' consultative body could be linked to this idea as proposals by the mixed institutional Committee could be submitted to this group for discussion. The Director-General would be entitled to process suitable proposals into diplomatic channels and the bodies of the WTO.

(d) The Committee could also take up matters submitted to it by WTO Committees and Negotiating Groups for advice and recommendation.

(e) The work of the Committee should also be made available to Members which, of course, would retain the right to take matters up and develop initiatives of their own, based upon the work of the Consultative Committee. It may also be taken up by dispute settlement panels and the Appellate Body in discharging their duties.

B. Standing committee on legal affairs

Members and the Director-General alike should be entitled to introduce recommendations of the Consultative Committee into the negotiating process. To this effect, a Standing Committee on institutional legal matters should be created. It could be combined with the Dispute Settlement Body assuming responsibility for all structural, horizontal and procedural matters. It would also be responsible for securing coherence between different draft treaty texts. It would be mandated to discuss proposals made by Members and the Consultative Committee.

This body is purely governmental and fully integrated into the regular decision-making process of the WTO. It would assume the responsibility for preparing treaty texts and decisions relating to horizontal structural issues. Matters pertaining to special committees would remain the domain of these bodies, but mutual interaction and consultation should be assured. The Standing Committee would report to the General Council and thus support it in discharging its responsibilities on horizontal and structural matters. Recommendations may entail changes in diplomatic practices and the operation of the agreement. They may also entail explicit changes in agreements and supplementary instruments relating to the structure and process of the organization and its interaction with domestic and other areas of international law.

IV. CONCLUSION

Building upon the traditions of incremental change and practices, case law and explicit changes brought about in treaty negotiations, structural reform may find its appropriate forms of progress. The WTO can build upon its tradition of combining different avenues. Yet, appropriate horizontal working bodies, other than the Ministerial Conference and the Council, to steer and monitor this process, need to be created first. Different avenues are possible, and models other than those briefly sketched here are conceivable. The need for structural reform can hardly be disputed. The multilateral system can no longer afford to leave horizontal issues aside due to a lack of appropriate fora for debate and decision-making. The traditional lack of attention paid to structural issues no longer serves the long-term interests of the WTO which has become deeply involved in complex areas of addressing non-tariff barriers to trade. Of course, it would be naïve to believe that the creation of bodies such as the Consultative Committee and a Standing Committee on Legal Affairs, as well as a more proactive and transparent role for the Secretariat is a purely technical matter. It affects allocation of powers and perhaps the traditional perceptions of sovereignty of Members. This is still truer if a hierarchy of rules and a more effective decision-making process is adopted in due course. Yet, inaction may accelerate the disintegration of the system, and may further promote relocation of regulatory efforts outside the WTO. No Member with a keen interest in a functioning multilateral system based upon MFN can see this as being beneficial and should make an attempt to rethink the traditional perceptions of a purely Member-driven organization. When this Journal celebrates twenty years of long-term thinking in the field of WTO law and policy in 2017, it is hoped that it might be able to look back at a decade characterized by enhanced attention being paid to substance–structure pairing in the WTO and to the efforts made to achieve enhanced coherence among the different layers and components of international economic law.

GOOD GOVERNANCE AT THE WORLD TRADE ORGANIZATION: BUILDING A FOUNDATION OF ADMINISTRATIVE LAW

*Daniel C. Esty**

ABSTRACT

Good governance lies at the heart of both the effectiveness and legitimacy of collective decision-making. In this essay, Professor Esty argues that, if the World Trade Organization (WTO) is to be successful in its designated role of promoting trade liberalization and helping to manage international economic interdependence, it needs a deeper commitment to good governance, advanced through a more refined structure of administrative rules and procedures. He identifies 14 core elements of good governance and traces how administrative law might promote each one in the WTO context. While acknowledging the difficulty of bringing administrative law to the supranational level, Esty concludes that there exists an emerging consensus around many of the underpinnings of good governance—and therefore places value in trying to build these elements in to the WTO policy-making process.

Good governance is a hot topic in many circles today.[1] But debate remains over exactly what constitutes 'good governance' and how the concept should be applied in various contexts. In this essay, I offer a template of 14 elements of good governance and argue that these concepts should be woven into the fabric of the World Trade Organization (WTO) through a more robust structure of administrative law. These elements matter because they contribute to institutional effectiveness and legitimacy.

To be clear, bringing good governance to the WTO is not the same as arguing for a bigger or stronger WTO. But trade liberalization and

* Hillhouse Professor of Environmental Law & Policy at The Yale Environment School and the Yale Law School, Email: daniel.esty@yale.edu.

[1] See, for example: Thomas F. Weiss, 'Governance, Good Governance, and Global Governance, Conceptual and Actual Challenges', 21 Third World Quarterly (2000) 795; Carlos Santiso, 'Good Governance and Aid Effectiveness: the World Bank and Conditionality', 7 The Georgetown Policy Review (2001) 1; John Dearlove, 'The Deadly Dull Issue of University 'Administration'? Good Governance, Managerialism and Organizing Academic Work',11 Higher Education Policy (1998) 59; Alvaro Cuervo, 'Corporate Governance Mechanisms: A Plea for Less Code of Good Governance and More Market Control', 10 Corporate Governance (2002) 84; Derick W. Brinkerhoff, 'Institutional Dualism and International Development', 37 Administration & Society (2005) 199.

successful management of economic interdependence require supranational governance with a measure of responsibility and authority. Even if one wanted a thinner international trade body with more limited reach, a commitment to good governance through carefully crafted administrative rules and procedures makes sense insofar as whatever role the WTO plays in fostering international economic cooperation, it should be designed to play well.[2]

Punctiliousness in the process of decision-making, which administrative law promotes, is itself a central component of good governance and legitimacy. Procedural rigour not only contributes directly to sound policy-making, it indirectly enhances other foundations of legitimacy. A well-designed structure of administrative law can partly substitute for weak democratic foundations, which many theorists see as the *sine qua non* for any exercise of power or governing authority.[3] In this regard, a deeper commitment to administrative law at the WTO could help to overcome the international trading system's perceived democratic deficit and the WTO's reputation for opaque decision-making that is susceptible to special interest manipulation. Appropriate rules and procedures might also improve public understanding of the trading system, promote global-scale 'politics' (notably, dialogue that yields a higher degree of convergence on policy ends and means), and enhance the WTO's capacity to deliver social welfare gains.

I. FOUNDATIONS OF LEGITIMACY

In the modern democratic tradition, going back to Rousseau, the right to exercise power has been connected to elections that provide a mechanism for determining majority will.[4] Despite occasional calls for a 'parliament of man' or a global legislature,[5] direct election of international officials seems some

[2] Only those who favour autarky would wish for a less rather than more functional and effective WTO. See, for example: Sophie Meunier, 'The French Exception', 79 Foreign Affairs (2000) 104; Jagdish Bhagwati, 'After Seattle: Free Trade and the WTO', 77 International Affairs (2001) 15; Jose Seoane, 'From Seattle to Porto Alegre', 50 Current Sociology (2002) 99.

[3] See Daniel Bodansky, 'The Legitimacy of International Governance: A Coming Challenge For International Environmental Law?', 93 The American Journal of International Law (1999) 596, at 599 (observing that democracy is 'touchstone of legitimacy'); David Held, *Democracy and the Global Order*, (Oxford: Blackwell Publishers Ltd, 1995) at 17–18.

[4] Jean-Jacques Rousseau, *The Social Contract*, Maurice Cranston (trans.), (Harmondsworth: Penguin Books, 1968); Heinz Hauser and Alexia Müller, Legitimacy: The Missing Link for Explaining EU Institution Building, 50 Aussenwirtschaft (1995) 17, at 29 [cited in Grainne de Burca, 'The Quest for Legitimacy in the European Union', 59 The Modern Law Review (1996) 349, at 352 (discussing lack of EU electoral legitimacy)]; Robert A. Dahl, 'Can International Organizations Be Democratic? A Skeptic's View', in Ian Shapiro and Casiano Hacker-Cordón (eds), *Democracy's Edges* (Cambridge: Cambridge University Press, 1999) at 19.

[5] Immanuel Kant, 'Perpetual Peace: A Philosophical Sketch', in Hans Reiss (ed) and H.B. Nisbet (trans.), *Political Writings* (New York: Cambridge University Press, 1991), 105;

distance off—and may not be a good idea in any case. But the lack of democratic underpinnings need not undermine the legitimacy of global-scale policy-making bodies. In fact, elections are neither entirely necessary nor fully sufficient for policy-making that has authority based on public acceptance.[6] Good governance, and thus at least some degree of legitimacy, can be built on other foundations.

I have argued elsewhere that justification for a degree of authority being lodged with international bodies can be derived from several sources.[7] In particular, legitimacy adheres to governance processes that offer:

- expertise and the promise of social welfare gains;
- order and stability;
- checks and balances;
- political dialogue and a 'right process' for decision-making.[8]

Weber argues that legitimacy emerges from a legal/rational governance process that generates social welfare gains because bureaucrats with an unbiased perspective and recognized expertise produce systematically superior results over time.[9] The modern American administrative state builds on this neo-Weberian logic of efficacy, efficiency, and neutrality in policy-making as a source of legitimacy. Legitimacy can also be derived from an institution's ability to promote cooperation and establish order in the face of a Hobbesian State of Nature. In his seminal volume, The *Morality of Law*, Lon Fuller notes that order emerges from a legal structure that provides clear, stable, transparent, and predictable decision-making.[10] Madison's vision of multiple branches and layers of government that disperse policy-making responsibilities among contending institutions generates legitimacy by disciplining those with power, institutionalizing the process of getting a 'second opinion', and helping to ensure that decisions are legally grounded,

---

Paul Kennedy, *Parliament of Man* (New Haven: Yale University Press, 2006). Richard Falk and Andrew Strauss, 'Toward Global Parliament', 80 Foreign Affairs (2001), at 212.

6 See, for example: Samuel Brittan, 'Democracy Alone is Simply Not Enough', *Financial Times*, 13 May 2005 (arguing that majority rule is an inadequate basis for governing authority); George W. Bush, 'Freedom and Democracy in Latvia' (speech given at Riga, Latvia on 7 May 2005) ('sovereignty and majority rule are only the beginnings . . . the promise of democracy starts with . . . elections. But it does not end there.').

7 See Daniel C. Esty, 'Good Governance at the Supranational Scale: Globalizing Administrative Law', 115 (7) Yale Law Journal (2006) 1490, at 1515–23.

8 Ibid, (discussing these bases for legitimacy); Thomas M. Franck, *The Power of Legitimacy Among Nations* (New York: Oxford University Press, 1990) (emphasizing 'right process').

9 Max Weber, *Economy and Society: An Outline of Interpretive Sociology* (1914) (Berkeley: University of California Press, 1968) (emphasizing the value of technical decision-making).

10 Lon Fuller, '*The Morality of Law*', (Rev. edn, New Haven: Yale University Press, 1964); Gunther Teubner, 'Juridification—Concepts, Aspects, Limits, Solutions', in Gunther Teubner (ed), *Juridification of Social Spheres: A Comparative Analysis in the Areas of Labor, Corporate, Antitrust, And Social Welfare Law* (New York: Walter de Gruyter and Co., 1987) (stressing similar concepts).

carefully explained, and supported by reason and analysis.[11] This web of checks and balances creates a systematic legitimacy in the governance structure as a whole, even for those institutions (e.g. the judiciary) that do not have electoral mandates. Habermas stresses the importance of political deliberation, transparency, and public participation as mechanisms to promote legitimacy through the exercise of authority in a context of due process and decision-making based on reason.[12]

These foundations of legitimacy correspond to various aspects of good governance as spelled out in Chart 1 below. Many of the elements of good governance I have identified contribute to more than one foundation for legitimacy—and all contribute to successful policymaking as well. The good governance 'menu' offered here emerges from a careful review of the burgeoning scholarly literature and numerous policy contributions to the debate over what is fundamental to sound collective decision-making.[13] While no definitive list can be provided, there is a surprising degree of consensus emerging across countries and cultures about most of the elements identified here.[14] Note that the elements in this template will sometimes be in tension and work at cross-purposes. Good governance thus depends on an appropriate blending and balancing of these elements in practice.

Chart 1: Elements of Good Governance

A. Rousseauian (democratic) legitimacy

1. representativeness
2. accountability

B. Weberian (expertise-based) legitimacy

3. rationality
4. efficacy
5. efficiency
6. neutrality

C. Fullerian (order-based) legitimacy

7. clarity
8. stability

[11] See James Madison, Alexander Hamilton, John Jay and Isaac Kramnick, 'The Federalist No. 10', *The Federalist Papers* (Harmondsworth: Penguin, 1987); Jerry L. Mashaw, *Greed, Chaos & Governance: Using Public Choice to Improve Public Law* (New Haven: Yale University Press, 1997) 4–6.

[12] Jürgen Habermas, *The Theory of Communicative Action: Reason and the Rationalization of Society*, Thomas McCarthy (trans.) (Boston: Beacon Press, 1981) 287 (explaining deliberation is critical); Jens Steffek, 'The Legitimization of International Governance: A Discourse Approach', 9 European Journal of International Relations (2003) 249, at 263 (explaining Habermas's discursive foundation for legitimacy).

[13] Esty, above n 7, at 1515–23.

[14] Esty, above n 7, at 1541–42.

D. Madisonian ('checks and balances' or systemic) legitimacy

9. power sharing
10. legality
11. fairness

E. Habermasian (procedural) legitimacy

12. deliberation
13. transparency
14. participation and due process

II. ELEMENTS OF GOOD GOVERNANCE

The optimal structure of rules and procedures at the WTO must be understood in the context of an international body that has limited direct authority—and where ultimate decision-making power continues to lie with the member states. This raises a deeper question about *who* the decision makers are at the WTO. Traditional trade scholarship often describes the WTO Secretariat as merely ministerial in its functions—with international bureaucrats simply carrying out the will of national trade officials.[15] But this picture is over-simplified. The work of the WTO secretariat is more complicated and nuanced. It involves important roles in agenda setting and structuring the policy dialogues that define the international trading system.[16] More importantly, as the WTO moves toward being a system of rules and away from being simply a forum for negotiation, the secretariat will wield even more power.[17] Thus, the governance procedures employed within the WTO significantly shape trade policy-making and need to be established with great care.

A. Representativeness

Whenever policy-making authority is delegated to unelected officials, questions arise about whether the decision makers are tracking the needs and advancing the wishes of the public. These representativeness questions

[15] Jeffrey J. Schott, 'Challenges Facing the World Trade Organization', in Jeffrey J. Schott (ed), *The World Trading System: Challenges Ahead* (Washington, DC: Institute for International Economics December, 1996) 23.

[16] Esty, above n 7, at 1545; Steve Charnovitz, 'The WTO and Cosmopolitics', 7 Journal of International Economic Law (2004) 675; Carrie Wofford, 'A Greener Future at the WTO: The Refinement of WTO Jurisprudence on Environmental Exceptions to GATT', 24 Harvard Environmental Law Review (2000) 563 (observing the professionalization of WTO adjudication).

[17] Marco C. E. J. Bronckers, 'Better Rules for a New Millennium: A Warning Against Undemocratic Developments in the WTO', 2 Journal of International Economic Law (1999) 547; Bernard Hoekman, 'Operationalizing the Concept of Policy Space in the WTO: Beyond Special and Differential Treatment', 8 Journal of International Economic Law (2005) 405; Chad P. Brown, 'Participation in WTO Dispute Settlement: Complainants, Interested Parties, and Free Riders', 19 World Bank Economic Review (2005) 287.

multiply with delegation at the international level that stretch the lines of accountability back to elected leaders.[18]

The WTO has launched a number of public dialogues designed to better connect the multilateral trade regime to public thinking around the world. The recent series of WTO-sponsored conferences and formal discussions about 'trade and the environment' and 'trade and development' as well as other topics represents a step toward greater connectedness.[19] Likewise, efforts to make the WTO website a better tool for information flow to and from the public promises to improve the link between WTO decision-making and public concerns.[20]

But the answer to questions about the representativeness of those engaged in the WTO policy process all too often comes down to an argument that real power is wielded only by national trade officials. Confidence in the WTO's policy-making cannot rest, however, on this thin reed of connectedness to the range of political perspectives that need to be understood.[21]

Alternative mechanisms must be developed to ensure that WTO decision processes are infused with information about the concerns, views, and circumstances of citizens around the world on whose behalf the trading system must deliver. Thus, the WTO needs a more robust set of requirements that mandate reporting on the international trading system's policy-making processes, disclosure of decisions made, and access to information. Although a full set of WTO administrative rules to promote this 'connectedness' agenda has not yet been developed, an important step was taken with the 2002 *Procedures for the Circulation and Derestriction of WTO Documents*, which facilitates the release of most official WTO documents within sixty days.[22] But still more needs to be done to open up the information flow, especially with regard to the monthly General Council meetings, dispute settlement procedures, and ongoing policy dialogues. A better defined role for NGOs within the WTO policy-making process might also help to ensure that both the WTO secretariat and the national officials engaged in policy debates on the shores of Lake Geneva are aware of

[18] Robert Howse, 'Transatlantic Regulatory Cooperation and the Problem of Democracy', in George A. Berman, Matthias Herdegen, and Peter A. Lindseth (eds), *Transatlantic Regulatory Cooperation: Legal Problems and Political Prospects* (New York: Oxford University Press, 2001).

[19] Records of these meetings are available on the WTO website. Relations with Non-governmental Organizations/Civil Society, http://www.wto.org/english/forums_e/ngo_e/intro_e.htm (last visited 25 February 2006); See Martin Wolf, *Why Globalization Works* (New Haven: Yale University Press, 2004) 211 (arguing for expanded outreach).

[20] The Community Forum on the website, for example, could prove to be very helpful. http://www.wto.org/english/forums_e/chat_e/chat_e.htm (last visited 15 June 2007).

[21] Daniel Esty, 'Linkages and Governance: NGOs at the World Trade Organization', 19 (3) University of Pennsylvania Journal of International Economic Law (1998) 709 (discussing 'connectedness').

[22] 'Procedures for the Circulation and Derestriction of WTO Documents', WT/L/452, Adopted on 14 May 2002.

the range of views on trade issues that exist and should be factored into policy choices.[23]

There is, of course, a risk that NGOs will become special interests.[24] Rather than illuminating issues and bringing useful facts and analysis to bear, they might distort policy dialogues and manipulate decision-making. But if properly channeled and constrained through appropriate disclosure requirements, NGO participation in WTO policy-making provides a mechanism for educating the public about the work of the international trading system and for connecting WTO officials to citizens around the world. The 2005 Sutherland Report offers a useful starting point for defining the administrative law framework needed to ensure a cooperative relationship between the WTO and NGOs. In particular, it recognizes that NGOs represent an important mechanism for influencing public opinion. It also recommends that the WTO allocate resources to expand the NGO engagement at the WTO.[25]

B. Accountability

Good governance requires that policy makers act in the public interest. In this context, Anne-Marie Slaughter stresses 'responsiveness to the people' as a fundamental governance principle. [26] Ruth Grant and Bob Keohane argue that the essence of such accountability lies in *ex post* opportunities for the public to hold decision makers 'to a set of standards, and to impose sanctions if they determine that those responsibilities have not been met.'[27]

In the domestic context, elections are the central accountability mechanism and the identity of the public is relatively clear. Those who do not meet the electorate's expectations are defeated at the ballot box and stripped of power. In the global context, electoral discipline is not available. And it is much harder to discern what the public interest is.[28] To be sure, elections are not the only mechanism for ensuring the accountability of those

[23] Daniel Esty, 'Non-governmental Organizations at the World Trade Organization: Cooperation, Competition, or Exclusion', 1 (1) Journal of International Economic Law (1998).

[24] Mashaw, above n 11, (suggesting that proceduralization may lead to policy-making breakdown by giving rather than taking power from special interests).

[25] The Future of the WTO: Addressing Institutional Challenges in the New Millennium (2004), Report by the Consultative Board to the Director-General Supachai Panitchpakdi (henceforth referred to as the Sutherland Report).

[26] Anne-Marie Slaughter, 'Agencies on the Loose? Holding Government Networks Accountable', in George A. Berman, Matthias Herdegen, and Peter A. Lindseth (eds), *Transatlantic Regulatory Cooperation: Legal Problems and Political Prospects* (New York, NY: Oxford University Press, 2000) 521–46 (defining accountability as 'responsiveness to the people.'); Ruth W. Grant and Robert Keohane, 'Accountability and Abuses of Power in World Politics', 99 American Political Science Review (2005) 29, at 31.

[27] Ibid, at 31.

[28] Esty, above n 7, at 1540–41 (highlighting the complexity of defining the 'public interest' in the supranational governance context).

exercising delegated authority. Markets, officials in other governmental bodies, NGOs, and the media can also force power-wielders to explain their actions and justify their policy choices.[29]

In administrative agencies, the link to the public is somewhat more attenuated.[30] In most domestic governance systems, the top officials are appointed and approved by elected officials. Those who fail to follow the Prime Minister or President's policies can be fired or reassigned.[31] Moreover, domestic legal systems often have provisions for oversight hearings or similar mechanism by which elected representatives review the work of appointed officials.

The more tenuous the link between delegated decision makers and those with electoral legitimacy, the greater the need to specify alternative ways to expose decision makers to scrutiny and potential sanction.[32] In this regard, Grant and Keohane identify seven possible accountability mechanisms that could serve to discipline supranational policy-making.[33] In concrete terms, the WTO could improve accountability through a range of administrative law mechanisms—structured policy review processes (of the sort the OECD conducts), oversight hearings (perhaps carried out by national legislators), as well as limited terms and carefully defined reappointment provisions for top officials.[34] A 'notice and comment' requirement, mandating that drafts of policy proposals be published and made available for review would also be helpful as would provisions for more clearly identified decision processes, better-documented decisions, and lobbying disclosure.[35]

[29] Mashaw, 'Reinventing Government and Regulatory Reform: Studies in the Neglect and Abuse of Administrative Law', 57 University of Pittsburgh Law Review (1996) 405.

[30] See, for example: Steve Charnovitz, 'Accountability of Nongovernmental Organizations (NGOs) in Global Governance', GWU Legal Studies Research Paper No. 145, (April 2005) (describing limited provisions in international institutions for representation).

[31] Note, however, that civil servants, with protected tenures, are somewhat immune to this sort of accountability. Thus, mechanisms used to ensure the accountability of civil servants may be useful in the international context.

[32] Susan Rose-Ackerman identifies five sorts of monitoring and participation tools to enhance accountability. Susan Rose-Ackerman, *From Elections to Democracy: Building Accountable Government in Hungary and Poland* (New York: Cambridge University Press, 2005) (looking at Poland and Hungary).

[33] Grant and Keohane, above n 26, at 23–26.

[34] See, for example: Gregory Shaffer, 'Parliamentary Oversight of WTO Rule-Making: The Political, Normative, and Practical Contexts', 7 Journal of International Economic Law (2004) 629, at 631 (discussing the potential benefits of a WTO parliamentary body and how such a body could *potentially* allow greater participation and impact of constituents) (Note, however, that Shaffer sees both costs and benefits to such increased accountability).

[35] Esty, above n 7, at 1527–28. See also Ngaire Woods and Amrita Narlikar, 'Governance and the Limits of Accountability: The WTO, the IMF, and the World Bank', 53 (4) International Social Science Journal (2001) 568, at 573.

C. Rationality

At the heart of Weber's emphasis on legal–rational policymaking lies the intuition that governance founded on careful consideration of relevant facts and good analysis is likely to stand up better over time. In brief, the Weberian technocratic model depends on bringing knowledge, information, and expertise to bear. It promotes efficiency and efficacy by requiring that decision makers give reasons for the policy options they choose to adopt.[36]

In pursuit of neo-Weberian legitimacy and improved social welfare, WTO administrative procedures should require careful construction of administrative records with full documentation of the key issues, findings of fact, assumptions made (including a statement of the 'public interest' being advanced), and analyses undertaken.[37] More emphasis on developing an array of policy options, screening out special interest pleading, and requiring that decisions be rule-based would also improve WTO policy-making.[38] Written explanation of decisions, particularly in dispute settlement, would force officials to justify their policy choices. This simple discipline would promote public understanding, support successful implementation of policy decisions, increase clarity, and cut costs by improving predictability. Efforts to expand understanding of the trade regime would, moreover, be useful as a way to build consensus around policy choices and to inculcate common values over time.[39]

D. Efficacy

Expert-based legitimacy rests largely on whether a governing body delivers results that are perceived to be social-welfare enhancing. The WTO has a history of success in this regard.[40] But in recent years, the WTO's reputation for 'getting it right' has slipped. By encouraging analysis from multiple perspectives, careful assessment and explanation of underlying assumptions, open deliberation on difficult issues, and continuous reassessment of past choices, better administrative procedures can improve the odds of future policy success. A variety of administrative law mechanisms are available in support of greater WTO efficacy including: conflict of interest rules to

[36] Benedict Kingsbury, Nico Krisch, and Richard B. Stewart, 'The Emergence of Global Administrative Law', 1 Law and Contemporary Problems (2005) 1, at 24 (discussing the need for reasoned decisions). See Steffek, above n 12, at 261–63 ('reasoning' or 'giving reasons' lies at the heart of the communicative process that legitimates governance).

[37] Esty, above n 7, at 1529–30.

[38] Steffek, above n 12, at 250 (discussing the need for justification to legitimize international governance. Avoiding 'arbitrary and capricious' policy choices stands at the heart of American Administrative Law); Jerry L. Mashaw, Richard A Merrill, and Peter M. Shane (eds), *Administrative Law: The American Public Law Process* (St. Paul, MN: West Group, 2003) 509–10. See also, Jürgen Schwarze, *European Administrative Law*, (London: Sweet & Merrill, 1992).

[39] Steffek, above n 12, at 251 (noting that good governance involves 'an institutionalization of rational communication about means, ends and values').

[40] Esty, above n 7, at 1543–45.

reduce 'agency' problems, mechanisms to draw in expert judgments as well as competing data and analyses, expanded public participation provisions, more use of inspections and audits, and power sharing to deepen political dialogues and maximize the chances of catching mistakes.[41]

E. Efficiency

Systematic analysis and political debate always entail transaction costs. But minimizing these and other policy-making costs is fundamental to good governance.[42] Decision making must not only be relatively low-cost but also timely. In brief, the transaction costs involved in governance must be low enough to justify efforts to achieve collective action in response to shared problems.[43] Making governance efficient is never easy. The divergence of economic circumstances, policy-making competence, values, and interests is often great in the national context—and will be even greater in the international domain. But the relative success of the EU demonstrates that supranational policymaking can be done successfully.[44]

The need for greater efficiency has been understood within the trading system since the Uruguay Round negotiations. And progress has been made. Time limits have been imposed on a number of procedures.[45] Unlike the GATT before it, the WTO has a provision that ensures that dispute settlement decisions cannot easily be buried. But more could be done to enhance WTO efficiency, from tighter time limits to more transparency designed to reduce obfuscation and expose foot-dragging.

Of course, efficiency will often be in tension with other elements of good governance such as the desire for robust deliberation and power sharing. A full airing of views takes time and resources, which cuts against the needs

[41] Ibid, at 1525–36. See also Steve Charnovitz, 'Transparency and Participation in the World Trade Organization'.

[42] Oran R. Young, 'Global Governance: Toward a Theory of Decentralized World Order', in Oran R. Young (ed), *Global Governance: Drawing Insights from the Environmental Experience* (Cambridge: MIT Press, 1997) 273, at 285.

[43] Efficiency in a pluralistic policy context is a central goal of the positive political theory of the 1970s and 1980s; Mashaw, above n 11, at 23; Peter Schuck, 'The Politics of Regulation', 90 (3) Yale Law Journal (1981) 702.

[44] Peter L. Lindseth, 'The Contradictions of Supranationalism: Administrative Governance and Constitutionalization in European Integration Since the 1950s', 37 Loyola Law Review (2003) 363 (arguing that the EU emerged as a successful administrative entity); Francesca Bignami, 'The Challenge of Cooperative Regulatory Relations After Enlargement', in George Bermann and Katharina Pistor (eds), *Law and Governance in an Enlarged European Union* (Portland: Hart, 2004) 97, at 98.

[45] Time limits are now in place on a number of WTO procedures. For example, Article IX, Section 7a of the Agreement Establishing the World Trade Organization (The WTO Agreement), adopted limits on the consideration of obligation waivers to ninety days; WTO Agreement, Article X Section 1 limits the consideration of amendment proposals to ninety days; and the Procedures for the Circulations and Derestriction of WTO Documents, WT/L/452, adopted on 14 May 2002, mandates that most official documents be derestricted within sixty days of their release.

of speedy decision-making. And multiple layers of decision-making and mechanisms for review inescapably slow down policy-making. So, while it is easy to say that the WTO needs to ensure that its rules and procedures produce efficient outcomes, how the balance with other elements of good governance is struck will require careful consideration and a degree of experimentation and refinement over time.

F. Neutrality

To be seen as legitimate, decision makers must be understood to be pursuing the public good in an objective, unbiased, and uncorrupted manner—not promoting powerful special interests or their own private gains. How best to overcome agency problems and public choice failures has been the subject of a great deal of scholarly focus.[46] The requisite objectivity and neutrality might be achieved in several ways. First, insulating decision makers from 'politics' and potential sources of bias may allow them to exercise their judgment with clarity and impartiality.[47] In this regard, conflict of interest rules, financial disclosure requirements, lobbying limits, and post-employment work restrictions for key decision makers all help to ensure that delegated policy-making stays focused on the public interest rather than having decisions influenced by prospects for private gain whether in the form of bribes, vacation travel, jobs for relatives, fancy meals, or promises of future employment.[48]

The WTO has in place provisions to address a number of these concerns.[49] But the conflict of interest rules and other provisions of administrative law are not as fully developed as they need to be. As a result, the WTO continues to be seen as a venue where special interests hold sway.[50] Many observers believe, for example, that the WTO's *Trade-Related Aspects of Intellectual Property* agreement pandered to pharmaceutical interests as a result of undue influence from drug companies.[51]

An alternative approach to neutrality is through balance—exposing decision makers to the political arguments on all sides of an issue.

[46] Mashaw, above n 11; Michael C. Jensen and William H. Meckling, 'Theory of the Firm: Managerial Behavior, Agency Costs and Ownership Structure', 3 Journal of Financial Economics (1976) 305; Sanford J. Grossman and Oliver D. Hart, 'An Analysis of the Principal-Agent Problem', 51 Econometrica (1983) 7.

[47] Stephen Bryer, *Breaking the Vicious Circle* (Cambridge: Harvard University Press, 2006) (on theoretical logic of insulating decision makers).

[48] Esty, above note 7, at 1524–26 (providing specific administrative law suggestions for limiting special interest influence at the global scale).

[49] These provisions can be found online at: http://www.wto.org/English/tratop_e/dispu_e/rc_e.htm (last visited 20 June 2007).

[50] Andreas Marschner, 'The New Lobbying: Interest Groups, Governments, and the WTO in Seattle', 11 SAIS Review (2001) 159 (arguing that special interest influence hinders the WTO's independence and strength).

[51] Caroline Thomas, 'Trade Policy and the Politics of Access to Drugs', 23 Third World Quarterly (2002) 251, at 254–55.

An emphasis on countervailing perspectives argues for open debate and broad public participation in decision processes. However, the 'interest group' model of governance raises important questions about fairness, capacity for political influence, and equality of access to the policy-making process. [52] These questions multiply in the international context.

Political participation has historically been difficult for those at a distance from the locus of decision-making, with limited means, or difficulty getting organized. These factors may undermine the potential neutrality of policy-making. But note that Information Age technologies are lowering the price of participation.[53] Anyone with internet access can today follow debates at the WTO and contribute comments on issues of the day. But even if basic access is available, theory tells us that diffuse interests and disadvantaged communities may not engage in the political process as fully or regularly as others.[54] And there remain a number of aspects of WTO policy-making that are conducted in secret and where access is controlled by national government officials who share information with those who they wish to bring into the policy-making process and not with others.

G. Clarity

Clarity is important both in the structure of the rule-making process and in the rules that emerge. The legitimacy of governance depends in no small part on having those who are governed understand how decisions are made and why particular outcomes emerge. Being clear on who has decision-making authority and on what basis they will exercise it is fundamental to governance being seen as fair and non-arbitrary.

In the WTO context, there are multiple layers of influence on policy-making that need to be better understood. WTO officials who are guiding decision-making processes—negotiations, policy-making dialogues, or dispute settlement panels—should be publicly identified. They should face more fully defined restrictions on *ex parte* contacts and have an obligation to

[52] Alan S. Blinder, 'Is Government Too Political?', 76 Foreign Affairs (1997) 115 (arguing that public interest may be threatened by the over-influence of interest groups); see also: 'Convention on Access to Information, Public Participation in Decision-Making and Access to Justice in Environmental Matters', (A Convention of the United Nations Economic Commission for Europe adopted in Aarhus, Denmark on 25 June 1998).

[53] See Joseph S. Nye, Jr. (ed), *Governance.Com: Democracy in the Information Age* (Washington, DC: Brookings Institution Press, 2002); Daniel Esty, 'Environmental Protection in the Information Age', 79 New York University Law Review (2004) 167; Slaughter, above n 26 (discussing online discussion procedures).

[54] Bruce Ackerman, 'Beyond Carolene Products', 98 Harvard Law Review (1985) 713, at 723–26 (noting the advantage of concentrated interests). See also Roger G. Noll, 'Economic Perspectives on the Politics of Regulation', in Richard Schmalensee and Robert D. Willig (eds), *Handbook of Industrial Organization* (Amsterdam: Elsevier, 1989) 1265; Buchanan and Tullock, *Calculus of Consent* (Ann Arbor: University of Michigan Press, 1962) (discussing this asymmetry).

'docket' all relevant materials that are provided to them as well as to report on all contacts they have with interested parties.[55]

H. Stability

In every institution rules and procedures occasionally need to be reworked or refined, but a careful process of amendment is essential to effective collective decision-making. No one wants to participate in a decision process where the rules of the game are constantly shifting. Thus, stability is an important element of good governance, especially in the international domain where order represents an important virtue.

In the WTO context, amendments to the *General Agreement on Tariffs and Trade* and other key 'contracts' are hard to get adopted.[56] Under the WTO Agreement, a consensus generally must be reached before a proposed amendment can be accepted.[57] The difficulty of amending the WTO structure creates a high degree of stability in the WTO rules and procedures, which helps ensure order and the rule of law in the supranational context. If anything, the current amendment process may be too stringent, making it too difficult to adopt changes that are needed to keep the trading system fresh and functioning.

I. Power Sharing

Dispersion of authority both vertically (across levels of government) and horizontally (over multiple institutions, agencies, or decision makers) limits the power of officials, disciplines abuses of authority, institutionalizes cross-checks on decisions, and, therefore, improves the quality of policy-making.[58] Such separation of powers also serves to soften the edge of all-or-nothing politics—by creating alternative decision-making 'spaces' in which issues can be considered. Multiple nodes of policy-making authority also produce regulatory competition along several dimensions that may generate innovation and efficiency.[59]

Of course, power sharing arrangements, such as those found in the EU,[60] the United States, and in other nation-states known for good governance, represent finely tuned systems that have evolved over many years. No such

[55] Esty, above n 7, at 1529–30 (for a full discussion of the provisions that might be adopted).

[56] John H. Jackson, 'The Role and Effectiveness of the WTO Dispute Settlement Mechanism', Brookings Trading Forum (2000) 179, at 203.

[57] *Agreement Establishing the World Trade Organization*, Article X.

[58] Dahl, *Preface to Democratic Theory* (Chicago: University of Chicago Press, 1956) (describing Madisonian democracy).

[59] See Esty and Damien Geradin (eds), *Regulatory Competition and Economic Integration: Comparative Perspectives*, (New York: Oxford University Press, 2001) (discussing multiple strands of horizontal and vertical regulatory cooperation).

[60] Joseph H.H. Weiler, *The Constitution of Europe*, (London: Cambridge University Press, 1999); Bignami, above n 44, at 73; René Seerden and Frits Stroink (eds), *Administrative Law of the European Union, its Member States and the United States*, (Antwerpen: Intersentia, 2002).

regime of checks and balances presently exists at the WTO or within other international bodies.

The success of the WTO's Appellate Body in providing a 'second opinion' mechanism and moving dispute settlement outcomes onto more secure legal grounds demonstrates the value of institutionalizing review processes.[61] Administrative structures that test assumptions, triangulate on the 'truth', and catch mistakes all contribute to good governance in a variety of ways. In this regard, the WTO would benefit from a broader set of mechanisms to cross-check outcomes. Most notably, the WTO might seek more links to other international organizations with recognized expertise so that it could share decisionmaking on 'trade *and*' issues with others such as United Nations Conference on Trade and Development (UNCTAD) or the International Labor Organization.[62]

J. Legality

Delegated decision-making is always circumscribed.[63] Decision processes must be structured to promote outcomes that are consistent with legal mandates and within the limits of authority that have been granted to those exercising power. One of the most important aspects of administrative law is the provision of mechanisms to test whether decision makers are acting within the scope of their authority and not over-reaching in ways that infringe upon the liberty of individuals, the rights of economic entities or, in the WTO context, the sovereignty of nation states.[64] The principle of legality helps check abuses of power and ensure that decision makers exercise restraint in their policy-making activities. Such restraint is especially important in the international realm—as over-reaching by supranational authorities quickly raises serious legitimacy issues.

The WTO has a strong Legal Affairs Division that helps to constrain the organization's activities. And national trade officials are vigilant about protecting their prerogatives and keeping the WTO within its proscribed legal bounds. Thus, concerns about the legality of decisions coming from the trading system are likely only to emerge in the context of disputes over whether the policies emanating from the WTO are in conflict with legal obligations imposed by other international bodies, such as mandates from environmental treaties.[65] Nevertheless, rules that require the WTO to be

[61] See Wofford, above n 16.

[62] Report of the Consultative Board to the Director-General Supachai Panitchpakdi, *The Future of the WTO: Addressing Institutional Challenges in the New Millennium* (Geneva: World Trade Organization, 2004); Stuart E. Eizenstat and Grant D. Aldonas, Co-chairs, *Transatlantic Leadership for a New Global Economy*, The Atlantic Council of the United States, Policy Paper April 2007 (Washington DC: The Atlantic Council of the United States, 2007), at 30.

[63] See Mashaw et al., above n 38, at 12–13, 17.

[64] See Kingsbury et al., above n 36 (discussing legal limits of delegation).

[65] John H. Jackson, 'World Trade Rules and Environmental Policies: Congruence or Conflict?,' 49 (4) Washington & Lee University Law Review (1992) 1245, at 1248.

more clear about the legal foundations on which decisions rest would be helpful. More generally, the move toward being a rules-based institution rather than a forum for ongoing negotiation helps to promote the sense that the WTO is legally rigorous.

K. Fairness

An essential element of governance legitimacy is an over-arching sense of balance and fairness.[66] Fairness entails both a procedural element that relates to questions of due process and a chance to be heard,[67] as well as a substantive element that asks whether the burdens and benefits of governance are being distributed in ways that meet agreed upon equity norms.[68] Embedded in the question of substantive fairness is a great deal of scope for normative dispute.[69] As governance moves into the supranational realm and values diverge, the potential for perceived unfairness grows.[70]

No structure of administrative law guarantees substantive fairness. But procedures that give all interested parties a chance to be heard and provide for careful deliberation are likely to generate outcomes that will be considered fair. Once again, the WTO has some distance to go in developing administrative structures that offer these elements.

Of particular concern is the participation of developing countries. While the Doha Round was launched with an emphasis on the needs of the developing world, there is no doubt that the outcomes of past rounds of negotiations have not always put the needs of developing countries first.[71] While the WTO's consensus-based policy-making has certain advantages, it gives particular weight to the strongest countries.[72]

[66] John Rawls, *Justice as Fairness: a Restatement* (Cambridge: Belknap Press of Harvard University Press, 2001) (highlighting requirements for fairness); Randy Barnett, *The Structure of Liberty: Justice and the Rule of Law* (New York: Oxford University Press, 1998).

[67] Debra P. Steger, 'The Struggle for Legitimacy in the WTO', Trade Policy Research (2003) 111 (arguing that due process increases perceptions of fairness and legitimacy).

[68] The emphasis on justice as an element of legitimacy highlighted earlier makes clear the importance of this issue. Bruce Ackerman, *Social Justice in the Liberal State* (New Haven: Yale University Press, 1980) (making the case for the centrality of justice); Thomas W. Pogge, *Realizing Rawls* (Ithaca: Cornell University Press, 1989) 227–39, 240–73 (showing how Rawls's conception of justice could be and should be globalized); Stephen Weatherford, 'Measuring Political Legitimacy', 86 American Political Science Review (1992) 150.

[69] See Rudolf Dolzer, *The Impact of Investment Treaties on Domestic Administrative Law* (draft paper presented at the NYU Conference on Global Administrative Law 21–22 April 2005) (discussing the difficulty of agreeing on an international definition of 'fair and equitable treatment' of foreign investment).

[70] Steffek, above n 12, at 271; Bignami, above n 43 (discussing this challenge in an expanded EU).

[71] Joseph E. Striglitz, 'Two Principles of the Next Round or, How to Bring Developing Countries in from the Cold', 23 The World Economy (2000) 437, at 437.

[72] Amrita Narlikar, 'Fairness in International Trade Negotiations: Developing Countries in the GATT and WTO' 29 The World Economy (2006) 1005, at 1014–15 (Narlikar points to three problems associated with consensus policy-making: lack of representation for some least developed countries, intimidation of least developed countries by developed countries, and

L. Deliberation

Procedural legitimacy depends on a careful structure of policy deliberation—the making of arguments, followed by responses and rebuttals, the checking of facts and reviewing of claims, ultimately leading to a thoughtful conclusion. Good governance depends, therefore, on having mechanisms that promote dialogue and debate. The importance of give-and-take as a path to superior results over time can be traced not only to political theory but also to the scientific method.[73] Procedures that promote the advancing of data, testing of theories, scrutiny of assumptions, review of policy results, and the refinement of thinking based on experience are all to be prized.[74]

WTO procedures provide some degree of structure for debate, but much more could be done to adopt a more sophisticated regime of administrative law in support of a healthy policy dialogue. In particular, the WTO should adopt a practice that potential trade rules or policies be advanced in draft form with public 'notice' and an opportunity for all interested parties to 'comment' on the draft.[75] Decision makers should then be required to respond to the comments and concerns put forward.

M. Transparency

Transparency is a key element of good governance.[76] Seeing the decision maker in action and observing who has influenced the decision process is essential to a sense of fairness, rationality, and neutrality, as well as public understanding of the policy results. Transparency is especially important in the international context where relationships of trust are not deeply established.[77] Transparency also tends to expose sub-par results and

exclusion of least developed countries in 'Green Room' meetings); Richard Blackhurst, Bill Lyakurwa, and Ademola Oyejide, 'Options for Improving Africa's Participation in the WTO', 23 The World Economy (2000) 491, at 497–98 (Blackhurst et al. catalogue the difficulty that least developed countries have in maintaining a qualified representative in Geneva).

[73] See Hugh G. Gauch Jr., *Scientific Method in Practice*, (New York: Cambridge University Press, 2003) (arguing that pressure from counter-arguments drives scientists to deeper understanding).

[74] See Wayne Sandholtz and Alec Stone Sweet, 'Law, Politics, and International Governance', in Christian Reus-Smit (ed), *The Politics of International Law* (New York: Cambridge University Press, 2004) 247.

[75] Esty, above n 7, at 1527–34.

[76] Francis Fukuyama, *State-Building: Governance and World Order in the 21st Century* (Ithaca: Cornell University Press, 2004) (highlighting transparency as an element of good governance); Slaughter, above n 26, at 524 (invisibility as a key critique of government networks); Francesca Bignami, 'Three Generations of Participation Rights Before the European Commission', 68 Law and Contemporary Problems (2004) 61, at 101, 102; (discussing the 'drive for transparency' in the EU led by the Netherlands, Sweden, and Finland).

[77] Abram Chayes and Antonia Handler Chayes, *The New Sovereignty: Compliance with International Regulatory Agreements* (Cambridge: Harvard University Press, 1995) 62;

discourage rent-seeking and other self-serving behaviour.[78] Some trade scholars argue that secrecy is critical to the ability of governments to overcome protectionist interest and achieve trade liberalizing agreements.[79] But this logic increasingly holds little sway in the face of mounting evidence that closed-door processes yield more, not less, special interest manipulation.

The WTO has taken important first steps toward being more transparent, but has a good distance to go toward full-fledged openness in support of good governance.[80] In this regard, the fact that dispute settlement decisions are now published is a progress. But the dispute settlement process should be opened up completely with the taking of evidence done in public.[81] Similarly, the monthly General Council meetings should be open to the public and media.

N. Participation and due process

Opportunities for 'voice' or public participation in some fashion or another are essential for legitimacy. [82] To be meaningful, a policy-making dialogue must be carefully structured so as to respect the interests of all those who might be affected by the outcome. Opportunities to be heard are critical to Habermasian legitimacy. Those affected by policy-making processes are much more likely to accept outcomes if they feel the procedures were fair.[83]

See also, Ronald B. Mitchell, 'Sources of Transparency: Information Systems in International Regimes', 42 International Studies Quarterly (1998) 109, at 111.

[78] Paul B. Stephan, 'Accountability and International Lawmaking: Rules, Rents and Legitimacy', 17 Northwest Journal of International Law and Business (1996–97) 729, at 729.

[79] For many years, trade experts argued that the GATT's opaque negotiating process was necessary as the 'only way conflicting, narrow (and often protectionist) domestic interests could be traded off, outside the scrutiny of domestic publics, to reach agreements that would liberalize trade, open markets, and enhance national and, ultimately, global prosperity.' Elizabeth Smythe and Peter J. Smith, 'Legitimacy, Transparency, and Information Technology: The World Trade Organization in an Era of Contentious Trade Politics', 12 Good Governance (2006) 31, at 34; see also, The Sutherland Report, at 44–45 (noting that transparency can increase domestic negotiations past the capacity of some Members).

[80] One report indicates that roughly 35,000 individuals were receiving daily information about the WTO. See Smythe and Smith, above n 79, at 42.

[81] Esty, 'The World Trade Organization's Legitimacy Crisis', 1 The World Review (2002) 7, at 13–14.

[82] Kal Raustiala and David G. Victor, 'Conclusions', in David G. Victor, Kaul Raustiala, and Eugene B. Skolnikoff (eds), *The Implementation and Effectiveness of International Environmental Commitments Theory and Practice* (Cambridge: MIT Press, 1998), at 659, 663; Harold Hongju Koh, 'The 1998 Frankel Lecture: Bringing International Law Home', 35 Houston Law Review (1998) 623, at 676 (discussing how empowering participation can lead countries to obey international law through the transnational legal process).

[83] J.L. Gibson, 'Understandings of Justice: Institutional Legitimacy, Procedural Justice, and Political Tolerance', 23 Law & Society Review (1989) 469, at 483–86 (discussing the

But participation has a potential downside that must be addressed squarely: the risk that special interests will take advantage of open decision-making processes to distort policy outcomes.[84] In this regard, 'comitology', the European style of consultative rule making with structured roles for business and NGO interests, has been criticized as 'corporativism' that may give undue sway to those with strong views, perhaps ignoring the public interest.[85] The US 'interest group' governance model could be faulted for the same reason.[86]

The WTO, therefore, needs a structured decision process that mandates disclosure of those who are lobbying officials or otherwise seeking to shape policy outcomes. At the same time, access must be provided for all those who are interested in the issues under debate. This balance between participation and mechanisms to control special interest distortions of policy-making must be struck with care. But it would make sense, for example, to provide more open forums for NGOs (of all sorts) to offer comments on ongoing WTO policy debates. And there should be a mechanism for NGOs and others to offer amicus briefs in the course of the dispute settlement processes.[87]

III. DIFFICULTIES IN ESTABLISHING WTO-SPECIFIC ADMINISTRATIVE LAW

Establishing administrative law procedures at the supranational level has many difficulties. Several distinct challenges make establishing a body of WTO administrative law hard to do.[88] As Kingsbury et al. note, international decision processes are inevitably multi-level; the informality of the decision processes may detract from the application of administrative law; private actors play an important role in many decision-making mechanisms

importance of fair decision-making procedures to legitimate outcomes—even outcomes that are disliked).

[84] Martin Shapiro, 'Administrative Law Unbounded: Reflection on Government and Governance', 8 Indian Journal of Global Legal Studies (2001) 369, at 369; Jim Rossi, 'Participation Run Amok: The Costs of Mass Participation for Deliberative Agency Decisionmaking', 92 Northwestern University Law Review (1997–98) 173, at 196–208.

[85] Susan Rose-Ackerman, above n 32; Peter L. Lindseth, '"Weak" Constitutionalism? Reflections on Comitology and Transnational Governance in the European Union', 21 Oxford Journal Of Legal Studies (2001) 145, at 145; John R. Bolton, 'Should We Take Global Governance Seriously?', 1 Chicago Journal of International Law (2000) 205, at 205 (rejecting 'corporatism' run rampant in participatory global governance).

[86] Cass R. Sunstein, 'Interest Groups in American Public Law', 38 Stanford Law Review (1985) 29 (noting that tension has been seen between public and private interest since the creation of the Constitution); Mashaw, above n 11 (describing the interaction between public interest and interest groups in American voting practices).

[87] See WTO document WT/L/162. See also, Gabrielle Marceau and Matthew Stilwell, 'Practical Suggestions for *Amicus Curiae* Briefs Before WTO Adjudicating Bodies', 4 Journal of International Economic Law (2001) 155 (exploring practical procedures for the use of amicus curiae by NGOs in the WTO).

[88] Kingsbury et al., above n 36, at 40–42.

(often with national government support); and the mix of government action and global governance can complicate the logic of using administrative law.[89] Similarly, Grant and Keohane suggest that the global challenge is greater because the abuse of power is more serious internationally, global governance lacks even minimal institutional constraints on power-wielders, and there is no 'constitutional system' of checks and balances at the global scale.[90] In particular, the influence of the prominent, industrialized nations on decisionmaking is unusually strong because of the WTO's preferred policy of consensus rather than voting. In moving forward with the development of WTO administrative law, the representation of developing nations must be carefully considered.

IV. CONCLUSION

A better functioning international trading system would yield benefits for most if not all countries. As a central part of the global governance regime, the WTO plays a critical role in helping to bring countries together to achieve collective action in the international economic realm. To build public confidence in the trading system, the structure of the WTO's decision-making processes needs to be refined to promote good governance and a greater degree of procedural rigour. The WTO has a somewhat uneven record with regard to these various elements of good governance, but a solid base on which to build a structure of administrative law that will enhance its legitimacy and improve its performance in managing international economic interdependence.

[89] Esty, above n 7, at 1537; James M. Rosenau and Ernst-Otto Czempiel, *Governance Without Government: Order and Change in World Politics*, (New York: Cambridge University Press, 1992).

[90] Esty, above n 7, at 1537; Grant and Keohane, above n 26, at 14.

MULTILEVEL JUDICIAL GOVERNANCE OF INTERNATIONAL TRADE REQUIRES A COMMON CONCEPTION OF RULE OF LAW AND JUSTICE

*Ernst-Ulrich Petersmann**

ABSTRACT

Since the establishment of the Permanent Court of International Justice in 1922, governments have consented to, and actively used, an ever larger number of international and transnational courts, quasi-judicial dispute settlement bodies and *ad hoc* arbitral tribunals for the settlement of disputes over the interpretation and application of rules of international law. Such judicial clarification of disputed interpretations of incomplete, intergovernmental agreements reduces not only the negotiation costs of governments by delegating the clarification of contested facts and legal claims to independent third-party adjudication. Judicial decision-making at intergovernmental, transnational, national and private levels also supplements rule-making and offers citizens judicial remedies for defending their rights and interests. Modern international economic law increasingly complements intergovernmental, legislative, and administrative governance by multilevel 'judicial governance' so as to protect rule of law more effectively for the benefit of citizens (Section I). This contribution criticizes the one-sidedly power-oriented perceptions of WTO law as 'international law among states' (Section II) and the related perceptions of international judges as dependent agents of states (Section III). Civil society, parliaments and democratic governments should encourage national and international judges to cooperate in their legal task of interpreting citizen-oriented international economic law 'in conformity with principles of justice and international law', as explicitly prescribed in the Vienna Convention on the Law of Treaties (VCLT). The legal coherence of multilevel judicial governance depends on protecting principles of procedural as well as substantive justice and a

* Professor for International and European Law and Head of the Law Department in the European University Institute at Florence, Italy. E-mail: Ulrich.Petersmann@EUI.eu. Former professor at the University of Geneva and its Graduate Institute of International Studies, legal advisor in GATT (1981–95) and legal consultant in the WTO (1995–2006). Former secretary, member or chairman of numerous GATT and WTO dispute settlement panels. Chairman of the International Trade Law Committee of the International Law Association.

common conception of 'rule of law' not only in intergovernmental relations among states, but also vis-à-vis their citizens engaged in, and benefiting from, international trade (Sections IV–VIII).

I. FROM 'MEMBER-DRIVEN GOVERNANCE' TO 'MULTILEVEL JUDICIAL GOVERNANCE' AND 'CITIZEN-DRIVEN' ECONOMIC INTEGRATION

The history of international economic law is characterized by the evolution from unilateral, authoritarian protection and regulation of transnational economic transactions (e.g. by ancient rulers and city republics) towards their progressive bilateral, regional and worldwide liberalization, intergovernmental regulation, and private self-regulation. The 'international law of coexistence' among states focusing on state sovereignty, as well as the 'international law of cooperation' promoting intergovernmental cooperation in international organizations,[1] have proven to be incapable of protecting human rights and democratic peace effectively. As emphasized by Kofi Annan in his final address as UN Secretary-General to world leaders assembled in the UN General Assembly on 19 September 2006, the power-oriented international legal system and many intergovernmental UN bodies are widely perceived today as 'unjust, discriminatory and irresponsible' because they failed to effectively respond to the three global challenges to the UN: 'to ensure that globalization would benefit the entire human race; to heal the disorder of the post-Cold War world, replacing it with a genuinely new world order of peace and freedom; and to protect the rights and dignity of individuals, particularly women, which were so widely trampled underfoot.' According to Kofi Annan, these three challenges—'an unjust world economy, world disorder and widespread contempt for human rights and the rule of law'—entail divisions that 'threaten the very notion of an international community, upon which the UN stands.'[2] Governments have only rarely challenged in the International Court of Justice (ICJ) the massive violations of UN human rights obligations in numerous UN member states. Likewise, prior to the more recent complaints (e.g. by Congo, Bosnia, and Croatia) against genocide and other gross violations of human rights (e.g. by Rwanda and Serbia), the ICJ has hardly ever based its less than one hundred judgments, since 1948 on human rights, notwithstanding references to human rights in *obiter dicta* and in advisory opinions by the ICJ. Civil society and parliaments widely share the criticism by Kofi Annan and perceive the UN and the ICJ as guardians of a power-oriented *ancien régime* that fails to contribute effectively to the protection of human rights and to reducing the unnecessary poverty of more than two billion people.

[1] On the distinction between 'international law of coexistence' and 'international law of cooperation' see: W. Friedmann, *The Changing Structures of International Law* (1964).

[2] The speech of Kofi Annan is reproduced in UN document GA/105000 of 19 September 2006.

The post-war leadership of the United States for a liberal (i.e. liberty-based) international order was characterized not only by US proposals for negotiating a UN Charter, the Bretton Woods institutions and the Universal Declaration of Human Rights, but also by democratic distrust vis-à-vis international law and insistence on constitutional powers (e.g. of the US Congress and US President) to adopt measures in violation of international law.[3] The US proposals for 'embedding international liberalism' into national constitutional democracies were based on communitarian conceptions of popular sovereignty, as reflected in the premise of the American legal philosopher John Rawls that 'the crucial element in how a country fares is its political culture—its members' political and civic virtues—and not the level of its resources.'[4] This emphasis on constitutional democracy and on the national roots of economic welfare and poverty contributed not only to the US refusal to ratify the 1948 Havana Charter of an International Trade Organization but also to the US insistence that the 1947 General Agreement on Tariffs and Trade (GATT) must remain a 'member-driven organization' where all decisions remain in the power of the Contracting Parties. The perception of GATT 1947 as an intergovernmental agreement for the promotion of national interests entailed that, for example,

- the 'member-driven GATT Rounds' of multilateral trade negotiations focused on the export interests of powerful producers in industrialized countries (e.g. of agricultural products, cotton, textiles, steel, services);
- and GATT diplomats and their 'diplomats' jurisprudence' interpreted GATT law as a 'self-contained regime' separate from UN law.[5]

The Agreement establishing the World Trade Organization (WTO), its compulsory dispute settlement system and the progressive development of WTO law by the already more than 200 panel, Appellate Body, and arbitration reports adopted by the WTO Dispute Settlement Body have legally limited this 'member-driven governance'.[6] There are also increasing political restraints resulting, for example, from the insistency by the more than one hundred less-developed WTO members that future consensus needed for concluding WTO negotiations must depend on transforming the

[3] Cf. J. Rubenfeld, 'The Two World Orders', in G. Nolte (ed.), *European and US Constitutionalism*, (2005), at 280, 283, 293: the post-war US support for internationalism and multilateralism was 'for the rest of the world, not for us', even though America's commitment to internationalism in economic affairs is recognized as serving US interests.

[4] J. Rawls, *The Law of Peoples* (1989), at 117.

[5] On my personal experiences, as the first 'legal officer' ever employed by GATT, which only happened in 1981, with GATT's anti-legal, diplomatic traditions see: E.U.Petersmann, *The GATT/WTO Dispute Settlement System* (1997), at Introduction.

[6] See: E. U. Petersmann, From 'Member-Driven Governance' to Constitutionally Limited 'Multi-level Trade Governance' in the WTO in G.Sacerdoti, A.Yanovich and J.Bohanes (eds), *The WTO at Ten. The Contribution of the Dispute Settlement System* (2006), at 86–110.

producer-driven WTO negotiations into a 'Development Round' protecting developing country interests more effectively.

Since the WTO Ministerial Conference at Seattle (1999), WTO negotiations are increasingly influenced by civil society and parliamentary pressures to make WTO negotiations more transparent and more responsive to general citizen interests. For example, the American legal philosopher F. J. Garcia has argued that the five 'circumstances of justice' (as identified by Rawls) necessitating legal principles of justice inside national communities exist increasingly also in international relations: scarcity of resources; shared geographical spaces; capacity to help and harm each other; non-altruistic behavior of most people; and conflicting claims whose peaceful settlement requires 'principles of justice'.[7] Just as principles of representative national democracy are increasingly complemented inside the European Community by EC law principles of participatory, deliberative, and international democracy in order to better legitimize and control the EC's governance mechanisms, so does the democratic legitimacy of intergovernmental UN and WTO governance increasingly depend on transforming the power-oriented 'society of states paradigm' into a more citizen-oriented paradigm of international law empowering citizens and addressing their common interests, common risks, and common responsibilities for the collective supply of international public goods and for an equitable sharing of the adjustment costs. Democratic discourse and justice must become political virtues not only of communities inside states, but also for functionally defined international legal communities, including the 'WTO community' benefiting from the international division of labuor and international adjustment processes made possible by WTO law. The less national constitutions and parliamentary governance remain capable of securing the well-being of national citizens, the stronger the need for promoting new forms of democratic self-government, 'transnational justice' and international rule-making for the collective supply of international public goods. If international governance becomes an indispensable 'fourth branch of governance' supplementing *national* legislative, administrative, and judicial governance mechanisms,[8] then *international governance mechanisms* must become consistent with democratic and social 'principles of justice'.

II. MULTILEVEL JUDICIAL TRADE GOVERNANCE WITHOUT JUSTICE?

Similar to Article 1 of the UN Charter, the Preamble to the Vienna Convention on the Law of Treaties (VCLT) prescribes that 'disputes concerning treaties, like other international disputes, should be settled by peaceful means and in

[7] F. J. Garcia, 'Globalization and the Theory of International Law', Boston College Law School, Faculty Paper 93 (2005).

[8] In this sense: E. U. Petersmann, 'Constitutionalism and International Organizations', 17 Northwestern Journal of International Law & Business (1996) at 398, 415 ff.

conformity with the principles of justice and international law.' The WTO Agreement recognizes 'basic principles and objectives ... underlying this multilateral trading system' (Preamble). Some of these principles are specified in WTO provisions, for instance in the GATT (e.g. Articles III.2, VII.1, X.3, XIII.5, XX (j), XXIX.6, XXXVI.9) and other WTO agreements on trade in goods (e.g. Article 7.1 Agreement on Customs Valuation, Article 9 Agreement on Rules of Origin), services (e.g. Article X of the GATS) and trade-related intellectual property rights (e.g. in the Preamble of the TRIPS Agreement, Articles 8 and 62.4). The WTO requirement of interpreting WTO law 'in accordance with customary rules of interpretation of public international law' (Article 3.2 DSU) refers not only to *formal* interpretative principles (such as *lex specialis, lex posterior, lex superior*) aimed at mutually coherent interpretations on the basis of legal presumptions of lawful conduct of states, of the systemic character of international law, and the mutual coherence of international rules and principles. The customary law requirement of interpreting treaties 'in conformity with principles of justice', and the related reference of the VCLT to 'universal respect for, and observance of, human rights and fundamental freedoms for all' (Preamble VCLT), also call for clarifying the *substantive principles of justice* underlying WTO law, like freedom, non-discrimination, rule of law, independent third-party adjudication, and preferential treatment of less-developed countries (LDCs). For, without clarification of the 'principles of justice' common to national and international law, national courts will continue to define 'rule of law' without regard to international law. The basic WTO principle of progressive liberalization and legal protection of liberal trade can be justified by all liberal theories of justice such as

- utilitarian theories defining justice, in terms of maximum satisfaction of individual preferences and consumer welfare;
- libertarian theories focusing on protection of individual liberty and property rights;
- egalitarian concepts defining justice more broadly in terms of equal human rights and democratic consent; and
- international theories of justice based on sovereign equality and effective empowerment of states to increase their national welfare through liberal trade.[9]

Hence, the diversity of libertarian, egalitarian, or utilitarian value preferences should not affect recognition that the WTO guarantees of freedom, non-discrimination and rule of law—by enhancing individual liberty, non-discriminatory treatment, economic welfare, and poverty reduction across frontiers—reflect, albeit imperfectly, basic principles of justice. In terms of the

[9] For overviews of these theories see F. J. Garcia, *Trade, Inequality and Justice: Toward a Liberal Theory of Just Trade* (2003); A. Beviglia Zampetti, *Fairness in the World Economy: US Perspectives on International Trade Relations* (2006).

Aristotelian distinction between 'general principles of justice' (like liberty, equality, fair procedures, promotion of general consumer welfare) and particular principles of justice requiring adjustments depending on particular circumstances, WTO rule-making and WTO dispute settlement procedures can also contribute to 'corrective justice' and 'reciprocal justice', just as the special, differential and non-reciprocal treatment of less-developed WTO Members in numerous WTO provisions may contribute to 'distributive justice'.

WTO law regulates 'the dispute settlement system of the WTO' (Article 3 DSU) as a multilevel system with compulsory jurisdiction for the settlement of international as well as domestic trade disputes by independent international as well as domestic dispute settlement bodies so as to promote 'security and predictability to the multilateral trading system' (Article 3 DSU) for the benefit not only of governments but also of their citizens. The increasing judicial recourse—in the case-law not only of WTO dispute settlement bodies but also of domestic trade courts—to 'principles' and 'balancing' for justifying interpretive choices is in line with modern constitutional theories of adjudication, such as Dworkin's 'adjudicative principle of integrity' which requires judges to regard law as expressing 'a coherent conception of justice and fairness'.[10] Yet, national and international judges often fail to cooperate in their judicial protection of the rule of law in international trade because they perceive international and domestic trade law as being based on mutually conflicting conceptions of justice.[11] For instance, just as US courts claim that WTO dispute settlement rulings 'are not binding on the United States, much less this court',[12] so has the EC Court refrained long since—at the request of the political EC institutions who have repeatedly misled the ECJ about the interpretation of WTO obligations so as to limit their own judicial accountability[13]—from reviewing the legality of EC measures in the light of the EC's

[10] Cf. R. Dworkin, *Law's Empire* (1986), at 225, 243: 'Law as integrity asks judges to assume, so far as this is possible, that the law is structured by a coherent set of principles about justice and fairness and procedural due process, and it asks them to enforce these in the fresh cases that come before them, so that each person's situation is fair and just according to the same standards.'

[11] On the pursuit of 'order' rather than 'justice' in international political relations see: R. Foot, J. L. Gaddis, and A. Hurrel (eds), *Order and Justice in International Relations* (2003); J. Thomson, *Justice and World Order* (1992).

[12] US Court of Appeals for the Federal Circuit, judgment of 21 January 2005 (Corus Staal), available at (http://www.fedcir.gov/opinions/04-1107.pdf). In the Corus Staal dispute, the US Supreme Court denied petition for certiorari on 9 January 2006 (http://www.supremecourtus.gov/docket/05-364.htm), notwithstanding an amicus curiae brief filed by the EC Commission supporting this petition ('We argue that the Federal Circuit went too far by construing the Uruguay Round Agreements Act to make considerations of compliance with international obligations completely irrelevant in construing a Department of Commerce anti-dumping determination, and further argue that the Department's "zeroing" methodology—held invalid by both a WTO Appellate Body and a NAFTA Binational Panel—is not entitled to Chevron deference because it would bring the United States into noncompliance with treaty obligations.' (available at http://www.robbinsrussell.com/pdf/265.pdf).

[13] Cf. P. J. Kuijper, 'WTO Law in the European Court of Justice', 42 Common Market Law Review (2005) 1313, who claims (at 1334) that 'it is difficult to point out one specific

GATT and WTO obligations. Even though the mandate of national and international judges to protect the rule of law includes a mandate to promote coherent interpretations of international and national law for the benefit of citizens, domestic judges—like international judges—often refrain from applying international rules unless they are explicitly required to do so. Similar to the *dictum* by US Supreme Court justice Oliver Wendell Holmes that his judicial task was not to administer justice but to apply the positive rules of law,[14] multilevel judicial governance in international trade tends to neglect the legal requirement and judicial task of interpreting international treaties 'in conformity with principles of justice', including 'universal respect for, and observance of, human rights and fundamental freedoms for all' (Preamble VCLT) as required by the universal human rights obligations of all WTO members under international treaty law (e.g. the UN Charter), customary law and 'general principles of law recognized by civilized nations' (Article 38 ICJ Statute). Multilevel judicial trade governance remains characterized by frequent legal and judicial incoherencies reducing rule of law, economic efficiency, and justice to the detriment of the rights and welfare of citizens.[15] Similarly, in the more than one hundred transnational arbitration awards in investor-state arbitration over private challenges of investment restrictions over the past years, hardly any of the arbitration awards has referred to the human rights obligations of the countries concerned. Just as *ad hoc* judges in the ICJ usually side with the state that has nominated the judge, investment arbitrators tend to construe their mandates narrowly and, unless specifically requested, prefer to avoid referring to human rights and a 'miscarriage of justice'.[16]

III. OBSTACLES TO IMPROVING COOPERATION AMONG INTERNATIONAL AND DOMESTIC JUDGES

Even though the WTO Agreement (e.g. Article XVI:4) commits all government organs of WTO Members to comply with WTO obligations, WTO members have only rarely accepted WTO obligations specifically *requiring* domestic courts to *apply* WTO rules at the request of private

moment at which it can be established beyond doubt that WTO rules have been breached, even after a decision of a panel or report of the Appellate Body', and 'that it is rarely or never possible to speak of a sufficiently serious breach of WTO law' by the political EC institutions justifying the EC's non-contractual liability for damages pursuant to Article 288 EC Treaty.

[14] For a discussion of this dictum by Justice Holmes see: T. Sowell, *The Quest for Cosmic Justice* (1999), at 169.

[15] Cf. E. U. Petersmann, 'Multilevel Judicial Governance in the WTO Without Justice?', in M.E. Janow (ed), *The WTO at 10: Governance, Dispute Settlement and Developing Countries* (2007).

[16] The quotation is from paragraphs 241–2 of the ICSID arbitration award of 23 June 2003 in the case *Loewen Group v. United States* (published in Journal of World Investment 2003, at 675 ff.), which concerned a Missisippi jury award of $500 million damages and procedural biases against a foreign investor.

plaintiffs (as provided for in Article XX of the WTO Agreement on Government Procurement). The prevailing view is that—in contrast to the judicial protection of economic freedoms inside constitutional democracies, in European integration law as well as in bilateral investment treaties providing for private rights of action and direct access to transnational investor-state arbitration if the capital-importing country engages in expropriation or related investment restrictions—WTO rules should be interpreted and applied as intergovernmental commitments about reciprocal market access without private rights of action.[17] Only a few international lawyers argue that—at least in those areas where WTO law provides explicitly for private legal and judicial remedies in domestic courts (as in the WTO Agreements on Government Procurement and Trade Related Intellectual Property Rights, the WTO Protocol on the Accession of China) or for private access to international arbitration (e.g. pursuant to Article 4 of the WTO Agreement on Preshipment Inspection)—intergovernmental disputes (e.g. about private rights) should be avoided by empowering citizens and domestic courts to apply and protect WTO rules at domestic levels.[18]

Just as UN diplomats, their legal advisors from national ministries of foreign affairs and ICJ judges (most of whom are former diplomats and legal advisors in national governments) derive broad discretionary powers from their conception of UN law as 'international law among states', so do WTO diplomats continue to defend their intergovernmental 'founding myth of GATT'[19] that member-driven governance requires all decisions to remain in the hands of government representatives and to respect also 'the sovereign decision of the violator'[20] of WTO obligations. The Machiavellian world-views of many WTO diplomats and their legal advisors are reflected in their opinion that, for example, judges should focus on the intergovernmental 'WTO law in action' rather than on the 'WTO law in the books' as ratified by domestic parliaments.[21] The perception of international economic law as 'international law among states' for advancing *national* interests in an anarchic world prompts many international lawyers and diplomats to argue that effective international tribunals must remain 'dependent' tribunals staffed by *ad hoc* judges closely controlled by governments, for example

[17] See A. O. Sykes, 'Public versus Private Enforcement of International Economic Law: Standing and Remedy', 34 Journal of Legal Studies (2005) 631.

[18] Cf. E. U. Petersmann, 'Prevention and Settlement of Transatlantic Economic Disputes', in E. U. Petersmann and M. Pollack (eds), *Transatlantic Economic Disputes: The EC, the US and the WTO* (2003), 3, 55ff.

[19] G.Abi-Saab, 'The WTO Dispute Settlement and General International Law', in R. Yerxa and B. Wilson (eds), *Key Issues in WTO Dispute Settlement: The First Ten Years* (2005), 7–8.

[20] Rufus Yerxa, '*The Power of the WTO Dispute Settlement System*', in Yerxa and Wilson, above n 19, 3–4.

[21] See the legal advice by the EC's legal advocate Kuijper, above n 13, at 1332–34.

through their power of reappointment and threats of retaliation; independent international courts are perceived with suspicion because independent judges risk allowing moral ideals and interests of third parties to influence their judgments; the domestic ideal of rule of law is seen as inappropriate for the reality of international power politics: 'Dependent tribunals' are more likely to 'render judgments that reflect the interests of the states at the time that they submit the dispute to the tribunal.'[22] In support of such visions of international judges as agents of the states which appoint them, reference is also made to the empirical voting patterns of *ad hoc* judges in international arbitral and other tribunals, who side much more often with the legal claims of the government nominating the judge than with the legal claims of the other party to the dispute.[23] The complaints in trade and investment disputes, like GATT and WTO panel reports and arbitral awards of investment tribunals, refer even less frequently to the human rights obligations of the states parties to the disputes than it is the case in complaints to the ICJ and in ICJ judgments.

WTO diplomats and their 'realist' legal advisors argue that the intergovernmental structures of WTO law make it impossible to limit the 'Member-driven governance' of WTO negotiations by new forms of constitutionally limited governance: 'the WTO is not constitutionalized, and nor, according to any current meanings of the term, should it be.'[24] WTO law tends to be perceived as mere 'global administrative law' and 'conflict of law' rules (e.g. GATT rules allocating the regulation of product standards to importing countries, and the regulation of production standards to exporting countries), from which constitutional democracies (e.g. the US Congress) should deviate whenever necessary for protecting national interests. EC trade politicians often emulate the power-oriented approaches to international law favored by their US counterparts, for instance by justifying violations of WTO obligations (e.g. as determined in GATT and WTO dispute settlement findings) on political grounds and rejecting judicial enforcement of international trade liberalization commitments as 'politically naïve.'[25] Both the EC and US governments have requested their respective domestic courts to refrain from applying WTO rules directly at the request

[22] See E. Posner and J. C. Yoo, 'Judicial Independence in International Tribunals', 93 California Law Review (2005) 1, at 6, who define the function of international tribunals as providing states with neutral information about the facts and the law in a particular dispute.

[23] Cf. E. A. Posner and F. P. de Figueiredo, 'Is the International Court of Justice Politically Biased?', 34 Journal of Legal Studies (2005) 599–630.

[24] D. Z. Cass, *The Constitutionalization of the WTO* (2005), at x. Following seven chapters arguing against constitutionalization of international relations, her Chapter 8 concludes that 'trading democracy, not merely trading constitutionalization, should be the key to WTO constitutionalization in this century' (at 242). Cass admits at the end that her 'received account' of Anglo-Saxon constitutionalism has, indeed, 'been revealed as neither descriptively adequate nor normatively appealing' (at 240).

[25] See, e.g. Kuijper, above n 13, 1313–41, who criticizes the rule-oriented 'Kupferberg jurisprudence' of the ECJ as politically 'naïve' (at 1320).

of citizens or non-governmental organizations;[26] in order to limit their own judicial accountability, they have repeatedly encouraged their respective courts to apply domestic trade regulations without regard to WTO dispute settlement findings on their illegality.[27] The simultaneous insistence by the same trade politicians that WTO rules can be enforced at their own request in *domestic courts* vis-à-vis member-states violating WTO law inside the EC or United States, illustrates the political rather than legal nature of such Machiavellian objections against judicial accountability for violations by trade bureaucracies of the rule of law.

IV. CITIZEN-ORIENTED CONCEPTIONS OF INTERNATIONAL ECONOMIC LAW

In Europe, the move to constitutional democracy and constitutional adjudication in most of the 46 member states of the Council of Europe, as well as the judicial clarification and progressive development of EC law by the EC Court (ECJ), of the Treaty establishing the European Economic Area by the European Free Trade Area before (EFTA) Court, and of the European Convention on Human Rights (ECHR) by the European Court of Human Rights (ECtHR), have led to 'constitutional modes' of multilevel governance, including 'governing with judges'[28] that increasingly limits national legislative and executive powers by multilevel judicial protection of constitutional rights. All 46 democracies cooperating in the Council of Europe, as well as their national courts, have progressively recognized that

- rule of law in the EC's common market requires new forms of governance, of democratic participation and of multilevel judicial protection,
- just as respect for the fundamental rights protected by the ECHR requires new forms of multilevel judicial governance;

[26] At the request of the political EC institutions, the EC Court has refrained long since from reviewing the legality of EC acts in the light of the EC's GATT and WTO obligations. In the United States, courts are barred by legislation from challenging the WTO-consistency of US federal measures.

[27] Cf. J. A. Restani and I. Bloom, 'Interpreting International Trade Statutes: Is The Charming Betsy Sinking?' 24 Fordham International Law Journal (2001) 1533. On the controversial relationship between the 'Charming Betsy doctrine' of consistent interpretation and the 'Chevron doctrine' of judicial deference see: A. Davies, 'Connecting or Compartmentalizing the WTO and United States Legal Systems? The Role of the Charming Betsy Canon', 10 Journal of International Economic Law (2007) 117–49.The European Court of Justice has a long history of ignoring GATT and WTO rules at the request of political EC bodies which have often misinformed the EC Court on the meaning of GATT/WTO rules and dispute settlement reports (e.g. in Case 112/80, Dürbeck, ECR 1981, 1095, the Commission misinformed the EC Court on an unpublished GATT dispute settlement finding against the EC, and the Court relied on this information without verifying the obviously wrong information submitted to the Court).

[28] Cf. A. Stone Sweet, *Governing with Judges: Constitutional Politics in Europe* (2000).

- European economic integration law rests on autonomous constitutional sources and legal structures which—even though rooted in the common *national* constitutional traditions of democratic governance and respect for fundamental rights—inevitably differ from national constitutional systems;
- national constitutional courts, the ECJ and the ECtHR mutually respect their respective constitutional autonomy and the reality of constitutional pluralism on the basis of principles of mutual coherence ('as long as'), deliberative democracy and mutual adaptation of national and European constitutional law, rather than only on the basis of claims to constitutional hierarchy and state sovereignty;
- governments accept that the constitutional checks and balances assign to independent courts autonomous, judicial functions that are different from democratic legislation and administrative governance functions.[29]

The supranational 'community methods' of EC governance and the judicial 'constitutionalization' of international law in Europe[30] have contributed to the fact that international movements of goods, services, persons, capital, and payments among more than 480 million EC citizens are now legally and judicially protected by fundamental rights, citizen-driven competition, and common EC trade law 'founded on the principles of liberty, democracy, respect for human rights and fundamental freedoms, and the rule of law' (Article 6 EU Treaty). Some of these constitutional and judicial EC guarantees have also been extended to the EC's free trade and customs union agreements with neighbouring European and Mediterranean countries (like Turkey). Similar to the transformation of the intergovernmental European system of international law (e.g. of the ECHR and the EEC Treaty) into citizen-centred integration law protected by multilevel judicial governance, so could a more coherent, multilevel judicial governance system of the WTO play a crucial role in protecting international rule of law in the worldwide division of labour for the benefit of citizens. Without such multilevel judicial protection of the law of international organizations (like the WTO), their statutory objectives of collectively supplying international public goods (like 'sustainable development' and international legal security) and protecting private rights (like intellectual property rights) can hardly be

[29] 'Dualist conceptions' of democracy as two-track processes are also widespread in the US, as shown by B. Ackerman, *We the People*, Vol. 1 (1991) and 2 (1998). C. L. Eisgruber, *Constitutional Self-Government* (2001), explains why democratic legislatures and elections provide only an incomplete representation of the people, and why judicial interpretation and application of the Constitution by courts are integral parts of constitutional self-government.

[30] Cf. A. Stone Sweet, *The Judicial Construction of Europe* (2004).

realized.[31] Just as national market economies and democracy are not sustainable without 'constitutional democracy', so is multilevel democratic governance for the collective supply of international public goods not sustainable without new forms of functionally limited 'multilevel constitutionalism' and multilevel judicial protection of the rule of law, with due respect for the reality and legitimacy of constitutional pluralism[32] and for the need to promote the mutual coherence of constitutional sub-systems by universalizable principles and rules (such as human rights). The legitimate functions of multilevel 'judicial governance'—and, more generally, of the multilevel legal and judicial WTO guarantees of freedom, non-discrimination, rule of law and national sovereignty in international trade—remain inevitably contested depending on the diverse, national conceptions of constitutional democracy and of international economic law.

Lawyers perceiving constitutional democracy as being inevitably limited to *national communities*, often analyse international trade law and transnational economic governance in terms of 'global administrative law'.[33] The increasing number of provisions in worldwide economic agreements (such as the Law of the Sea Convention and the WTO Agreement), regional trade agreements (RTAs) and bilateral investment treaties for additional legal safeguards of *private rights* and judicial remedies prompt, however, many international lawyers in Europe and North-America to acknowledge potential 'constitutional functions' of international economic law and of multilevel 'judicial governance'[34] for the collective supply of international public goods.

[31] Cf. A. M. Slaughther and W. Burke-White, 'The Future of International Law is Domestic (or, the European Way of Law)', 47 Harvard International Law Journal (2006) 327, 329: 'the future effectiveness of international law will turn on its ability to influence and alter domestic politics.' The authors define the major functions of international law in terms of 'strengthening domestic institutions', 'backstopping domestic governments' where they fail to act, and 'compelling action by national governments.' My own publications focus less on the *inter-state* functions of international guarantees of freedom, non-discrimination, due process of law and human rights than on their potential *intra-state* functions and 'domestic policy functions', for example, in terms of strengthening the 'enabling constitution' and 'limiting constitution' of states, empowering citizens and courts vis-à-vis abuses of foreign policy powers, and requiring all state organs to contribute to the collective supply of international public goods, cf. E. U. Petersmann, *Constitutional Functions and Constitutional Problems of International Economic Law* (1991).

[32] On national and European 'constitutional pluralism' as foundation of European integration law see: M. Poiares Maduro, 'Contrapunctual Law: Europe's Constitutional Pluralism in Action', in N.Walker (ed.), *Sovereignty in Transition* (2003), 501–37.

[33] Cf. N. Krisch and B. Kingsbury, 'Global governance and Global Administrative Law in the International Legal Order', 17 European Journal of International Law (2006) 1–15.

[34] On the notion of 'judicial governance' and the legal and democratic functions of courts see, e.g. A. Stone Sweet, *Governing with Judges: Constitutional Politics in Europe* (2000), according to whom (at 137) constitutional courts perform four basic functions: (i) they operate as a 'counterweight' to majority rule; (ii) they 'pacify' politics; (iii) they legitimize public policy; and (iv) they protect human rights.

For instance, lawyers refer to a 'WTO Constitution' in view of

(a) the comprehensive rule-making, executive and (quasi-) judicial powers of WTO institutions;[35]
(b) the 'constitutionalization' of WTO law resulting from the jurisprudence of the WTO dispute settlement bodies;[36]
(c) the *domestic* 'constitutional functions' of GATT/WTO rules, for example, for protecting constitutional principles (like freedom, non-discrimination, rule of law, proportionality of government restrictions) and domestic democracy (for instance, by limiting the power of protectionist interest groups) for the benefit of transnational cooperation among free citizens;[37]
(d) the *international* 'constitutional functions' of WTO rules, for example, for the promotion of 'international participatory democracy' (e.g. by holding governments internationally accountable for the 'external effects' of their national trade policies, by enabling countries to participate in the policy-making of other countries)[38] and of the enhancement of 'jurisdictional competition among nation states'[39] and 'the allocation of authority between constitutions';[40]
(e) in view of the necessity of 'constitutional approaches' for a proper understanding of the law of comprehensive international organizations that use constitutional terms, methods and principles for more than fifty years (see, e.g. the 'Constitutions' of the ILO, WHO, FAO, EU);[41] or
(f) in view of the need to interface and coordinate different levels of governance on the national and international level.[42]

[35] See J. H. Jackson, *The World Trade Organisation: Constitution and Jurisprudence* (1998).

[36] See D. Z. Cass, 'The Constitutionalization of International Trade Law: Judicial Norm-Generation as the Engine of Constitutionalization', 12 European Journal of International Law (2001) at 39–75.

[37] See J. O. McGinnis and M. L. Movsesian, 'The World Trade Constitution', 114 Harvard Law Review (2000) 511–605; P. M. Gerhart, 'The Two Constitutional Visions of the World Trade Organisation', 24 University of Pennsylvania Journal of International Economic Law (2003) 1–75, contrasts the 'inward-looking, economic vision of the WTO' in helping member countries addressing internal political failures with the 'external, participatory vision of the WTO' helping WTO members to address concerns raised by policy decisions in other countries.

[38] See, for example, P. M. Gerhart, 'The WTO and Participatory Democracy: The Historical Evidence', 37 Vanderbilt Journal of Transnational Law (2004) 897–934.

[39] See J. O. McGinnis, 'The WTO as a Structure of Liberty', 28 Harvard Journal of Law and Public Policy (2004) 81–8.

[40] J. Trachtman, 'The WTO Constitution: Toward Tertiary Rules', 17 European Journal of International Law (2006).

[41] See, for example, Petersmann, above n 31, Oxford: Hart Publishers; N. Walker, 'The EU and the WTO: Constitutionalism in a New Key', in G. de Búrca and J. Scott (eds), *The EU and the WTO: Legal and Constitutional Issues* (2001).

[42] T. Cottier and M. Hertig, 'The Prospects of 21st Century Constitutionalism', 7 Max Planck Yearbook of United Nations Law (2003) at 261.

V. CONSTITUTIONAL FUNCTIONS OF INTERNATIONAL ADJUDICATION

In international economic law, commercial arbitrators, national, transnational, and intergovernmental judges tend to define their respective 'judicial functions' and 'rule of law' differently depending on their diverse mandates and 'applicable law'. Independent, tenured judges deriving their mandate from *multilateral* (rather than bilateral) agreements for the collective supply of 'international public goods' (rather than the pursuit of *national* interests), and permanent multilateral tribunals with compulsory jurisdiction, offer important advantages,[43] for example by promoting rule of law through judicial 'checks and balances' and by rendering international law and compliance with judgments more effective not only in *intergovernmental* relations but also vis-à-vis citizens:

- compulsory international adjudication can enhance the credibility of international commitments, promote compliance and rule of law, and reduce international transaction and enforcement costs, especially in fields (like international economic law) that regulate autonomous actions of citizens (e.g. the daily decisions by billions of producers, investors, traders and consumers relying on rule of law in their worldwide division of labour);
- in contrast to *ad hoc* tribunals and *ad hoc* judges, permanent courts and tenured judges have stronger incentives to promote legal coherence by deciding disputes on the basis of consistent case-law and predictable interpretations;
- independent judges acting as trustees of international communities may convey better informed judgments on the limits of 'national interests' (e.g. in case of harmful external effects on third parties) and on the rational long-term interests of states in cooperating for the collective supply of 'international public goods';
- the publicity of international court proceedings and other discursive, legal and political constraints can constrain abuses of the independence of judges;
- the permanence of tribunals and independence of their judges also facilitate cooperation with domestic courts and with other domestic constituencies who may press national governments to comply with the rulings of international courts.

The establishment of new international courts (such as the EC Court of First Instance, the EC Civil Service Tribunal, the EFTA Court), the recognition by ever more countries of existing courts (such as the ECJ and ECtHR), the extension of their jurisdiction, their ever more frequent use and rising caseload have been of crucial importance for the transformation of the

[43] Cf. L. R. Helfer and A. M. Slaugther, 'Why States Create International Tribunals: A Response to Professors Posner and Yoo', 93 California Law Review (2005) 1–58.

intergovernmental ECHR and EC Treaty into citizen-oriented European integration law. The advantages of permanent, independent international courts are obvious in respect of those supranational European tribunals (like the ECJ, the EctHR, and the EFTA Court) which grant direct access not only to states but also to private parties for judicial protection vis-à-vis state restrictions as well as intergovernmental measures, including those of international organizations (like the EC and the EFTA Authority).[44] Through the intergovernmental regulation of the composition of the tribunals, of the admissible actions, procedures, fact-finding capacity, judicial powers, applicable law, and kinds of judgments, the governments creating supranational tribunals have manifold possibilities of limiting abuses of judicial powers and ensuring the effectiveness of supranational adjudication for the benefit of rule of law not only in intergovernmental relations, but also among their citizens. Also the judges themselves have strong incentives to avoid (e.g. by the quality and autonomy of their legal reasoning) appearances of arbitrariness, and to promote confidence by the legal and political communities that are subject to supranational tribunals. The high rates of compliance with judgments by the ECtHR—even in member states of the Council of Europe that are only nominally constitutional democracies and lack strong traditions of domestic courts committed to the rule of law—suggest that the advantages of supranational judicial review of government measures in response to direct actions from private citizens are not necessarily limited to tribunals operating in constitutional democracies, but may extend to 'functional legal communities' for the promotion of human rights, democratic peace and mutually beneficial economic cooperation—provided national, transnational and international judges and courts cooperate in their protection of rule of law based on a common conception of justice.[45]

VI. NEED FOR GLOBAL DISCOURSE ON THE DEMOCRATIC LIMITS OF MULTILEVEL JUDICIAL PROTECTION OF INDIVIDUAL RIGHTS

Since the democratic revolutions during the eighteenth century, an ever increasing number of constitutional democracies share the view that the constitutional rights of citizens depend on the separation of government powers, on the judicial protection of citizen rights by independent courts, and on

[44] Cf. L. R. Helfer and A. M. Slaugther, 'Toward a Theory of Effective Supranational Adjudication', 107 Yale Law Journal (1997) 273–391.

[45] The claim by Posner and and Yoo, above n 22, at 55 that the success of the ECJ and the ECtHR cannot be replicated outside "political communities" overlooks the potential of functionally limited, citizen-driven 'legal and economic communities' protected by multilevel judicial governance based on common 'principles of justice'. On the important role of national and European courts in the progressive 'judicialization' and 'constitutionalization' of international law in Europe see A. M. Slaugther, A. Stone Sweet, and J. H. Weiler (eds), *The European Courts and National Courts* (1997).

complementing representative forms of democracy by more direct forms of democratic self-government, citizen participation, and deliberative democracy. Democratic self-government by citizens requires that only those rules may claim democratic legitimacy that can meet with the assent by rational citizens in discursive processes of 'deliberative democracy' equally open to all affected persons.[46] One-sidedly power-oriented conceptions of international law as an intergovernmental system of rights and obligations are rightly challenged by citizens, parliaments and civil society for disfranchising citizens, treating them as mere objects and neglecting the universal human rights obligations of all governments. The 'constitutional failures' of the 'international law among states' to protect the rights and welfare of citizens more effectively call for additional constitutional and judicial restraints on *foreign policy* powers similar to those on *domestic policy* powers. If the legitimacy of governments and their limited powers derive from respect for, and protection of, the inalienable human rights of their citizens—as universally recognized not only in the UN Charter, in more than one hundred UN and regional human rights instruments as well as in general international law, but also in the national laws of most UN member states—then the intergovernmental structures of international law must be constitutionally limited more effectively by national and international human rights law and constitutional law.[47]

WTO law fundamentally differs from GATT 1947 by its legal limitations of 'member driven governance' and the compulsory jurisdiction of WTO dispute settlement bodies for judicial protection of the legal primacy of the WTO legal guarantees of freedom, non-discrimination and rule of international law over other intergovernmental rules[48] as well as domestic laws and regulations.[49] Some parts of WTO law reflect intergovernmental 'conflict of law approaches' (e.g. Articles II, III, VI, XI GATT on product standards of importing countries, production standards of exporting countries) and 'global administrative law approaches' (e.g. in the WTO agreements on technical barriers, sanitary and phyto-sanitary standards, customs valuation, anti-dumping, and safeguard measures). Other parts of WTO law (such as the WTO rules on dispute settlement and authoritative interpretations, the WTO agreements on TRIPS, government procurement, accession of China) protect the rule of international law more comprehensively by means of 'constitutional checks and balances' (e.g. between intergovernmental,

[46] Cf. J. Habermas, *Between Facts and Norms: Contributions to a Discourse Theory of Law and Democracy* (1996) at 315–328. This constitutional concept of democracy limits alternative, majoritarian conceptions of democracy.

[47] Cf. E. U. Petersmann, 'Human Rights, Markets and Economic Welfare: Constitutional Functions of the Emerging UN Human Rights Constitution', in F. M. Abbott, C. Breining-Kaufmann, and T.Cottier (eds), *International Trade and Human Rights. Foundations and Conceptual Issues* (2006) 29–68.

[48] Cf. e.g. Article XVI:3 WTO Agreement, Article11 Agreement on Safeguards.

[49] Cf. e.g. Article XVI:4 WTO Agreement, Article 1 Agreement on TRIPS.

supranational, and judicial governance in the WTO), commitments to the protection of individual rights (e.g. access to domestic courts, protection of freedom of trade and property rights in China) and to their judicial protection by independent, national and international dispute settlement bodies.[50]

Most of the more than 240 legal rulings by WTO dispute settlement bodies in the context of the already more than 360 WTO dispute settlement proceedings since 1995 have been regularly adopted and implemented by WTO members; non-implementation occured only exceptionally when, for example, the EC Council or the US Congress lacked the necessary political majorities for amending domestic legislation. Courts in most WTO member countries accept legal obligations to *interpret* domestic trade rules (e.g. on customs valuation, antidumping, intellectual property rights) in conformity with the WTO obligations of the country concerned. In European economic integration law governing already more than 480 million EC citizens and millions of additional citizens in associated European states (like the EFTA countries and Turkey), the recognition of human rights and democratic governance have led to the legal recognition of individuals as legal subjects of European integration law, to increasing access of 'market citizens' to judicial protection of their 'market freedoms' and other constitutional rights by national and international courts, and to the transformation of the intergovernmental EC Treaty and of the ECHR into 'constitutional instruments of European public order'.[51] Inside Europe, 'judicial governance' (e.g. by the ECJ, the EFTA Court, the ECtHR) and judicial protection of an international community based on rule of law and respect of citizen rights have become accepted by governments as well as by citizens as necessary complements of democratic governance so as to protect the rule of international law for the benefit of the rights and welfare of citizens. The small number of only three ECJ judgments on disputes among states over the past fifty years confirms that—depending on the legal and institutional framework regulating international trade—many intergovernmental trade disputes can be avoided (e.g. by authorizing domestic courts to decide disputes over private rights with due regard to the WTO obligations of the country concerned) and depoliticized (e.g. by stronger legal and judicial remedies for the enforcement of certain categories of legally binding WTO dispute settlement rulings in domestic courts).

[50] On these complementary 'conflict of laws' approaches, 'global administrative law approaches' and 'constitutional approaches' in the WTO regulation and limitation of trade policy powers see: E.U.Petersmann, 'Introduction and Overview', in C. Joerges and E. U. Petersmann (eds), *Constitutionalism, Multilevel Trade Governance and Social Regulation* (2006), xxi–xxxviii.

[51] This concept continues to be used not only by the EC Court, but also in many judgments of the European Court of Human Rights since the Court's decision in *Loizidou v Turkey* (preliminary objections), Series A No 310 (1995) 20 EHRR 99 Section 75(2).

VII. WHY CITIZEN-ORIENTED APPROACHES TO INTERNATIONAL ECONOMIC LAW ARE 'REALISTIC'

The understanding of law as a struggle for just rules and fair procedures goes back to ancient Greece[52] and is today widely shared in constitutional democracies; as explained by L.Fuller, law must order social life not only by 'subjecting human conduct to the governance of rules';[53] law must also aim at establishing a *just* order and procedures for the *fair* resolution of disputes.[54] Since the American and French democratic revolutions in the 18th century, fairness and justice are increasingly defined not only in terms of rule-following and procedural justice (such as rights to a fair hearing, democratic participation, access to courts), but also in terms of substantive justice and human rights.[55] The universal recognition of human rights entails that claims to 'legal authority' by national and international legal systems must be evaluated also in terms of their contribution to the protection and fulfillment of human rights and to the empowerment of citizens. Goods and services tend to be produced and traded by private actors on the basis of national laws and international private law rules which, in case of conflicts, tend to be interpreted and enforced by national courts and privately agreed arbitration ensuring a high degree of rule of law among private economic actors. If the major purpose of public international trade law is defined from a citizen perspective as (i) to empower domestic citizens to increase their individual and social welfare through trade (e.g. by limiting national border discrimination and other 'government failures'), and (ii) to legally protect mutually beneficial trade transactions by means of international legal guarantees of market access and rule of law beyond state borders, then these 'empowerment functions' and 'legal security functions' of public international trade law argue for decentralized international dispute settlement mechanisms: primarily, it should be left to the citizens concerned to enforce international trade law in domestic courts; for, it is in the rational self-interest of citizens and their governments to depoliticize international trade disputes (e.g. over private intellectual property rights) and reduce international transaction costs by mandating domestic courts to protect the rule of law in international trade.

[52] On the ancient Greek concept of 'law as participation in the idea of justice' see C.J.Friedrich, *The Philosophy of Law in Historical Perspecitve* (1963), Chapter II. The Greek and Roman words for 'law' (dikaio, jus) and 'justice' (dikaiosyni, justitia) have an identical core.

[53] L.L.Fuller, *The Morality of Law* (1969), at 96.

[54] For Fuller's criticism of positivist conceptions of law, see L.L.Fuller, 'Positivism and Fidelity to Law – A Reply to Professor Hart', 71 *Harvard Law Review* (1958) 630.

[55] Cf. James Madison, *The Federalist* (1790), 51: 'justice is the end of government. It is the end of civil society. It ever has been and will be pursued until it is obtained, or until liberty be lost in the pursuit.'

International relations theory and international law doctrine distinguish realism, institutionalism, liberalism, and constructivism as the four major theoretical approaches to, and explanations of, international relations and international law.[56] When, based on my personal experiences as legal advisor in the Uruguay Round Negotiating Groups which elaborated the WTO Dispute Settlement Understanding and the institutional framework of the WTO Agreement, I published one of the first books on the GATT/WTO dispute settlement system following the entry into force of the WTO Agreement, I emphasized the need to use these simplifying theories in complementary rather than mutually exclusive ways and to focus on citizen interests:[57]

A. Realism

The 'realist' focus on states as the principal actors in international politics, and on their power-oriented pursuit of national security and other state interests, is consistent with the intergovernmental structures of WTO law, with the 'Member-driven' nature of reciprocal bargaining in GATT and WTO negotiations, and with the reliance of the WTO dispute settlement system on self-help in case of violations of WTO obligations (e.g. recourse to WTO dispute settlement procedures and to countermeasures *vis-à-vis* WTO Members refusing to implement WTO dispute settlement rulings). Yet, the prevailing realist approaches to international relations often define 'national interests' too narrowly (e.g. without adequate regard for transnational 'external effects' of agricultural protectionism) and offer no coherent theory for the collective supply of international public goods.

B. Institutionalism

The institutional changes from GATT to the WTO confirm the premise of institutional theories that rational governments can reduce the collective action problems (like uncertainty and free-riding) in intergovernmental negotiations for the collective supply of international public goods (like international rule of law and open markets) by deliberately changing the legal and institutional incentives for non-cooperation. The compulsory jurisdiction of WTO dispute settlement bodies for independent, factual as well as legal dispute settlement findings and the creation of the WTO Appellate Body, for instance, have helped WTO Members to legally limit their welfare-reducing recourse to unilateral self-help and trade sanctions (cf. Article 23 DSU).

[56] Cf. K. W. Abbott, 'Toward a Richer Institutionalism for International Law and Policy', 1 Journal of International Law and International Relations (2006) 9–34; S. R. Ratner and A. M. Slaugther (eds), *The Methods of International Law* (2004).

[57] Cf. Petersmann above n 5, at 4–24.

C. Rational choice theory

Economists, political scientists, and lawyers tend to agree today that, inside citizen-driven markets and constitutional democracies, analyses of the economy, the polity, and of law should proceed from normative individualism (i.e. values must be derived from individual consent) and from the assumption of rational choices of individuals confronted with scarcity of resources (e.g. individual income) and with competition among rational egoists for scarce goods and services (e.g. educational and medical services, job opportunities).The trade policies of constitutional democracies are primarily shaped by the liberty-based, normative arguments of economic, political and legal liberalism and welfare economics, as illustrated by the pursuit of individual interests (utility maximization) in economic and political markets and the strong political influence of export industries and import-competing producers on reciprocal market access negotiations among governments that must respond to the pressures, demands and rational choices of their domestic constituencies. The liberal criticism of treating states as 'black boxes' offers important insights into the domestic origins of intergovernmental negotiations (e.g. the influence of private rent-seeking), their 'domestic policy functions', and the policy-impact of non-governmental organizations on intergovernmental relations.

D. Constitutionalism

The impact of constitutions, human rights, democratic procedures, international as well as non-governmental organizations on intergovernmental relations reveals that international power politics can be legally limited and 'constitutionalized'.[58] The successful transformation of the European 'international law among states', and of centuries of power politics among the 27 EC member states, into a European 'community law' protecting peaceful cooperation among more than 480 million free 'EC citizens' across national frontiers, confirms that changes in the constitutional rights of citizens, in policy incentives and perceptions of human relations can be of constitutive importance for individual and social conduct not only *inside* states, but also in transnational relations beyond states. The 'realist' focus on state power in intergovernmental relations must become part of a broader constitutional and democratic discourse integrating the diverse policy approaches to international economic regulation.

VIII. TOWARDS INTERNATIONAL CONSTITUTIONAL ADJUDICATION?

Internationally traded goods and services tend to be produced and consumed by individuals on the basis of private law contracts regulating production,

[58] Cf. E. U. Petersmann, 'Multilevel Trade Governance in the WTO Requires Multilevel Constitutionalism', in Joerges and Petersmann (eds), above n 50, at 5–57.

investments, trade, distribution and consumption. The universal recognition of human rights has transformed this 'private law society' cooperating in the worldwide division of labor into 'civil societies' asserting their human rights not only vis-à-vis their respective national governments, but also vis-à-vis intergovernmental regulation of international economic transactions among citizens. The more citizens all over the world benefit from the enormous consumer welfare and freedom of choice made possible by modern international economic law, the more they insist on their human right 'to a social and international order in which the rights and freedoms set forth in this Declaration can be fully realized', as recognized already in Article 28 of the 1948 Universal Declaration of Human Rights (UDHR). Two centuries earlier, this need for constitutional coherence of national and international law was already emphasized by the philosopher Immanuel Kant, according to whom—just as 'enlightenment' requires 'man's leaving his self-caused immaturity' by having the courage to 'make public use of one's reason in all matters' as an individual member of a cosmopolitan world society—individual freedom and democratic self-development require antagonistic human struggles for ever more precise national, transnational and international constitutional guarantees of equal freedoms protecting individual and democratic self-government, 'democratic peace' and mutually beneficial cooperation among citizens.[59]

Modern international law recognizes that 'everyone has the right to take part in the government of his country, directly or through freely chosen representatives' (Article 21 UDHR). Democratic elections and representative parliaments offer only indirect ways of democratic participation whose effectiveness is ever more limited by globalization and multilevel governance. Constitutional democracies and international law, therefore, protect ever more additional forms of representative, participatory and deliberative democracy and limit governmental border restrictions and border discrimination in order to protect and facilitate mutually welfare-increasing cooperation among citizens across frontiers. The human rights ideal of constitutionally protected, individual and democratic self-government challenges not only the authoritarian traditions of legal positivism (as justified e.g. by *Hobbes*, *Austin* and *Hart*) defining law as those rules enacted by the competent law-maker whose compliance can be enforced, regardless of the morality and content of the rules. The universal recognition of human rights and of international legal guarantees of voluntary exchanges among citizens across national frontiers also demonstrate the inadequacy of Hobbes' conception of 'negative freedom' (e.g. in terms of absence

[59] The quotations are from I. Kant, 'What is Enlightenment? (1784)', in C. J. Friedrich (ed), *The Philosophy of Kant. Immanuel Kant's Moral and Political Writings* (1993) at 145–8. On Kant's conception of an international and cosmopolitan 'law of freedom' see, e.g. Parts V and VI in B. Sharon Byrd and J. Hruschka (eds), *Kant and Law* (2006).

of legal prohibitions).[60] Human rights law and international economic law perceive the task of law in *protecting* individual freedom and voluntary cooperation among individuals against abuses of public and private power, such as the centuries-old abuses of trade policy powers restricting individual freedom and consumer welfare for the benefit of rent-seeking interest groups (like import-competing producers, trade bureaucracies, periodically elected trade politicians), including abuses by democratically elected parliaments (as in the case of the infamous 'Smoot-Hawley Tariff Act' adopted by the US Congress in 1930). Parliaments and courts increasingly accept the need for constitutional and international legal limitations not only of monetary policy powers (e.g. in European monetary law) but also of protectionist abuses of trade policy powers (e.g. in European customs union law and WTO law). The judicial protection of the EC Treaty's intergovernmental prohibitions of restrictions on international movements of goods, services, persons, capital, payments and non-discriminatory conditions of market competition as individual 'market freedoms',[61] like the judicial protection of the human rights guarantees in the ECHR, illustrate this legal change from 'negative freedom' to 'positive freedom' protected by multilevel constitutional adjudication.

The international 'constitutions' (*sic*) establishing the International Labor Organization, the World Health Organization and other UN Specialized Agencies increasingly acknowledge the universal human rights obligations of all UN member states and the need for 'international constitutional restraints' on abuses of government powers.[62] Bilateral investment treaties and more recent RTAs concluded by the EC and the US focus on strengthening legal and judicial remedies for private economic actors.[63] Also, outside the close cooperation among national a international courts in Europe, international courts with overlapping jurisdiction increasingly cooperate among each other, for example by referring to related judgments (e.g. references by the ICJ to judgments of international criminal tribunals, references in WTO dispute settlement reports to ICJ judgments, references

[60] Cf. T. Hobbes, *Leviathan* R. Tuck (ed.), (1991), Chapter 21, at 146: 'A free man is he that... is not hindered to do what he has a will to.' On the concept of freedom as legal non-interference in classical English political philosophy see: I. Berlin, *Liberty* H. Hardy (ed.), (2002), 170ff.

[61] On the interrelationships between human rights, fundamental rights, fundamental freedoms and 'market freedoms' in European constitutional law see the contributions by J. Kühling, Fundamental Rights, and T. Kingreen, Fundamental Freedoms, in A. v. Bogdandy and J. Bast (eds), *Principles of European Constitutional Law* (2006), 501ff, 549ff.

[62] See Petersmann, above n 54 and R. S. J. Macdonald and D. M. Johnston (eds), *Towards World Constitutionalism. Issues in the Legal Ordering of the World Community* (2005).

[63] Cf. E. Ramirez Robles, 'Political and Quasi-Adjudicative Dispute Settlement Models in EU Free Trade Agreements', WTO Staff Working Paper 2006–09.

of Law of the Sea tribunals to ECJ).[64] Similar to the pioneering role of the ECJ and of the ECtHR in the progressive emergence of citizen-oriented integration law in Europe, such multilevel cooperation among courts can contribute to the emergence of functionally limited, citizen-oriented integration law beyond Europe[65] holding governments accountable for their universal human rights obligations and constitutional obligations vis-à-vis their citizens.

IX. CONCLUSION

The US Constitution of 1789 was the first successful historical experiment in realizing a constitutional, representative democracy for a large people (e.g. compared with the preceding paradigm of Athenian democracy). The EC and EU treaties were the first successful effort at creating a constitutionally and functionally limited 'international democracy'. The increasing tensions between *national polities* and the *global economy*, and the impossibility of recreating parliamentary democracies at the global level, call for new forms of citizen-driven, constitutional self-government in the worldwide division of labour. European integration law has demonstrated that the multilevel governance necessary for a democratic foundation of an international market economy can, and must, be based on rights-based, multilevel constitutionalism compensating the ineffective parliamentary control of international economic governance by transnational, participatory, and rights-based constitutionalism. This article argues that democratic self-government can, and must, be extended beyond national polities by means of functionally limited, economic integration law and multilevel, judicial protection of citizen rights based on common conceptions of rule of law, social justice and respect for universal human rights. Without such common conceptions of rule of law, national judges are likely to continue ignoring WTO dispute settlement findings that WTO guarantees of freedom, non-discrimination, and rule of law should be respected by all domestic government institutions for the benefit of their citizens.

[64] A recent example of concurrent jurisdiction of international dispute settlement bodies for environmental disputes is the ECJ judgment of 30 May 2006 (Mox-Plant Case C-459/03, *Commission v Ireland*), in which the Court decided that EC member states are not allowed to submit disputes potentially involving EC law to dispute settlement bodies other than the ECJ; EC member states must inform and consult EC bodies prior to seizing other international tribunals. For additional examples of concurrent jurisdiction of international arbitral tribunals and the ECJ for environmental disputes among EC member states see: N. Lavranos, 'The Mox Plant and Ijzeren Rijn Disputes: Which Court is the Supreme Arbiter?', 19 Leiden Journal of International Law (2006) 223–46.

[65] Cf. E. U. Petersmann, Justice in International Economic Law? From the 'International Law among States' to 'International Integration Law' and 'Constitutional Law', (I) The Global Community Yearbook of International Law and Jurisprudence (2006) 105–46.

WTO FOR TRADE AND DEVELOPMENT POST-DOHA

Seung Wha Chang★

ABSTRACT

The WTO Members' negotiations under the Doha mandate on special and differential treatment ('SDT') and development issues have made little progress. The gap between developed countries and developing countries in this regard seems too wide to be bridged. This gap originates from a fundamental difference in their basic stances on cross-cutting issues. In principle, without prejudice to currently available SDT under individual WTO Agreements, developing countries should be given flexibilities in implementing WTO rules, which may result in the rebalancing of rights and obligations of WTO Members but only when policy measures at issue can contribute to particular developing countries' development needs and no alternative less-trade restrictive measures are reasonably available. After reviewing WTO Members' discussions since the adoption of the Doha Ministerial Declaration, this article suggests a 'measure-specific *ex ante* approach' for a workable solution to bridging the gap between developed countries and developing countries on SDT and development issues.

INTRODUCTION

Currently, developing countries account for more than three-fourths of the WTO membership. With more than a dozen years of WTO history, developing country Members of the WTO have expressed their discomfort with the end-results of the implementation of the Uruguay Round and subsequent negotiations under the WTO. It is generally understood that most developing countries, in particular, the Least Developed Countries ('LDCs'), have been unable to harvest benefits from the multilateral trading system to the same extent as the developed countries. In the view of developing countries, developed countries are unresponsive to their development needs. A World Bank study demonstrated that more than 50% of the whole WTO members are having serious problems in effective representation

★ Professor of Law at Seoul National University. Currently Visiting Professor of Law at Harvard University (2007) and Yale University (2008). E-mail: changsw@snu.ac.kr.

and participation in WTO activities.[1] All of these factors seem to threaten the credibility of the WTO as an international institution governing the multilateral trading system.

One of the most contentious and critical issues currently facing the WTO is the debate over whether and to what extent differentiated rights and obligations will be recognized between developed and developing countries. In order to bridge the gap between developed and developing countries, the GATT system introduced the concept of special differential treatment (SDT), which was further developed and expanded under the WTO system. The roughly 155 SDT provisions scattered throughout the WTO Agreements are typically classified into several categories: (i) trade preference, (ii) safeguarding the interests of developing countries, (iii) flexibility, (iv) transition periods, and (v) technical assistance.[2] In exchange for these SDT provisions, the developing countries accepted the Uruguay Round 'single package' deal, which included (i) effectively binding disciplines in old areas (e.g. anti-dumping, subsidies, technical barriers to trade, etc.), (ii) new disciplines in services, intellectual property and investment-related measures, and (iii) an effective dispute settlement mechanism. However, it is widely agreed that the Uruguay Round approach to SDT—based upon (i) preferences with unilaterally imposed non-economic conditions and exclusion of 'sensitive products', (ii) opt-outs from WTO rules, (iii) uniform and arbitrary transition periods without economic foundation, and (iv) technical assistance without consideration of supply-side constraints—has not been helpful in promoting economic development in most developing countries.[3] Consequently, many developing countries and LDCs are still unprepared to be fully integrated into the multilateral trading system. From the developing countries' perspective, most of the SDT provisions are not mandatory, and therefore unenforceable through dispute settlement procedures.

Against this background, the Doha Ministerial Declaration tackled this fundamental and critical issue. In particular, Paragraph 44 of the Doha Ministerial Declaration mandates the WTO Members to review all SDT provisions 'with a view to strengthening them and making them more precise, effective and operational,' while reaffirming that 'provisions for special and differential treatment are an integral part of the

[1] See Constantine Michalopoulos, 'Developing Countries' Participating in the World Trade Organization,' World Bank, Policy Research Working Paper 1906 (1998), at 22, available at http://www-wds.worldbank.org/servlet/WDSContentServer/WDSP/IB/1998/03/01/000009265_3980429111520/Rendered/PDF/multi0page.pdf.

[2] See WTO Secretariat, Implementation of Special and Differential Treatment Provisions in WTO Agreements and Provisions, (12 September 2001), WT/COMTD/W/77/Rev.1, para 3.

[3] Ernst-Ulrich Petersman, 'Introduction (to Mini-Symposium on Developing Countries in the Doha Round)' 8 JIEL (2005), 347, at 351.

WTO Agreements.'[4] In addition, the WTO established the Committee on Trade and Development Special Session (CTDSS) in early 2002 that undertook the mission to carry out the Doha mandate on SDT and more generally to increase the development relevance of the WTO.

While there is a broadly shared agreement amongst WTO Members that developing country Members should be accorded some kinds of SDT, WTO Members have failed to reach consensus on the forms and contents of such treatment in spite of several years of hot debates at the CTDSS. Although SDT aims to preserve flexibility and policy space for developing countries so they can pursue their development goals, the current SDT is not sufficient to fully integrate developing countries into the multilateral trading system and to address their development needs.

This article takes the position that, in principle, without prejudice to currently available SDT under individual WTO Agreements, developing countries should be given flexibilities to implement WTO rules, which may result in rebalancing of rights and obligations of WTO Members, but only when policy measures at issue can contribute to particular developing countries' development needs and no alternative less-trade restrictive measures are reasonably available. After critically assessing divergent views of WTO Members and scholarly proposals on SDT and development issues, this article suggests an approach for a workable solution to bridging the gap between developed countries and developing countries on SDT and development issues, which may kill two birds with one stone: increasing development relevance of the WTO and minimizing deviations from the basic principles of the WTO.

This article is organized as follows: Part I describes how the WTO Members have made efforts to fulfill the Doha development mandate thus far. Part II critically reviews the WTO Members' contrasting views on the future directions for WTO SDT and evaluates the current status of works at the CTDSS. Part III evaluates scholarly proposals on SDT and then suggests a 'measure-specific *ex ante* approach.' Part IV concludes this article with a summary of policy suggestions.

I. WTO NEGOTIATIONS UNDER THE DOHA MANDATE

A. From Doha to Cancun

The CTDSS undertook the mission to carry out the Doha mandate on SDT and development. It divided the subjects of debate into two categories: cross-cutting issues and Agreement-specific issues. Cross-cutting issues mean general issues applicable to the SDT negotiations as a whole, including the principles and objectives of SDT; the issue of eligibility

[4] WTO Ministerial Declaration, WT/MIN(01)/DEC/1 (20 November 2001), adopted on 14 November 2001.

(differentiation); benchmarking; technical assistance and capacity building; transition periods; coherence in international organizations; integration of SDT into the WTO rules; and the monitoring mechanism. Agreement-specific issues indicate discussions on 88 Agreement-specific proposals principally made by the African group.[5] In May 2003, the then Chairman of CTDSS, Ambassador Perez del Castillo, divided the 88 proposals into three categories. Category I covered 38 proposals that were relatively easier subjects and, therefore, could be agreed upon at or before Cancun. Category II dealt with another 38 issues that were supposed to be more appropriately discussed at relevant WTO bodies. Category III contained issues on which Members were mostly unlikely to reach consensus due to their sensitive and difficult nature.

Most fundamentally, the developed and developing countries expressed contrasting views on the interpretation of the mandate. Developing countries took the position that the Doha mandate requires meaningful amendment to the current WTO Agreements, and thereby a rebalancing of the WTO Members' rights and obligations. In contrast, developed countries stated that the Doha mandate on SDT did not authorize new negotiations that fundamentally alter balances of rights and obligations of the Members.[6] In light of the background of the adoption of the Doha Declaration on SDT, it seems doubtful that the drafters of Paragraph 44 intended to limit the scope of the mandate so as to disallow any rebalancing of the rights and obligations of the Members.

Not surprisingly, developed and developing countries also clashed on several cross-cutting issues. First of all, developed countries proposed discussing the 'principles and objectives' of SDT before discussing Agreement-specific proposals. Their underlying motivation was to clarify the main goals of SDT discussions, which in their view should be to fully integrate developing countries into the single package multilateral trading system.[7] If that was the case, SDT would probably be treated as a temporary and exceptional device to help developing countries eventually comply with one set of unitary WTO rules. Developing countries argued that basic principles and objectives were already codified in Part IV of the GATT and after Doha they wished to recognize SDT as a legal or political right inherently embedded in the GATT/WTO system. Consequently, their different stances on principles and objectives further led to contrasting views on the extension of transition periods. Developing countries argued for automatic rights for renewal of transition periods at the choice of relevant

[5] Joint Communication from the African Group in the WTO, 'Special and Differential Treatment Provisions,' TN/CTS/W/3/Rev.2 (17 July 2002), at 22.

[6] For individual country Members' divergent views see e.g. Chairman's Note on the Meetings of 7 and 18 October 2002, TN/CTD/M/7 (30 April 2003) at 28–31; Chairman's Note on the Meeting of 1 June 2006, TN/CTD/M/25 (3 August 2006), at 3–4.

[7] Ibid.

developing countries, whereas developed countries perceived transition periods as exceptions to basic principles and obligations of the Members and, therefore, contended that extension should be given through individual negotiations under relevant WTO bodies.[8]

Developed country Members, in particular European countries, raised the issue of 'graduation' or differentiation amongst developing countries. In their opinion, since SDT is designed to help developing countries become fully integrated into the multilateral trading system, advanced developing countries capable enough to fully assume WTO obligations should graduate from the category of developing countries.[9] This issue was raised mainly because, unlike the LDCs, the concept of 'developing countries' is not defined in the WTO Agreements, but is rather self-designated. As expected, some of the advanced developing countries strongly opposed opening discussion on differentiation. Other developing countries also protested because they thought the issue would be more appropriately put on the table after the completion of the Agreement-specific mandate.[10] Putting aside political implications and its sensitive and disruptive nature, the idea of differentiation amongst developing countries situated at different economic development levels cannot be easily dismissed because it seems to be consistent with the basic underlying rationale for SDT, which is differential treatment to different countries. How to differentiate and what criteria to apply, however, are a totally separate matter.[11]

With heated controversies over cross-cutting issues, resulting in no agreement, the CTDSS focused on the 88 Agreement-specific proposals. Out of the 88 original proposals, the Chairman of the CTDSS made a constructive deal on 28 Agreement-specific proposals, as evidenced by Annex C to the draft Cancun Ministerial Declaration. This deal was called the 28 'in-principle agreed' proposals. Due to the failure of the Cancun Ministerial Conference in September 2003, the decision on the 28 proposals was not officially adopted either.

B. From Cancun to Hong Kong

After the Cancun Ministerial Conference, discussions on SDT did not resume until April 2004. The CTDSS discussions at that time centred more around a time-consuming procedural issue of relative priority between Agreement-specific and cross-cutting issues. The July Package of 2004

[8] See e.g. Communication by Kenya on behalf of the African Group, 'Analysis of the Twenty-Eight Agreement-Specific Proposals,' TN/CTD/W/29 (9 June 2006).

[9] See e.g. Communication from Switzerland to the CTD in Special Session, 'Special Session on Special and Differential Treatment,' TN/CTD/W/14 (13 September 2002).

[10] See e.g. Chairman's Note on the Meeting of 21 and 25 November 2002, TN/CTD/M/13 (1 April 2003), at 3–5.

[11] See below n 37–38 and accompanying texts.

reaffirmed that development concerns form an integral part of the Doha Ministerial Declaration. It simply noted that some progress had been made in the SDT negotiations, but again did not formally adopt the 28 Agreement-specific proposals. In the July Package, the General Council instructed the CTDSS to expedite its review of outstanding Agreement-specific proposals while addressing other works, including cross-cutting issues, the monitoring mechanism and the incorporation of SDT into the WTO rules.[12] In addition to SDT, the July Package focused on four more development-related issues: (i) Technical Assistance, (ii) Implementation, (iii) Other Development Issues, and (iv) LDCs.[13] Most notably, it attempted to address development concerns of small and vulnerable economies. However, due to strong resistance from some of the large and advanced developing countries that feared differentiation, the General Council reached a compromise and made it explicit that this issue would not create a sub-category of Members.

The controversy over the relative priority between cross-cutting and Agreement-specific issues continued after the General Council decision in August 2004. In an effort to move forward, the then Chairman of the CTDSS, Ambassador Faizel Ismail, presented a new approach in December 2004.[14] This approach was originally designed to address both cross-cutting issues and Agreement-specific issues at the same time. He suggested considering a few elements that could be useful in addressing the remaining SDT proposals. In essence, such elements emphasized (i) the importance of export interests to developing countries, (ii) flexibilities in the rules that are consistent with a multilateral rule-based system, and (iii) enhanced capacity-building programmes that address supply-side constraints. Regarding enhanced flexibility in WTO rules, in particular, he suggested the following element:

> [E]nhanced flexibility in WTO rules, with appropriate transitional arrangements, should enable the development of developing countries. These additional flexibilities should be made available to those Members that were in need of them to address particular development challenges whilst ensuring that there was no a priori exclusion of any developing country from such a situational flexibility. There should be multilateral monitoring of the use of those flexibilities.[15]

[12] WTO General Council, Decision on Doha Work Programme, adopted on 1 August 2004, WT/L/579 (2 August 2004).

[13] For an evaluation of the July Package, see Faizel Ismail, 'A Development Perspective on the WTO July 2004 General Council Decision,' 8 JIEL (2005) 377, at 398–403.

[14] For this approach, see Chairman's Note on the Meeting of 7 December 2004, TN/CTD/M/18 (27 January 2005), at 1–2.

[15] Ibid, at 2.

Due to this element, the Chairman's approach is often called a 'situational flexibilities' approach.[16] A number of Members questioned how the concept of situational flexibilities could be placed into actual practice, considering the difficulty in pre-determining all possible situations. Many developing countries also expressed concerns about the possibility of this approach leading to an implicit differentiation amongst developing countries and possibly incorporating the controversial graduation issue.[17]

Failing to reach an agreement on the earlier suggested approach, in February 2005 the WTO Members decided to focus on the remaining Agreement-specific proposals, giving priority to proposals made by the LDCs. In the Hong Kong Ministerial Conference held in December 2005, the Ministers agreed to adopt the decisions contained in Annex F to the Ministerial Declaration, which dealt with the five LDC proposals.[18] In addition, WTO Members decided to provide LDCs with improved SDT including (i) duty-free and quota-free (DFQF) market access for all products originating from all LDCs by 2008; (ii) effective implementation of the Integrated Framework (IF) that can contribute to reducing LDCs' supply-side constraints while enhancing institutional coherence with the World Bank and the International Monetary Fund; and (iii) improved technical assistance through the Technical Assistance and Training Plans (TATP) with appropriate needs assessment mechanisms and reinforced coordination with other agencies and programmes such as the Joint Integrated Technical Assistance Programme (JITAP). On issues of SDT in general, the Hong Kong Ministerial Declaration once again repeated almost the same language as that contained in the July Package.

C. After Hong Kong

To date, excluding the five LDC proposals harvested in Hong Kong and the 28 in-principle agreed proposals, the CTDSS has focused on the remaining 18 proposals under Categories I and III. Little progress has been made on proposals under Category II. Out of the 18 proposals, two proposals related to the Agreement on Textiles and Clothing have since expired. Of the 16 remaining proposals, eight were Category I proposals and the other eight fell under Category III.[19] On 7 May 2007, the Chairman of the CTDSS, Ambassador Burhan Gafoor, reported to the General Council that further

[16] This approach apparently was influenced by a research paper which was presented on 6 December 2004 by International Center for Trade and Sustainable Development (ICTSD), entitled 'Situational Approach to Special and Differential Treatment in the WTO: An Exploratory Exercise,' http://www.ictsd.org/dlogue/2004-12-06/Situational%20Approach%20Revised.pdf (visited on 16 June 2007)

[17] See above n 14, at 3.

[18] Ministerial Declaration, Doha Work Programme, adopted on 18 December 2005, WT/MIN(05)/DEC (22 December 2005).

[19] Chairman's Note on the Meeting of 6 March 2006, TN/CTD/M/23 (10 April 2006), at 2.

discussions led to revised texts on six proposals without complete consensus in any final way, but represented an important step forward for the agreement. Members have yet to come up with revised text on the 7th proposal. On the remaining nine Agreement-specific proposals, wide divergence still existed and thus the Chairman intended to set aside these proposals for the time being.[20]

As for remaining outstanding issues, including cross-cutting issues, some progress was reported only with respect to the Monitoring Mechanism. Members seem to agree on its basic aim, that is, to monitor the implementation and effectiveness of SDT provisions in the existing agreements as well as those that will result from the Doha Round negotiations. Members believed that the monitoring process could function at the technical level (e.g. CTD) and the political level (e.g. General Council).[21]

II. ASSESSMENT OF CURRENT WORKS AT THE WTO

What CTDSS has harvested so far under the Doha mandate is the following:

(i) the five LDC proposals adopted in Hong Kong;
(ii) the 28 proposals agreed in principle before Cancun;
(iii) the six (or possibly seven) proposals under negotiations; and
(iv) an agreement to establish the Monitoring Mechanism.

A core benefit that LDCs could draw from the above item (i) is DFQF market access. To implement this, further actions such as an adoption of common preferential rules of origin are required. Unfortunately, there seems to be no progress in that direction.[22] Although an in-principle agreement was reached on the 28 proposals, many developing countries expressed their dissatisfaction with the final text on most of the 28 proposals and objected to an official adoption of the final text. In their view, the final text of the proposed decisions did not fully reflect their original proposals or would not produce meaningful economic value for them.[23] Six or possibly seven proposals are currently being negotiated, but alternatively proposed texts for several of those proposals seem to be a difficult point of reconciliation between developed countries and developing countries. Discussions on the Monitoring Mechanism are at an early stage and the scope of its mission has yet to be developed. Then, how can we evaluate the current status of the WTO's progress on SDT and development issues?

[20] Report by the Chairman to the General Council, Special Session of the Committee on Trade and Development, TN/CTS/19 (7 May 2007), at 1–2.
[21] Ibid, at 2–3.
[22] Ibid, at 2.
[23] See above, n 8, at 25.

A close examination of the final texts, which were agreed upon with respect to the above items (i) and (ii), reveals that developed countries have been receptive and flexible in dealing with LDCs with respect to their special needs. For instance, out of the 28 Agreement-specific proposals, at least five original proposals made for the LDCs were fully accepted without textual changes in the final proposed decisions.[24] Nonetheless, as pointed out by the African Group, the wording of the final text for the proposed decisions would not obligate developed countries to take positive measures to increase market access opportunities for developing countries.[25] To put it differently, developed countries did not agree to rebalance rights and obligations of WTO Members, while granting automatic rights for developing countries to be exempted from basic GATT/WTO obligations.[26] For instance, as noted earlier, whereas the original proposal made by the African Group granted an automatic right for the LDCs to extend transition periods, it was not the same case under the proposed decision.[27]

Then why did CTDSS fail to succeed in reaching a final outcome that would be mutually satisfactory to both developing and developed countries? In my opinion, the answer is that both sides harboured different dreams when negotiating through CTDSS. For instance, they interpreted the Doha mandate differently. They also perceived the principles and objectives of SDT differently. Developed countries did not intend to make fundamental changes to basic rights and obligations of Members via the CTDSS under the Doha mandate. They believed that the basic objectives of SDT were to integrate developing countries into the multilateral trading system. In contrast, developing countries construed the Doha mandate as an explicit authorization for CTDSS to rebalance rights and obligations of WTO Members and to rectify imbalances of rights and obligations between developing countries and developed countries that were embedded as a result of a single package system. To developing countries, the aim of SDT was to preserve or expand flexibilities and policy space for them to pursue their development goals. Accordingly, developing countries, in particular LDCs, should be given automatic, open-ended, and self-granted rights to deviate from some of the WTO obligations.[28] All of the conflicting views revolve around cross-cutting issues. In other words, the lack of agreement or compromise between both sides on cross-cutting issues ultimately produced

[24] See above, n 8.

[25] Ibid, at 25.

[26] See e.g. Chairman's Note on the Meeting of 1 June 2006, TN/CTD/M/25 (3 August 2006), at 3–4.

[27] See above, n 8, at 22–23.

[28] For the CTDSS Chairman's summary of divergent views on this, see Report by the Chairman to the General Council, Special Session of the Committee on Trade and Development, TN/CTD/12 (28 July 2005), at 1.

dissatisfaction of developing countries with the result of negotiations at CTDSS on Agreement-specific issues.

Furthermore, between developing countries and developed countries, which group is right? In my opinion, neither side is perfectly right. Developed countries interpreted the Doha mandate too narrowly. Strengthening SDT provisions and making them effective and operational under certain circumstances will inevitably involve changes in the rights and obligations of Members. The developed countries' position that the mandate can be carried out without altering the balance of Members' rights and obligations remains doubtful and unpersuasive. Developed countries also stated that the ultimate aim of SDT provisions is to integrate developing countries into the multilateral trading system. This statement in itself may be correct. However, it should be noted that the current WTO rules, including existing SDT provisions, are not effective for promoting the economic development of developing countries and then integrating them into the WTO single package system. Moreover, the current WTO rules as such are not perfect and ideal. Although those rules were crafted with the aim of promoting free trade and trade liberalization, many rules still allow Members to maintain their protectionist measures. This applies to the developed countries' trade barriers that protect their domestic industries against primary products from developing countries and LDCs. In this sense, developed countries were not quite right when they assumed that the current WTO rules are an ideal package into which all the Members should be integrated without altering a balance of right and obligations. If developed countries wish to maintain their position that SDT be provided on a provisional and exceptional basis and that the aim of SDT is to fully integrate developing countries into the WTO rules, then developed countries should first agree to amend the current rules to lift up their protectionist barriers which may be detrimental to the export interests of developing countries. A number of developed countries also take the view that any flexibility in implementing the WTO obligations should be provided on the need basis that is assessed collectively by Members.[29] This view was reflected in the decisions adopted in Hong Kong on the LDCs' five proposals. For instance, *Decision on Measures in Favour of Least-Developed Countries—Paragraph 1* reads:

> Least-developed country members, whilst reaffirming their commitment to the fundamental principles of the WTO and relevant provisions of GATT 1994, and while complying with the general rules set out in the aforesaid instruments, will only be required to undertake commitments and concessions to the extent consistent with their individual development, financial and trade needs, and their administrative and institutional capabilities. Should a least-developed country Member find that it is not

[29] Ibid.

> in a position to comply with a specific obligation or commitment on these grounds, it shall bring the matter to the attention of the General Council for examination and appropriate action.[30]

According to the above decision, LDCs will be allowed to deviate from the WTO obligations to the extent consistent with their development needs, but it will not be an automatic right. Whether a particular LDC Member can deviate from specific obligations will depend on a collective decision made by the General Council, which as a matter of fact requires all Members' consensus. The legal implication of this provision is to grant a veto to any Member that was adversely affected by a LDC Member's derogation from its specific obligations. Even without this kind of veto, a collective decision at the General Council will inevitably be made on the basis of a political consideration rather than an objective assessment of individual countries' development needs and their relevance to non-compliance with specific obligations. Without obtaining a consensus decision at the General Council, the LDC Member in question would not be able to avoid a judicial challenge under the Dispute Settlement Understanding ('DSU'). Under this scenario, the earlier proposed decision will be practically useless from the LDCs' point of view. This suggests that it is necessary for the WTO to create a mechanism that enables an objective assessment of individual developing countries' development needs and whether and how specific WTO obligations at issue are positively or negatively related to the economic development of that Member.

The developing countries' positions that emerged in the course of negotiations on Agreement-specific proposals are not perfectly right, either. First of all, although the WTO must address development concerns of developing countries and LDCs, it cannot be denied that WTO is in essence a trade organization. In other words, even if the Doha mandate is construed as an affirmative decision to assist developing countries in promoting their economic development, it should preferably be carried out through means that can minimize the extent of undermining the basic objectives of the multilateral trading system. Although some criticisms may be cast over the single package system, it is still generally agreed that that is the backbone of the multilateral trading system and is certainly better than the 'code approach' under the GATT system. In that sense, with some caveats for the LDCs, it seems to be unrealistic and inappropriate to provide blanket, automatic and open-ended exemptions to developing countries from WTO obligations without an assessment of individual developing countries' development needs and how individual measures at issue are relevant to economic development. While it is vital to provide developing countries with a certain degree of flexibility and assistance to implement WTO Agreements,

[30] See above, n 18, Annex F.

such flexibility can be properly granted only when an objective assessment indicates a positive relationship between such flexibility (e.g. exemptions from certain WTO obligations) and economic development in the national economy of the beneficiary.

III. PROPOSALS AND ASSESSMENT

A. Proposals involving differentiation

Several scholars have suggested some options for possible reforms of the current SDT provisions and for enhancing development relevance of the WTO.[31]

Stevens:[32] The cost imbalance in implementing the WTO Agreements is the basis of SDT, and the idea of 'one size does not fit all' is the underlying standard for SDT. Stevens proposed several criteria to determine which country is eligible for flexibilities in implementing WTO obligations. Potential indicators include political costs, relevant market share in the world market, the extent of market distortion and spillover effects to other countries, government expenditures, implementation costs, etc. He endorsed a methodology for sub-grouping individual developing countries, although he proposed an Agreement-specific approach for areas such as the agricultural sector. Stevens also argued that supply-side constraints must be considered in providing SDT to individual developing countries.

Prowse:[33] While pointing out that WTO SDT provisions lacked an assessment of a Member's overall economic policies in a comprehensive manner, Prowse suggested a country-specific approach. When an implementation of resource-intensive obligations is involved, a developing country Member would be required to fulfill specific obligations only when this conforms to the accomplishment of development goals.

Wang and Winters:[34] Where more implementation costs are incurred to developing countries, new types of SDTs such as longer transition periods, more flexible rules, and specific commitments to technical assistance, would have to be allowed for those developing countries. In particular, monitoring and phased transitions should be introduced to make a longer transition period effective. Developed countries' obligations to provide technical assistance should become mandatory and subject to dispute

[31] For a brief summary of these proposals, see Bernard Hoekman, 'Operationalizing the Concept of Policy Space in the WTO: Beyond Special and Differential Treatment,' 8 JIEL (2005) 405, at 412–15.

[32] Christopher Stevens, 'The Future of SDT for Developing Countries in the WTO, Institute for Developing Studies,' Sussex, Working Paper 163 (May 2002).

[33] Susan Prowse, 'The Role of International and National Agencies in Trade-Related Capacity Building,' 25(9) World Economy (2002) 1235–61, also available at http://www.unido.org/file-storage/download/?file_id=12962 (visited on 16 June 2007).

[34] Zhen Kun Wang and Alan Winters, 'Putting 'Humpty' Together Again: Including Developing Countries in a Consensus for the WTO,' CEPR Policy Paper No. 4 (2000).

settlement procedures. These authors endorsed an Agreement-specific approach. They suggested specific criteria under each WTO Agreement to determine whether an individual Member can be exempted from certain WTO obligations.

Hoekman, Michalpoulos, and Winters:[35] Hoekman in his recent article summarized these authors' approach as follows:

> A simple rule-of-thumb approach that would allow opt-outs for resource-intensive agreements for all countries satisfying broad threshold criteria such as minimum level of per capita income, institutional capacity, or economic scale... As countries come to surpass thresholds over time, disciplines automatically would become applicable.[36]

While criticizing Agreement-specific and country-specific approaches, these authors proposed to create a new developing country sub-group including LDCs and other smaller and vulnerable economies.

As pointed out by Hoekman, all of the above approaches, to some degree, involve differentiation amongst developing countries. As noted earlier, such an attempt made by European countries at WTO CTDSS faced strong opposition from almost all developing countries. In addition, differentiation amongst developing countries inevitably requires setting out specific criteria by which some countries are included and others are excluded. In some sense, such criteria are 'inherently arbitrary.'[37] Some years ago, the OECD Working Party of the Trade Committee submitted a report suggesting specific criteria that can be used for country differentiation.[38] Relevant indicators include (i) GNI per capita; (ii) trade share of a country in world trade; (iii) share of manufacturing and services in total GDP; (iv) share of total trade in GDP; and (v) governance indicators. Regarding analysis methodology, this report used both the cluster analysis and the index approach. An application of such criteria led to the result that small-sized economies relying heavily on trade are at the top of the rankings. Subject to relative weight given to individual indicators, in general, Singapore, Hong Kong, and South Korea were ranked at the top, leaving the United States, Japan, and West European countries behind. This result was not surprising because the nature of the above specific indicators drove the final result in that direction. It confirms that country sub-grouping would go in

[35] Bernard Hoekman, Constantine Michalpoulos, and L. Alan Winters, 'Special and Differential Treatment in the WTO After Cancun', 27(4) The World Economy (2003) 481.

[36] Bernard Hoekman, above, n 31, at 413.

[37] Ibid.

[38] See OECD, 'Analytical Criteria for Calibrating Provisions for Special and Differential Treatment Across Different Beneficiaries,' (28 April 2003), TD/TC/WP(2002)44/Rev2 & ANN. For an initial publication of the OECD that suggested differentiation, see OECD, *The Development Dimension of Trade* (2001).

different directions, depending on which specific indicators are applied, which demonstrates that this approach would pose a high risk of arbitrary results.

B. New proposals: situational or measure-specific approaches

Since a number of WTO Members raised strong objections to the concept of country differentiation at the CTDSS, alternative approaches have been suggested.

1. A situational approach

As noted earlier, this approach was introduced by ICTSD in December 2004 as a theoretical back-up for the then CTDSS Chairman Ismail's 'situational flexibilities' approach.[39] Most of all, this approach suggests that SDT should be provided to address individual developing countries' problems with a focus on 'developmental situations' instead of developing countries' 'levels of development.' This approach is also aimed at removing the idea of country differentiation or graduation from the WTO system. A description of the situation is Step 1 for this approach. Only a country that fits a pre-defined situation may be eligible for SDT. Step 2 is to define particular development-related objectives that should be pursued. Step 3 is to provide SDT in order to accomplish the specific objectives defined in Step 2.

The situational approach seems to provide more sophisticated methodologies than the previous approaches. Nonetheless, in terms of how the concept of situational flexibility could be applied in actual practice, this approach would face the difficulty in predetermining all possible situations and the risk of implicit country differentiation in that process. This was obviously the main reason why Former Chairman Ismail faced objections from a number of Members and gave up this conceptual approach in the end.[40] However, one should not totally dismiss some of the merits of the situational approach. This approach actually tackles one of the most challenging and demanding tasks involved in the current debates at the WTO on SDT. The situational approach was designed to provide developing countries with enhanced flexibilities in implementing WTO rules, but only when such flexibilities were necessary to address particular development needs and challenges. Former Chairman Ismail also made it clear that 'there was no a priori exclusion of any developing country from such a situational flexibility.'[41] This situational approach is not a blanket approach with the aim of developing country sub-grouping. Thus it should be differentiated from other previous approaches, although this approach may entail a practical difficulty in pre-determining all possible situations.

[39] See above n 16.
[40] See above, n 14, at 3.
[41] See above n 14.

2. A measure-specific approach

In an effort to avoid politically insurmountable objections from many developing countries, an alternative approach was proposed by staff members of the WTO Economic Research and Statistics Division.[42] While noting that all the previous approaches with strong emphasis on the creation of new country groupings are politically unacceptable, this approach suggests that a focus be made on 'measures' rather than on country status. This particular approach resembles in many respects an Agreement-specific approach proposed by other scholars, but it has some merit in that it emphasizes that SDT provisions should be adequately 'customized' and responsive to national development interests.

Bernard Hoekman, while noting the political difficulty of the 'differentiation' proposals, recently suggested a 'more cooperative approach', that is in essence a measure-specific approach with additional elaboration of its relationship to dispute settlement procedures.[43] As far as development-related measures are concerned, he tried to make fundamental changes in the dispute settlement scheme. His new approach makes recourse to the DSU conditional on a 'development test'. Hoekman proposed setting up an independent body at some point in the dispute settlement procedures that primarily focuses on an economic assessment of challenged measures while applying a development test. Such an assessment would include an analysis of the likely net benefits of (non-)implementation from a development perspective and the magnitude of negative spillovers associated with the use of relevant policy measures that potentially do not comply with specific WTO disciplines. A policy measure failing a development test would face a normal judicial challenge under the dispute settlement procedures. Even if a policy measure passes a development test, it would nevertheless be subject to DSU as long as such a measure produced a 'significant' negative spillover effect on other developing countries.[44]

Although Hoekman's approach seems reasonable from a theoretical mirror, it may pose a series of practical problems. First, dispute settlement procedures can be invoked only when certain government measures nullify benefits of other Members arising under the WTO agreements. Whether the extent of such nullification is significant will be dependant on particular situations facing affected developing Members. In my view, even an independent assessment body would be unable to set out objective and consistently applicable standards by which it can make such judgment on the level of nullification. Hoekman also suggested that as far as developed countries are concerned even a significant negative externality should

[42] Alexander Keck and Patrick Low, Special and nhDifferential Treatment in the WTO: Why, When and How?, WTO Staff Working Paper ERSD-2004-03 (May 2004), also available at http://www.wto.org/english/res_e/reser_e/ersd200403_e.doc.

[43] See above, n 31.

[44] Ibid, at 417.

be tolerated and recourse to the DSU should not be allowed. It would be very difficult for an affected developed country Member to persuade its adversely affected domestic industry to simply tolerate negative spillover effects after a developing country Member's specific measure had been applied and actually hurt that domestic industry.

This practical problem originates from the inherent nature of his approach, which can be appropriately called an *ex post* approach. This demonstrates that the acceptability of an SDT measure would preferably be determined on an *ex ante* basis. In other words, a decision whether to provide flexibilities in implementing WTO rules should be made in advance of actual occurrence of nullification of benefits regarding specific interest groups of any WTO Members. The provision of SDT is a policy decision, whereas recourse to DSU is a very legalistic process. Injecting development concerns into the middle of, or right before, judicial disputes would cause significant confusion in the already well established dispute settlement system.

For all these reasons, although I support Hoekman's idea of establishing an independent body that makes an objective assessment of the development relevance of developing countries' policy measures, I suggest an *ex ante* approach where that body can function before the policy measures in question would actually be introduced by relevant developing country Members. The job of the independent body would be triggered by a relevant developing country's voluntary notification of a policy measure. That Member would be required to prove a policy measure's development relevance. If placing a burden of proof on developing countries is perceived to be unreasonable, a development-related international institution or another WTO sub-body in charge of technical assistance or capacity building may provide some assistance in that process. In cases where the relevant measures are generally applicable and potential targets cannot be ascertained in advance, the independent assessment body may invite participation of any third country Members that have trade interests affected by the relevant policy measures. On the other hand, if a potentially aggrieved Member can be identified in advance of actual application of a policy measure, such a Member must be consulted in advance and given an opportunity to express its views in this assessment process. In this process, if it is determined that a less-trade restrictive alternative measure can accomplish the same development goal, after considering implementation costs and other supply-side constraints, such alternative measures that are reasonably available would be recommended.

This assessment process would be triggered only by a developing country Member's voluntary request. In the early part of the assessment process, an assessment body or other relevant international institutions may play some advisory role. For this purpose, institutional coherence between the WTO and other institutions will be essential. In this connection, the currently available IE and JITAP may function to assist developing countries, in particular LDCs, in the notification and assessment procedures. Since the neglect of notification would result in possible exposure to dispute settlement procedures in the end, developing countries would have strong incentives to work with the assessment body or other relevant international institutions at an early stage of adopting policy measures that might have relevance to both trade and development. This also would contribute to decreasing the number of trade disputes that would normally be subject to dispute settlement procedures.

Of course, the assessment body should be composed of independent experts whose political neutrality is preserved. Once this assessment body finds that a policy measure at issue would not be helpful, or even irrelevant or detrimental, to the development needs of the developing country Member in question, this body should recommend alternative measures to properly address particular development needs after consultation with that Member, or simply recommend that flexibility to WTO rules with respect to a policy measure at issue should not be granted. If a policy measure is found to be eligible for flexibilities to WTO rules, for instance SDT, then an assessment body shall recommend that such a measure will be exempted from challenges under the dispute settlement procedures. In this case, the assessment body may designate the time period for this special treatment and impose some workable conditionalities on the flexibility. This recommendation shall be adopted by relevant WTO bodies such as General Council or CTDSS on the basis of a reverse-consensus rule. Finally, the assessment body should monitor the post-recommendation stage, for instance, by checking the fulfillment of conditionalities, and also play an advisory role in conjunction with relevant international institutions having expertise in development issues.

IV. CONCLUSION

As far as development-related issues are concerned, the position gap between developed and developing country Members seems too wide for reconciliation. Neither side is perfectly right in their respective position. The width of the gap could be narrowed or hopefully be removed only when both sides take a big step towards the other. It is recommended that developed country Members accept that the Doha development mandate should lead to some rebalancing of rights and obligations of current Members. Developing country Members also need to agree that such a rebalancing will not come in an automatic, open-ended, and self-invoked manner. With some caveats for LDCs and without prejudice to currently available SDT under individual WTO Agreements, flexibilities to WTO rules should be provided when a certain policy measure can contribute to development goals of individual developing countries and in a manner that can minimize adverse impact on the multilateral trading system.

Various proposals involving differentiation amongst developing countries are objectionable not only because of their political unacceptability but also because of their inherent limits due to arbitrary criteria. A situational approach is more sophisticated in its methodology, but still cannot avoid the risk of pre-determining particular situations. Accordingly, a measure-specific approach is a preferable option, but in consideration of its practicality, it is recommended that WTO Members adopt an *ex ante* approach. A decision whether flexibilities are provided should be made by an independent expert body on the basis of an objective assessment, rather than by a political body that would require consensus among Members. In this process, an independent assessment body would preferably make recommendations in a manner that the adverse impact on the multilateral trading system is minimized. The Monitoring Mechanism, which WTO Members agreed to establish, may take the administrative role in these assessment and monitoring processes.

A NEW DOMINANT TRADE SPECIES EMERGES: IS BILATERALISM A THREAT?

Frederick M. Abbott[*]

ABSTRACT

Over the past decade, government trade and finance ministries have increasingly turned toward negotiating bilateral and regional trading arrangements, and away from negotiations in multilateral forums like the WTO. There are several reasons for this shift, including changes in the global political environment and negotiating obstacles encountered by the multinational business community at the multilateral level. This shift appears to be an embedded phenomenon. Positive and negative aspects of preferential trading arrangements (PTAs) are in evidence. Trade creation-trade diversion economic analysis suggests the results may be net global welfare enhancing, although such analysis does not readily assess distributional effects. The global economy is enjoying a period of sustained—and widely distributed—economic growth, suggesting that the PTA phenomenon is not an immediate economic threat. On the negative side, the PTAs lead to administrative complexity, and may be somewhat destabilizing as businesses are encouraged to relocate. Some countries may suffer if left out, but this risk is ameliorated by the wide availability of potential negotiating partners. The PTA negotiating environment strongly favors powerful economic actors like the United States and European Union, which are largely dictating terms to developing (and developed) countries. Developing countries, particularly the less economically powerful, are losing autonomous decision-making authority. The consequences of this are difficult to quantify, and may raise questions better attuned to moral philosophers than economists. The WTO continues on its way, relegated to a less central status. A return to the WTO might reinvigorate the role of less powerful actors, but such return does not appear an immediate prospect. The PTA phenomenon, on balance, does not appear aggressively threatening. We may, however, be underestimating the positive role of multilateralism.

* Edward Ball Eminent Scholar Professor of International Law, Florida State University College of Law. Member of the Board of Editors. Email: FAbbott@law.fsu.edu

One objective of this special issue is to identify the major changes in the world trading system over the ten years this Journal has been published, and to explore the implications of those changes. This essay addresses the shift away from multilateralism as the preferred government trade policy option, toward bilateral and regional trade negotiations as the central focus of government trade ministries. This trend is not newly "discovered" here. It is well known to participants and commentators in the trade arena. It was addressed at some length in the Sutherland Report,[1] the results of which were commented upon in this Journal.[2] The fact that a trend is well known does not make it less important. The emergence—or re-emergence—of a new dominant species in the world trading system, the bilateral and regional trading arrangement, is certainly worthy of attention here.

I. SHIFTING TRADE POLICY PRIORITIES

From the 1700s through the 1930s, countries conducted their trade relations largely on the basis of bilateral treaties.[3] By the start of the Second World War, bilateral arrangements underlay imperial trading systems covering much of the world. Conventional wisdom is that the architects of the post-war institutional architecture established a preference for multilateralism—in the trade context grounded in most-favoured-nation (MFN) treatment—in order to guard against a recurrence of conflict among competing systems of colonial preference.[4] The MFN principle was embedded in the GATT 1947, now the WTO, to institutionalize this policy preference.

We are today confronted with substantial, and perhaps compelling, evidence that the post-War commitment to the MFN principle is deteriorating. Most countries of the world—in all regions—are actively pursuing bilateral and regional trade deals (hereinafter sometimes referred to as 'preferential trading arrangements' or "PTAs"). The European Commission and the Office of the US Trade Representative devote most of their trade attention to bilateral and regional negotiations. The European Union—itself a manifestation of preferential regionalism—is comprised of 27 member states, but this vastly understates the scope of the EU preferential trading sphere, when the African, Caribbean and Pacific (ACP) group and other EU-related PTAs are included. The United States is rapidly expanding its

[1] Peter Sutherland, et al., The Future of the WTO, Addressing Institutional Challenges in the New Millennium, Report by the Consultative Board to the Director-General Supachai Panitchpakdi (2005).

[2] Regarding preferential trade agreements, or PTAs, see, e.g. Gary Hufbauer, 'Inconsistency Between Diagnosis and Treatment', 8 Journal of International Economic Law 291 (2005).

[3] Frederick M. Abbott, Crosscurrents in European Union External Commercial Relations: The Controversy Over the Germany-United States Treaty of Friendship, 54 Zeitschrift für Ausländisches öffentliches Recht und Völkerrecht (Zaörv) (1994) 756.

[4] See, e.g., Stefan A. Riesenfeld, The Changing Face of Globalism, in F. Abbott and D. Gerber (eds), *Public Policy and Global Technological Integration* (Kluwer Law International, 1997).

network of bilateral and regional preferential agreements, Israel, Canada, Mexico, Chile, Jordan, Singapore, Australia, Morocco, Bahrain, Costa Rica, El Salvador, Honduras, Guatemala, Nicaragua, Dominican Republic, Panama, Peru, Colombia, and Korea (and onward to Malaysia, Thailand, and so forth).[5]

But the PTA phenomenon is by no means limited to the EU and the United States. The countries of Asia are dramatically expanding formal preferential arrangements among themselves, and with other regions.[6] Even Japan, which long considered its better interests served by multilateral negotiations,[7] has joined the crowd.[8] The countries of Latin America are strengthening their already existing ties in the Mercosur and elsewhere.[9] This expansion of preferential relations, previously well documented by the WTO Secretariat, appears to be an embedded phenomenon.[10]

II. FACTORS UNDERLYING THE SHIFT

There is no single factor underlying the shift. Rather, a number of political and economic forces have combined to produce the change.

A. Geo-political movement

In hindsight, that the GATT 1947 was comprised of one block among several global political and economic antagonists may have been underestimated as 'glue' holding the multilateral trading system together. The GATT was not truly a 'global' trading system. It was a key institution of a Western liberal political bloc confronting a perceived threat from a Second World of 'communist' and 'socialist' countries.

The deterioration of the military power of the Soviet Union and the dismantling of the ideological underpinning of the communist Chinese government has led to a wide expansion of participation in the multilateral trading system embodied in the WTO. Yet, at the same time, it seems to have diluted the 'multilateralism glue' holding it together. Without a

[5] See USTR website, at Trade Agreements, at <http://www.ustr.gov.>

[6] See, e.g. *ASEAN to Push for More FTAs As Global Trade Talk Pace Slows*, BNA INT'L TR. DAILY, 8 June 2007. See the Asia-Pacific Trade and Investment Agreements Database (APTIAD), at United Nations Economic and Social Commission for Asia and the Pacific, at <http://www.unescap.org/tid/aptiad/default.aspx>.

[7] See report of this author's discussions in Japan in 1994, shortly following entry into force of the NAFTA, in Frederick M. Abbott, *Law and Policy of Regional Integration, The NAFTA and Western Hemispheric Integration in the World Trade Organization System* 139–51 (Kluwer/Martinus Nijhoff, 1995) [hereinafter 'Abbott, Regional Integration'].

[8] See, e.g. See Japan-Mexico FTA Comes Into Force, UNCTAD-ICTSD, 9 Bridges Weekly Trade News Digest, 6 April 2005.

[9] See information regarding developments in Latin American regional integration at websites of the Organization of American States (<http://www.sedi.oas.org/dttc/>) and Inter-American Development Bank (<http://www.iadb.org//int/1_English/2_Divisions/a_ITD.htm>).

[10] See, e.g. Jo-Ann Crawford and Roberto V. Fiorentino, 'The Changing Landscape of Regional Trade Agreements', WTO Secretariat Discussion Paper No. 8 (2005).

common ideological and economic enemy, the West appears to have lost interest in multilateralism as a policy principle.

Governments are seeking to establish new bilateral and regional alliances to advance their particular geopolitical interests. Europe, Latin America, and Asia are not keen on a political (or economic) world dominated by the United States. It may be hard to empirically demonstrate that political power considerations, in addition to mercantile considerations, are driving the new bilateral and regional negotiating wave, because governments are not generally so explicit about these objectives. But the shifting constellations of political and economic power in Latin America being played out in regional trade alliances should provide some backup for this thesis. Similarly, the ongoing bilateral economic and political negotiations between United States and India, including nuclear power-related discussions, suggest that economics and politics are not so far apart.

B. Redirection of the multinational business community

It has become exceedingly difficult for the multinational business community to achieve its preferred economic agenda at the multilateral level. This is true at the WTO, as evidenced by lack of progress on the Doha Development Agenda (DDA). It is also true at the World Intellectual Property Organization (WIPO).[11] Even limited membership multilateral organizations such as the Organization for Economic Cooperation and Development (OECD) have failed in efforts to move on issues perceived as important to the multinational business community; in particular the Multilateral Agreement on Investment (MAI).

The preferred agenda of the multinational business community is not the preferred agenda of many other stakeholders in multilateral governance. Multinational business enterprises are typically pursuing mercantile agendas designed to enhance their returns on investment. Other stakeholders in multilateral governance have much different agendas. The difference between the multinational business community and most other stakeholders is that the former can elect to transfer its negotiating agenda to more favorable forums because it generally has the power to direct the focus of trade negotiators. Other forums may be 'second-best', but that is just a fact of business to which enterprises can adapt.

To take just a few examples: Although negotiations on the MAI may have failed at the OECD, negotiations on investment protection have been successfully carried out by the United States in its series of bilateral and regional agreements, and; while there is little present prospect for negotiating higher levels of intellectual property protection at the WTO and WIPO,

[11] Observe stalled negotiations on the Substantive Patent Law Treaty and other proposals. See generally, Barton et al., *Views on the Future of the International Intellectual Property System*, ICTSD Selected Issue Briefs No. 1, June 2007.

the United States and the European Union have been successfully negotiating higher levels of protection in various bilateral and regional settings. While governments hardly make offers in DDA services negotiations at the WTO, services market access commitments in the bilateral and regional context are far-reaching, suggesting that governments are reserving their most valued concessions for these latter forums.

C. Seeking higher growth

In light of the reduced impetus for multilateral cooperation, and the present inability of private enterprise to promote consensus on 'improved' rules at the multilateral level, government economic planners looking for ways to stimulate domestic economic growth might well be justified in concluding that alternative forums for negotiating are required. The 'second-best' solution is negotiations on a bilateral or regional basis which, from the perspective of Treasury Departments and Trade Ministries, may well reflect the present national interest. Of course, this reflects a certain circularity in reasoning: bilateral and regional trade agreements have become the 'new first best' option because the Ministries turned away from the 'old first best' option.

III. REWARDS AND RISKS

A. Rewards

There is a substantial 'classical' economics literature explaining the potential benefits and costs of PTAs.[12] This classical literature focused on the dual effects of 'trade creation' and 'trade diversion' that follow from the establishment of localized trade preferences among a group of countries. Jacob Viner laid the foundation of the trade creation–trade diversion analytical approach, concluding that if the trade creating effect of a PTA exceeded the trade diverting effect (i.e., if it was 'net trade creating'), the global economic welfare effect would be positive. It is also understood that Viner's analytic approach did not account for the distributional effects of the arrangement. That is, net positive welfare gains might accrue disproportionately to a particular region, yet still increase overall global welfare.

Viner's original analytic work was done in an era when tariffs and quotas remained the principal concerns of the trading system. More recent work by economists necessarily has taken into account the broader range of economic activity covered by PTAs. Today, reducing barriers to the free movement of services, enhancing the protection of investment and strengthening the rules governing intellectual property rights (IPRs) account for a substantial part of

[12] See discussion in Abbott, Regional Integration, above n 7, Ch. 9. The seminal document is Jacob Viner, *The Customs Union Issue* (New York: Carnegie Endowment for International Peace, 1950), at 41–81.

new PTA texts, and typically involve the more contentious aspects of negotiations. Yet, taking into account the expanded scope of subject matter interest, the basic idea that a PTA will have a 'net positive' impact on the global economy if it creates more trade than it diverts appears to remain sound. We continue to expect that greater trade flows are a signal of increasing efficiencies as lower-priced goods and services, reflecting comparative advantage and specialization, displace higher-priced less efficiently produced goods. In this overall calculation, IPRs are something of a conundrum, because strengthening protection of IPRs tends to increase prices and may constitute a drag on economic growth, unless offset by efficiency gains.

The phenomenon commonly known as 'globalization' is thriving on an apparent increase in the security of foreign direct investment (FDI) which facilitates investment in plants and equipment. One of the main elements of many new PTAs is increased investor protection, including possibility for third party dispute settlement. Similarly, globalization is thriving on the basis of relatively free capital flows that are stimulated by PTA rules liberalizing the establishment of banks and other financial institutions, as well as the inward and outward flow of capital. This increasingly open flow of global capital is benefiting individual consumers who are more likely to obtain credit for purchases of homes and consumer goods, further stimulating localized and global economic growth.

All of the 'positives' referred to above are part of the rule-making pursued in PTAs presently being negotiated. And, we are in the midst of a relatively unprecedented era of widely-shared global economic growth. We could well be satisfied to conclude that the trend toward increased regionalization embodies the creation of a series of 'mini-engines' of growth that are driving the global economy to greater heights.

B. Risks

There are some fairly apparent disadvantages to the present focus on bilateral and regional trade negotiations, and perhaps some less apparent, and even greater, difficulties.[13]

[13] The world has changed a great deal since 1947, and the wealth of nations may not be so nearly dependent on particular trading constellations as it was then. Advances in transportation and communications technologies have reduced the transaction costs of trade. The success of the GATT and WTO in reducing tariff rates and quotas means they may not play the role in trade relations they once did. Goods and services are flowing across national boundaries. The multilateral trading system may not be as important as it once was, due to its own success.
And, perhaps a good part of this success can be attributed to the benign influence of a relatively open multilateral trading system. We may all be taking for granted the fact that the GATT and WTO have worked—and are working. But that is okay, because the WTO is not a celebrity seeking adulation—it does not need recognition and praise. It only needs to keep working.

1. Complexity and inefficiency

Perhaps the most obvious problem presented by the plethora of new PTAs is the sheer complexity of the rules now confronting the international trader, and the government officials seeking to implement the rules. How a good or service is to be treated from a tariff, quota or regulatory standpoint depends on its origination, the determination of which may involve significant factual issues. Once the originating country or region is determined, the applicable set of bilateral or regional rules must be found and applied. Multiplying this activity into the millions and billions of transactions presents obvious prospects for inefficiency, delay and error.

The difficulties confronting customs and related regulatory authorities in identifying and applying relevant rules are mirrored in the increasing complexity of choice of forum and law for dispute settlement. This is not to suggest that the 'tail' of dispute settlement should 'wag the dog' of international trade, but evidence of conflict of norms problems is growing.[14]

2. Rapid change and destabilization

Business enterprises calculate opportunities based on their expected costs, and those costs include applicable tariffs, quotas, and regulatory norms. It is commonplace today to read of businesses that are shifting production from one country to another because of shifts in tariff or quota preferences under PTAs. As governments increasingly pursue bilateral and regional trade arrangements, the rate of change in applicable preferences is likely to accelerate, and with it the rates at which businesses shift their locations. The consequence is increased instability for national and local economies, employees, families, etc. While net global trading activity may be increased, this may not adequately offset the negative social consequences of economic destabilization.

3. Potential isolation and the 'domino effect'

It has long been noted that the major potential 'losers' from regional or bilateral trade arrangements are the countries which, for one reason or another, are left on the sidelines of the negotiations.[15] A country not receiving preferential treatment may find itself in some economic difficulty if competitor countries are so benefiting.

Recall that the 'net trade creation' analytical approach to PTAs does not capture their distributional effects. The United States and European Union may benefit substantially more from PTAs than their smaller trading partners, and countries outside these PTAs may suffer from trade diversion. PTAs may be overall increasing in world trade, but that does not mean that all countries are benefiting, or are benefiting in a proportional way.

[14] For example, in the Mexico–US high fructose corn syrup saga involving NAFTA and WTO claims.

[15] See concerns expressed by Singapore Ambassador Tommy T.B. Koh in 1990, recounted in Abbott, Regional Integration, above n 7, at 167–18.

Yet with the proliferation of regional alliances today, it may be that almost any country which seeks a preferential trading partner can find one. There is, in fact, a 'domino effect' in operation around the world. Trade Ministries, perhaps legitimately, fear that domestic economies will suffer if their countries do not join the wave of PTAs. The trend towards preferential arrangements is self-reinforcing. Joining a PTA out of perceived necessity may be an improvement over being left out, but it reflects part of an overall loss of independence being suffered by less powerful economic actors, discussed under the next heading.

4. Loss of sovereign control

Perhaps, the most dramatic negative consequence of the recent trend toward bilateral and regional negotiations is the loss of economic and political control facing developing countries, as a whole, and especially smaller and less economically powerful developing countries. When the United States or European Union tenders a draft PTA to a developing country, it expects the basic template of its proposal to be followed, and in some areas (such as investment rules or strengthening of IPRs protection), the possibilities for effective counterproposal arc almost non-existent.

Countries such as Argentina and Brazil have rejected meaningful participation in negotiations with the United States and EU on PTAs (such as the proposed Free Trade Area of the Americas) because they are unwilling to accept the basic template, and there is little present room for further discussion. In Latin America, the push of the United States to secure FTAs with countries of Central America and the Andean Community is viewed as part of a strategy to isolate Argentina and Brazil, and ultimately to cause them to rethink their own policy preferences. Argentina and Brazil, however, are exceptions to the general rule among developing countries. They are large economy countries that can withstand some economic pressure from the United States and EU, and have been in that position for a long time. Even then, the United States is holding out some increasingly valuable carrots to Brazil,[16] and at some stage the incentives might be great enough to bring that country into the PTA program.

Jordan, Morocco, Dominican Republic, El Salvador, Guatemala, Peru and the like do not have leverage to bargain with the United States. In much the same way the ACP countries have very limited leverage with the EU.[17] As a consequence, these countries accept economic and regulatory policies 'made in the USA' and 'made in the EU'. The recent agreement between the Bush

[16] For example, the prospect of large-scale sugar-based Ethanol imports implicit in discussions in a recent visit by President Bush to Brazil. See, e.g. White House Office of the Press Secretary, *President Bush and President Lula of Brazil Discuss Biofuel Technology*, São Paulo, Brazil, 9 March 2007.

[17] The ACP countries are in the midst of negotiating an Economic Partnership Agreement with the European Commission, the proposed terms of which have drawn considerable criticism from the European Parliament and NGOs.

Administration and congressional leaders to modify the terms of concluded FTAs with Panama, Peru, Colombia, and South Korea so as to reflect new labour, environmental and IPRs-related conditions precisely illustrates the lack of bargaining power on the other side of the table.[18] These changes to bilateral agreements are being dictated by the US Congress as a condition of ratification. While Panama et al. are being 'asked' to renegotiate, it is doubtful anyone is under the illusion that Panama et al. will draft the new conditions, or even have the chance to say much about them.

United States and EU trade negotiators might well acknowledge the imbalanced nature of these negotiations—the facts are too well known to allow otherwise—but presumably would argue that there is little cause for concern because the rules of the FTAs are beneficial to all sides. Developing countries may be forced to take certain medicine, but since the medicine is beneficial where is the cause for complaint?

Here, we tread on some pretty treacherous moral, political, social, and economic ground. I cannot suggest to you with any certainty what the implications of all this 'pushing around' may be. Some former British colonies get along pretty well with their former imperial leader. Imbalanced power relations may be the natural order of things, and the weak may not resent the strong for their efforts.

The precise nature of the problem is difficult to define, but there is something not quite right about one-sided trade negotiations. In his essay on the Sutherland Report, Gary Hufbauer invoked Shakespeare's Julius Caesar.[19] I might follow suit by invoking the Chinese philosopher, Lao Tzu:

> To be overbearing when one has wealth and position
> Is to bring calamity upon oneself.
>
> Lao Tzu, *Tao Te Ching*, Book I, Chapter IX[20]

Lao Tzu can be a bit obtuse, and he does not always seem constrained to explain his reasoning.[21] It is hard to elaborate more on this particular point: the current negotiating environment for PTAs is heavily imbalanced in favour of the large economy actors that are effectively dictating the terms of the agreements. In my own view, there is something not quite right. But, I cannot—or I prefer not attempting to—explain the problem in terms of economic science.

It can of course be argued that this current situation does not represent a significant change from the GATT 1947. In the old GATT environment,

[18] See, e.g. USTR, Bipartisan Agreement on Trade Policy: Intellectual Property, May 2007, Trade Facts, available at <http://www.ustr.gov>.

[19] Hufbauer, above n 2, at 294.

[20] Translated by D.C. Lau, Penguin Classics (1963).

[21] Gautama Buddha's karmic wheel may have suggested much the same thing, but the Buddha was not grounded in empirical science either.

rules and terms of trade were largely dictated by the EU and United States. In this sense, power relations in the PTA environment are not much different.

That may be true, but the shift away from the WTO took place at precisely the point when developing countries had managed to secure one of their first multilateral successes—the Doha Declaration on the TRIPS Agreement and Public Health of 14 November 2001.[22] The moment developing countries demonstrated some mastery of WTO diplomacy, the rug was pulled out from under them, as if the prospect of negotiating at the WTO on more equal terms was too much for the OECD countries to bear. This does not shed a better light on the current PTA situation.

C. What if things go wrong

The rewards and risks of the PTA phenomenon so far seem to be in rough balance, and the dangers not too great. The DDA is making scant progress, but the global economy is thriving in relative terms, and emerging economy countries are enjoying virtually unprecedented economic growth. The PTAs may be stimulating some cross-border investment and capital flows, and encouraging a general air of economic progress and security. Many developing countries are accepting the terms of PTAs dictated to them by the United States and EU, but perhaps only a few ancient philosophers would worry (as I do) about the unconstrained exercise of power.

We are in the midst of a benign global economic environment, where most boats seem to be rising, and we may need to be reminded that things can change. An Avian flu pandemic, a disruption of Mid-East oil flows or the sudden collapse of a major currency could change the global economic environment pretty quickly. Is the PTA phenomenon likely to influence the course of a serious global economic contraction, for better or worse?

Viewed through the lens of 1910, or the lens of the 1930s, we might well be concerned that severe stresses on the global economy will pressure countries to revert to the kind of political, military, and trade alliances that foretold global conflict. Bilateral and regional trade agreements might form the basis for such renewed alliances. Yet, without suggesting that the human condition (and capacity for aggression) has moderated, it seems doubtful that today's PTAs would play a similar role to those of the competing imperial empires of the early 1900s or 1930s. This largely has to do with the evolution of military, communications and transportation technologies.

The outcome of 'serious' military conflict today seems more likely to be determined in a matter of days and weeks, as opposed to years. It seems doubtful that the regional identity of suppliers of raw materials and foodstuffs will be a decisive factor in such events. There likewise does not

[22] See Frederick M. Abbott, 'The Doha Declaration on the TRIPS Agreement and Public Health: Lighting a Dark Corner at the WTO', 5 Journal of International Economic Law 469 (2002).

seem much likelihood that the United States or EU would initiate an armed conflict to defend a trade preference with particular developing countries. (This should not be confused with a war to defend the integrity of oil supplies.) All in all, it seems doubtful that the pre-occupation of the architects of the GATT 1947 with avoiding renewal of systems of colonial preference should be of equal concern in today's age of the Internet and routine airfreight. (I hope I am right about that.)

IV. WHERE DOES THIS LEAVE THE WTO?

A. The WTO continues on its way

The WTO is still operating in Geneva, overseeing the implementation of rules agreed to in the Uruguay Round, and refereeing disputes between its members. World tariff rates, generally speaking, are low; many quotas have been eliminated; some agricultural subsidies have been reduced; global textile trade is opening up; telecommunications and banking markets have been liberalized; basic standards of IPRs protection have been widely recognized; membership continues to expand. Unless one is a strong adherent to the 'bicycle theory', the WTO does not appear in any great danger of going away.

The movement of the world's trade negotiators away from the WTO and into bilateral and regional negotiating forums may well reduce the prospects for new WTO agreements, including results of the DDA, but at least for the near-to-medium term it seems doubtful that the WTO as an institution is at any great risk from the PTA phenomenon. It has simply been relegated to a less central status.

B. The Doha development agenda

It appears virtually incontestable that the focus on PTAs is diminishing prospects for successful conclusion of the DDA, if for no other reason than that trade negotiators are working on other matters. Since the trade concessions being sought by the United States and EU in the PTAs are more extensive in scope than those they are seeking in the DDA—and they are being asked for less in return—one might well ask what incentive the United States and EU have for demanding that the DDA once again take center stage.

One possible answer is that major concessions on non-agricultural market access (NAMA) (e.g., tariff spikes on OECD goods) are being withheld by the major developing country economic actors like Brazil, India and Egypt, and the United States and EU may not be able to secure these concessions on a bilateral basis any time soon. So, there is at least some reason to try to complete the DDA. On the other hand, since the EU and United States are not serious about reducing agricultural subsidies, and since major concessions on agriculture are a condition to success on NAMA, the game at the WTO may not be so much worth playing.

While it seems most likely that the PTAs are perceived as a viable alternative to the DDA, and are almost certainly impeding its conclusion, it is not so clear that this is very important. Developing countries long ago gave up the illusion that the DDA was in fact a 'development round', and it is not as if failure to complete this venture would make a tremendous difference to them in an immediate economic sense.

C. PTAs as models for future WTO negotiations

It is not beyond possibility that a sufficient critical mass of new rules at the PTA level will have emerged over the next five or ten years such that transposing these rules to the WTO will be comparatively easy.[23] A country that has already agreed to protect foreign direct investment in a regional forum, including provision of third party investment dispute settlement, may not balk at negotiating the same rules among a wider group of countries. The WTO might, in effect, 'free ride' on all the PTA activity taking place. To the extent that the PTAs could lead to new 'progressive' agreements at the WTO, this would be perceived as a net benefit to the WTO.

Of course, the developing countries that are presently being pressured to accept PTA terms dictated by the United States and EU may find such a development less than wholly satisfactory, and NGOs would be ready to oppose a 'WTO-encirclement' strategy.

D. WTO reform

What would be needed for the WTO to regain its central role as a forum for trade negotiations? As many have suggested, including in the Sutherland Report, probably some change to the voting structure to enable 'less than consensus' agreements. There is a lot of territory to address in respect to such reform—including especially the implications for the less powerful countries. This brief essay will not attempt to address these difficult issues.

V. ARE PTAS THREATENING?

PTAs have emerged as the dominant new trade species, today surpassing the WTO as the primary focus of trade negotiators. We are in the midst of a sustained period of global economic growth that is raising standards of living in developed and developing countries. In the present circumstances, it is hard to make a compelling case that the PTAs represent an immediate economic danger.

[23] It seems doubtful that the United States and EU are consciously engaging in a 'grand strategy' to create this specific momentum for the WTO because the prospects are rather uncertain.

The most troubling aspect of the PTA phenomenon is the exercise of virtually unconstrained political and economic power by the United States and EU to secure concessions from developing (and developed) countries. While this phenomenon might (or might not) have negative economic implications for developing countries, that is not at the heart of the problem. The heart of the problem is that it deprives developing countries of the capacity to make autonomous decisions about the way their affairs should be governed. Presumably, most imperial leaders have believed they were acting in the best interests of their vassal states, and no doubt in some cases they were. But this does not justify subjugation.

Perhaps, the best case that can be made for encouraging a return to multilateralism is that the weaker actors have a better chance to have their voices heard, and their policy choices taken into account, than in the PTA negotiating environment. In that regard, the present WTO rule of consensus may not be such a bad thing. Some compromises on governance might still be made that would improve the capacity of the WTO to 'move forward', while at the same time preserving the decision-making authority of its less powerful Members.

We are living in a trading environment of bilateralism. It does not appear to be an aggressively threatening environment, but even seemingly benign environments need careful watching. In the late 1940s, the grounds for multilateralism appeared compelling. It is possible we are too optimistic in thinking that those grounds have weakened.

ENSURING THAT REGIONAL TRADE AGREEMENTS COMPLEMENT THE WTO SYSTEM: US UNILATERALISM A SUPPLEMENT TO WTO INITIATIVES?

*Matthew Schaefer**

ABSTRACT

In the mid-1990s, the policy debate within the WTO focused on whether regional trade agreements (RTAs) were building blocks or stumbling blocks for the WTO system, essentially questioning whether regionalism was appropriate at all from an economic policy perspective. Given the proliferation of RTAs since that time and the inability to roll back the clock, that policy debate has been replaced by a search for strengthened constraints on RTA activity that might ensure it complements the WTO system. Three major controversies within many existing RTAs are the exclusion of agriculture from coverage, complex and restrictive rules of origin, and varied treatment of the application of trade remedies. Despite some competing policy considerations, it is likely, on balance, that the WTO system would benefit if agriculture was required to be included in RTA coverage, if RTA rules of origin were simplified and liberalized, and if the controversy surrounding RTA treatment of trade remedies was cleared up. However, the search for constraints within the WTO system to achieve these results, either through the Doha negotiations or the dispute settlement system seems unlikely to succeed in the near future. Accordingly, enhanced and extended efforts by the US, either unilaterally or in conjunction with its RTA partners utilizing its negotiating leverage, may be a necessary supplement to efforts within the WTO in ensuring a more harmonious relationship between RTAs and the WTO system.

INTRODUCTION

Virtually every important WTO member is now party to a Regional Trade Agreement (RTA)[1] and roughly one-half of world trade occurs under

* Professor of Law, University of Nebraska College of Law.
Email: mschaefer1@unlnotes.unl.edu

[1] The term RTA is used throughout this article to refer to customs unions (CU), free trade agreements (FTA) and interim arrangements leading to either a CU or FTA as those terms are

preferential tariff rates. Through the end of 2006, over 368 RTAs were notified to the WTO of which over 260 occurred after January 1995, reflecting a surge in RTA activity that actually began in the late 1980s/early 1990s. It is estimated that by 2010, over 400 RTAs will have been implemented worldwide.[2] The debate in academic and policy circles in the 1990s focused on whether RTAs were building blocks[3] or stumbling blocks[4] for the multilateral system. Specific criticism was directed at the United States for its pursuit of regionalism because of its undue bargaining power in bilateral and small group negotiations. However, US abstinence from RTA negotiations from 1995–2000 did nothing to stem the tide of regionalism. Moreover, the US has traditionally only turned to a robust regional agenda when the WTO system has stalled in achieving further trade liberalization.

Given the proliferation of RTAs, the inability to turn back the clock and the political and diplomatic capital the US has invested in reinvigorating its RTA agenda, the policy debate has moved to an acceptance of the existence of RTAs and a focus on mechanisms both within the WTO system and outside that system that might ensure that this robust RTA activity complements, rather than detracts from, the WTO system. Part I of this article examines *three major controversies associated with RTAs*: the exclusion of agriculture from significant liberalization in many RTAs, complex and restrictive rules of origin established by RTAs, and the varied treatment of trade remedy laws within RTAs. Part II examines existing WTO constraints

---

understood within GATT Article XXIV. The use of the term carries no geographic connotations (i.e. it applies to agreements between countries in different regions, such as the US–Jordan FTA).

2 See www.wto.org (click on trade topics and click on regional trade agreement).

3 Arguments include: (i) the domino effect – creating incentives for third countries, i.e. those outside a given RTA, particularly one featuring a large market such as the US or EU, to participate in multilateral liberalization to reduce negative preference margins they face; (ii) serving as laboratories for experimentation with rules in new areas, e.g. services, intellectual property, etc and (iii) locking in reforms in developing countries. For a discussion of many of these arguments, see, generally, Robert Z. Lawrence, 'Emerging Regional Arrangements: Building Blocks or Stumbling Blocks?' in Richard O'Brien (ed.), *Finance and the International Economy* (1991); Richard E. Baldwin, 'A Domino Theory of Regionalism', in Baldwin et al. (eds), *Expanding Membership of the EU* 25 (1995).

4 Arguments include: (i) those countries in RTA relationships with big markets have less incentive to engage in multilateral liberalization efforts within the WTO and thereby lessen their margins of preference; (ii) an alternative response for third countries is to pursue an RTA with the large market, i.e. become an 'insider' rather than 'outsider'; (iii) RTAs use up necessary political capital and attention, as well as negotiating capacity, to the detriment of multilateral trade liberalization within the GATT/WTO system; and (iv) RTAs create a spaghetti bowl of trade regimes adding large administrative cost to traders and governments alike. See, generally, Jagdish Bhagwati and Arvind Panagariya, 'Preferential Trading Areas and Multilateralism—Strangers, Friends or Foes?' in Bhagwati and Panagariya (eds), *The Economics of Preferential Trade Agreements* (1996); Jagdish Bhagwati and Anne O. Krueger, *The Dangerous Drift to Preferential Trade Agreements* (1995).

on the use of RTAs and explores the possibility of strengthening WTO constraints, in particular to eliminate some of the negative consequences flowing from these controversies. Part III considers what efforts the US could undertake either unilaterally or in conjunction with RTA partners to help ensure that regionalism complements the global trading system. The analysis in Parts II and III reveals a potentially large irony: unilateral actions by the US and actions in conjunction with its RTA partners using the significant negotiating leverage of the US in bilateral and regional negotiations may be more successful than efforts within the WTO, or at least a necessary supplement to efforts within the WTO, at ensuring that RTAs better complement the WTO system.

I. MAJOR CONTROVERSIES REGARDING RTAS

The original GATT (1947–94) and subsequently the WTO system (1995 to present) both allow an exception for RTAs in part because it was thought that the trade creation effects of an RTA that complied with certain conditions laid out in the GATT/WTO system would outweigh any trade diversionary effects (i.e. the growth in trade between the RTA countries would outweigh the loss of trade between third countries and the RTA countries).[5] However, the ambiguities in the conditions laid out in the GATT/WTO system for RTAs have lead to at least three major controversies in the way RTAs have been structured: (i) many RTAs exclude agriculture from coverage, at least to some exent; (ii) many RTAs have highly complex and restrictive rules of origin that might divert trade from third countries as RTA partner countries use inputs from partner countries rather than cheaper inputs from third countries to comply with the rules of origin necessary to gain the preferential tariff rates under the RTA and (iii) many RTAs do not eliminate the application of trade remedies to products from RTA partner countries, thus not leading to full liberalization of internal trade within the RTA, but may give some special treatment in this regard, potentially creating third country impacts. Aside from the legal ambiguities allowing for these controversies, each of these major problems has many economic nuances and numerous competing policy considerations as not only must the trade creation v trade diversion issue be considered *but also the impact of these RTA features on countries incentives to be forthcoming in WTO negotiations.*

[5] See John Jackson, *World Trade and the Law of GATT* 576 (1969)(discussing whether GATT Art. XXIV conditions actually implement this trade creation v trade diversion test); Ken Dam, 'Regional Economic Arrangements and the GATT: The Legacy of Misconception,' 30 University of Chicago Law Review. 615 (1963)(questioning whether GATT Art. XXIV utilizes this test).

A. The exclusion of agriculture

A WTO study early in the Doha Round of negotiations confirmed, both in terms of percentage of trade and duty-free tariff lines, that agriculture is not liberalized nearly as much as industrial products in RTAs.[6] Many RTAs utilize a negative list approach (covered unless specifically excluded) for industrial products and, in contrast, employ a positive list approach (not covered unless specifically included) for agricultural products. Additionally, when an agricultural product is included in an RTA, it tends to be subject to tariff reduction but not duty elimination.[7] Finally, there is less harmonization across overlapping RTAs in agriculture[8] and tariff peaks are more likely to remain in the agricultural sector.

The reason for this phenomenon is that the behavior of countries within their RTAs on agricultural issues tends largely to parallel their behavior on agricultural issues in the WTO.[9] Under this line of thinking, the exclusion of agriculture is merely another symptom or manifestation of the same political sensitivities that prevent significant liberalization in the WTO. However, it may be that allowing RTA activity that largely excludes agriculture is indeed harming multilateral liberalization efforts within the WTO. RTAs that exclude agricultural products allow countries to obtain increased market access in industrial products and engage in new rule development without having to engage in the politically tough liberalization of agriculture – something that they could not get away with in the WTO's 'package deal' framework of negotiations. Assuming the countries pursuing RTAs without agricultural liberalization would chose not to pursue them if they were required to include agricultural goods in a more fulsome manner, then the WTO would be the exclusive forum for them to pursue industrial goods liberalization and new rules creation, and they would only obtain this

[6] See WTO Doc. WT/REG/W/46, 5 April 2002.

[7] According to the WTO study, more than three-quarters of the RTA relationships had less than 50% of agricultural tariff lines at zero duty rates. See WTO Doc. WT/REG/W/46, 5 April 2002.

[8] Particularly low levels of harmonization occur with EC, Israel and Turkey RTAs. See ibid.

[9] Of course, for the small percentage of RTAs that constitute customs unions and achieve deeper levels of integration, such as the EU, the behavior in the WTO may be even more protectionist because of the potential for their negotiating position to gravitate towards the most protectionist country in the customs union. Experience seems to back this view up, although some commentators have argued the opposite –that creation of customs unions with deeper integration, as with the EU, actually leads to greater liberalization because the views/votes of the most protectionist member are offset by other members of the customs union and 'national champions in every industry' are no longer ensured. See Lawrence, above n 3. Which view is correct can depend on a variety of factors within the customs union, including voting practices, informal decision making practices, and other political and economic issues under consideration by member countries of the customs union at the time.

liberalization and the new rules in exchange for agricultural liberalization.[10] Alternatively, countries might actually pursue RTAs that include agriculture more fully and thus start chipping away at the enormous protectionist sentiment in this sector, albeit with some potential for significant trade diversion as high MFN tariff rates charged to third countries impact demand from those countries as compared with RTA partner country products subject to preferential rates. Another possible scenario is that countries with defensive interests in the agricultural sector might simply pursue RTAs with countries that do not threaten their agricultural sectors, but this would at least reduce the amount of RTA activity and still increase the pressure on governments to utilize the WTO forum. Regardless of which of these scenarios played out, a requirement to include agriculture in RTAs would be a net benefit for the WTO system.

B. Complex and restrictive RTA rules of origin

RTAs include rules of origin to ensure that products more closely connected with a third country do not receive preferential treatment under the RTA without the third country paying reciprocal tariff concessions. RTA rules of origin tend to be more restrictive (stringent) than non-preferential rules of origin utilized by countries, particularly on sensitive items. Concerns have been expressed that overly restrictive RTA rules of origin magnify the trade and investment diversionary effect of RTAs. The more complex and restrictive the RTA rules of origin, the more they can lead to companies within the region using partner country inputs rather than cheaper third country inputs in order to ensure compliance with the rules of origin necessary to obtain the preferential tariff treatment afforded by the RTA.

The shear complexity of the rules, particularly when one considers that many countries are parties to numerous overlapping RTAs, creates substantial administrative and compliance costs for traders and customs administrators (often referred to as the spaghetti bowl effect[11]). Indeed, for products in which the MFN tariff rate is low (and thus there is a low preference margin) some traders simply elect to pay the MFN rate than suffer the administrative costs of complying with the RTA rules of origin (e.g. a significant amount of US-Mexico trade occurs at the MFN rate).

[10] While some might counter that forcing agricultural liberalization in RTAs would simply use up countries' political capital and reduce the chances for liberalization multilaterally, on balance, it appears that requiring RTAs to include agriculture would be a boost for multilateral liberalization, both in agricultural and other areas.

[11] Professor Bhagwati (Columbia) coined this term. See Jagdish Bhagwati, 'The Agenda of the WTO,' in van Dijck and Faber (eds), *Challenges to the World Trade Organization* (1996) 27, 49. On the impact of rules of origin, see also WTO Secretariat, Rules of Origin in Regional Trade Agreements, WTO Doc. WT/REG/W/45, 5 April 2002.

However, one irony is that further RTA activity may lessen this spaghetti bowl effect as 'consolidation' occurs among overlapping RTAs. Broad regional RTAs, such as the expansion of the EU from 15 to 25 countries after the enlargement of the EU to include most of central and eastern Europe in 2004, and the now-stalled Free Trade Agreement of the Americas (FTAA) negotiations among 34 countries, may reduce, although clearly not eliminate, the complexity. Another competing consideration is that stringent rules of origin maximize the incentives of third countries to engage in multilateral liberalization since they have little opportunity to 'free ride' on preferences in the RTA. Despite these competing considerations, on balance, it is generally agreed from a policy perspective that less stringent and less complex RTA rules of origin would be better at achieving GATT Article XXIV's goal of creating trade among RTA partners without diverting it from third countries.

C. The treatment of trade remedies (safeguards, anti-dumping)

RTAs vary widely in how they address the application of trade remedy laws among members – from virtual exclusion from such remedies (although usually in the case of safeguards with the establishment of a lesser RTA-specific emergency remedy) to continued application of both global safeguards and anti-dumping laws. However, exclusion from trade remedy laws is rare compared to continued application of such laws.

Many countries are of two minds on the issue of trade remedies in RTAs. Most greatly desire to be excluded from the application of such laws, particularly by large market countries such as the US, in their RTAs with those countries as it would lead to greater trade liberalization. However, when they are outside an RTA offering exclusion, partial or full, from a trade remedy law, they believe their interests are hurt by such exclusion, i.e. they 'take a bigger hit' when remedies are applied. The WTO Appellate Body has not ruled on whether excluding RTA partners from the application of trade remedy laws is required, allowed or prohibited by GATT's exception for regional trade agreements, but they have lessened the latter concern by ruling that there must be parallelism between the imports investigated and the remedy (i.e. a country cannot include RTA partner imports in the investigation—thereby making it more likely that imports will be viewed as a cause of injury to domestic industry—and then exclude them at the remedy stage).[12]

The treatment of trade remedy laws within US and other large market RTAs can have a significant impact on countries' willingness to pursue

[12] See, e.g. WTO Appellate Body Report, United States—Definitive Safeguard Measures on Imports of Wheat Gluten From the EC, WTO Doc. WT/DS166/AB/R, adopted 22 December 2000.

multilateral liberalization. The US continues to be the largest user of anti-dumping laws (although the EU is also a large user and many developing countries are significantly increasing their use of such laws). If the US were to begin offering exclusion from anti-dumping laws in its RTAs, then those RTA partner countries would have a reduced incentive to engage in the multilateral liberalization processes. Similarly, safeguard remedial actions have substantially increased since the creation of the WTO in 1995 (and the banning of so-called gray measures such as voluntary restraint agreements). Thus, exclusion from application of global safeguards is also something desirable for US RTA negotiating partner countries.[13] The US market, in terms of MFN tariff rates, is relatively open. Thus, the largest complaint of foreign trading partners of the US tends to focus on extensive use of so-called 'contingent protectionism' or trade remedy laws.

Of course, one could make similar arguments regarding exclusion of trade remedies to those made with respect to the inclusion of agriculture. If countries were required to exempt RTA partners from trade remedies, then at least some countries, such as the US, might largely cease RTA activity due to the political sensitivity of changing or weakening trade remedy laws. Alternatively, they may conclude RTAs that exempt partner countries from trade remedies, thus slowly chipping away at the protectionist sensitivities, although possibly increasing third country impacts. On balance, however, it is likely that multilateral liberalization efforts will benefit from the US preserving at least the anti-dumping negotiating chip for the Doha Round as this chip is one of the few significant ones the US maintains to force further MFN tariff liberalization within other countries (US MFN rates, as mentioned before, generally being quite low already).[14] Because application of US safeguards remedies is not as big a negotiating chip as anti-dumping laws, it is probably not too harmful to the WTO trade liberalization process if the US replaces global safeguards remedies with RTA-specific emergency remedies vis a vis its RTA partner countries.

II. STRENGTHENED WTO CONSTRAINTS ON RTAS

The three major controversies surrounding RTAs persist due to the lack of clarity surrounding the existing constraints within the WTO. Institutional mechanisms within the WTO system do exist for clarifying and strengthening these existing constraints, however, numerous complications have previously

[13] For example, Australia, having been affected already by US safeguards actions on lamb and steel, showed a great interest in the question of application of US safeguards law in its FTA negotiations with the US.

[14] Of course, the concern of other countries is that the US will not be able to make significant enough concessions on anti-dumping in the Doha negotiations given the enormous resistance to changing anti-dumping laws in the US Congress.

prevented and may continue to prevent the mechanisms from being successfully utilized.

A. Existing constraints[15]

GATT Article XXIV permits the formation of customs unions, free trade agreements and interim agreements leading to the formation of such agreements 'within a reasonable length of time'. However, the language of Article XXIV is broad, imprecise language that, when combined with inadequate review and monitoring, leaves considerable room in practice for auto-interpretation by members to an RTA. (The corresponding language in General Agreement on Trade in Services (GATS) Article V and the language in the Enabling Clause permitting RTAs between developing countries are filled with as much if not more uncertainty and wiggle room). Article XXIV declares that the purpose of an RTA should be to facilitate trade between its members and 'not to raise barriers to the trade' of third countries. In terms of internal requirements for an RTA, Article XXIV requires that 'duties and *other restrictive regulations of commerce* (except, where necessary, those permitted by Art. XI, XII, XIV, XV, and XX)[16] are eliminated with respect to *substantially all trade*'. In terms of external requirements, an RTA cannot impose 'duties and *other regulations of commerce* that are higher or more restrictive' than the general incidence of duties and regulations of commerce existing in the RTA members' territories prior to the formation of the RTA.[17] The Uruguay Round Understanding on Article XXIV clarified certain issues related to compensation negotiations and assessing tariff barriers affecting third party trade upon the formation or enlargement of a customs union[18] and also clarified that a

[15] For a lengthy and detailed analysis, see Robert Hudec and James Southwick, 'Regionalism and WTO Rules: Problems in the Fine Art of Discriminating Fairly,' in Mendoza, Low and Kotschwar (eds), *Trade Rules in the Making: Challenges in Regional and Multilateral Negotiations* (1999) 47–81; WTO Secretariat, Compendium of Issues Related to Regional Trade Agreements, WTO Doc. TN/RL/W/8/Rev.1, 1 August 2002. See generally, John Jackson, *World Trade and the Law of GATT* 576 (1969); John Jackson, *The World Trading System* (1997) 163–173.

[16] These exceptions relate to certain agricultural programs (the scope of which has been reduced by the Uruguay Round Agriculture Agreement), balance of payments considerations, and the so-called general exceptions clause of GATT (protection of human health, conservation of exhaustible natural resources, etc.). The question is raised whether this list of exceptions is exclusive or not. One strong argument that the list is not exclusive is that it fails to list the so-called national security exception found in Art. XXI. It seems unlikely the drafters envisioned preventing a country joining an RTA from applying a security- related measure to its RTA partners. See Hudec and Southwick, above n 15, at 66.

[17] While quite similar, the language regarding customs unions is not identical to that regarding FTAs, for the simple reason that customs unions adopt common regimes vis a vis third party trade while FTAs do not. See, e.g. the language 'on the whole' inserted with respect to customs unions but not FTAs.

[18] The US basically succeeded in having its position on the three issues in contention at the time Spain and Portugal joined the EU in 1986 incorporated into the Uruguay

reasonable period of time for an interim arrangement was generally to be taken to mean ten years. However, the Understanding did *not* clarify several terms related to the specific problems arising out of the increased RTA activity described above.

First, the term 'substantially all trade' was not clarified, leaving open the question of whether such a determination should be based on trade coverage or tariff lines or some combination. For example, the question can be raised whether an RTA that excludes agriculture meets the substantially all requirement if agriculture is a small percentage of trade between the RTA members (perhaps because of high trade barriers) and taking account of the fact that agricultural products constitute roughly 15% of tariff lines. The preamble to the Uruguay Round Understanding states that WTO members recognize that the contribution of RTAs to the expansion of world trade is 'diminished if any major sector is excluded'. While this language might help influence the interpretation of the term 'substantially all', it is not an obligation in and of itself.

Second, the Understanding did not clarify whether the exceptions list to the substantially all requirement is an exclusive list or not. Thus, the question can be raised whether, internally, an RTA would be required (or at least permitted) to eliminate the application of trade remedy laws (e.g. safeguards authorized by GATT Article XIX and anti-dumping duties authorized by GATT Article VI) among members.

Third, the terms 'other regulations of commerce' and 'other restrictive regulations of commerce' were not clarified, leaving open the question of whether RTA rules of origin are included within the meaning of these terms. For example, the question can be raised whether rules of origin should be included in an assessment of whether barriers to third country trade are higher or more restrictive than pre-RTA barriers[19] or even taken into

Round Understanding. For the US and EU positions at the time, see Working Party Report, Accession of Portugal and Spain to the European Communities, GATT 35th Supp. BISD (1989) 295–300. The assessment of whether barriers are higher after the accession is to be based on an overall assessment of weighted average tariff rates and duties collected (not based on trade coverage), is to be done by WTO country of origin, and is to be based on the applied rates of duty.

[19] However, as Hudec and Southwick point out, there are some 'conceptual problems' in considering whether RTA rules of origin to fit within the term 'other regulations of commerce'. Specifically, in considering whether such rules are 'higher or more restrictive' after the FTA than before, we run into the problem of what is the 'before' – because prior to the RTA there were no RTA rules of origin. While one might look to rules of origin of other preferential programs or another RTA, the rules in those programs are designed to determine eligibility to a program with a fundamentally 'different purpose or scope than the RTA' under consideration. See Hudec and Southwick, above n 15, at 57. Note that there may also be complications in comparing different rule of origin regimes existing under different programs and agreements to determine whether one is more restrictive than the other. See ibid, at 59.

account when determining whether substantially all trade has been liberalized among RTA members.[20]

B. Existing review and monitoring procedures[21]

GATT Article XXIV requires countries to 'promptly notify' other WTO members when deciding to enter an RTA and to make available such information as will enable WTO members to make reports and recommendations. In practice, many notifications occur after RTAs are finalized. Under the GATT, individual working parties were established to examine RTAs that were notified to the body. In virtually every review, the working parties were unable to come to any consensus on the consistency of the RTA with Article XXIV requirements. In February 1996, the General Council created the Committee on RTAs in an effort to improve the review and monitoring of RTAs. However, significant problems remain. The committee has only reached consensus on WTO consistency in one case and even most factual examinations of RTAs prepared by the Committee have been held up from adoption. Further, the chairmen of the committee complained in 2002 of the unwillingness of countries to provide, or significant delays in providing, information on their RTAs for the factual examination reports. Some of this unwillingness was alleged to be a result of so-called 'dispute settlement awareness' (i.e. fear that the information will lead to and/or be used against them in a future dispute settlement case).

C. Forums for strengthening constraints

Two possible avenues exist for strengthening the current WTO constraints on RTAs: the broad Doha Round negotiations (originally launched in 2001) and the WTO dispute settlement system.[22]

1. Negotiations

The Doha Ministerial Declaration launching the current round of WTO negotiations provides for the following mandate for negotiations on RTAs: 'clarifying and improving disciplines and procedures under the existing WTO provisions applying to regional trade agreements'.[23] The literature on RTAs is filled with many far-reaching proposals for improving WTO disciplines.

[20] For instance, if a high percentage of trade continues to occur under MFN rather than RTA rates because of complex rules of origin, one might argue that this portion of trade has not been liberalized within the RTA.

[21] Information in this section comes from the WTO web site, www.wto.org (click on regional trade agreements).

[22] I leave aside the slight possibility of the WTO membership utilizing its formal interpretation or amendment powers because such powers have rarely been utilized and would almost surely not occur in the context of RTA disciplines with negotiations in the Doha Round occurring that allow for trade-offs among many issues.

[23] See Doha Ministerial Declaration, para. 29, adopted 14 November 2001.

Most of these are not politically feasible, although some far-reaching proposals in the literature have actually seen reflection in government proposals.

For example, in an effort to end the discrimination against third countries created by RTAs, it has been suggested that the WTO should require that an 'open accession' clause be included in all RTAs.[24] The proposal ignores the key question of what concessions would be required of countries wishing to join, keeping in mind that the phase out periods on tariffs on certain goods is important even if all trade were to be liberalized within an RTA. Such a requirement also ignores the non-trade goals that are important considerations when choosing RTA partners (e.g. Cuba is not a participant in FTAA negotiations).[25] Yet, Taiwan proposed that the WTO require such a clause to be put in all RTA agreements, explaining in response to criticism, that it simply would require an opportunity to negotiate.[26] There have also been suggestions that the WTO should hold negotiations to harmonize *preferential* rules of origin.[27] However, the exceedingly slow progress in the harmonization negotiations of *non-preferential* rules of origin (initially due to be concluded in 1997 but continuing today) cautions against proceeding with negotiations on the trickier topic of preferential rules of origin.

Another proposal in the literature was a proposal that all RTA tariff cuts be extended on an MFN basis five years from the cut thereby limiting the length of time preferences under an RTA could remain in place to five years.[28] This proposal, if adopted wholesale, might lead to 'dirty' RTAs with even more numerous carve-outs and/or dramatically reduce the incentive of third countries to engage in multilateral liberalization (and simply free-ride on RTA tariff cuts as they are multilateralized). However, a US proposal in the Doha Round in 2003 for elimination of all tariffs globally by the year 2015 would have achieved the advantages of the academic proposal (by limiting the length of time that RTA preferences would remain in place) but without the disadvantages because it would not allow for any free riders. Of course, most other countries considered the US proposal too far-reaching and politically infeasible as well because developing countries would lose their preferences under GSP and other schemes

[24] See, e.g. Meredith Lewis, 'The Free Trade Agreement Paradox', 21 New Zealand Universities Law Review (2005) at 554, 574.

[25] It should be noted that the US Administration previously explored with Congress the idea of 'docking' agreements in which the US would negotiate a deal with one nation in a region and another country in the region 'could join into the basic set of rules and structure – probably with a separate market access agreement', according to former USTR Ambassador Zoellick.

[26] See WTO Doc. TN/RL/W186, 3 August 2005.

[27] See Joseph A. LaNasa III, 90 American Journal of International Law (1996) at 625, 637, fn 60 (not proposing it, but describing that it was at one point considered).

[28] See T.N. Srinivasan, 'Regionalism in the WTO: Is Non-Discrimination Passe?', in Anne Krueger (ed.), *The WTO as an International Organization* (1998).

in the industrialized countries' markets and there would be adverse consequences for those developing countries heavily dependent on duties as a source of government revenue (in the absence of improved tax structures and enforcement). To date, only very modest transparency proposals have succeeded in the Doha negotiations and even modest substantive or systemic proposals continue to create significant disagreement among WTO members.

a. Transparency agreement. The Doha negotiations led to an agreement among governments to increase transparency regarding RTAs.[29] In July 2006, WTO members agreed to provisionally implement, pending conclusion of the negotiating round, an agreement that requires WTO members to: (i) inform other members of the launch of negotiations of an RTA; (ii) inform other members of the signature of an agreement and (iii) formally notify an RTA immediately upon ratification. Thus, other members become aware of and can track an RTA's progress from start to finish. The transparency agreement also requires notification to the WTO of changes in implementation or operation of an RTA that occur after the original notification. Information flow is improved by the transparency agreement as it lays out the information that must be provided in notifications including tariff-line data on concessions made in the agreement, trade volume data, rule of origin formulations, etc. Additionally, the dispute settlement awareness problem is partially resolved because factual reports are now prepared by the WTO Secretariat in consultation with the relevant parties.[30]

While this transparency agreement is a potentially useful step forward, it does not resolve any of the substantive differences over key terms in Article XXIV. Moreover, it must be kept in mind that implementation of the transparency agreement is still dependent on the good faith of members (as well as enhanced peer pressure) for compliance and that, generally, there are not any significant penalties for failing to comply with notification/transparency obligations (as many countries have found out with notification obligations in other WTO agreements).

b. Substantive/Systemic proposals. Government proposals on substantive or systemic issues have generally focused on clarifying the term 'substantially all' trade (and the related issues of 'other regulations of commerce' and 'other restrictive regulations of commerce'). As regards the issue of

[29] Proposals submitted by the governments during the negotiations included the following: (i) notification in advance of RTA texts being finalized or ratified; (ii) providing information not just on a trade flow basis, as is currently done, but also a tariff line basis; (iii) biennial reporting on implementation of RTAs; (iv) having the WTO Secretariat or independent groups of experts prepare the factual reports on RTAs and (v) clarifying the legal status of factual examination reports (so as to end virtual paralysis in adopting such reports and perhaps eliminate the 'dispute settlement awareness' problem).

[30] See WTO web site at www.wto.org/english/news_e/news07_e/rta-May07_e.html

'substantially all' trade, members are still in discussions as to whether to use a trade volume-based test or a tariff-line based test or some combination of the two. The problem with a pure tariff-line based test is that parties to an RTA could liberalize a very high percentage of tariff lines but still not liberalize a high percentage of trade if the tariff lines they refuse to liberalize currently constitute a large percentage of the trade between the countries to the RTA. The problem with a pure trade-based test is that trade volumes can fluctuate (and thus an agreement's consistency under a trade-based test might fluctuate as well).[31] A trade-based test might also allow countries to an RTA to exclude many tariff lines from liberalization that currently do not have much trade but might in the future were tariffs to be lowered.[32] Thus, many countries are leaning towards some sort of combined test, particularly those interested in curing the agriculture-exclusion problem riddling many current RTAs. For example, Australia, a significant agricultural exporter, has proposed a type of combined test.[33] Australia's submission suggests that at least 70% of tariff lines be liberalized immediately upon entry into force of an RTA and that 95% of tariff lines be fully liberalized within ten years of conclusion of an RTA. To address, the problem of a few tariff lines with high trade volumes being excluded, Australia would supplement its tariff line approach with a requirement that the top 50 tariff lines in terms of trade volume be included in the duty elimination under the RTA or that any tariff line that constituted 0.2% of total imports be included in the liberalization.

Other countries are not satisfied with a pure quantitative test and want to at least supplement any quantitative test with qualitative factors. For example, Japan proposed that the following qualitative factors be considered: (i) the exclusion of any major sector (although the combined quantitative test of Australia would do a good job of ensuring this does not occur in an RTA); (ii) the influence of trade remedy measures; (iii) the extent of tariff reduction; (iv) an assessment of tariff rate quotas and (v) tariff elimination with long implementation periods.[34] These qualitative factors obviously tie into other issues such as what constitutes 'other regulations of commerce' and the 'reasonable period of time' to implement an interim agreement leading to an RTA. The European Union also favors a qualitative as well as quantitative assessment of RTAs adding a few other factors that might be considered, including special safeguards in RTAs and seasonal restrictions on products.[35] However, qualitative factors might lead to the same ambiguity regarding the consistency of the RTAs with WTO disciplines as occurs today

[31] See, e.g. the Japanese submission, WTO Doc. TN/RL/W/190, 28 October 2005.

[32] See ibid.

[33] See WTO Doc. TN/RL/W/180, 13 May 2005.

[34] See WTO Doc. TN/RL/W/190, 28 October 2005.

[35] See WTO Doc. TN/RL/W/179, 12 May 2005.

and some countries may be suggesting such factors to keep the 'waters muddy' and protect non-robust RTAs from challenge.

With respect to clarifying the term 'other regulations of commerce', India has proposed that it be explicitly agreed that RTA rules of origin fall within the term 'other regulations of commerce'. India's proposal also suggests a requirement that RTA rules of origin be no more restrictive than the most liberal GSP scheme operated by any country member to the RTA. Very few, if any, RTAs, would currently comply with such a condition so one can imagine the distance that still needs to be bridged in the negotiations on this issue.

Perhaps unsurprisingly, given the variations in RTAs, not much compromise or consensus has been achieved on substantive and systemic issues to control RTAs. No draft consensus text has been prepared; indeed, governments have even been reluctant to submit text-based proposals.

c. 'Grandfathering' issue. Some countries, including the European Union, suggested early in the negotiations that existing RTAs should be 'grandfathered', i.e. exempted from any new constraints developed in the course of negotiations.[36] This should be strongly resisted for several reasons. First, it could affect the second avenue to strengthening constraints within the WTO system, namely, it may, depending on how phrased, directly or indirectly affect the ability of a WTO member to successfully challenge an existing RTA in the WTO dispute settlement system. Second, to the extent new substantive constraints only impact or deter future RTAs, those constraints may lock in place a worse state of affairs than would exist with further regional activity for, as noted above, some of the broader regional initiatives currently underway may actually help reduce the existing spaghetti bowl effect. Third, as China pointed out in its submission, grandfathering of existing RTAs would discriminate against countries only recently entering into RTA activity.[37]

2. *WTO dispute settlement system*

The Uruguay Round Understanding on Article XXIV eliminated the uncertainty that existed within the GATT system over whether challenges to RTAs within the dispute settlement system were possible[38] by explicitly

[36] More recently, the EU has stated that 'any future clarifications would have to take into account such variations in approaches by Members, while going beyond lowest common denominator'. WTO Doc. TN/RL/W/179, 12 May 2005.

[37] WTO Doc. TN/RL/W/185.

[38] Under the GATT, there was only one case brought against an RTA within the dispute settlement system. 'In the early 1980s, the United States complained of a series of regional agreements concluded between the EC and Mediterranean countries because they lacked a plan or schedule for completion within a reasonable time and were not reciprocal in some aspects. After a long delay in the proceedings, the panel issued a report in 1985 in which it said that it would not review the conformity of the agreements with GATT Art. XXIV

declaring that the dispute settlement system is open to such challenges. Indeed, the Appellate Body stated (or at least very strongly hinted) in the 2000 Turkey Textiles case that they would examine the conformity of an RTA with the internal and external requirements of Article XXIV if presented with such a claim.[39] Additionally, GATT/WTO jurisprudence does not recognize the concept of latches (i.e. a long delay in challenging an RTA does not lead to a presumption of conformity of the RTA with Article XXIV).[40] Therefore, a case against an RTA is a legal possibility. However, whether such a case becomes a reality depends on several factors. While at least some lawyers in the DC trade bar believe that a government could successfully pursue an RTA challenge, bringing such a case carries several risks. First, because nearly all WTO members are party to a RTA and the standards for reviewing conformity are so broad and imprecise, most members will see at least some defensive interests on the issue. Second, potential plaintiffs will need to consider the interaction between the negotiations and an on-going dispute settlement case. If negotiations on RTAs within the Doha Round are leading to nothing fruitful, then a dispute settlement case might be the only hope for moving towards tangible constraints. It is a strategy not without risk, however, because if a case fails, then there will be even less motivation in the negotiations. Third, there is some institutional risk to the Appellate Body being viewed as 'law making'

---

because this could only be done within Art. XXIV:7 review proceedings. However, the panel seemed to accept a so-called non-violation nullification and impairment argument by the United States and so the EC blocked adoption of the report. After a series of retaliatory actions, a settlement was negotiated in 1986 in which the US pledged no further legal challenges in exchange for reduction in orange and lemon tariffs.' Robert Hudec, *Enforcing International Trade Law* (1993). Note that the Bananas I (1991) and Bananas II (1994) GATT panels (both leading to unadopted reports) also apparently faced Article XXIV defense issues being raised at the margins of the dispute.

39 The WTO Appellate Body has examined Article XXIV's RTA provisions in the 2000 Turkey Textiles case. See Appellate Body Report, Turkey—Restrictions on Imports of Textile and Clothing Products, WTO Doc. WT/DS34/AB/R, adopted 19 November 1999. Turkey imposed quantitative restrictions on Indian textiles because otherwise the EU would not have agreed to include textiles in its RTA with Turkey. (Turkey indicated that if textiles were not included in the RTA, then the RTA would not meet the requirement of liberalizing substantially all trade since such a large amount of EU-Turkey trade is in textiles). However, the Appellate Body did not examine whether the EU-Turkey RTA met the internal (substantially all) and external (barriers not on the whole higher or more restrictive) requirements of Art. XXIV because India did not present such a claim. Rather, the AB only decided that the QRs were not necessary, or more specifically that their absence would not have 'prevented' the formation of a CU between the EU and Turkey, since a certificate of origin scheme would have been a satisfactory alternative to prevent Indian textiles from being transshipped into the EU under the EU-Turkey RTA.

40 See, e.g. panel report in Turkey – Restrictions on Imports of Textile and Clothing Products, WTO Doc. WT/DS34/R, 31 May 1999 (stating that 'it would be erroneous to interpret the fact that a measure has not been subject to Art. XXIII over a number of years as tantamount to tacit acceptance by the contracting parties').

given the broad, imprecise language such a claim would be based upon (similar to the controversy surrounding the Appellate Body's rulings in the area of amicus briefs).[41] Indeed, while the Appellate Body does not like to backtrack, it is possible that they would use a tool of judicial restraint to avoid actually directly addressing a complaint of this nature.[42]

Beyond these general considerations, the most likely plaintiff countries seem to have somewhat mixed interests in pursuing such a case. The countries historically most opposed to increased RTA activity (Japan, Korea, Singapore and Hong Kong), and most likely to be plaintiffs for systemic reasons, are now negotiating and concluding RTAs themselves (signaling a 'if you cannot beat them, join them' mentality). One potential claim that might be made in a challenge to an RTA is that its failure to liberalize a major sector such as agriculture runs afoul of the 'substantially all' criteria for internal liberalization. However, Japan and Korea are defensive on agriculture issues and unlikely to make that particular challenge. Indeed, Japan is having trouble making rapid progress in its RTA negotiations due to its agricultural sensitivities. Korea's paper on RTAs in the Doha Round suggests it has many concerns with RTAs but it is unclear that they would choose to go the dispute settlement route (at least until progress in the negotiations can be more clearly assessed).

The United States is another potential plaintiff. As evidenced by the 1980s challenge to the Euro-Med agreements (EC agreements with Mediteranean countries), a complaint by the United States against an RTA has been taken in the past and continues to be a possibility in the future. An EU RTA would be the likely target of any such case[43] as the United States would surely not want to challenge a Latin American RTA for fear of further harming possibilities of reviving FTAA negotiations at some point in the future. However, the overall status of EU–US relations and some fatigue with other controversial cases suggests that another explosive case, such as an RTA complaint, is likely not in the cards in the near future either.

Australia (or another Cairns group member) is another possible plaintiff. Traditionally, it was thought third country agricultural exporters had no interest in challenging agricultural-exclusions within RTAs (in essence asking to be subject to negative preference margins) but the impact of the large

[41] On the risks of 'law making', see generally Robert Hudec, *Enforcing International Trade Law* 364 (1993). But see also, John Jackson, *Sovereignty, the WTO, and Changing Fundamentals of International Law* (2006) 184–186 (noting that 'gaps and ambiguities' do exist in all treaties, and that in some situations they are appropriately filled in by dispute settlement bodies).

[42] On tools of judicial restraint in the WTO, see generally William Davey, 'Has the WTO Dispute Settlement System Exceeded Its Authority?', 4 Journal of International Economic Law 79 (2001).

[43] As a sign that the EU is aware of their potential exposure to such a claim, they tried at the very end of the Uruguay Round negotiations in December 1993 to have the Art. XXIV Understanding's provisions on dispute settlement deleted.

number of agricultural-excluded RTAs on multilateral liberalization (and/or the view that any RTA-induced agricultural reforms may eventually benefit or expand to third countries) may change this traditional calculation, although to date it has not.

III. EFFORTS THE US CAN UNDERTAKE UNILATERALLY OR REGIONALLY TO ENSURE RTAS COMPLEMENT MULTILATERALISM

With fairly wide disagreement within the WTO negotiations as to how to ensure that RTAs complement the WTO system, and no plaintiff yet willing to step forward within WTO dispute settlement system to challenge the broad legality of an RTA, the question is left as to what actions the United States, as the largest economy in the world and with much negotiating leverage, could take to ensure that at least its own growing regionalism complements the WTO system. Specifically, the question is whether the United States has tools at its disposal as it pursues its regional agenda to ensure that other countries it partners with maintain an incentive to be forthcoming and cooperative in the WTO negotiations and that its RTAs are not overly trade diverting. In fact, there are a series of measures the United States could take unilaterally or in cooperation with their RTA partners using its negotiating leverage to minimize the harmful effects of regionalism on the WTO system, some of which the United States is already undertaking but that could be further emphasized. These measures include the following:

- Explore the possibility of including obligations, not just preambular language, in RTAs requiring WTO partner countries to cooperate positively within WTO negotiations, not just on specific issues but also more generally.[44] While it might be hard to enforce such an obligation, it would certainly provide further negotiating leverage within the WTO when the United States asks for cooperation on progress in the WTO from an RTA partner country.
- Emphasize in broader diplomatic discussions with potential RTA partner countries, the need for those countries to participate actively and positively in WTO negotiations,[45] and continue to make WTO membership and cooperation a condition of launching RTA negotiations with a given country.

[44] Article 3.16 of the US-Chile FTA is an example of where the parties pledge to cooperate in the WTO negotiations on a specific issue area, namely agricultural export subsidies disciplines.

[45] For example, apparently, the US was originally hesitant about 'docking' the Dominican Republic to the FTA with Central American countries because of positions the Dominican Republic was taking within WTO negotiations.

- Explore the possibility of linking, either explicitly or *de facto*, RTA tariff cut accelerations (that reduce the amount of time it takes under an RTA to fully eliminate tariffs on a given product) to progress/concrete results in the WTO multilateral negotiations. In other words, say to RTA partners 'you keep your preference margins for the same amount of time even if you are forthcoming and cooperative in multilateral negotiations because we will reduce the preferential rate under the RTA faster as you cooperate to reduce MFN rates faster within the WTO'.[46]
- Continuing to explore and negotiate sectoral customs unions (i.e. harmonize the tariffs charged to third countries) with RTA partners. Sectoral customs unions reduce the problems and costs associated with applying rules of origin. The United States already has a sectoral custom union with Canada on computers and, given the similarity in MFN rates between the two countries, other sectoral customs unions are possible.[47]
- Continuing to liberalize rules of origin within existing RTAs where possible (e.g. as was done in 2002 and again in 2006 within NAFTA).
- Maintain and improve the high standards of trade coverage in the RTAs it concludes so as to minimize any defensive interests it has with respect to RTAs as regards WTO-compliance but continue to resist exempting RTA partner countries from US anti-dumping law.

It is important to realize that some of these measures are potentially politically difficult, such as tariff accelerations and rule of origin liberalization, depending on what products are involved. Additionally, unlike WTO efforts, these US unilateral efforts cannot 'clean-up' or make more robust those RTAs to which it is not a party. Thus, these US efforts must be viewed as a supplement, rather than a replacement, for efforts within the WTO to improve disciplines on RTAs. However, these US efforts could potentially have a more immediate impact than efforts within the WTO.

IV. CONCLUSION

RTA activity by the United States and even other countries traditionally opposed to regionalism has rapidly expanded in the past decade. This trend is unlikely to be halted as political and diplomatic considerations will require future FTAs even if the WTO negotiations process for further multilateral

[46] Of course, there is already some linkage between the broad regional (but now stalled) FTAA negotiations and the Doha negotiations being demanded by countries such as Brazil that may drive these two negotiations to be concluded at or around the same time. Brazil wants agricultural subsidies issues and anti-dumping issues addressed prior to concluding the FTAA negotiations and the U.S. has made clear that these two issues can only (or largely) be addressed within the WTO negotiations.

[47] See, e.g. Robert Kunimoto and Gary Sawchuk, 'Moving Towards a Customs Union: A Review of the Evidence', at http://policyresearch.gc.ca

liberalization is reinvigorated. Proponents of the WTO system have concerns that this RTA activity, as currently structured, may not be fulfilling the original economic conditions creating the basis for the exception in the WTO system for RTAs. Specifically, there is much concern over the exclusion of agriculture from many RTAs, the use of highly complex and restrictive rules of origin within RTAs, and the varied treatment of trade remedies within RTAs. While the WTO has two mechanisms to cure these controversies, specifically its negotiating rounds and dispute settlement system, doubts exist as to how much progress can be made utilizing these two mechanisms. As a result, and somewhat ironically, US unilateral efforts and use of US negotiating leverage with its RTA partners may be, at the very least, a necessary supplement to efforts in the WTO to ensure that RTAs are complementing the WTO system.

SERVICES TRADE: PAST LIBERALIZATION AND FUTURE CHALLENGES

*Gary Hufbauer** and *Sherry Stephenson***

ABSTRACT

Services trade has truly become an engine of world growth. Over the past two decades, international trade in services has grown faster than world merchandize trade, which in turn has grown faster than world output. A combination of policy liberalization and technological progress has facilitated trade in many previously untradable services. However, very little progress has been made towards new policy liberalization in the ongoing Doha Development Round. This article discusses trade in services in five sections. Following a short introduction, Section I presents data on the past growth of services trade flows and makes rough projections of future expansion. The second and third sections summarize the achievements of the WTO in the service field, both as a negotiating forum and a dispute settlement system. The third section also emphasizes how FTAs are now playing the leading role in services liberalization. The fourth section critiques the absence of progress in the Doha Round and the fifth section examines the hot issue of services outsourcing. The concluding section offers policy recommendations for containing a possible protectionist backlash and promoting new liberalization.

INTRODUCTION

Services trade has truly become an engine of world growth.[1] Over the past two decades, international trade in services has grown faster than world

* Reginald Jones Senior Fellow at the Peterson Institute for International Economics. E-mail: ghufbauer@petersoninstitute.org

** Acting Director of the Department of Trade, Tourism and Competitiveness at the Organization of American States. E-mail: SStephenson@oas.org. Agustin Cornejo and Costantino Pischedda, Research Associates at the Peterson Institute, made substantial contributions to this article. The opinions expressed are the views of the authors and not their affiliated institutions.

[1] Bosworth and Triplett calculate that the services sector was a major contributor to US economic growth in the period between 1995 and 2005, accounting for three-quarters of the gains in total factor productivity. The global expansion of services trade doubtless spread these gains far beyond the United States. Barry P. Bosworth and Jack E. Triplett. 'The Early 21st Century US Productivity Expansion is Still in Services'. International Productivity Monitor, 14 (2007), at 3–19.

merchandize trade, which in turn has grown faster than world output. A combination of policy liberalization and technological progress has facilitated trade in many previously untradable services. If current trends continue, by 2020 recorded services trade flows will reach the level of merchandize trade flows—even though large volumes of services trade are not captured in statistical records. The academic literature points to huge potential payoffs from services liberalization. So far, however, very little progress has been made in the ongoing Doha Development Round. In fact, after an initial spurt of activity, the services area has lagged behind advances in both agricultural and non-agricultural market access discussions.

This article is organized as follows. Section I, following this short introduction, presents data on the past growth of services trade flows and makes rough projections of future expansion. The second and third sections summarize the achievements of the WTO in the service field, both as a negotiating forum and a dispute settlement system. The third section also emphasizes how FTAs have come to play the leading role in services liberalization. The fourth section critiques the absence of progress in the Doha Round and the fifth section examines the hot issue of services outsourcing. The concluding section offers policy recommendations for containing a possible protectionist backlash and promoting new liberalization.

I. A SNAPSHOT OF SERVICES TRADE

A. The picture in 2005

In 2005, world trade in services—broadly defined to include cross border trade in commercial services, consumption abroad, commercial presence abroad, remittances and the income of individuals working abroad on a temporary basis—is estimated to have reached $7.8 trillion, approximately three quarters the size of world merchandize trade. The figures are summarized in Table 1.

Foreign sales of service providers—boosted by huge flows of foreign direct investment in the wake of liberalization and privatization during the 1990s—stood at $5.2 trillion in 2005, accounting for nearly two-thirds of world services trade. Large as it is, this estimate represents a conservative measure of commercial presence (Mode 3 in the GATS typology): it reflects the foreign sales receipts of just the world's top 300 multinational enterprises (MNEs) in the services sector rather than sales of the entire set of foreign-owned service affiliates operating abroad.[2]

[2] It should be noted that a more restrictive measure of Mode 3 would yield a much lower estimate. For example, one could measure 'commercial presence abroad' through repatriated profits of foreign sales of service providers. However, since neither merchandize trade nor any of the other services modes are measured in terms of profits generated, this approach seems too conservative.

Table 1. World Trade in Services (Exports in billions of current US dollars)

	Actuals			Forecasts[a]			Average annual growth			
	1990	2000	2005	2010	2020	2050	81-05	90-05	95-05	00-05
'Modes 1 & 2' (cross-border trade & consumption abroad)[b]	**781**	**1,491**	**2,414**	**3,690**	**8,760**	**130,230**	**8.0%**	**8.6%**	**8.2%**	**9.6%**
Transportation	223	348	569	810	1,610	12,990	6.2%	7.2%	7.4%	10.0%
Travel & tourism	265	479	685	980	2,030	17,930	8.1%	7.5%	6.4%	7.0%
Other commercial services	292	665	1,161	1,900	5,120	99,310	9.4%	10.4%	9.9%	11.2%
'Mode 3' (commercial presence abroad)										
Investment income (BOP)	689	1,431	2,248	3,330	7,330	78,000	na	8.2%	9.1%	10.9%
Foreign sales of top 300 service-sector MNEs[c]	na	na	5,191	8,450	22,410	417,380	na	na	na	na
Broad 'Mode 4' (individuals working abroad)	**69**	**113**	**223**	**360**	**900**	**14,380**	**na**	**10%**	**11%**	**13%**
Workers' remittances	46	73	151	240	590	8,760	na	9%	12%	15%
Compensation of employees	23	40	72	120	310	5,620	na	10%	9%	10%
Total service trade	**na**	**na**	**7,829**	**12,500**	**32,070**	**561,990**	**na**	**na**	**na**	**na**
Addenda										
World merchandise exports	3,449	6,452	10,431	15,420	33,730	352,680	7.0%	8.1%	8.6%	10.9%
Total sales of MNEs (all sectors)	6,045	15,680	22,171	36,100	95,690	1,782,580	12.6%	10.2%	10.9%	14.7%

na = not available.

[a] Forecast based on average annual growth 1990–2005.

[b] Commercial services excluding government services. Consumption abroad entails expenditures of foreign citizens admitted to the country on a temporary basis (mostly tourism).

[c] We estimate a value for 2005 based on the assumption that foreign sales of the top 300 service-sector MNEs represent 50 per cent of their total sales. as reported by UNCTAD's 2004 World Investment Report. The value for total sales for each service-sector MNE is derived from the 'Global 500' database of Fortune Magazine.

The forecast is based on the growth of sales of all MNEs (all sectors).

Sources: IMF (Balance of Payment Statistics); WTO (Trade Statistics Database).

Apart from foreign sales of companies operating in third markets, world trade in services is dominated by cross-border trade in commercial services and consumption of services abroad (Mode 1 and Mode 2 of the GATS). Current statistics record these two modes (partially in certain cases such as tourism) for transport (7% of the world total), travel and tourism (7%), and other commercial services (14%). Again many services provided under Mode 1 and Mode 2—such as educational and health services, recreation, sports and entertainment services—are not captured in the data, yet have become important exports for some countries.

Traditional estimates of Mode 4 (natural persons working abroad on a temporary basis) are based on remittances sent home plus earnings of individuals temporarily residing in foreign countries; together these account for a small share of world services trade.[3] Immigrant remittances, as measured by balance of payment statistics, stood at $151 billion in 2005. Income earned by *temporary* workers was another $72 billion.[4] The estimate would be much larger if the definition of Mode 4 was expanded to include permanent as well as temporary immigrants, and if one considered the income (not just the remittances) of all immigrants as Mode 4 trade.[5]

B. Forecasts based on past growth

Services trade, particularly in Modes 3 and 4, has grown rapidly, even by the standards of world merchandize trade and with all of the current statistical limitations that understate the service flows. Table 1 offers speculative forecasts, based on 1995–2005 average growth rates for each of the components. If the forecasts are roughly right, world service trade could reach the level of world merchandize trade by 2020. By 2050, trade in

[3] Remittances as recorded in international statistical publications and earnings of individuals resident in foreign countries can include income earned from service as well as non-service activities (such as agricultural or factory workers). At the present time it is impossible to separate the sources of the remittance income, so the estimates for Mode 4 may in fact be overstated.

[4] Balance of payment statistics seriously underestimate remittances. The International Organization for Migration (OIM) puts the most recent figure at $233 billion, a 50% discrepancy. The figures on income earned by temporary workers could also be on the low side. Consider for example that, in 2005, the United States admitted just below half a million workers under the H1-B and NAFTA professional worker programs. Assuming a median salary of $55,000, these temporary workers alone would account for $26 billion of annual earnings.

[5] For example, just in the United States the immigrant population is estimated at about 40 million people. Assuming that half of these individuals are employed at an average salary of $35,000, then the hypothetical estimate of US Mode 4 trade, under an alternative broad definition, would increase by some portion (corresponding to service activities) of their total estimated earnings of $700 billion annually. The OIM estimates 191 million migrants worldwide, more than half of which are in 'more developed countries'. Of course most of these persons are permanent, not temporary, residents of their adopted countries and thus would not fall under the category of Mode 4 as currently defined by the GATS.

services under Mode 3 alone (commercial presence) could overtake world merchandize trade.

Two features of the world economy suggest that these projections are not outlandish. First, demographic trends in some advanced countries may soon cause serious labor shortages. Second, if experience in the 1990s is repeated, the world will see substantial unilateral liberalization as well as bilaterally negotiated liberalization of services trade, which is currently much more restricted than goods trade by nearly all countries; perhaps the world will also see multilateral liberalization within the GATS framework.

The International Organization for Migration (OIM) calculates that, by 2030, Europe alone will need twenty million additional workers. Labor shortages will be recorded in Japan, South Korea and Russia as well. In advanced countries both business firms and public officials will likely take population dynamics on board in their planning. Outsourcing (Mode 1) is one response, but Mode 4 trade could also be boosted as a result of active recruitment programs carried out through bilateral, short-term labor agreements (outside the permanently binding context of the multilateral GATS), and more liberal immigration rules. Several bilateral trade agreements have taken timid steps in this direction.

C. Potential gains from liberalization

Significant policy barriers remain on services trade, and progress at the multilateral level has so far been modest. Barriers to trade in services are difficult to quantify because of the sector's characteristics, particularly the regulatory nature of services restrictions. Since many services are highly regulated, barriers often take the form of overtly or covertly discriminatory regulations affecting foreign service providers. Liberalizing services trade, unlike liberalizing goods trade, often involves the movement of factors of production, requiring both capital and labor mobility. Behind-the-border, regulatory barriers on these two factor flows are hard to capture in a single index.[6] As a consequence, most modeling exercises have generated rough estimates of the impact of liberalization on economic welfare

[6] One example would be the various indices estimated by the Australian Productivity Commission (http://www.pc.gov.au/research/rm/servicesrestriction/index.html). Mattoo, Rathindran and Subramanian (2006) and Findlay and Warren (2000) likewise provide a range of estimates. A. Mattoo, R. Rathindran and A. Subramanian, 'Measuring Services Trade Liberalization and Its Impact on Economic Growth: An Illustration'. 21(1) Journal of Economic Integration, (2006), at 64–98. C. Findlay and T. Warren (eds), *Impediments to Trade in Services; Measurement and Policy Implications* (London and New York: Routledge, 2000). The OECD has also recently tried to measure the relative restrictiveness of regulatory barriers to services trade for its member countries in some interesting studies. See OECD (2005), *Modal Estimates of Services Barriers*, as prepared by Nora Dihel and Ben Shepherd, TD/TC/WP(2005)36, OECD, Paris.- OECD (2005), and *Modal Estimates of Services Barriers – Annex*, TD/TC/WP(2005)36/ANN, OECD, Paris. For studies on how to quantity the impact of services regulatory barriers, see OECD (2005a), *The Economy-Wide Effects of Services Trade Barriers*, TD/TC/WP(2005)7, OECD, Paris; OECD, Services Barriers and their

(measured by GDP gains) rather than measuring its impact on trade flows and sales, which would require better data. Robinson *et al.* suggested that '[t]he welfare gain for the world as a whole from a 50% cut of protection in the service sectors is 5 times larger than that from non-service sector trade liberalization. . . .'[7] Stern calculated that free trade in services could result in a global welfare gain of $1.7 trillion.[8]

In his literature review of trade in services, Hoeckman concludes that, despite methodological differences, most indices of services barriers reveal that the highest barriers are found on Modes 3 and 4.[9] Winters *et al.* argue that high barriers on Mode 4 should make this sector especially attractive for negotiations by both advanced and developing countries.[10] Given the large differentials in the relative wage levels between developed and developing economies (which translate into large differences in comparative costs) an enormous potential exists for countries of all income levels to gain through greater labor mobility. The authors conclude that if advanced countries were to grant an annual immigration quota for both skilled and unskilled *temporary* workers equivalent to just 3% of their labor force, the resulting global gains would be about $150 billion annually.[11]

II. WTO FRAMEWORK FOR SERVICES

The original GATT 1947 did not cover trade in services, beyond a few services absolutely essential for the conveyance of goods. Indeed in 1947, few services were tradable, apart from sea and air transport, and tourism. A combination of communications technology, regulatory reform, and privatization of erstwhile state-owned monopolies has substantially increased the range of services trade since the 1970s. The General Agreement on Trade in Services (GATS), adopted as a major part of the Uruguay Round, came into force on 1 January 1995 as an integral part of the new World Trade Organization. The GATS provides a general MFN obligation (subject to exceptions) and a framework of obligations for scheduled services,

---

Economic Impact: Examples of Banking and Telecommunication Services in Selected Transition Economies, OECD Trade Working Paper No.7, OECD Paris (2004).

[7] S. Robinson, Z. Wang and W. Martin, 'Capturing the Implications of Services Trade Liberalization'. Paper presented at the Second Annual Conference on Global Economic Analysis, Ebberup, Denmark, 20–22 June 1999.

[8] Robert Stern, 'The Places of Services in the World Economy', University of Michigan Discussion Paper No. 530, 15 February 2005.

[9] Bernard Hoeckman, 'Liberalizing Trade in Services: A Survey', World Bank Policy Research Working Paper 4030 (2006).

[10] L. A. Winters, T.L. Walmesley, Z.K. Wang and R. Grynberg, 'Liberalizing Temporary Movement of Natural Persons: An Agenda for the Development Round'. 26 (8) World Economy (2003), at 1137–61.

[11] Temporary workers would be required to return to their country of permanent residence after working in the host country for two to four years.

it creates a forum for negotiating further liberalization, and it establishes (through the Dispute Settlement Understanding) a mechanism for countries to settle their differences.

The GATS framework extends fundamental tenets of the GATT to services, including national treatment and most-favored-nation (MFN) principles, and transparency in regulations as part of the basic rules. This is not always done in the same way, however.[12] With respect to actual market opening, the crafters of the GATS opted for a very cautious approach and adopted a 'positive list' approach with respect to market access (Article XVI) and national treatment (Article XVII). Under a positive list approach, the obligations that are voluntarily undertaken by WTO Members apply only to the specific service sectors that are included in individual schedules of commitments. Moreover, the commitments may be circumscribed by limitations that a member enumerates in its schedule. Both the commitments and the limitations are defined on a sector-by-sector and mode-of-supply basis.

WTO Members have many options with respect to the degree of their own services trade liberalization that they choose to pursue under the multilateral GATS system. The agreement in its Preamble references the aim of 'progressive liberalization' no fewer than twice in four paragraphs. Thus WTO Members were given a wide range of choice, with no firm guidelines. They can decide to open markets fully and adopt no limitations on market access and national treatment for their services activities; they can go to the other extreme and make no commitments; or they can make partial commitments in specific sectors and particular modes of delivery (subject to scheduled limitations that in turn become legally binding). There is no rule or understanding in the GATS as to how many sectors or modes of supply need to be included in a schedule of commitments.

The third option (partial commitments) was most widely chosen during the Uruguay Round, a fact that makes it quite difficult to quantify the extent of liberalization accomplished by GATS. The prevailing view among economists, however, holds that only modest results were achieved, as most countries made only partial commitments for limited sectors and accepted binding at existing levels of openness or even less.

While a significant degree of unilateral services liberalization and regulatory reform has occurred in the last decade, the GATS has in fact played little or no role in this process, nor has it yet locked in the results.[13]

[12] For example, WTO Members can qualify the MFN principle through limited exceptions taken out for ten years. These MFN exceptions have tended to become permanent features of the GATS system. And the national treatment provision is not a generalized obligation but rather a specific obligation, applying only when a WTO member schedules a service sector among its commitments, and then only to the extent that national treatment is indicated.

[13] Bernard Hoekman, 'Transatlantic Cooperation on Services: Supporting Multilateralism', Paper presented at the conference 'Sleeping Giant: The Transatlantic Services Market', Washington, 8 February 2007.

Indeed, with the exception of WTO agreements on telecommunications (February 1997) and financial services (December 1997), no multilateral liberalization has occurred under the GATS framework for more than a decade. The provisional offers made to date in the service negotiations under the auspices of the Doha Development Round contain few new market access commitments, but instead, for the most part, would lock in past liberalization.[14] The process of plurilateral services requests that was attempted in 2006 as a catalyst to spur interest in the services negotiations has sputtered out. A central problem in liberalizing services within the multilateral GATS framework of 150 members is to define commitments that are viewed both as beneficial to the countries that undertake them and as significant to their negotiating partners.[15]

The lack of forward movement on services liberalization under the GATS and in the Doha Round is particularly unfortunate given the large potential benefits that might otherwise accrue. A WTO study estimates that services sector liberalization could yield a welfare gain for developing countries of US $6 trillion from 2005–16, four times more than goods liberalization.[16] Another economic model indicates that free trade in services could yield a potential welfare gain to the global economy of $1.7 trillion, more than double that from goods liberalization and thirty times the gain from agricultural liberalization.[17]

III. ACHIEVEMENTS OF THE GATS

With so much potential welfare gains to be had from services trade liberalization, yet so little of it yet realized under the multilateral system, the question arises: What have been the achievements of the GATS? From our point of view, the achievements of the GATS were important, but they lie more in the area of breaking new ground for rules and inspiring further progress in other fora than in actually opening markets. We posit three major accomplishments of GATS which we comment on below:

- The GATS has provided a framework of rules for services at the multilateral level, thus marking the equal importance of trade in goods and services, and heightening the awareness of services internationally;

[14] Rudolf Adlung and Martin Roy, 'Turing Hills into Mountains? Current Commitments Under the General Agreement on Trade in Services and Prospects for Change'. 39, Journal of World Trade, (2005), at 1161–94.

[15] Aaditya Mattoo, 'Services in a Development Round: Three Goals and Three Proposals', 39, Journal of World Trade, (2005), at 1223–38.

[16] See 'Services Negotiations Offer Real Opportunities for all WTO Members and More so for Developing Countries' WTO NEWS, 2002 Press Release (28 June 2002) available from http://www.wto.org/english/news_e/pres02_e/pr300_e.htm, cited in *Making the Most of the Doha Opportunity: Benefits form Services Liberalization (2006)*, U.S. Coalition of Service Industries Research and Educational Foundation, Washington DC, page 1.

[17] See Stern, above n 8, at 7.

- The GATS has been successful in resolving trade disputes involving services through the WTO panel process; and
- The GATS has inspired negotiators at the regional level to improve upon both its rules and liberalizing mechanisms.

A. GATS has heightened the awareness of services trade

The negotiation of the GATS and its incorporation as part of the Uruguay Round Agreement under the World Trade Organization in 1995 marked the end of nearly half a century in which trade had been defined under the GATT only in terms of merchandize. The widely held perception of services as 'invisibles' or 'non-tradeables' was finally uprooted with the creation of GATS. Services thus began to acquire the legal importance that they merited in economic terms for many years. And the understanding of the ways in which services could be traded, together with the applicability of the theory of international trade and comparative advantage to the service sector, slowly spread to academics and policy-makers around the world. In just a decade, the importance of services trade to modern economies and to international trade is no longer doubted.

Placing services on an equal footing with goods in world trade rules through the GATS agreement also underscored the importance of building national statistical institutes capable of recording the data along the lines of the four modes of service supply. This has proven to be a more challenging task than simply recording the entry of goods under a specific tariff nomenclature. The need to better grasp the quantitative aspect of services trade led to the creation of an inter-agency task force on service statistics that labored for several years to improve and disaggregate the categories of services trade to be captured for Modes 1 and 2 (cross-border trade and consumption abroad) and to create ways to capture services trade for Mode 3 (commercial presence).[18] The fruit of this labor was the 2002 Manual on Statistics of International Trade in Services, published by the United Nations, which defines a new set of service sector products for statistical reporting. These categories follow closely those that have been defined in the WTO for the purpose of the GATS services negotiations (known as the list

[18] See United Nations, *Manual on Statistics of International Trade in* Services (2002), ST/ESA/STAT/SER.M/86, Department of Economic and Social Affairs, Statistics Division, Statistical Papers Series M No. 86, Geneva, Luxembourg, New York, Paris, Washington DC. The Manual can be found at http://unstats.un.org/unsd/tradeserv/manual.htm. The inter-agency task force that developed the Manuel was composed of the following organizations: OECD, IMF, WTO, UNCTAD and the United Nations Statistical Department. The Manual is being gradually implemented by all United Nations members. Data on Modes 1 and 2 are reported in the IMF Balance of Payments Manual while data on Mode 3 can be found in national statistical publications setting out the activities of foreign affiliates (FATS statistics).

W/120 of July 1991).[19] Due to these efforts, which were inspired by the GATS, in a few more years it will be possible to have a much more precise account of the actual magnitude of services trade. Already the thirty-four members of the Organization for Economic Cooperation and Development (OECD) are collecting and publishing their service statistics on a much more disaggregated basis.[20]

B. GATS has successfully resolved trade disputes over services

The WTO has played an important role in establishing the importance of services trade through its dispute settlement system. The GATS was placed on an equal footing with the GATT 1994 and the TRIPS with respect to the WTO dispute settlement mechanism. Any dispute arising in the context of the agreements listed in the Dispute Settlement Understanding (DSU), including the GATS, can be brought to the WTO. Interestingly, the WTO also envisages the possibility of cross-retaliation in the case of non-compliance of panel decisions, as between the three WTO pillars—the GATT 1994, the GATS and the TRIPS.[21] To date, there have been three major service disputes adjudicated by WTO panels, as well as a number of trade disputes involving goods with services dimensions.[22]

Three of the high profile cases invoking obligations within the GATS framework are the US–EU *Banana* case, the Antigua–US *Gambling* case, and the US–Mexico *Telecoms* case. In the first case, EU compliance with its commitment on wholesale distribution services was brought into question, though the case focused on the EU banana regime; in the second case, US compliance with its commitment on recreational services was brought into question, as well as the definitional aspect of the commitment; in the third case, the dominant Mexican telecom carrier, Telmex, sought to preserve its monopoly by thwarting Mexico's commitment to national treatment for foreign carriers. In all three cases, whose main elements are summarized below,

[19] The W/120 list is based on a condensed version of the United Nations Commodity Classification Product Listing for Services. Although there is now a revised version of the UN CCP, the WTO Members have preferred to stay with the original listing rather than to adopt the revised version for fear of disputes over reclassification and definition of legally binding commitments.

[20] OECD Statistics on International Trade in Services: Detailed Tables by Service Category, 1996–2005, 2007 Edition. This publication shows the value of each member country's exports and imports of services by category of service. See http://www.oecd.org/document/43/0,3343 and 3355. A complimentary publication, OECD Statistics on International Trade in Services: Detailed Tables by Partner Country 2001–04, shows partner country breakdowns for trade in services as a whole, transport services, travel, other commercial services and government services (balance of payments basis). Information about how to purchase it can be found at: http://www.oecd.org/document/18/0,3343.

[21] TRIPS is the acronym for the WTO agreement on Trade Related Intellectual Property Rights.

[22] Hector Millan-Smitmans, 'Dispute Settlement in the Services Area under GATS', in Sherry Stephenson (ed.), *Services Trade in the Western Hemisphere*, Washington DC: Brookings Institution (2000), at 105–36.

the DSB held that the respective legally binding GATS commitments had to be respected. One decision (*Gambling* case) may even allow for cross-retaliation.

1. The EU Banana case[23]

In the mid-1990s, the United States and a few Latin American countries filed several complaints against the European Union's banana regime, which afforded preferential entry to the prized EU market for bananas from overseas territories and former colonies, while restricting entry from other regions, in particular Latin America. US banana wholesalers—Chiquita Brands International and Dole Food Company—are major actors in Latin America.

The US angle of the larger dispute over banana trade centered on the supply of wholesale services through commercial presence (Mode 3), with respect to which the EU had scheduled a fully open commitment under the GATS, with no limitations on national treatment or an MFN exception. The United States claimed that the EU banana regime violated GATS Articles II (MFN) and XVII (national treatment), to the detriment of US wholesalers. In May 1997, a WTO panel found the EU banana regime inconsistent with these GATS provisions; the Appellate Body (AB) substantially confirmed the panel's ruling in September 1997. Importantly, the AB ruled that a measure affecting the supply of a service, or a service supplier, also falls within the scope of the GATS when the measure in question directly regulates trade in goods, rather than trade in services. The panel and the AB went on to find that the EU banana regime violated national treatment and MFN commitments, because, *de facto*, it offered less favorable conditions in terms of import licenses to the US banana wholesalers than to the EU wholesalers.[24]

2. The Antigua Gambling case[25]

In 2003, tiny Antigua and Barbuda brought a WTO case against US measures that prohibit online gambling.[26] The dispute was triggered by a US court decision in 2000 to sentence a US national to twenty-one months in jail for selling gambling services to US citizens from the island of Antigua.

[23] *European Communities—Regime for the Importation, Distribution and Sale of Bananas* (WT/DS27).

[24] For a detailed legal analysis, see Zdouc (1999). Werner Zdouc, 'WTO Dispute Settlement Practice Relating to the GATS', 2 (2) Journal of International Economic Law (1999), at 295–346. After the 1997 rulings, the EU modified its banana import regime, but the United States objected and, in 1999, a WTO arbitration panel found against the new system. In April 2001, the dispute was temporarily resolved with a bilateral agreement. See Eliza Patterson, 'The US-EU Agreement to Resolve the Banana Dispute'. ASIL Insight (April 2001) and Charles E. Hamrahan, 'The US–European Union Banana Dispute', CRS Report for (December 2001). However, the banana case is now back on the WTO plate. It is worth noting that a similar issue as to the discriminatory treatment of wholesalers arose in *Canada-Certain Measures Affecting the Automotive Industry* (WT/DS142), but in that dispute the Appellate Body reversed the panel's finding of a violation because of inadequate proof that the GATS was implicated by Canada's duty exemption scheme.

[25] *United States—Measures Affecting the Cross-border Supply of Gambling and Betting Services* (WT/DS285).

[26] Gambling services are Antigua's second largest industry, after tourism.

Antigua's case was based on the fact that the United States had committed under GATS not to impose restrictions on the import of 'recreational services', and on the claim that online gambling belonged to this category. The United States defended its position by arguing that gambling services should be considered 'sporting services' (subject to restrictions in the US schedule in GATS). In addition, the United States contended that its ban was justified under GATS Article XIV, which allows trade restrictions to 'protect public morals or to maintain public order.'

In November 2004, a WTO panel held that the US ban was tantamount to a quantitative restriction on service imports from Antigua and thus violated GATS market access provisions (Article XVI).[27] The panel also held that US enforcement efforts were skewed in favor of US-based suppliers of gambling services, thus the panel rejected US arguments based on public order and morals (Article XIV). In April 2005, the AB upheld the panel's definitional finding that online gambling should be considered a recreational service rather than a sporting service, and thus concluded that the ban violated GATS Article XVI. The AB also found that the US ban on online gambling was applied in a discriminatory way as between US-based and offshore suppliers.[28] At the end of March 2007, a WTO compliance panel found that the United States had failed to comply with the previous WTO recommendations and rulings.[29]

In May 2007, the United States took the novel approach of announcing that it would 'comply' by modifing its schedule of national treatment commitments to exclude online gambling from 'recreational services'.[30] It seems doubtful that the WTO will find that such a retroactive change represents compliance; the US 'solution', if accepted, would radically devalue the worth of scheduled commitments.

3. *Cross-retaliation*

The Antigua-US dispute is particularly interesting because it might establish a precedent, based on a panel decision in the services area, for the adoption of 'cross-retaliation' measures. WTO rules allow a prevailing member to retaliate, by imposing restrictions on its bilateral trade flows, if the losing member does not abide by the DSB ruling (DSU Article 22.3). Standard retaliation measures normally entail punitive duties against items

[27] The interdiction to conduct internet gambling was viewed by the panel as a zero quota, or thus a quantitative restriction, falling under GATS Article XVI on Market Access.

[28] For concise summaries of the panel and AB findings, see Joost Pauwelyn (2004 and 2005). Joost Pauwelyn, 'WTO Condemnation of US Ban on Internet Gambling Pits Free Trade Against Moral Values'. ASIL Insight (November 2004) and Joost Pauwelyn, 'WTO Softens Condemnation of US Ban on Internet Gambling, but Confirms Broad reach into Sensitive Domestic Regulation'. ASIL Insight (12 April 2005).

[29] Brendan McGivern, 'WTO Compliance Panel Report: United States—Gambling',White & Case International Law (31 March 2007).

[30] *International Herald Tribune* (22 May 2007).

imported from the losing member under the violated agreement (and, when possible, against products within the sector that is the subject of the dispute). Cross-retaliation refers to countermeasures applied under a different WTO agreement than the locus of the dispute. The WTO may allow cross-retaliation when it is not 'practicable' or 'effective' for a member to impose penalties under the violated agreement.

Only limited precedents exist for cross-retaliation. In 2000, a WTO dispute arbitrator granted Ecuador permission to adopt cross-retaliation measures against the European Union because the EU had failed to comply with the WTO ruling on its banana import regime. Ecuador was authorized to suspend some of its obligations under the WTO TRIPS Agreement involving patents and copyrights, and the suspension was valued at $200 million. However, Ecuador chose not to avail itself of its cross-retaliation rights. In the *Gambling case*, Antigua will reportedly ask the WTO for permission to copy and export US-content DVDs.[31] Antigua is prepared to argue that retaliation against US exports would have no impact on the US economy, given the huge disproportion in economic size between the two parties. On the other hand, says Antigua, interruption of intellectual property rights might prompt a forthcoming US response, because Hollywood and software companies would lobby the US government to find an acceptable solution.[32]

4. The Mexican Telecoms case[33]

In terms of commercial importance, the Mexican telecoms case dwarfs the other services disputes so far resolved by the WTO, but the legal issues were relatively straightforward. In its GATS schedules, Mexico committed to national treatment for access by foreign carriers to its telecommunications network. The commitments were taken in the Telecommunications Agreement of 1997 (Protocol IV of the GATS), at a moment when Mexico eagerly anticipated cheap, reliable and innovative telecom service.

Telmex, the dominant national carrier which was privatized in the early 1990s and soon came under the control of Mexico's richest billionaire, Carlos Slim, had a different agenda. Telmex did everything in its power to block foreign carriers and maintain sky-high rates. Prompted by US telecom carriers, the United States launched a WTO case against Mexico in 2000. The panel completed its report in April 2004, and easily found that Mexico violated its GATS commitments by failing to ensure interconnection at cost-oriented rates, by failing to prevent anti-competitive practices, and by failing to ensure reasonable and non-discriminatory access to its

[31] Paul Blustein, 'Against All Odds: Antigua Besting U.S. in Internet Gambling Case at WTO'. *The Washington Post*. 4 August 2006.

[32] Sallie James, 'US Response to Gambling Dispute Reflects Weak Hand', Free Trade Bulletin no. 24 (6 November 2006).

[33] *Mexico—Measures Affecting Telecommunications Services* (WT/DS204).

telecommunications networks. Mexico prevailed on one important issue, however: the panel ruled that Mexico had not committed to national treatment for non-facilities based services (notably, cross-border telecom services relayed by satellite).

Since the facts were clear and the legal issues straightforward and since the Mexican government was happy to break the Telmex monopoly and give Mexico the benefit of lower rates and better service, no appeal was taken. Mexico and the United States reached an agreement in June 2004, at the same time that the DSB adopted the panel report, and in August 2005, Mexico published a new set of telecom resale regulations.

C. GATS has inspired a new generation of regional trade agreements

The GATS can ironically also count among its major achievements the inspiration of a new generation of regional trade agreements that have improved upon its own limitations and developed an alternative model for liberalizing services trade. The GATS framework reflected experience with the US-Israel FTA (1985), the Canada-US FTA (1989) and NAFTA (1994).[34] However, due to strong opposition from developing countries in the GATT, the GATS Agreement could only be finalized in the form of a significant compromise that embodies a weak set of rules and a very fluid mechanism for services liberalization. In fact, the GATS model is almost diametrically opposed to that which the US and other countries have followed at the regional level. It has been the NAFTA model and not the GATS that has inspired subsequent United States free trade agreements and that is now being duplicated throughout the world by the United States and its trading partners, particularly Mexico and Chile.[35]

This alternative model for services agreements differs considerably from the GATS in important ways. FTA negotiators developed an integrated framework, setting out chapters on investment, standards, transparency, government procurement, competition policy, electronic commerce and dispute settlement that cover both goods and services. In addition, they devised chapters on cross-border services trade, telecommunications, financial services and other subjects that apply to services alone. Negotiators also incorporated disciplines that are cross-referenced in the

[34] Gary C. Hufbauer and Sjamsu Rahardja, *Toward a US-Indonesia FTA. Policy Analyses in International Economics 83*. Washington: Peterson Institute for International Economics (2007). Sherry Stephenson, 'Regional versus Multilateral Liberalisation of Services', 1 (2) World Trade Review (2002), at 187–209.

[35] Sherry Stephenson, 'Regional Agreements on Services and Multilateral Disciplines', in Sherry Stephenson (ed.), *Services Trade in the Western Hemisphere*. Washington: Brookings Institution Press (2000) 86–105. Sherry Stephenson, 'Services', in Maryse Robert and Jose Manuel Salazar (eds), *Towards Free Trade in the Americas*. Washington: Brookings Institution Press (2003), at 163–86.

areas of domestic regulation and transparency for investment both in services and goods.

The strength of the NAFTA template for services trade resides in two main features: the comprehensive coverage of the agreement as it applies to all service sectors and all service measures (other than reserved sectors such as air transport and services provided under government authority on a non-competitive basis), and the generalized application of its disciplines. These core disciplines include MFN, national treatment, market access, and a provision guaranteeing cross-border trade without restrictions (no local presence requirement). Additionally, the discipline on domestic regulation is permanent, applies to regulations affecting all services activities, not just those included in scheduled commitments (as under the GATS). The comprehensiveness and depth of disciplines are strong distinguishing features of this regional approach championed by the United States.

To date there have been twenty-two FTAs (involving twenty-three countries) negotiated post-2000 by the United States and other nations that include services and have followed the negative-list approach.[36] The United States has negotiated more than half of these, some twelve agreements. Four of these FTAs are in the process of Congressional approval at the time of writing this article.[37] US trading partners that have adopted this alternative approach for services trade liberalization are found in Latin America, the Middle East and in East Asia. Future FTAs on this model are contemplated. In fact, a stand-alone agreement on services between the United States and the European Union is being discretely viewed as an option if the Doha Round negotiations stall.

In terms of actual services liberalization, the various FTAs negotiated by the United States and other countries that follow this template set a high standard. The objective of these FTAs is to remove all limitations on market access and all discrimination connected with national treatment, so as to make service markets in partner countries fully contestable. This is carried out through the negative-list approach, which means that the only exceptions to the core disciplines mentioned above are those listed in the annexes to the agreement in the form of non-conforming measures. Since all of the national

[36] The negative-list approach to services trade liberalization in FTAs has been adopted by the following countries: (i) in the Western Hemisphere: United States, Canada, Mexico, Costa Rica, Guatemala, El Salvador, Honduras, Nicaragua, Dominican Republic, Panama, Colombia, Peru, and Chile; (ii) in North Africa and the Middle East: Jordan, Bahrain, Oman, Morocco, and the UAE; and (iii) in Asia and the Pacific: Japan, Korea, Singapore, Australia and New Zealand. The FTAs negotiated under the negative-list approach in the Western Hemisphere comprise 87.5% of all services trade for that region of the world (Source: calculations carried out by OAS Department of Trade, Tourism and Competitiveness, May 2007).

[37] These are the FTAs between the United States and Peru, Colombia, Panama and Korea. The President has notified Congress of his intention to sign all four, and they are awaiting Congressional votes (as of July 2007).

regulatory measures constituting the legal framework affecting services are examined during the negotiating process, this procedure means that governments must justify and clearly document any restrictions that they would wish to remain. The documentation is based on actual laws, regulations and decrees in place. Thus the annexes to these regional agreements, in stark contrast to the opaque complexity of the GATS schedules of commitments, clearly set out all of the remaining restrictions affecting services trade, at least at the federal level and often at the state or provincial level as well. This makes the FTAs not only more liberalizing instruments but also more 'user-friendly' to service exporters who need to know the local legal framework.

An example of the extent to which these negative-list FTAs have worked to liberalize services trade can be illustrated by the financial services and telecoms chapters in the US–Singapore FTA. In the realm of securities, the FTA grants market access, MFN and national treatment, thereby opening Singapore's market to US investment firms. US investment firms that establish mutual funds in Singapore are allowed to use personnel based in the United States to manage the securities held in the fund portfolios. Singapore pledged to ease the local staffing rules for US asset management and insurance companies that offer their investment products to the Central Provident Fund, Singapore's mandatory national savings scheme.

In telecoms, the FTA addresses interconnection, resale of services, and non-discriminatory access. It grants all US telecommunication companies market access to all of Singapore's telecommunications sectors and vice versa.[38] However, the United States adopted a reservation to maintain its restrictions on ownership of US radio licenses, and Singapore took a similar reservation. The FTA also guarantees further liberalization of Singapore's express delivery services by granting market access to US firms and improving customs administration (even though Singapore took a reservation on its postal services).

In spite of their progress on the services liberalization front, FTAs have not been able to crack the tough barriers associated with Mode 4 (more on this subsequently). As a corollary, this has meant that bilateral trade in professional services area has not progressed as rapidly as it might have. For example, in the US–Singapore FTA, the agreement sets out a best endeavor clause to ease entry procedures for legal, architectural, engineering and other professions, but without specific or binding obligations, while

[38] By contrast, under the WTO, Singapore has committed to giving market access in select telecom markets to only three foreign telecom providers. For a comprehensive review of East Asian Service agreements, see Carsten Fink and Martin Molinuevo, *Liberalization of Trade in Services*, World Bank (June 2007).

a number of reservations remain in place regarding residency and registration requirements and other national treatment differences.

IV. DOHA DEVELOPMENT ROUND NEGOTIATIONS

By their continuous emphasis on agricultural barriers, the negotiators in the Doha Development Round have implicitly assigned a secondary priority to barriers that hamper services trade. The resulting absence of significant offers for new services trade opportunities through the request-and-offer process of the negotiations, begun in 2002, has meant that US and EU service firms have little incentive to act as political counterweights against the protectionist aspirations of their national agricultural lobbies.

As of early 2007, the proposals put forward by the major trading nations would not result in substantial cuts in trade and investment barriers to services.[39] The European Union and other developed WTO Members have made very narrow offers on the temporary provision of labor services (Mode 4), an issue central to the demands of developing countries (the United States has made no new offer on Mode 4). On the other hand, emerging economies like Brazil, Mexico, South Africa, Malaysia, Thailand and Indonesia, have made few concrete offers to reduce their current levels of protection for domestic service firms, in particular concerning financial services, telecommunications, air transport, and distribution.

The plurilateral negotiating process that began in 2006 after the Hong Kong Ministerial Meeting (held in December 2005) was viewed as a way of providing renewed energy to the services negotiations. While the process helped WTO Members to build upon their initial discussions, the plurilaterals ended after several months with little to show in concrete progress toward revised offers.[40] Given the regulated nature of services trade, the time required to reach agreement on liberalizing reforms at the national level—an indispensable prerequisite to making substantial offers in the WTO talks—is much longer than in the goods area. Agreement at the national level involves a large number of actors—government ministries, service regulators, service providers, and services professional associations—and it takes time for consultations to forge a consensus among so many players.

At the time of this writing (June 2007), the foreseeable content of a Doha deal in services is limited, consisting mainly of 'lock in' provisions for reforms already undertaken.[41] However, even limited progress would create

[39] Jeffrey J. Schott, 'Completing the Doha Round', in *Policy Briefs in International Economics* (October). Washington: Institute for International Economics (2006).

[40] Johannes Bernabe and Shuaihua Cheng, 'The Doha Round Negotiations on Services: An Overview', document prepared for the German Marshall Fund of the United States and presented at the Salzburg Seminar, Austria, 16 February 2007.

[41] An important exception to this gloomy scenario is a possible agreement (comprising a 'critical mass' of WTO members) to liberalize computer services; such an agreement does not seem far-fetched at the time of this writing (Steve Steward, presentation on 'Expanding services

a more predictable and stable policy environment for trade and investment in many developing economies, some of them desperate to attract foreign investment. One option at this point for the Doha negotiations that was used in the telecommunications negotiations of the Uruguay Round might entail 'pre-commitments' that would be phased in over time. Pre-commitments have the advantage of locking governments into a reform program but allowing this to be carried out in an acceptable time frame.

V. SERVICE OUTSOURCING: THE NEXT FRONTIER

One of the new frontiers of services trade is that of internet-based services. During the short existence of the GATS, there has been a tremendous boom in the supply of services traded cross-border, (Mode 1) through the internet. This is due to new economic opportunities as well as changes in technology so that firms are able to more easily source service inputs from foreign suppliers.[42] As part of Mode 1, internet services and thus outsourcing would fall under the legal disciplines of the GATS, as seen earlier in the discussion of the *Antigua Gambling case*. However, the lines of application of GATS disciplines are not always as clear as they should or could be, largely due to the very general manner in which services commitments are described in national schedules.

The growth of internet services poses challenges both for the international trading system, as well as for the internal political economy debate on trade and the impact of internet-traded services on employment and wages. With respect to the former, Zleptnig argues that WTO Members should make a greater effort to clarify the scope and interrelationship of the application of the main GATS obligations to internet services, particularly as between the market access, national treatment and domestic regulation obligations, so as to clearly delineate in which way an internet service is covered, regulated or prohibited.[43]

---

trade in Doha: computer services', for the Conference 'Services Trade and the Doha Round', 13 April 2007, Washington).

[42] In this article, service 'outsourcing' and 'offshoring' are used as synonyms, referring to a firm's purchase of services from abroad. We are not concerned whether the service provider abroad is an independent party or an affiliate of the firm purchasing the services; in other words, for our purposes we ignore the distinction between so-called 'outsourced offshore activity' and 'captive offshore activity' (also known as 'arms-length' and 'intra-firm' offshoring respectively). For a brief discussion of definitional issues, see GAO (2005) and McKinsey (2005). McKinsey (Global Institute). *The Emerging Global Labor Market*. June 2005, http://www.mckinsey.com/mgi/publications/emerginggloballabormarket/(accessed on 13 March 2007).

[43] Stefan Zleptnig, 'The GATS and internet-based services: between market access and domestic regulation' 20 *Cambridge Review of International Affairs* (2007), Routledge, London.

The growth of internet services in the form of outsourcing has come to the forefront in national economic discussion as well as at the WTO. While global production networks have existed for decades, traditionally they involved the use of imported material inputs for domestic production. Material outsourcing is still quantitatively dominant for advanced economies, but in the recent years services offshoring has captured the political debate.[44] This section discusses the size of the outsourcing phenomenon and whether or not it is a legitimate cause of concern for jobs and wages in developed economies.[45]

Using US imports of computing and other business services as a proxy for service outsourcing, Amiti and Wei calculate that the offshoring of services doubled in each of the past two decades as a share of US GDP, from 0.1% in 1983, to 0.2% in 1993, to 0.4% in 2003.[46] By contrast, the share of material outsourcing is about 12% in the United States (steadily increasing but more slowly than service outsourcing).[47] Alternative measures of outsourcing, calculated on an industry basis using input/output coefficients, suggest a similar picture: services offshoring by manufacturing industries is still at very low levels compared to materials outsourcing, but services outsourcing grew at an average rate of 6.3% between 1992 and 2000, compared to 4.4% for materials outsourcing.[48] Insurance (2.8% of total sales) and business services (2.2%) are the most intensively outsourced in the United States, followed by communications (1.2%), computer and information services (0.6%), and financial services (0.5%). However, the range of jobs sent offshore has broadened to encompass not only less skilled activities like call centers and insurance claims, but also more skilled professions like

[44] David Hummels, Ishi Jun and Kei-Mu Yi, 'The Nature and Growth of Vertical Specialization in World Trade', 54 (1) Journal of International Economics (2001), at 75–96. For example, it is claimed that over 80% of the Boeing 787 will be outsourced, and that only final assembly will take place in the United States (Dominic Gates, 2005. 'Boeing 787: Parts from around world will be swiftly integrated', *Seattle Times*. September 11; David Pritchard and Alan McPherson, 'Strategic Destruction of the North American and European Commercial Aircraft Industry: Implications of the System Integration Business Model', Canada-United States Trade Center Occasional Paper No. 35, January 2007).

[45] One of the most respected living economists, Nobel laureate Paul Samuelson, has given these concerns prominence. Paul Samuelson, 'Where Ricardo and Mill Rebut and Confirm Arguments of Mainstream Economists Supporting Globalization', 18 (3) *Journal of Economic Perspectives* (2004), at 135–46.

[46] Mary Amiti and Shang-Jin Wei, 'Fear of Outsourcing: Is It Justified?', CEPR Discussion Paper No. 4719 (October). London: Center for Economic Policy Research (2004).

[47] Similar relationships are observed in the United Kingdom: service outsourcing (growing fast) was calculated at 1.2% of GDP in 2003, and material outsourcing (actually shrinking) at 27% of GDP. Ekholm and Hakkala (2006) present an analogous picture for Sweden, with service offshoring growing faster (again from a much smaller base) than material offshoring. Carolina Ekholm, and Katariina Hakkala, 'The Effect of Offshoring on Labour Demand: Evidence from Sweden', CEPR Discussion Paper No. 5648 (April). London: Center for Economic Policy Research (2006).

[48] Mary Amiti, and Shang-Jin Wei, 'Service Offshoring, Productivity and Employment: Evidence from the US', CEPR Discussion Paper No. 5475 (February). London: Center for Economic Policy Research (2006).

accounting, consulting, computer software, architecture, and health and financial services.

The management consulting firm McKinsey found that, over the period 1980–2002, offshoring of services from advanced economies to developing countries grew faster than international trade in manufacturing and services.[49] McKinsey went on to forecast a 30% annual growth of services outsourcing to emerging markets between 2003 and 2008 (raising the outsourcing share of world trade in services from 3% to 10%). The wider range and enhanced volume of industrial services being offshored reflects foremost the digitization of information, but also rising education levels in the developing world and broad integration in the world economy.

A different but also rapidly growing form of service outsourcing is 'medical tourism'. In 2003, an estimated 350,000 people traveled to Cuba, India, Jordan, Malaysia, Singapore, and Thailand to purchase health services.[50] Patients from industrialized countries travel to world-class medical centers in developing countries to receive high-quality treatments, sometimes at a fraction of prices charged at home.[51] As with other forms of service outsourcing, the price differentials reflect much lower labor costs in developing countries.[52]

The growth of private service outsourcing has generated objections in advanced economies, voiced in the political debate. Widespread fears have taken hold over the supposedly inexorable disappearance of white-collar jobs, to the benefit of well-educated but underpaid workers in the developing world, particularly India and China. [53] In the US media, stories abound over the seemingly invincible competition of Indian call-center workers, software engineers, insurance claim workers and accountants (paid one-fifth to one-tenth the US rate).[54]

But the common perception of outsourcing as a one-way flow of jobs from advanced economies towards developing nations is misinformed. Using imports of business services as a proxy for service outsourcing, Amiti and Wei found that, in 2002, the United States was the top outsourcer in dollar

49 See McKinsey, above n 42, at 20.

50 Aaditya Mattoo and Randeep Rathindran, 'Does Health Insurance Impede Trade in Health Care Services?' World Bank Policy Research Working Paper 3667 (July 2005).

51 *The Guardian* reported an estimate of 50,000 UK patients going to Thailand, South Africa, India, and Cuba in 2003 to receive a variety of medical treatments ('Sun, sea, sand... and surgery'. 11 May 2004). Woodman (2007) estimates the number of American medical tourists in 2006 at 150,000. Josef Woodman, *Patients Beyond Borders: Everybody's Guide to Affordable, World-class Medical Tourism*. Chapel Hill, NC: Healthy Travel Media (2007).

52 Over 70% of US hospital costs are labor related. See Matto and Rathindran, above n 50, at 22.

53 For example, a study by the University of Maryland (cited by Amiti and Wei 2006, above n 46) found that support for free trade dropped from 57% in 1999 to 28% in 2004 among white-collar workers earning over $100,000 a year.

54 See, for example, Robert J. Samuelson, 'The Specter of Outsourcing', *The Washington Post*. 14 January 2004, A19.

amount, followed by Germany, Japan, the Netherlands, Italy, France, and the United Kingdom. India and China occupied the eleventh and the eighteenth positions, respectively in the world ranking. However, when the value of service offshoring is measured as a share of GDP rather than raw dollars, smaller countries like Angola, the Democratic Republic of Congo, Mozambique, and Ireland appear as top outsourcers, while the United States and the United Kingdom rank 117th and 85th, respectively, while India and China rank 44th and 99th, respectively. In 2006, insourced skilled work in India grew faster (42%) than call-center work (34%).[55] This situation is in stark contrast to the very few commitments (or none at all) that developing countries have made in their service schedules on Modes 1 and 2.

Industrial countries are also major insourcers in raw dollar terms. Using exports of business services as a proxy for insourcing, Amiti and Wei (2004) rank the United States, the United Kingdom, Germany, France, and the Netherlands as the top five insourcers. India and China occupy the sixth and the fourteenth positions respectively.[56] Relative to its economic size, the United States ranks higher as an insourcer than as an outsourcer (90th vs 117th); the same is true for the United Kingdom (33rd vs 85th).

A. The impact of outsourcing on employment and wages

Available evidence suggests that widespread fears of massive job losses in industrial countries due to outsourcing are overblown. While large cost differentials are a driving determinant of outsourcing to developing countries, not all services can be traded across the border: some services are location insensitive (e.g. computer programming) while others are much more difficult to outsource (not only haircuts and taxi drivers, but also divorce lawyers and office managers).

Moreover, as Ricardo's comparative advantage reminds us, it is a combination of productivity and cost differentials, not labor costs alone, that determine whether a country will specialize in a certain economic activity. Jensen and Kletzer found that US workers in tradable services activities have significantly higher wages and skill levels than workers in either non-tradable services or manufactures.[57] This finding is entirely consistent with the common understanding of US comparative advantage. Thus, contrary to the fears of Lou Dobbs and Alan Blinder, the fact that a certain high-skill service activity *can*

[55] Jared Sandberg, 'How Long Can India Keep Office Politics Out of Outsourcing?', *The Washington Post*. 27 February 2007, B1.

[56] See Amiti and Wei above n 46, at 21.

[57] J. Bradford Jensen and Lori K. Kletzer, 'Tradable Services: Understanding the Scope and Impact of Services Outsourcing', Institute for International Economics Working Paper number WP 05-9 (September 2005).

be outsourced to a developing country does not predict that the activity is *likely* to be outsourced.[58]

The McKinsey study estimated that, in 2008, the theoretical maximum number of service jobs that could be performed remotely and therefore outsourced world-wide will be 160 million out of 1.46 billion service jobs, or about 11%. McKinsey estimated the share of US service jobs that could be outsourced at 9%, or about 10 million jobs. The study did not predict that all of these jobs will actually be outsourced, due to multiple regulatory and company-specific barriers. In fact, the report argued that company-specific barriers are usually a bigger obstacle than regulatory barriers, although in some sectors regulatory barriers are critical.[59]

McKinsey estimated that about four million jobs in 2003 were performed in developing countries for companies and customers in *all* industrial countries. Forrester Research estimated the total number of US service jobs outsourced to both developed and developing countries in 2005 at 0.8 million; Forrester Research also projected an increase to 3.4 million by 2015.[60] These figures look less dramatic when one considers that the US economy each year turns over about thirty million jobs.[61]

Again, despite fears, service outsourcing will probably not exert a significant impact on wages in industrialized countries, given the relatively small percentages of workers affected. The maximum number of US services jobs that might be outsourced, based on the McKinsey calculations mentioned earlier, amounts to 9% of total US services jobs. If half of these jobs move offshore within the next thirty years, the annual rate of offshoring comes to under 200,000 jobs, under 1% of the thirty million-plus jobs annually created by the US economy.

The other side of the globalization of labor markets is represented by the rapidly increasing number of insourced service jobs in the United States.

[58] Lou Dobbs, *Exporting America: Why Corporate Greed is Shipping American Jobs Overseas*. New York: Warner Books, (2004). Alan S. Blinder, 'Offshoring: The Next Industrial Revolution?' *Foreign Affairs*. New York: The Council on Foreign Relations (2006) vol 85 (2).

[59] In the case of medical tourism, US regulatory barriers are a major obstacle. The major federal insurance programs, Medicaid and Medicare, as well as most private health plans, cover medical treatment received abroad only under exceptional circumstances. See Mattoo and Rathindran n. 50, at 22. However, there are signs of changing attitudes on the part of US health insurers, which are eager to contain soaring costs ('Medical Tourism: Sun, sand and scalpels', *The Economist*. 8 March 2007). Regulatory barriers include labor and product market regulations at home, plus weak protection of intellectual property rights in the offshore market. Company-specific barriers can be operational (some companies have business processes that are too convoluted to be performed remotely) or structural (some companies operate on too small a scale to benefit from offshoring).

[60] 'Forrester finds near term growth of offshore outsourcing accelerating', Press release on 17 May 2004. Available at http://www.forrester.com/ER/Press/Release/0,1769,922,00.html (accessed on 13 March 2007).

[61] 'Trade disputes: Nagging doubts about the benefits of globalization, and a look at the evidence', *The Economist*, 18 September 2004. The figure for jobs turned over includes all persons leaving their employment, both voluntary and involuntary quits.

In 2004, overall US employment at insourcing companies (i.e. US affiliates of foreign companies) amounted to 5.1 million jobs, of which approximately 2.9 million (or nearly 57%) were in the service sector.[62] These numbers are not exactly comparable with their outsourcing counterparts. Services outsourcing generally refers to services performed abroad but destined for consumption at home, while many of the insourced jobs are designed to serve the US domestic market (for example, a local branch of a large Swiss or Dutch insurance company). But these statistics have the merit of balancing the image of services trade as a one-way street from advanced economies to developing countries.

VI. THE FUTURE ROLE OF THE WTO

The GATS was a path breaking instrument when it was negotiated in the mid-1990s. In the services area, however, the world has moved quickly since then, and the GATS is no longer at the forefront of either rules-making or services trade liberalization, its two most important functions. For the GATS to maintain its relevance and hopefully reacquire prominence at the services frontier, it will need to confront and move forward positively on four main challenges, as set out below.

A. Keeping channels open for the electronic delivery of services

Although the public image of outsourcing may be exaggerated and inaccurate, the alarmed attitude of policy makers in advanced countries, particularly the United States, could trigger new protective measures. What can the WTO do, if anything, to forestall a possible protectionist backlash?

As seen earlier, electronic delivery of services is part of services trade through Mode 1. Electronic outsourcing at present takes place in a context of low applied barriers. The issue facing the WTO over the next decade is whether the current open regime, in applied terms, can be locked in, to forestall the possibility of discriminatory regulation and taxation. Locking in this openness could be achieved through an agreement among WTO Members to adopt a negative-list approach for national treatment and market access for agreed service sectors under Modes 1 and 2, apart from agreed and narrow exceptions.[63]

Another approach would combine liberalization in cross-border trade with comparable initiatives in Mode 3 (commercial presence abroad). This would

[62] US Bureau of Economic Analysis (BEA). 'Employment by Majority-Owned Nonbank U.S. Affiliates, Industry of Affiliate by Country of Ultimate Beneficial Owner, 2004.' Available at www.bea.gov (accessed on 13 March 2007). The BEA data covers only majority-owned nonbank US subsidiaries of foreign companies. Therefore the reported number of insourced jobs is conservative, as it excludes a large number of jobs in banking.

[63] Aaditya Mattoo and Sacha Wunsch, 'Preempting Protectionism in Services: The GATS and Outsourcing', World Bank Policy Research Working Paper 3237 (March 2004).

be more balanced in market access terms, as illustrated by services trade between India and the United States. Indian software firms and call centers could continue and expand their access to the US market; while US financial firms, big box retailers, and other service providers could establish their commercial presence in India. However, this would effectively amount to a radical strengthening of GATS disciplines, as it would involve a movement from a positive to a negative-list basis for scheduled commitments on Modes 1, 2 and 3.

B. Liberalizing temporary labor movement, Mode 4

Liberalization of GATS Mode 4 (temporary presence of natural persons abroad) would offer big economic benefits both to host and source countries. Yet no form of services trade is more controversial.[64] An old dictum holds that nothing is more permanent than a temporary worker. Immigration, whether temporary or permanent, raises the specter of downward pressure on wages in the host country and cultural clashes. Labor ministries, and their supervising parliamentary committees, stoutly resist ceding jurisdiction over immigration to trade officials.

The stringent barriers facing Mode 4 liberalization have so far proved almost immune to liberalizing initiatives under the GATS framework, with the notable exception of intra-corporate transferees. While the GATS provisions for Mode 4 service delivery do not enumerate minimum levels of skill, nevertheless most national regimes allow the temporary presence of certain categories of skilled or professional labor only. The services negotiations in the Doha Round have therefore not covered categories of semi-skilled or unskilled workers (by the implicit choice of WTO Members).

The GATS needs to find a way to move the discussion on Mode 4 forward in a mutually beneficial manner. The challenge is to make progress on the area of professional services in the first instance, by expanding the categories included in national schedules and fostering the further liberalization of intra-corporate movements, as well as expanding coverage to independent professional service providers. Most countries already offer quite liberal conditions of access for managers, executives and specialists who are transferring between locations within the same MNE; a meaningful deal should extend these benefits to a broader range of skilled employees.[65]

Liberalizing efforts under the WTO should also extend to the movement of high-skill, professional and business personnel working on a contract basis.

[64] Mode 4 liberalization lies at the core of the disagreements between the United States and India in the ongoing Doha negotiations. Until April 2007, India conditioned its acceptance of US demands for substantial market access concessions in agriculture and financial services on US offers in Mode 4, a very touchy political issue in the United States. However, in April 2007, the Indian Minister of Commerce and Industry, Kamal Nath, somewhat relaxed his stance. Bruce Stokes, 'India's Paradox', National Journal (2007).

[65] Mattoo offers recommendations along similar lines. See Mattoo, above n 15, at 9.

In these cases, an employee of a foreign-based company travels to the host country to provide services pursuant to a contract between his employer and a foreign customer. By its nature, contract-based presence is more likely to be temporary, and therefore more acceptable politically in host countries.[66] Requiring a bond as an enforcement mechanism would give additional assurance that the foreign employee is working on temporary basis.[67]

Outside the WTO, bilateral trade and labor agreements often regulate short-term flows of *low-skill* workers.[68] Such provisions have been kept outside the GATS framework because they are highly idiosyncratic and addressed at cyclical economic needs. They also respond to specific immigration pressures within countries. GATS Article V and Article V *bis* allow MFN exceptions respectively for economic integration and labor market integration agreements, and the latter should be granted special MFN exceptions upon request (though to date this has rarely been solicited).[69] Given existing political sensitivities, this 'division of labor' between the WTO and bilateral agreements is a reasonable one.

C. GATS and future developments in dispute settlement

The discipline of cross-retaliation may represent the most important evolution of the WTO dispute settlement mechanism, insofar as services are concerned. The need for cross-retaliation is a direct consequence of the huge disparity that exists between WTO Members (illustrated by the contrast between the United States and Antigua). Allowing a small country to suspend the enforcement of certain intellectual property rights within its territory may induce the large country to comply with an adverse WTO ruling. Moreover, in some circumstances (e.g. trade between the European Union and Egypt) trade in commercial services may essentially be a one-way flow (except for tourism). Unless the European Union, in this example, can retaliate against Egyptian merchandize, it might have no practical means to induce compliance if Egypt breaches a commitment in financial services.

However, tension exists between the need to give more 'bite' to the WTO in asymmetrical disputes and the general mission of the WTO to assure predictability in the world trading system. Clear criteria need to be developed, guiding the arbitration panels that decide actual cases, so as to identify circumstances when cross-retaliation is permissible and the form it

[66] Ibid, at 27.

[67] Mark Hatcher, 'Draft Model Schedule for Mode 4: A Proposal', in Aaditya Mattoo and Antonia Carzaniga (eds), *Moving People to Deliver Services*. Washington: Oxford University Press and the World Bank (2003).

[68] Julia Nielson, 'Labour Mobility in Regional Trade Agreements,' in Aaditya Mattoo and Antonia Carzaniga (eds), *Moving People to Deliver Services*. Washington: Oxford University Press and the World Bank, (2003).

[69] In bilateral agreements, as a *quid pro quo* for host country liberalization, source countries may commit to take on pre-movement screening and selection, accept and facilitate return, and fight illegal migration (Mattoo, 2005, above n 6).

should take. WTO arbitration panels need to ground their decisions on sound and predictable economic calculations, a feature sometimes missing from past arbitral rulings. When cross-retaliation is authorized, the need for sound calculations is particularly important; for this purpose, arbitration panels need to be serviced by highly competent economists lodged in the Secretariat.

D. GATS and future services trade liberalization

Possibly the main challenge of services at the multilateral level will be to bring about greater services trade liberalization. The GATS has been static for the past ten years, while services trade has progressed tremendously, both technologically and in volume. Meanwhile, the depth and breadth of services commitments (very limited in the case of most developing WTO Members) have remained the same since 1997. The positive-list approach of the GATS has not brought about significant liberalization; the burning question is how to improve upon this approach so that such liberalization can actually be forthcoming at the multilateral level. The difficult, time-consuming and unwieldy request-and-offer technique is still the vehicle for services negotiations, but it has effectively stymied all progress. WTO Members need to realistically assess this situation and bring about useful improvements. In the absence of adopting a negative-list across-the-board approach, sectoral negotiations could be pursued that would offer greater potential for significant liberalization. Proceeding by sectors would offer the opportunity to coalesce the main service exporters and importers around a common and well-focused set of liberalizing and regulatory objectives.

Until WTO Members decide to make the GATS a vehicle for real services liberalization, much of the policy innovations and actual market-opening in services trade over the next decade is likely to take place within the framework of bilateral and regional FTAs. The WTO should certainly keep abreast of these developments, with a view to encouraging the compatibility of these agreements with the highest standard possible under the GATS and promoting the MFN application of resulting liberalization whenever feasible. In addition, the WTO could offer to make its dispute settlement mechanism available, if parties so wish, to resolve questions that might arise under bilateral and regional FTA commitments.

REGULATORY JURISDICTION AND THE WTO

*Joel P. Trachtman**

ABSTRACT

The WTO is not explicitly concerned with the problem of regulatory jurisdiction in connection with prudential regulation (as opposed to industrial policy regulation). However, as the WTO has addressed increasingly complex regulatory barriers to trade, it has developed several devices that have the implicit effect of allocating regulatory jurisdiction among states. This article reviews a few illustrative cases in WTO law, including *Helms–Burton*, *Shrimp*, and *Gambling*. This review suggests how these cases may be understood as dealing with allocation of regulatory jurisdiction. Negative integration rules such as national treatment or proportionality may serve as devices applied by tribunals for allocation of regulatory authority. The WTO has very limited rules of positive integration—whereby states either harmonize regulation or agree on more specific allocations of regulatory authority, such as mutual recognition. However, it has developed a modest degree of capacity to engage in positive regulation, or to refer to positive integration rules developed in other contexts, such as Codex Alimentarius. Finally, this article examines theoretical bases for allocating and reallocating regulatory jurisdiction in order to establish a framework by which to analyse the role of the WTO in this context.

INTRODUCTION

In the international setting, questions often arise as to the scope of application of national law. These questions are often examined under the heading of 'choice of law' relating to private law, such as contract or tort, or 'extraterritoriality' or 'prescriptive jurisdiction'[1] relating to public law, such as anti-trust, securities law, or export controls.

* E-mail: joel.trachtman@tufts.edu

[1] Restatement (Third) of Foreign Relations Law 401 (1987) [hereinafter, Restatement Third], distinguishing prescriptive jurisdiction, on the one hand, from judicial or enforcement jurisdiction. Prescriptive jurisdiction is the state's power 'to make its law applicable to the activities, relations, or status of persons, or the interests of persons in things, whether by legislation, by executive act or order, by administrative rule or regulation, or by determination of a court.' For an economic analysis of prescriptive jurisdiction, *see* Joel P. Trachtman, 'Economic Analysis of Prescriptive Jurisdiction and Choice of Law', 42 Virginia Journal of Internation Law (2001) 1.

On the other hand, public international law has generally not directly addressed the issue of choice of law or extraterritoriality. While there are some notable exceptions, including international tax treaties, and some private international law treaties that deal with choice of law either directly or indirectly, many issues are not addressed by public international law. Although there are some arguments to the effect that customary international law provides limits of reasonableness,[2] the scope of these limits is at least debatable.

However, with the growth of economic integration, and with the growth of national regulation, the question of the scope of application of regulatory law may increasingly be understood as a trade issue, and has increasingly been addressed in international trade law.[3] This seems appropriate to the extent that the greatest concern raised by the exercise of regulatory authority is protectionism. However, it is important to note here that other concerns are raised by the exercise of regulatory authority.

It should come as no surprise that the main role of international law is to restrain the scope of action by the state, and so it is natural that we would find that international law already restrains the scope of national regulation in some contexts and to some degrees. Furthermore, to the extent that further restraints on national autonomy to regulate are desirable, it would be useful to assess the types of international legal instruments available to do so.

Trade law traditionally imposed only a narrow set of limits on national autonomy. It restricted measures 'at the border', such as tariffs and quotas. It also prohibited export subsidies. This indeed may be understood to be a reduction of regulatory autonomy, but the regulatory autonomy addressed is a particular kind of industrial policy, with pronounced external effects. Trade law did not traditionally address regulation with more 'prudential' purposes, with more incidental external effects, except to require that it be applied to imported and domestic goods on a non-discriminatory basis.

However, especially since the conclusion of the Uruguay Round and the advent of the WTO in 1995, trade law has become more intrusive. Its intrusion seems to be a response to what might be called the first law of trade dynamics: the law of conservation of protection. Protection exists at an equilibrium of demand for protection and supply of protection. It follows that if the supply of protection from one instrument is reduced, the supply from another instrument will be increased to meet demand. Thus, as tariffs and other more traditional protection was reduced, negotiators could expect, and did expect, an increase in other forms of protection. To the extent that

[2] According to sections 402–403 of the Restatement Third, and according to a number of states and scholars, there are substantial limits on a state's right to assert extraterritorial jurisdiction.

[3] For an early work examining trade law in regulatory jurisdiction terms, *see* Joel P. Trachtman, 'Trade in Financial Services under GATS, NAFTA and the EC: A Regulatory Jurisdiction Analysis', 34 Columbia Journal of Transnational Law (1995) 37.

these other forms are more costly to use, we may see an overall decrease in protection.

It thus appears that domestic regulation may be the next frontier of protection. And so, the WTO Agreement on Sanitary and Phytosanitary Measures (SPS Agreement) and the Agreement on Technical Barriers to Trade (TBT Agreement) began to discipline domestic regulation more intensively. While the WTO General Agreement on Trade in Services (GATS) did not impose substantial disciplines on domestic regulation, the recent *Gambling* case at least raises some questions about the extent to which the WTO Appellate Body will fill this gap through interpretation.

Part I of this article provides three case examples of instances in which the allocation of regulatory authority was at least implicitly at stake in WTO disputes. Part II examines the possibility of mutual recognition in connection with WTO rules, and describes mutual recognition as a type of transaction in regulatory authority. Part III of this article explains how analysis of these types of WTO disputes, in terms of allocation of regulatory authority allows the invocation of a theoretical perspective that understands WTO legal rules as transactions in regulatory authority. Once we understand WTO law as being concerned with transactions in regulatory authority, a normative perspective based on property rights theory becomes available.[4] This normative perspective indicates that (i) some types of allocation of authority may best be addressed through adjudication under various standards, while (ii) some types of allocation of authority may best be negotiated under rules of essential harmonization and mutual recognition.

I. CASES OF ALLOCATION OF REGULATORY AUTHORITY

This part shows that many important types of WTO cases deal with allocation of regulatory authority. This is not just a gloss. Rather, my claim is that the core substantive issue in these cases is that of allocation of regulatory authority. In fact, it can be argued that all WTO cases are concerned with allocation of regulatory authority, just as all applications of international law are concerned with the question of whether the respondent state retained or transferred authority to effect the measures at issue. But the cases discussed here can be understood more directly than the typical trade remedies case as relating to allocation of regulatory authority.

A. Shrimp three ways

At the core of the *Shrimp*[5] case is the jurisdictional question: can the United States regulate the way in which Indian, Malaysian, Pakistani, and Thai

[4] See Trachtman, above n 1.

[5] Appellate Body Report, *United States—Import Prohibition of Certain Shrimp and Shrimp Products*, WT/DS58/AB/R, adopted 6 November 1998, DSR 1998:VII, 2755.

fishermen fish for shrimp, as a condition for access to US markets? So, immediately we must recognize that this is not direct regulation by the United States: it is not the direct exercise of regulatory authority to require specified behaviour by private persons. In fact, it is indirect in two ways. First, United States requirements are merely a condition for the right to export to the United States Depending on the elasticity of demand, and the availability of other markets, the US law might not affect behaviour. Second, the US conditions access to its markets on whether these fishermen's governments specified acceptable rules for the protection of sea turtles. So, the United States did not directly seek to influence the behaviour of these fishermen, but of their governments.

Nevertheless, the indirectness of the US attempt to regulate fishing by Indian, Malaysian, Pakistani, and Thai fishermen does not mean that the United States did not seek to exercise regulatory authority. Perhaps one would argue that if the United States decided to apply its law directly, a customary international law rule would have prevented it doing so. In fact, this case is not so different from the *Lotus* case, which remains the leading reference for the public international law of jurisdiction. In that case, it will be recalled, the master of the Lotus, a French vessel, made the mistake of landing in Constantinople (now Istanbul). Just so, we might say that the fact that the Malaysian shrimp landed in US ports provides a similar 'hook' for the exercise of jurisdiction (*in rem*, if not *in personam*). But no general international law argument was made, and this case was decided based on a nuanced understanding of at least four parts of GATT. The rest of this section will show that this nuanced understanding included elements that can be identified as relating to allocation of jurisdiction.

1. National treatment and the product-process distinction

In the *Shrimp* case, the United States essentially conceded that its measure either violated Article III of GATT, or was not covered by Article III of GATT, because it was a 'process' regulation. Although there was no argument regarding Article III in this case, it is important to my discussion of the *Gambling* case, below, that, pursuant to an interpretation of the *ad note* to Article III, measures *subject to* Article III are not subject to Article XI. The United States conceded that its measure violated Article XI of GATT, prohibiting quantitative restrictions on imports of goods, and went on to argue that Article XX of GATT provided an applicable exception.

The first, and rather modest, point that I wish to make here is that a rule of national treatment can be understood as a rule of allocation of regulatory authority: the importing state may treat imported goods precisely the way that it treats domestic goods, and cannot treat the imported goods worse. Thus, the importing state is empowered to exercise territorial authority over imports. This allocation of authority is the opposite of a rule of recognition, by which the importing state must accept the exclusive application of home state regulation.

Second, the product–process distinction[6] can be understood in jurisdictional terms. The product/process distinction serves as a kind of territorially-based allocation of jurisdiction, in which the product, which travels to the importing state, is permitted to be regulated by the importing state. WTO jurisprudence has not yet clarified whether Article III 'applies' to or covers process-based regulatory distinctions. If Article III does not cover process-based regulations, then, pursuant to the understanding mentioned earlier of the ad note to Article III, these regulations will be viewed as border import restrictions (a ban of relevant products), controlled by Article XI. If Article III covers process-based regulations, the Appellate Body's application of a competition-based test in *Asbestos* suggests that in many cases, different PPMs would be insufficient to make products 'un-like'. The test under Article III would then prohibit treating like products differently on the basis of process-based considerations. In this sense the product/process distinction may often serve as a proxy to control the extraterritorial application of national measures which extra-territorial application is perhaps exceptionally permitted under the circumstances set forth in Article XX.

2. Article XX territoriality?

Nor do we have a definitive interpretation as to whether relevant provisions of Article XX, such as Article XX(b), of GATT, allow exceptions for actions by importing states to protect values outside their territory.[7] In *Shrimp*, the Appellate Body avoided addressing this issue on the grounds that the relevant 'exhaustible natural resource'—sea turtles—were migratory and might enter US waters. Again, we are left with uncertainty as to whether the exception is available, and so whether the importing state will be able to regulate, in order to protect non-territorial concerns. This question is functionally similar to the product–process distinction question.

All this uncertainty may be viewed as making for a relatively tense, and contentious, regulatory terrain. However, as we will see subsequently, uncertainty is not always bad.

[6] For discussions of the product/process distinction, see Robert E. Hudec, The Product-Process Doctrine in GATT/WTO Jurisprudence, in Marco Bronckers and Reinhard Quick (eds), *New Directions in International Economic Law: Essays in Honour of John H. Jackson* (The Hague: Kluwer Law International, 2000); Robert Howse and Donald Regan, 'The Product/Process Distinction-An Illusory Basis for Disciplining 'Unilateralism' in Trade Policy', 11 European Journal of International Law (2000) 249, and the cogent response to the Howse and Regan article from John Jackson at 11 European Journal of International Law (2000) 303.

[7] For a useful discussion in the human rights context, *see* Lorand Bartels, 'Article XX of GATT and the Problem of Extraterritorial Jurisdiction: The Case of Trade Measures for the Protection of Human Rights', 36 Journal of Word Trade (2002) 353.

3. Locating a line of equilibrium in the chapeau of Article XX

In a more subtle way, the Appellate Body's interpretation of the chapeau of Article XX may be viewed in jurisdictional terms as well. This allocation of authority relates the contention between the respondent and the complainants on a horizontal level to contention over how WTO law deals with norms from other treaty systems.

In *Shrimp*, the Appellate Body stressed the fact that the chapeau of Article XX is a recognition of the need to maintain a balance between the right of a member state to invoke one of the exceptions in Article XX and the substantive rights of other members under GATT rules. It noted that the task of applying the chapeau is a delicate one of finding and marking out a 'line of equilibrium'[8] between these two sets of rights in such a way that neither will cancel out the other. How is this line of equilibrium to be identified? In *Shrimp*, the Appellate Body found that the parties to the Inter-American Convention for the Protection and Conservation of Sea Turtles had 'marked out' the line in that convention.

Thus, under what might otherwise be uncertainty regarding the allocation of authority, as between the United States and the complainant states, a pre-existing international agreement may form the basis for allocation.

B. Gambling with the future

In 1994, when the GATS was agreed, there was little understanding that the internet would provide such a wide avenue for the cross-border provision of services. Much has been written about how the rise of the internet has challenged traditional ideas about regulatory jurisdiction, fracturing notions of basing jurisdiction on either territorial conduct or territorial effects. The core issue in the *Gambling* case[9] was whether US regulation of internet gambling or Antiguan regulation of internet gambling would prevail, in connection with cross-border internet-based provision of services from Antigua to the United States. And like the *Shrimp* case, this case was not considered a case of allocation of regulatory jurisdiction. Rather, like *Shrimp*, it was a case regarding market access.

The *Gambling* case had other similarities to the *Shrimp* case. First, the United States was found to have violated Article XVI of GATS, which was read to impose restrictions in this case that are similar to those under Article XI of GATT. I have argued elsewhere that this reading is simply inconsistent with the plain meaning of Article XVI.[10] Second, the exceptional provisions of GATS, which are very similar to Article XX of GATT, came into play.

[8] Appellate Body Report, *US—Shrimp*, WT/DS58/AB/R, at paras 156–160.

[9] Appellate Body Report, *United States—Measures Affecting the Cross-Border Supply of Gambling and Betting Services*, WT/DS285/AB/R, adopted 20 April 2005.

[10] Joel Trachtman, 'International Decisions–United States: Measures Affecting the Cross-Border Supply of Betting and Gambling Services. WT/DS285/AB/R', 99 American Journal of International Law (2005) 861.

So we have a similar pattern of uncertainty as to the scope of regulatory authority.

C. Helms–Burton: close, but no cigar

The Helms–Burton Act was signed into law in March 1996, after Cuba shot down two planes flown by members of a US-based anti-Castro organizations. Helms–Burton had several chapters, imposing several different types of sanctions against Cuba and those who did business with Cuba. The main complaint against Helms-Burton was that it was extraterritorial: the European Union, Canada, Mexico, and other US trade partners were concerned that the United States was reaching out to regulate the way that their companies did business with Cuba.[11] In the broadest terms, while this is analytically similar to the *Shrimp* facts, 'extraterritoriality' is not directly cognizable under WTO law. Nevertheless, the European Union brought a case against the United States, alleging several bases for violation of WTO law. However, the United States argued that the national security exception in WTO law, under both GATT and GATS, applied to deprive the WTO dispute settlement system of jurisdiction.

Among other things, Title I of the Helms–Burton Act codified the pre-existing US trade embargo, and other sanctions, against Cuba. Title I is vulnerable to attack under Articles I (MFN), III (national treatment), V (right of transit), XI (elimination of quantitative restrictions), and XIII (MFN administration of quantitative restrictions).[12] In a case brought by Cuba, these would be bases for invalidating the embargo provisions of Title I. Furthermore, section 110(a) of the Helms–Burton Act confirms long-standing regulations that bar entry into the United States of goods 'made or derived in whole or in part of any article which is the growth, produce, or manufacture of Cuba.' While raising questions about rules of origin, this provision can be viewed as a partial secondary boycott: those who purchase inputs from Cuba will not be permitted to send goods incorporating those inputs to the United States. In a case brought by a third country, such as the EU, this provision might be attacked under Articles III, XI, or XIII. Whether this case would be successful would hinge on the analytical approach taken by the panel or Appellate Body. On the one hand, the Helms–Burton Act might be viewed as a legitimate domestic regulation, enforced at the border, and subject to Article III, excluding the

[11] OAS Inter-American Juridical Committee Opinion Examining the U.S. Helms–Burton Act, 35 ILM (1996) 1322. The Committee found that the Helms–Burton Act violated international law for a number of reasons, including by extending US jurisdiction 'extraterritorially,' by improperly assigning domestic courts to deal with state-to-state claims, by espousing claims of persons who were not nationals at the time of injury, and by attributing liability to third-state nationals for claims against a foreign state.

[12] See John A. Spanogle, '*Can Helms-Burton be Challenged Under WTO?*', 27 Stetson Law Review (1998) 1313, 1318–28.

application of Article XI. Provided that the focus is on the question of discrimination between US manufacturers, prohibited from using Cuban ingredients, and foreign manufacturers, similarly restricted, this measure could be found legal under Article III. On the other hand, if the US measure is understood as regulation of a production process, and found on that basis to be in violation of, or outside the coverage of Article III, and also subject to the stricter scrutiny of Article XI, it might be invalidated (subject to the exceptional provisions discussed below). Alternatively, if the US measure is understood to be purely a border measure, it would simply violate Articles XI and XIII.

Title III provides a private right of action for US nationals whose property was expropriated by the Cuban government, against persons who 'traffic' in the expropriated property. Title III has been suspended since its enactment. Its suspension may or may not insulate it from review under WTO law, especially as liability of 'traffickers' under Title III began to accrue as of 1 November 1996.[13] However, it is not clear what grounds for attack exist under WTO law. While this provision may certainly be argued to be 'extraterritorial,' WTO law does not proscribe extraterritoriality *per se*. It might be argued that the United States was improperly burdening the import or export of such expropriated property, perhaps in violation of Articles II, III or XI, or perhaps resulting in non-violation nullification or impairment. However, the linkage of this measure to trade in goods might not be direct or strong enough to establish a violation.

The United States threatened to decline to appear in connection with the WTO proceedings brought by the EU.[14] The US based its defense on Article XXI(b), arguing that the availability of this defense is self-judging, and hence non-justiciable.[15] In relevant part, Article XXI(b) provides that nothing in the GATT shall be construed to prevent any contracting party from taking any action *which it considers* necessary for the protection of its essential security interests taken in time of war or other emergency in international relations.

Given the limited possibility for recourse at the WTO against the Helms–Burton Act, one might simply recognize that this is a problem that lacks a forum, and perhaps rules. However, it is open to states to negotiate conventional limitations on these activities, and indeed, the United States and EU began to do so, in connection with the failed negotiations for a Multilateral Agreement on Investment.

[13] See 22 U.S.C. Sections 6082(a)(1), 6085(a).

[14] Paul Blustein and Anne Swardson, U.S. Vows to Boycott WTO Panel, Wash. Post, 21 February 1997, at A12.

[15] See John H. Jackson and Andreas F. Lowenfeld, *Helms-Burton, the U.S., & the WTO*, ASIL Insight (March 1997), available at http://www.asil.org/insights/insight7.htm. See also GATT Panel Report, U.S–Trade Measures Affecting Nicaragua, GATT Doc. L/6053, 13 October 1986 (not adopted).

D. Summary

What do *Shrimp*, *Gambling*, and *Helms–Burton* have in common? They all involve jurisdictional disputes that arise as trade disputes. And yet, the 'trade' or market access issues involved in each are not the only issues, and issues of allocation of regulatory authority may appear to be even more important in these and perhaps other cases. *Shrimp* and *Gambling* are more normal fact patterns, and are replicated in many ways. *Helms–Burton* is more abnormal: a case that is centrally concerned with limitations on prescriptive jurisdiction, repackaged as a trade case.

In each of these cases, allocation of regulatory authority was not a peripheral issue, but was the core issue. WTO rules were called upon to mediate in connection with these disputes regarding allocation of regulatory authority.

II. MUTUAL RECOGNITION, HARMONIZATION, AND REGULATORY AUTHORITY

WTO negotiators have indeed recognized that regulatory jurisdiction is an important issue in connection with trade negotiations. In the negotiations for the WTO, in the TBT Agreement, the SPS Agreement, and the GATS, they included provisions to support mutual recognition and harmonization of regulation. These are rules regarding allocation of regulatory authority, while the negative integration provisions considered in Part I are understood as broader 'standards.'[16]

Recognition, in simple legal terms, is a choice of law rule. Recognition is a selection by importing (or host) states of the rule of the home or exporting state, to the exclusion of the rule of the importing state. Pure recognition regimes diminish barriers to trade, by dismantling importing country regulatory barriers: because the importing country law is inapplicable, it cannot serve as a barrier. Finally, in this sense, recognition is by its nature purely deregulatory (presuming that the exporting country rules are less onerous than the importing country rules). Recognition, at its core, entails an agreement to compromise local regulatory autonomy, by accepting that the exporting state regulation is 'good enough.'

The context of recognition arrangements—in terms of the possibility for externalization, the possibility for detrimental regulatory competition, and the possibility for discrimination against outsiders—is critical to an understanding of the utility of recognition arrangements. States may have regard to these concerns as they determine whether to engage in recognition arrangements. Institutional mechanisms may be established to reduce potential harmful effects of externalization. Essential harmonization is a

[16] On the distinction between 'rules' and 'standards', see Joel P. Trachtman, 'The Domain of WTO Dispute Resolution', 40 Harvard International Law Journal (1999) 333.

critical component of these mechanisms.[17] It should be clear that the value of engaging in mutual recognition will depend entirely on the context, both factual and institutional.

When added to 'recognition,' the word 'mutual' denotes narrow reciprocity in the sense described by Keohane (1986): a specific exchange of equivalent promises. You recognize my regulation, and I will recognize yours. In this sense, it is a trade concept—a concept of reciprocal liberalization—much more than it is a governance or regulatory concept. This type of narrow reciprocity exists in specialized bilateral agreements, but regional and multilateral integration agreements generally provide simply for recognition, without specifically conditioning Country A's recognition on Country B's compliance with its recognition obligations. Under this type of diffuse reciprocity (in the sense described by Keohane) the bargain is supported by a broad exchange, and narrow reciprocity—mutuality—is unnecessary. The question answered by mutuality is how does one state compensate the other for its recognition.

Essential harmonization is not formally necessary to recognition, but host or importing states would be expected before agreeing to recognition to check the partner's regulation to ensure that it satisfies the host or importing state's regulatory goals, and, to the extent that it does not, require modifications to the partner's regulation to ensure that it does. Insofar as a general minimum standard of harmonization can be agreed in a legislative context, this is understood as 'essential harmonization.'

In this context, essential harmonization plays two roles. First, it is a product of multilateral or plurilateral legislation. Exporting states, or at least their exporting firms, are required to comply with harmonized standards, or to forego the benefits of exporting the relevant goods or services. In regulatory jurisdiction terms, authority is allocated to a centralized harmonizing legislator, to the exclusion of individual states.

Second, by serving as a predicate for recognition, essential harmonization serves as an agreement on the scope or depth of regulatory competition. States are permitted to apply higher standards to their own suppliers, but regulatory competition might be expected to suppress the application of standards above the level of the essential harmonization. To the extent that this regulatory competition is expected, essential harmonization may be understood as simply 'harmonization.' The political process of essential harmonization provides an opportunity to decide collectively how far states will accept pressure on their standards from regulatory competition. By accepting recognition on the basis of essential harmonization, states accept competitive incentives to reduce the cost of the regulation that they apply to their own producers to the level required by the essentially harmonized rule.

[17] The measure of harmonization necessary as a predicate for mutual recognition in the EC is known as 'essential harmonization,' meaning that the essence or the core of the regulatory purpose is harmonized.

The WTO has extended its reach from anti-discrimination to more extensive forms of negative integration, requiring necessity or least trade restrictive character, and rational bases for regulation, under the TBT Agreement and the SPS Agreement.

The WTO has itself effected little positive integration, either in the form of harmonization (other than in intellectual property rights) or in the form of requirements of mutual recognition. (While Article 4.1 of the SPS Agreement, for example, calls for a kind of conditional equivalence, predicated on proof of equivalent protection, it is unclear that this provision has had significant effect.) These two types of positive integration—harmonization and recognition—are complementary, or synergetic. (Here it should be made clear that recognition, and not equivalence, is a type of positive integration, as it is general and is provided by broader regulation. On the other hand, equivalence is case-based, and is determined by courts as part of a determination that a national regulatory measure is excessive because it fails to take into account the equivalence of foreign regulation.) States would not agree to recognition without some degree of harmonization (known as 'essential harmonization'), or some opportunity to check in advance the protective qualities of the home country regulation. Recall that essential harmonization in the EC did not become common until the advent of majority voting under the 1987 Single European Act.

GATT itself contains no explicit equivalence requirement or facility of recognition. However, it is possible that necessity requirements under the exceptions provided in Article XX (b) or (d) (exceptions for protection of life or compliance with law) could require recognition. These provisions, which provide a defense after a finding of violation, have been found to require that the national measure be the least trade restrictive alternative. Sometimes, the least trade restrictive alternative will be simple recognition of the effectiveness of home country regulation.

In addition, the Appellate Body in *Shrimp (Article 21.5)* seems to have identified an embryonic equivalence requirement in the chapeau of Article XX (exceptions). The Appellate Body held as follows:

> In our view, there is an important difference between conditioning market access on the adoption of essentially the same programme, and conditioning market access on the adoption of a programme *comparable in effectiveness*. Authorizing an importing Member to condition market access on exporting Members putting in place regulatory programmes *comparable in effectiveness* to that of the importing Member gives sufficient latitude to the exporting Member with respect to the programme it may adopt to achieve the level of effectiveness required. [18]

[18] Appellate Body Report, *US—Shrimp* (Article 21.5), WT/DS58/AB/R, at para 144 (emphasis in original).

A measure requiring United States and foreign regulatory programs to be 'comparable in effectiveness', as opposed to being 'essentially the same' would comply with the prohibition against arbitrary or unjustifiable restrictions on trade. This appears to function as a 'soft' equivalence discipline, which only arises after a violation of another provision of GATT.

A. SPS Agreement

Article 4.1 of the SPS Agreement requires that equivalence be accorded other states' regulations. In 2001, the WTO's SPS Committee adopted a decision on the implementation of Article 4 on equivalence to 'make operational the provisions of Article 4 of the SPS Agreement.[19] It sets up the possibility for other states to serve as 'regulatory laboratories' to come up with alternate means to achieve the same regulatory goals. It imposes an obligation on an importing Member, upon the request of the exporting member, to explain the objective and rationale of the SPS measure, to identify clearly the risks that the relevant measure is intended to address, and to indicate the appropriate level of protection, which its SPS measure is designed to achieve.[20] In addition, the exporting member must provide reasonable access, upon request, to the importing member for inspection, testing, and other relevant procedures for the determination of equivalence. Such requests should proceed rapidly, especially with traditional imports, and should not in themselves disrupt or suspend on-going imports.

B. TBT Agreement

The requirement of the SPS Agreement is stronger than the more hortatory provision of Article 2.7 of the TBT Agreement, which simply requires Members to give positive consideration to accepting foreign regulation as equivalent, if the foreign regulation fulfils the importing state's objectives. In the Second Triennial Review, the TBT Committee considered that 'Members may find it useful to further explore equivalency of standards as an interim measure to facilitate trade in the absence of relevant international standards.'[21]

Since Article XX requires that members maintain an appropriate level of flexibility in the administration of their regulatory distinctions,[22] it is probable that Article 2.7 (or Article 2.2 in a manner parallel to Article XX) will be interpreted as requiring sufficient flexibility in normative

[19] See document G/SPS/19. This document was clarified in 2004, in G/SPS/19/Rev.2.

[20] It adds that in doing so, members should take into account the *Guidelines to Further the Practical Implementation of Article 5.5* adopted by the Committee on Sanitary and Phytosanitary Measures at its meeting of 21–22 June 2000 (document G/SPS/15, dated 18 July 2000).

[21] *TBT Triennial Review*, para 23, G/TBT/9.

[22] Appellate Body Report, *US—Shrimp*, WT/DS58/AB/R, at para 165; and Appellate Body Report, *US—Shrimp (Article 21.5)*, WT/DS58/AB/RW, at paras 135–152.

determinations and good faith consideration of the alternative and equivalent standards suggested by the exporting country.

C. GATS

Article VI:4 of GATS calls on the Council for Trade in Services (CTS) to develop any necessary disciplines to ensure that measures relating to qualification requirements and procedures, technical standards and licensing requirements do not constitute unnecessary barriers to trade in services. Prior to the agreement and entry into force of more specific rules under Article VI:4, disciplines on national measures are available under Article VI:5 in sectors in which the importing member has undertaken specific commitments. In order for these disciplines to apply, two sets of criteria must be satisfied:

(i) the licensing or qualification requirements or technical standards must nullify or impair specific commitments in a manner that could not reasonably have been expected at the time the specific commitments were made; and
(ii) the measure must be (a) not based on objective and transparent criteria, or (b) more burdensome than necessary to ensure the quality of the service, or (c) in the case of licensing procedures, in itself a restriction on the supply of the service

Note that Article VII of GATS and paragraph 3 of the Annex on Financial Services do not require recognition, but merely authorize it. Although a strong GATS standard of necessity might eventually lead to judicially required equivalence, this is unlikely to be the case under current treaty language. But the necessity test might nevertheless mandate equivalence of some regulations and not others, whereby partial equivalence becomes the operational consequence of the principle of proportionality.

D. The WTO legality of mutual recognition

WTO law may conceivably restrict the ability of states to engage in mutual recognition arrangements that exchange authority by providing for exclusive home country regulatory jurisdiction. This is because mutual recognition may be discriminatory in the MFN sense.[23] Mutual recognition under the GATS requires that equivalent opportunities be offered to other states. It seems clear that mere mutuality is not a permissible basis for discrimination. There is even a question under WTO law regarding the degree to which regional trade agreements may limit mutual recognition

[23] *See* Lorand Bartels, '*The Legality of the EC Mutual Recognition Clause under WTO Law*', 8 Journal of Internation Economic Law (2005) 691.

arrangements to their members, as opposed to making recognition available to other WTO member states.

III. EFFICIENT ALLOCATION OF REGULATORY AUTHORITY: PROPERTY RIGHTS THEORY AND THE THEORY OF THE FIRM

A rationalist approach to the problem of prescriptive jurisdiction or allocation of regulatory authority would begin with the theory of property rights and externalities.[24] When states regulate, they cause and encounter regulatory externalities: costs are imposed on outsiders without commensurate benefit or without legitimation by their consent or another basis. The outsiders may wish to come to an accommodation regarding these costs, but in theory the parties will only agree if the accommodation enhances their aggregate welfare. It is important to note, with Coase, that all problems of externalities are reciprocal: if I am required to stop taking action that has bad effects on you, then I bear a cost.

While all regulatory externalities will not be worth internalizing, due to transaction costs, the existence of regulatory externalities suggests the evaluation of the utility of transactions in regulatory authority. States also encounter regulatory economies of scale and scope. These possible costs and benefits drive the search for the optimal regulatory unit. We may understand all sorts of concerns about extraterritoriality in competition law, labour law, environmental law, or securities law, as well as debates about jurisdiction to tax, in terms of externalities.

In the trade arena, there are ordinary externalities as well as pecuniary externalities. The ordinary externalities are not fully within the trade sphere, as they exist in connection with environmental protection, human rights, and other 'linked' contexts. So, for example, an ordinary externality exists where one state's method of fishing for tuna causes environmental harm in the form of incidental mortality of dolphins that adversely affects another state. This is an externality because or to the extent that it is not fully accounted for in market or legal interaction.

On the other hand, a pecuniary externality, sometimes referred to as a competitive externality, occurs where adverse effects are transmitted through the market system. Thus, where the first state's method of fishing for tuna is less costly and therefore its products can be sold more cheaply than the products of states with more stringent regulation, the adverse effect on jobs in the tuna fishing industry in the second state is a pecuniary externality. These types of externalities are often understood as fully within the trade sphere.

The point here is that states may wish to engage in transactions regarding both types of externality. The WTO has often served as a mechanism for

[24] For a more complete exposition, see Trachtman, above n 1.

transactions relating to pecuniary externalities, but to the extent that pecuniary externalities are tied up with ordinary externalities, or even in other contexts, it may be useful for the WTO to deal with ordinary externalities.

Once we recognize that jurisdiction of states is at least somewhat analogous to property of individuals—in the sense that both are allocations of power and responsibility—we may assess the extent to which certain allocations or transactions may result in greater efficiency. Property rights literature has developed a number of bases for allocation relating to transaction costs, and has also examined the strategic constraints on transactions in this context.

The transaction costs methodology, supplemented to include considerations of strategic behaviour under asymmetric information, provides four basic potential strategies described here. The basic goal is to allocate authority to those to whom it is most valuable—those most greatly affected—at the lowest transaction costs. I describe the types of transaction cost circumstances in which a particular strategy might best achieve this goal.

(i) Strategy A—Anticipate Transactions. This strategy, seeks to minimize transaction costs by allocating property rights so as to anticipate, and thereby obviate, transactions. This strategy is dependent on the ability to determine *ex ante* which state is most greatly affected by a particular circumstance. This strategy can be implemented by a legislature or a court. To the extent that the WTO (efficiently) leaves authority over areas considered to be 'sovereign' with states, we might say that it anticipates transactions. It presumably leaves authority in the hands of those who value it the most. (While this formulation is circular, the point is about suggesting categories, not about identifying the contents of those categories.)

(ii) Strategy B—Clear Entitlements. Where the costs of transfer is low, transaction costs can be minimized by providing clear and complete property rights, amenable to transfer with the least transaction costs. The right to charge tariffs is clear and complete, and is amenable to transfer (by virtue of bindings) at what appear to be low transaction costs.

(iii) Strategy C—Muddy or Solomonic Entitlements. Where the cost of formal transfer is very high, it may be better to provide unclear and incomplete ('muddy') formal property rights, in order to reduce deadweight losses and encourage reallocative transactions through informal means or through adjudication. The question of whether, for example, states have the authority to block imports of goods due to the way that they are produced is not clearly answered in WTO law, thereby inducing states to reveal information in order to bargain. The Appellate Body's decision in *Shrimp* may be understood in these terms.

(iv) Strategy D—Organizational Solutions. An alternative to the above strategies would call for the establishment or use of organizations that can make allocative decisions, facilitate negotiations toward reallocative transactions or override holdouts. To the extent that power is allocated to the WTO (instead of merely exercised through the WTO by virtue of clear and self-executing rules), we might say that the WTO itself represents an organizational solution to certain cooperation problems.

While I illustrate these strategies with examples from WTO law, it is important to note that they are exhibited elsewhere, including at general international law and in other treaty or organizational settings. Moreover, an allocation that may be made clearly within the confines of WTO law may be muddied by other legal rules. For example, assume for a moment that the product–process distinction operates within the WTO to deprive importing states of authority to regulate the manner of production of imported goods, including whether these goods are made by child labour. Even if this allocation were uncontested, it would still be necessary to examine separate international labour and human rights standards to determine whether the importing state has any right to take any action in respect of child labour in the exporting state.

The property rights analysis suggested above provides an initial analytical technique[25] for determining the source of gain from transactions in jurisdiction, as well as a transaction costs and strategy-based method of discriminating among allocative techniques.

The varying rules of negative integration applied in WTO litigation may be understood in terms of maximization—in terms of efficiently prohibiting domestic measures that fail to pass a test that may be explained in cost–benefit analysis terms. Furthermore, these negative integration tests may be understood as dynamic mechanisms of multilevel choice: of subsidiarity. We can consider the judicial 'trade-off devices' developed in interjurisdictional settings, such as national treatment tests, least-trade restrictive alternative tests, proportionality tests and balancing tests, to be dynamic devices or heuristics for allocation of jurisdiction: as dynamic components of constitutions.

While our first question is how should authority be allocated horizontally for greatest efficiency, our second question asks when the best horizontal allocation is actually a vertical allocation. But these tradeoff devices teach us that we need not decide at the outset: it may be more efficient to develop a heuristic for future determination, and to assign to courts the job of making

[25] Trachtman, above n 1.

this determination. Thus, it is worth examining to what extent these tradeoff devices may be understood as heuristics to determine, *ex post*, to which level of governance responsibility should be assigned.

These questions are critical to the economics of federalism, which addresses the utility of congruence between effects and governance, and would seek to establish governmental units based on such congruence, subject to the costs of fragmentation of authority. It is essential to recognize that each tradeoff device serves as a heuristic to allocate authority in particularistic, fact-specific ways over time, and thus may provide a more complex solution to the level of authority problem than a simple static and/or broad allocation, such as is expected to be found in other parts of constitutions.[26]

The WTO treaty *ex ante* allocates certain authority as between member states and the organization itself. Furthermore, the WTO treaty provides mechanisms for deciding the allocation of authority in more particularistic ways *ex post*.

The WTO is an agreement by which states commit to suppress certain kinds of protectionism, and do other things. As the exercise of regulatory authority may be intended to protect, or may have other adverse consequences for trade even where there is no specific intent to protect, it is not surprising that states address at least some components of the exercise of regulatory authority within the WTO.

Many commentators are concerned that the WTO's main pre-occupation with liberalization may insufficiently respect the valid exercise of regulatory authority. However, in the *Shrimp* case, the Appellate Body upbraided the initial panel for failing to recognize the intent of the member states to provide useful exceptions to liberalization in connection with certain types of exercise of regulatory authority. Under *Shrimp*, there are circumstances under which states would be permitted to forbid importation of goods produced in a way that adversely affects exhaustible natural resources.

The WTO's negative integration 'trade-off devices,' including national treatment, least-trade restrictive alternative testing and balancing testing, may be understood simply as mandates to judges to exercise discretion in the allocation of jurisdictional authority.[27] The goal of states in delegating this discretion to judges is presumably to allow member states to exercise unrestricted regulatory authority where this exercise does not impose 'excessive' costs on foreign states in trade terms. The question is how to determine the excessive nature of the costs. While none of these tradeoff devices involve great precision, and a legal realist must recognize that they

[26] See Eugene D. Cross, 'Pre-Emption of Member State Law in the European Economic Community: A Framework for Analysis', 29 Common Market Law Review (1992) 447.

[27] See Joel P. Trachtman, 'Trade and... Problems, Cost-Benefit Analysis and Subsidiarity', 9 European Journal of International Law (1998) 32.

leave much discretion to judges, they may plausibly be understood to orient and constrain judges towards, if not to, an approximation of efficiency. They do so under circumstances where it is difficult to imagine an alternative approach, other than one of positive integration. Positive integration has its own costs.

As described earlier, property rights theory, including the theory of the firm, suggests that there will be circumstances in which it is efficient to share power over a particular element of jurisdiction: to establish and empower an international organization. While the WTO generally lacks powers to engage in positive regulation, the broader international legal system has the capacity to do so. Of course, the broader international legal system is driven by its individual members. However, once these members establish rules of law collectively, the rules of law may have binding effect on them individually.

The WTO has directly effected little positive integration in the form of harmonization, outside the rather distinct realm of TRIPS. However, WTO law contains important incentives for harmonization in other contexts. These incentives are not simply to encourage harmonization for its own sake. Rather, they are intended to assist in achieving liberalization through harmonization. In addition, they are intended to insulate from the scrutiny of negative integration domestic regulation that is assumed either non-protectionist or efficient, because it conforms to international regulation. So, this is an important mechanism of multilevel choice. Of course, it must be analysed in conjunction with mechanisms of negative integration.

One of the core problems facing the WTO is the imbalance between its dispute resolution authority, on the one hand, and its extremely limited legislative capacity. The legislative capacity of the WTO is limited by virtue of both legal constraints and a network of informal expectations and attitudes. Moreover, there are substantial questions about the subject matter competence of the WTO—the extent to which the WTO can or should address areas outside of its 'core competency' of international trade. Increasingly, the core of international trade is inseparable from its penumbra of traditionally domestic regulatory prerogatives in environment, health, labour, culture, tax, etc.

At the Singapore Ministerial in 1996, the WTO (informally) referred certain trade-related labour issues to the International Labor Organization; this referral was reaffirmed more recently at Doha. However, not to decide is to decide, and the WTO's abdication of authority has certain substantive results. While this article points to certain *negative integration* powers available in WTO dispute settlement, to be exercised through the application of general standards, the WTO has much more limited powers of *positive integration*, available to be exercised through the legislation of specific rules.

Interestingly, in the Uruguay Round, in the area of sanitary and phytosanitary measures, the WTO formally referred certain quasi-legislative authority to certain other functional organizations. That is, the definition of 'international standards' contained in Annex A to the SPS Agreement appoints Codex Alimentarius (Codex), International Office of Epizootics (OIE) and International Plant Protection Convention (IPPC) as 'quasi-legislators' of these standards in relevant areas. What do I mean by 'quasi-legislators'?

First, the standards developed by Codex, OIE, and IPPC for human, animal, and plant health, respectively, are, under the terms of their own constitutive documents, non-binding. However, Article 3.1 of the SPS Agreement provides that 'Members shall base their sanitary or phytosanitary measures on international standards, guidelines or recommendations, where they exist, except as otherwise provided for in this Agreement, and in particular in paragraph 3.'

Moreover, Article 3.2 states that SPS measures of WTO members that are in conformity with international standards, guidelines, or recommendations shall be 'presumed to be consistent with the relevant provisions of this Agreement.' In its *Hormones* decision, the Appellate Body found that the terms 'based on' in Article 3.1 and 'in conformity with' in Article 3.2 have different meanings. 'Based on' means simply derived from, and provides greater flexibility to members.[28] On the other hand, reversing the panel, the Appellate Body found that Article 3.2 was a safe harbour, but did not establish the converse presumption: the panel erred in presuming that measures that did not conform to international standards were inconsistent with the SPS Agreement.

So, while Codex, OIE, and IPPC do not by any means legislate in the normal, or full, sense, the norms that they produce have certain lesser binding force—they provide incentives that guide conduct. They are safe harbours, with characteristics similar to those used, for example, in US tax or securities law regulations to guide conduct. The SPS Agreement provisions mentioned earlier provide important incentives for states to base their national standards on, or conform their national standards to, the Codex, OIE, and IPPC standards. Article 3.3 provides an important exception in certain circumstances, including where a state adopts a higher 'appropriate level of sanitary or phytosanitary protection.' This is a refined system of applied subsidiarity, subtly allowing national autonomy subject to certain constraints.

[28] In the *Hormones* decision, the Appellate Body rejected the panel's finding that 'based on' and 'conform to' have the same meaning. Report of the Appellate Body: EC Measures Concerning Meat and Meat Products (Hormones), WT/DS26/AB/R, WT/DS48/AB/R, para 165, adopted 16 January 1998.

Article 2.4 of the TBT Agreement requires members to use international standards as a basis for their technical regulations, unless the international standards are an inappropriate or ineffective means to achieve legitimate objectives; so deviations from international standards is discouraged. This provision was interpreted in *Sardines*.[29] Article 2.4 of the TBT Agreement requires that Members use 'relevant international standards' 'as a basis for' their technical regulations. In *Sardines*, the European Communities argued that the EC regulation at issue was based on Codex Stan 94 because it adopted the portion of Codex Stan 94 that reserves the term 'sardines' exclusively for *sardina pilchardus*.[30] It argued that this relationship satisfies the requirement, in the European Communities' view, for a 'rational relationship' between the international standard and the technical regulation.

The Appellate Body rejected the European Communities' arguments. It recalled its decision in *Hormones*, addressing the meaning of 'based on' in Article 3.1 of the SPS Agreement. The Appellate Body here agreed with the panel's use of the *Hormones* decision, finding that in order for a standard to be used 'as a basis for' a technical regulation, it must be 'used as the principal constituent or fundamental principle for the purpose of enacting the technical regulation.'[31] Furthermore, one thing cannot be the 'basis' for another if the two are contradictory.[32] Article 2.4 requires that members use relevant international standards, 'or the relevant parts of them, as a basis for their technical regulations.'

Referring to the situation prior to 1994, and to the situation outside of the SPS and TBT Agreements, we note that GATT does not specifically require the use of international standards at all. However, the least trade restrictive alternative requirements under Article XX and or the good faith requirement under the chapeau of Article XX may include a requirement to attempt to create an international or regional standard before applying a unilateral one. As the Appellate Body stated in *Shrimp*,

> 'Clearly, and 'as far as possible', a multilateral approach is strongly preferred. Yet it is one thing to *prefer* a multilateral approach in the application of a measure that is provisionally justified under one of the subparagraphs of Article XX of the GATT 1994; it is another to require the *conclusion* of a multilateral agreement as a condition of avoiding 'arbitrary or unjustifiable discrimination' under the chapeau of Article XX. We see, in this case, no such requirement.'[33] (emphasis added)

[29] Appellate Body Report, *European Communities—Trade Description of Sardines (EC—Sardines)*, (WT/DS231/AB/R), adopted 26 September 2002.

[30] Ibid at para 241 *quoting* European Communities Appellant's Submission, para. 150.

[31] Ibid at para 243.

[32] Ibid at para 248.

[33] See Appellate Body Report, *US—Shrimp (Article 21.5 DSU)*, at para 124.

IV. CONCLUSION

We may understand all WTO law as being concerned with the allocation of regulatory authority: even when a state enters into a tariff binding, it is ceding a portion of its authority to set tariffs to the WTO, and indirectly to other WTO members. This is nothing new. However, as the WTO has been required to address more 'behind the border' issues, it has been required to determine regulatory authority in areas that have traditionally been outside its scope. It seems appropriate to recognize this expanded function of the WTO, and to analyse it. This article has given some examples of the WTO's function in allocating regulatory authority, and has suggested a theoretical framework for analysing this function.

ENFORCING WTO OBLIGATIONS: WHAT CAN WE LEARN FROM EXPORT SUBSIDIES?

*Andrew Green and Michael Trebilcock**

ABSTRACT

Export subsidies provide a good example for discussing some interesting questions underlying the debate over reforming the current system of remedies for violations of World Trade Organization (WTO) obligations. If the purpose of trade agreements is to maximize economic welfare, discussion of violations of WTO obligations will need to take account of the form of both the requirement and the remedy. The requirement could take the form of a standard or a rule and may be more or less complex. The remedy could take the form of a property rule or a liability rule. Further, both the level and the form of the remedy will be important. Each type of violation needs to be examined separately to determine whether flexibility to adapt to new circumstances should come through the requirement or the remedy. In the case of export subsidies, the current simple rule prohibiting export subsidies is likely optimal but the remedies which support this rule need to be reformed. They are currently both over-inclusive and under-inclusive and do not provide sufficient flexibility or incentive for efficient adjustment. This article considers some alternative remedies for export subsidies and discusses the general lessons for the debate on remedies for violations of WTO obligations.

INTRODUCTION

There has been a flurry of articles in recent years discussing the World Trade Organization (WTO) system for enforcing obligations under the various WTO agreements.[1] Many of these articles attempt to establish a general

* Assistant Professor, Faculty of Law, University of Toronto. E-mail: a.green@utoronto.ca. Michael Trebilcock, University Professor, Faculty of Law, University of Toronto. The authors wish to thank Michael Rosenberg for excellent research assistance and thoughtful comments on this article. E-mail: michael.trebilcock@utoronto.ca

[1] Some recent examples include Warren Schwartz and Alan O. Sykes, 'The Economic Structure of Renegotiation and Dispute Resolution in the World Trade Organization', 31 Journal of Legal Studies S179 (2002); Joel P. Trachtman, 'The WTO Cathedral' (43(1) Stanford J. of International Law 127(2007)); Marco Bronckers and Naboth van den Broek, 'Financial Compensation in the WTO: Improving the Remedies of WTO Dispute Settlement', 8(1) Journal of International Economic Law 101 (2005); Jide Nzelibe, 'The Case Against Reforming the WTO's Enforcement Mechanism' (Northwestern University School of Law

framework for discussing remedies for non-compliance with WTO obligations.[2] Emerging from this literature is a variety of recommendations for reforms such as permitting monetary remedies or the auctioning or trading of the ability to take countermeasures.[3] However, what is also clear from this literature is that the context of the particular remedy is important—i.e. the same remedy or reform option may not work for all WTO obligations.[4] The remedy that is optimal for non-compliance with tariff bindings may be different from that for non-compliance with requirements relating to adoption of international standards for regulatory measures. There may be reasons why, e.g., remedies for some types of non-compliance should focus on forcing compliance while others should focus on permitting non-compliance, subject to compensation or rebalancing of commitments.

This article examines the debate concerning optimal remedies from the perspective of the rules concerning export subsidies. If context is important, export subsidies provide an interesting example as they are subject to a specific per se prohibition under the Subsidies and Countervailing Measures (SCM) Agreement.[5] The prohibition itself is controversial as, at first glance, export subsidies seem only to increase trade and harm only the subsidizing country. Trachtman notes that because of these effects, the ban on export subsidies is a 'bit of a puzzle'.[6] Further, the enforcement system for

Public Law and Legal Theory Series No. 07–12, 2 April 2007); Joost Pauwelyn, 'Optimal Protection of International Law: Navigating Between 'European Absolutism' and 'American Voluntarism'' (Draft, 15 November 2006 on file with the author); Kyle Bagwell, 'Remedies in the WTO: An Economic Perspective' (manuscript, 9 January 2007) and Robert Z. Lawrence, *Crimes and Punishments? Retaliation under the WTO*. (Washington, DC: Institute for International Economics, 2003).

[2] For example, Trachtman, above n 1 and Pauwelyn, above n 1 adopt a law and economics framework based on Calabresi and Melamed's analysis of domestic remedies; Bagwell, above n 1 uses an economic (terms of trade) model; and Nzelibe, above n 1 and Schwartz and Sykes, above n 1 discuss the application of public choice analysis to enforcement issues.

[3] See, e.g. Trachtman, above n 1 (arguing for cash compensation); Bagwell, above n 1 (discussing disproportionate retaliation, monetary compensation and auctioning retaliation rights); Joseph Pelzman and Amir Shoham, 'WTO Enforcement Issues', 7(1) Global Economy Journal 1 (2007) (efficient fines); Bronckers and van den Broek, above n 1 (arguing for financial compensation) and Kyle Bagwell, Petros Mavroidis and Robert Staiger, 'The Case for Tradable Remedies in WTO Dispute Settlement,' in S.J. Evenett and B.M. Hoekman, (eds) *Economic Development and Multilateral Trade Cooperation* (Washington, DC: Palgrave Macmillan and the World Bank, 2006) (discussing tradable remedies). But see Nzelibe, above n 1 (arguing on public choice grounds that neither monetary remedies nor collective enforcement are superior to the existing system).

[4] Trachtman, above n 1, at 8; Pauwelyn, above n 1, at 38 and Bagwell, above n 1, at 2.

[5] Lawrence, above n 1, at 54–57.

[6] Trachtman, above n 1, at 133. See also Robert Z. Lawrence and Nathaniel Stankard 'Should Export Subsidies be Treated Differently?' (Conference on WTO Dispute Settlement and Developing Countries: Use, Implications, Strategies, Reforms, University of Wisconsin, 20, 21 May 2005) http://wage.wisc.edu/uploads/WTO%20Conference/Export%20Subsidies%20-%20Lawrence%20Stankard.pdf; Bagwell, above n 1, at 22 and Donald Regan, 'What are

subsidies as a whole under the SCM Agreement is different from, and stricter than, the general provisions under the Dispute Settlement Understanding (DSU), with shorter time lines and potentially more severe penalties. Despite, or perhaps because of, this prohibition and different remedial system, the export subsidies provisions have given rise to a relatively large number of disputes. Examination of these rules aid in understanding the various arguments put forward by commentators concerning the WTO's enforcement system more generally.

Interestingly, export subsidies have given rise to differing opinions. Bagwell and Lawrence believe that the stricter rules for export subsidies are not appropriate.[7] They each argue that the economic case for both the prohibition on export subsidies and the stronger penalties for non-compliance is weak at best. On the other hand, Sykes argues that the ban on export subsidies is justified economically.[8] The focus of the current export subsidies remedies on deterrence also fits with the broader view of the function of WTO remedies as ensuring compliance.[9]

This article enters this debate both to analyse the appropriateness of the remedies for violating the ban on export subsidies, and to discuss the implications of the analysis of export subsidies for the broader remedies debate. Section I examines the rules concerning export subsidies. It briefly sets out the prohibition and then discusses the difference between the specific dispute settlement provisions under the SCM Agreement and the general provisions under the DSU. Section II then discusses the purpose of the export subsidies provisions and whether there are any situations in which we would want to permit them. As we conclude that there may be instances where export subsidies are efficient, this Section then sets out various factors that need to be considered in designing the optimal export subsidy provisions. Section III examines how these factors are relevant to a number of options for addressing export subsidies: a complete ban with deterrence-based penalties, flexibility built into the rule or standard but not the remedy; and flexibility in the remedy but not the rule or standard. Section IV extends the discussion in Section III to the issue of the form (as opposed to the level) of remedy and discusses some possible reforms to the export subsidies provisions. Section V concludes.

Trade Agreements For? Two Conflicting Stories Told by Economists, with a Lesson for Lawyers', 9(4) Journal of International Economic Law 951 (2006), at 979.

7 Bagwell, above n 1, at 30 and Lawrence above n 1, at 59–60.

8 Alan O. Sykes, 'The Economics of WTO Rules on Subsidies and Countervailing Measures', in A. Appleton, P. Macrory and M. Plummer (eds) *The World Trade Organization: Legal, Economic And Political Analysis* (New York: Springer Verlag, 2005).

9 See Pauwelyn, above n 1 (discussing 'European Absolutism') and John H. Jackson, 'International Law Status of WTO Dispute Settlement Reports: Obligations to Comply or Option to 'Buy Out'?', 98(1) The American Journal of International Law 109 (2004), at 123.

I. EXPORT SUBSIDIES

The SCM Agreement prohibits 'subsidies contingent, in law or fact, whether solely or as one of several conditions, upon export performance'.[10] This blanket prohibition on export subsidies is stricter than the treatment of most other domestic measures such as domestic subsidies (subsidies that are not contingent on export performance), taxes or regulations.[11] Domestic subsidies are 'actionable' rather than prohibited (except for import substitution subsidies which are also prohibited).[12] 'Actionable' subsidies may be challenged by another member only if they are 'specific' (i.e. narrowly targeted at a particular range of firms or industries) and cause 'adverse effects' to other members.[13] Taxes and regulations are permitted, subject to certain constraints such as that they are not discriminatory (i.e. do not violate the most favoured nation principle or the national treatment principle),[14] do not create unnecessary obstacles to international trade,[15] or are necessary for the protection of human, animal or plant life or health.[16] Furthermore, many WTO agreements provide for 'exceptions' under which members can maintain measures which otherwise violate WTO obligations where the measures are related to some permitted objective such as environmental protection.[17] The SCM Agreement does not provide for any such exceptions to its provisions.[18]

[10] Agreement on SCM Agreement, Article 3. The various requirements for whether a measure is a 'subsidy' that is 'contingent, in law or fact,... upon export performance' have given rise to a number of disputes but will not be discussed in detail in this article. See Andrew Green, Michael Trebilcock, and Vivien Milat, 'The Enduring Problem of WTO Export Subsidies Rules' (manuscript, 27 April 2007) for a discussion of these requirements under the SCM Agreement.

[11] But see Lawrence, above n 1, at 59 (noting that there are other outright prohibitions in WTO law—but not many).

[12] SCM Agreement, Article 3 prohibits import substitution subsidies.

[13] SCM Agreement, Article 5. 'Adverse effects' include injury to the domestic industry of another member, nullification or impairment of benefits under WTO agreements of another member and serious prejudice to the interests of another member. Actionable subsidies therefore can only be challenged if there is an injury, unlike export subsidies which are prohibited whether or not an injury occurs to another member.

[14] General Agreement on Tariffs and Trade (GATT), Articles I and III; Agreement on Technical Barriers to Trade (TBT Agreement), Article 2.1 and Agreement on the Application of Sanitary and Phytosanitary Measures (SPS Agreement), Article 2.3.

[15] TBT Agreement, Article 2.2.

[16] SPS Agreement, Article 2.1.

[17] See, e.g. GATT, Article XX.

[18] The SCM Agreement used to have a category of 'non-actionable' subsidies including certain research and development, environmental or regional subsidies but this category has expired. SCM Agreement, Article 31. See Andrew Green, 'Trade Rules and Climate Change Subsidies' 5(3) World Trade Review 377 (2006) (discussing environmental subsidies and the non-actionable category). Similarly, the phase-out period for developing country export subsidies has now expired. SCM Agreement, Article 27.2(b). Nonetheless, there is a continued exception for LDC export subsidies. SCM Agreement, Article 27.2(a).

The remedies for breach of the export subsidies provisions are also stricter than remedies for violations of most other WTO obligations.[19] The DSU sets out the process for and content of remedies for non-compliance with most measures. The first obligation of members found to not have complied with most WTO obligations is to bring the challenged measures into compliance 'within a reasonable period of time' proposed by the respondent, agreed to by the parties or, absent agreement, set by arbitration.[20] For subsidies other than export subsidies (and import substitution subsidies), the member granting the subsidy 'shall take appropriate steps to remove the adverse effects or shall withdraw the subsidy', essentially within six months of the adoption of the panel or Appellate report by the Dispute Settlement Body (DSB).[21] A finding that a member is maintaining export subsidies, on the other hand, leads to the requirement that the member 'withdraw the subsidy without delay' with the panel specifying the requisite time period.[22]

Under the general provisions of the DSU, if a member does not bring its measure into compliance within a reasonable period of time, it is required (if requested) to enter into negotiations 'with a view to developing mutually acceptable compensation'.[23] The DSU states that compensation is a temporary measure where there is no compliance.[24] Similarly for subsidies other than export subsidies (and import substitution subsidies), if the member does not take the appropriate steps to remove the adverse effects or remove the subsidy, the SCM Agreement contemplates that the parties may agree on compensation.[25] However, the SCM Agreement does not provide for agreements on compensation where a member is found to be providing export subsidies.

Finally, under the DSU, if the member has not brought its measures into compliance and cannot agree with the complaining member(s) on compensation, any party that invoked the dispute settlement procedure may request authorization from the DSB to suspend application to the respondent of concessions or obligations under the WTO agreements.[26] The level of suspension is to be 'equivalent' to the level of nullification or impairment caused by the measure.[27] For domestic subsidies (other than import substitution subsidies), the DSB may authorize 'countermeasures,

[19] Trachtman, above n 1, at 133.
[20] Understanding on Rules and Procedures Governing the Settlement of Disputes (DSU), Article 22.2. Trachtman, above n 1, at 132 notes the requirement of compliance is not clearly set out in the DSU.
[21] SCM Agreement, Articles 7.8 and 7.9.
[22] SCM Agreement, Article 4.7.
[23] DSU, Article 22.2.
[24] DSU, Article 22.1.
[25] SCM Agreement, Article 7.9.
[26] DSU, Article 22.2.
[27] DSU, Article 22.4.

commensurate with the degree of the adverse effects determined to exist'.[28] In the absence of withdrawal of export subsidies, on the other hand, the DSB may authorize the complaining member to take 'appropriate countermeasures'.[29] The only explanation of this term is the unhelpful footnote stating that 'this expression is not meant to allow countermeasures that are disproportionate in light of the fact that the subsidies dealt with under these provisions are prohibited'.[30]

Export subsidies are therefore subject to stricter requirements (in terms of the prohibition) and stricter remedies than other WTO obligations. Interestingly, they are also subject to stricter time lines for dispute settlement, with the SCM Agreement stating that other than as specifically provided in the SCM Agreement, the time periods for the conduct of disputes over export subsidies are half the time specified in the DSU.[31] Of course, the actual impact of the differences in these provisions depends on how they are interpreted by panels or the Appellate Body. For example, one of the key distinctions is between 'equivalent' suspension of concessions or obligations under the DSU and 'appropriate' countermeasures under the SCM Agreement.[32] Panels and the Appellate Body have not measured 'appropriate' countermeasures in terms of either the harm to the complaining member or benefit to the subsidizing member but by the size of the subsidy.[33] Moreover, in *US–FSC*, the EU was permitted to impose countermeasures in the full value of the subsidy, even though it was not the only member affected by the subsidy.[34] Further, in *Canada—Aircraft*, the panel added a further 20% penalty to the countermeasure as Canada had indicated it had no intention of withdrawing the subsidy.[35]

II. EFFICIENCY, COSTS AND INSTITUTIONS

Bagwell argues that in order to understand what type of enforcement system is optimal, the first step is to understand the purpose of the

28 SCM Agreement, Article 7.9 (stating the DSB shall on request grant such authorization unless it decides by consensus to reject the request).

29 SCM Agreement, Article 4.10.

30 SCM Agreement, above n 9.

31 SCM Agreement, Article 4.12.

32 Trachtman, above n 1, at 135–36.

33 WTO Arbitration Report, *United States—Tax Treatment for 'Foreign Sales Corporations' – Recourse to Arbitration by the United States under Article 22.6 of the DSU and Article 4.11 of the SCM Agreement (US–FSC (arbitration report))*, WT/DS18/AB/R, circulated 30 August 2002, paras 5.24, 5.41, and 6.19. See Green, Trebilcock and Milat, above n 10, at 48–49 and Trachtman, above n 1, at 11–12 for a discussion of the case law concerning the level of 'appropriate' countermeasures.

34 *US–FSC*, ibid, paras 6.19 and 6.28.

35 WTO Arbitration Report, *Canada—Export Credits and Loan Guarantees for Regional Aircraft—Recourse to Arbitration by Canada under Article 22.6 of the DSU and Article 4.11 of the SCM Agreement (Canada—Aircraft (arbitration report))*, WT/DS222/ARB, circulated 17 February 2003, para 3.12.

WTO agreements.[36] There are two principal competing views of the purpose of WTO agreements. First, the agreements could be seen as joint welfare enhancing for the members.[37] Determining the optimal remedies regime would then require analysing the underlying reason why the agreements may enhance welfare and what remedies are consistent with these reasons. For example, Bagwell argues that the purpose of trade agreements is to allow governments to lower tariffs and raise trade volumes in the presence of a potential negative terms of trade externality of one country's trade measures on another's welfare.[38] Second, trade agreements could be seen as maximizing the member governments' welfare and, as Schwartz and Sykes argue, in particular the welfare of political officials (such as the probability of re-election).[39]

Related to the discussion of the purpose of trade agreements is a debate about the proper function of the enforcement provisions.[40] One view is that obligations under WTO agreements are mandatory and members should always be in compliance with these agreements.[41] Under this view, the purpose of remedies is enforcing compliance. The remedies would be seen as akin to penalties or property rules backed by specific performance.[42] The contrary view is that the WTO agreements are incomplete contracts and that compliance is not mandatory in all cases as the members have built-in flexibility mechanisms to allow adjustments to new situations (either political or welfare-based).[43] On this view, the remedies should be aimed at permitting breach or adjustment when efficient (again either politically or on a welfare basis). The underlying concern could be re-balancing or efficient breach. Efficient breach and re-balancing are related concepts but not necessarily identical. Re-balancing involves ensuring that the parties to the agreement end up in the same position that they would have been had

36 Bagwell, above n 1, at 2. See also Trachtman, above n 1, at 152–55 and Henrik Horn and Petros Mavroidis, 'A Survey of the Literature on the WTO Dispute Settlement System' (Research Institute of Indistrial Economics Working Paper Series, No. 684, 2006), at 5.

37 Bagwell, above n 1, at 2 (arguing that the WTO should be seen as increasing welfare to the member governments relative to absence of agreement). See also Trachtman, above n 1, at 129–30, 33 and 147–50.

38 Bagwell, above n 1, at 2–3 (arguing for a terms of trade approach to WTO agreements with the negative externality created through the impact of the trade measure on relative world prices).

39 Schwartz and Sykes, above n 1, at 180. Note that Bagwell, above n 1, at 5–6 argues that the terms of trade approach is compatible with the political economy approach where political factors can be captured through changes in local prices.

40 Pauwelyn, above n 1 terms these differences in approaches to international law as 'European Absolutism' and 'American Voluntarism'.

41 Jackson, above n 9, at 123.

42 Ibid, at 118; Pauwelyn, above n 1 at 42 and 61–69.

43 Bagwell, above n 1, at 9; Trachtman, above n 1, at 152–53, and Schwartz and Sykes, above n 1, at 187. See also Henrik Horn, Giovanni Maggi, and Robert W. Staiger 'Trade Agreements as Endogenously Incomplete Contracts' (NBER Working Paper Series, No. 12745, December 2006), http://www.nber.org/papers/w12745 (on incomplete contracts).

the breach never occurred—in the sense that the mutual benefits of the agreement are the same.[44] Efficient breach involves ensuring that the breaching party faces the full cost of the harm it imposes (so it can determine if there is an ultimate increase in political or economic welfare from breach).[45] Under this incomplete contract approach, WTO remedies could be either property rules or liability rules, depending on which better promoted the underlying goal (re-balancing or efficient breach).[46]

This article adopts the view that the purpose of trade agreements should be maximization of economic welfare and that WTO agreements are incomplete so that the core issue is how remedies should be structured to allow for optimal adjustment. However, there is an important overlap with the absolutist view. If a particular government measure is seen as always inefficient, the rules should then be structured so as to ensure that there is no breach. The subsequent discussion analyses how to structure the rules where there is a desire for compliance as the ultimate objective in such cases.

If the purpose of trade agreements is to maximize economic welfare, the first question to ask about export subsidies is whether they are ever efficient? Should we be structuring the provisions (including the remedies) concerning export subsidies to allow their use in some cases? The incomplete contract view would permit members to breach their obligations if it is efficient (in global welfare or political economy terms). However, if the measure or action is always inefficient, there would be no point in permitting members to breach. Of course, it is important to understand where the inefficiency arises. As Bagwell notes, under the terms of trade approach, the inefficiency arises from the negative terms of trade externalities imposed on other countries by a particular countries' measures that impact world prices.[47] There may also be other reasons why particular measures can be considered consistently inefficient.[48]

Are export subsidies inefficient? In general, with some limited exceptions, we argue that export subsidies are inefficient. Export subsidies may have some benefits from a welfare perspective. They provide a terms of trade benefit to other countries, thereby aiding consumers in other countries (the consumers in other countries face a lower price). The subsidy increases the domestic supply (and therefore the world supply if it is not a small economy) of the good and decreases domestic demand. As a result of this change in demand and supply, the relative world price of the good falls

[44] Holger Spamann 'The Myth of 'Rebalancing' Retaliation in WTO Dispute Settlement Practice', 9 (1) Journal of International Economic Law 31 (2006).

[45] See Trachtman, above n 1, at 147–52; Bagwell, above n 1, at 9; Pauwelyn, above n 1, at 6–7, and Schwartz and Sykes, above n 1, at 184–5 (discussing efficient breach).

[46] See, e.g. Schwartz and Sykes, above n 1, at 185, 189, and 192 (arguing for a liability rule).

[47] Bagwell, above n 1.

[48] Pauwelyn, above n 1 (discussing various reasons why certain obligations should be considered inalienable).

benefiting other countries.[49] Export subsidies may also allow for expansion of markets for experience goods where foreign buyers are unaware of the quality of an exporting firm's product. Subsidies allow the exporting firms to sell at a low price until consumers become acquainted with the higher quality of the good.[50] From a political economy perspective, export subsidies allow government officials to provide benefits to concentrated interests which may in turn provide benefits to the officials such as funds for election campaigns, graft, or future employment.[51] These benefits are provided at the expense of more diffuse interests such as consumers or taxpayers.

However, export subsidies also have drawbacks from both a welfare and political economy perspective. First, export subsidies can create a prisoner's dilemma for governments. While they wish to reward certain domestic producers, if all governments wish to protect their industries through subsidies, the result is merely increased government expenditures and expenditures by firms on rent seeking without altering exports.[52] Such subsidies wars may arise in a strategic trade context where export subsidies are thought to be potentially beneficial to a country despite the terms of trade impact. Under strategic trade theory, governments may enable firms to gain control of a market by providing or threatening to provide a subsidy which would allow the domestic firm to produce more cheaply than firms in other countries. Brander and Spencer argued that such benefits may arise in a simple oligopoly model such as may be the case for large commercial aircraft.[53] Such subsidies wars are inefficient.

Second, an export subsidy may undercut market access expectations of other countries.[54] If a country subsidizes its exports, it permits its exporters to provide the product to consumers in other countries at lower prices. Exporters in other countries which have negotiated market access to those

[49] See, e.g. Bagwell, above n 1, at 27, Paul Krugman and Maurice Obstfeld, *International Economics: Theory and Policy*, (7th ed., Boston: Addison Wesley, 2005) 99–102 and 186–7.

[50] Kyle Bagwell and Robert W. Staiger, 'The Role of Export Subsidies When Product Quality is Unknown', 27 Journal of International Economics 69 (1989).

[51] Krugman and Obstfeld, above n 49, at 101–2, J.M. Finger, H. Keith Hall, and Douglas R. Nelson 'The Political Economy of Administered Protection', 72(3) The American Economic Review 452 (1982).

[52] Alan O. Sykes, 'The Economics of WTO Rules on Subsidies and Countervailing Measures' (University of Chicago John M. Olin Law & Economics Working Paper No. 186), http://www.law.uchicago.edu/Lawecon/WkngPprs_176-200/186.aos.subsidies.pdf.

[53] James A. Brander and Barbara J. Spencer, 'Export Subsidies and International Market Share Rivalry' 18 Journal of International Economics 83 (1985) and Elhanan Helpman and Paul R. Krugman, *Trade Policy and Market Structure* (Cambridge: The MIT Press, 1989) 83–115. See, e.g. Krugman and Obstfeld, above n 49, at 262–3 (using a hypothetical dispute between Airbus and Boeing to explain strategic trade theory). But see Kyle Bagwell and Robert W. Staiger, *The Economics of the World Trading System* (Cambridge: The MIT Press, 2002) 168–79 (adding a political economy component to the basic Brander–Spender framework in order to apply it to agricultural export subsidy disputes (a perfectly competitive market)).

[54] Sykes, above n 52, at 7 and Bagwell, above n 1, at 22.

countries will experience harm (equivalent to the other countries giving preferential tariff treatment to the subsidizing country). As a result states will, in general, be less willing to enter into trade agreements as they would not be assured that they would receive the benefit of the bargains they had struck.

Third, and perhaps most importantly, export subsidies distort resource allocation.[55] Consider a single closed economy. If the government provides a subsidy to a firm or industry (such as the electricity generation industry), the firm or industry produces too much of the good and consumers consume too much of the lower-priced good.[56] Production is diverted away from more efficient firms or industry to the subsidized firm or industry. The same holds true in a three-country model. If firms in two countries (A and B) produce a good that is exported to a third country (C), an export subsidy to a firm in A will mean the firm in A will produce more of the subsidized good than is optimal (diverting some or all production from B) and consumers in C will consume too much of the now lower-priced good.[57] Bagwell agrees that production may be diverted to less efficient firms by an export subsidy but notes that these welfare costs can arise with tariffs as well.[58] There is a difference, however, stemming from the baseline from which these measures are approached. Bagwell argues that export subsidies should be permitted (or at least that there is a less solid rationale for the ban on export subsidies than for reductions in tariffs) as they expand trade. However, a reduction in tariffs expands trade by removing a distortionary measure while an export subsidy expands trade by introducing a distortionary measure. The ban on export subsidies is, in this sense, consistent with the reduction in tariffs despite the fact that the former decreases trade volumes and the latter increases trade volumes.

Export subsidies thus appear on balance to be globally inefficient. However, some have argued that export subsidies should be permitted. For example, Bagwell uses a terms of trade approach to argue that export subsidies should be permitted as they expand trade and that the ban on export subsidies may be the result of countries creating a cartel to increase profits by restricting trade.[59] Such increase in profits would then come at the expense of importing countries. However, Bagwell bases his model on export subsidies where governments have political economy objectives that favour export profits over the costs attributable to the subsidy. These subsidies are

[55] Ibid at 7–8 and Bagwell, above n 1, at 40.

[56] See Green, above n 18 and Sykes, above n 52, at 20 for a discussion of some rationales for domestic subsidies in particular instances. See also Sykes, above n 52, at 19 (while there may be reasons (such as correcting market failures) for domestic subsidies, there do not appear to be economic reasons why these subsidies need to be contingent on exports).

[57] Sykes, above n 52, at 11–12.

[58] Bagwell, above n 1, at 40.

[59] Bagwell, above n 1, at 28–29.

then based more generally, on the political economy objectives of the government as opposed to welfare.[60] The resulting cartel may be in the interests of the governments involved but not welfare maximizing for the world as a whole. The initial export subsidy regime (i.e. prior to the elimination of the subsidy) may then have been inefficient from a welfare perspective causing too much production (likely from inefficient firms and resulting in too much consumption and the ban would then move towards a more efficient resource allocation despite being inefficient in terms of the political economy objectives of the governments). Schwartz and Sykes argue that, as a positive matter, the WTO agreements should be seen as maximizing the political gains of the members' governing officials. However, it is a very different matter to argue that whatever is efficient for such government officials is normatively defensible.[61]

Lawrence raises a second argument in favour of export subsidies. He argues that export subsidies are important to developing countries which have set up 'export zones'.[62] He notes that the special rules in these zones may allow greater growth where it is difficult to introduce more wholesale institutional and policy changes in the rest of the country. He further argues that there may be knowledge spillovers from exporting that are promoted by export subsidies.[63] These arguments fit within the broader infant industry literature, where Chang has argued that export subsidies are an important part of a targeted protectionist agenda designed to generate sufficient economies of scale and overcome the initial learning period in the production of experience goods.[64] Even if these arguments have some validity, however, given the potential for injury to other countries, Lawrence acknowledges that not all export subsidies should be permitted. Rather, there may be certain cases in which developing countries should face more lenient penalties than other countries.[65]

Export subsidies therefore appear in general to be inefficient from a welfare perspective. Even on the alternative criteria of political welfare

[60] See Regan, above n 6, at 953–5 (discussing the distinction in approaches to welfare under the terms of trade and the more traditional protectionist models) and Schwartz and Sykes, above n 1, at 183–4.

[61] Regan, above n 6, at 965; Trachtman, above n 1, at 151–52; Nzelibe, above n 1, at 9, and Pauwelyn, above n 1, at 27–28 (discussing how a breach may be public choice efficient, but not welfare efficient).

[62] Lawrence and Stankard, above n 6, at 30–31.

[63] Lawrence and Stankard, above n 6, at 30–31. See also Devesh Roy and Arvind Subramanian, 'Who Can Explain the Mauritian Miracle: Meade, Romer, Sachs, or Rodrik?' (IMF Working Papers Series, No. 01/116, 2001).

[64] Ha-Joon Chang, 'Industrial Policy and East Asia – The Miracle, the Crisis, and the Future' (World Bank workshop on 'Rethinking the East Asian Miracle', 16, 17 February, 1999, San Francisco), http://www.econ.cam.ac.uk/faculty/chang/wbip-pdf.pdf, at 10.

[65] Lawrence and Stankard, above n 6, at 31 (arguing for relaxed rules, especially where the developing country has a small share of world trade). See below n 126 for a discussion of the transitional provisions for developing countries in the SCM Agreement.

maximization, the ban on export subsidies may be efficient where it either constrains subsidy wars or permits the cartelization of an industry. There may, however, be cases where export subsidies have positive welfare effects such as in the case of experience goods.

Lawrence has taken the potential for such instances as evidence that theory does not justify the ban on export subsidies.[66] However, even if it is true that export subsidies are efficient in some circumstances (i.e. that we may want some flexibility concerning their use), the optimal export subsidy provisions will depend not only on the efficiency of export subsidies in certain cases but also on a number of other factors. As Kaplow noted in his discussion of rules versus standards, the optimal form and content of legal commands will depend on relative costs and benefits.[67] First, there are *ex ante* costs of promulgating a law and, in particular, the information costs related to identifying and specifying the various aspects of a rule in advance of it being applied.[68] Second, the parties subject to the legal command face costs in obtaining information about what the command requires. Third, there are enforcement costs including the costs of monitoring compliance and litigating any enforcement action. Finally, Kaplow discusses the benefits that arise from the complexity of the legal command. These benefits can be thought of as a benefit to complexity or as a cost where there are errors as to the appropriate rule. A related issue, which arises from the law and economics literature concerning remedies generally and trade remedies in particular, is the cost of bargaining between the affected parties after a violation has occurred.[69]

In order to design the optimal provisions (including remedies) concerning export subsidies, each of these sets of costs must be examined. One of the interesting factors will be the interaction of these costs and the various institutions and parties that are involved in export subsidies disputes. These include the WTO membership acting as a body in negotiating and drafting agreements, the panels and/or Appellate Body in hearing complaints and the individual members involved or affected by the dispute. The identity of the institution or party involved in decision making will affect the various costs including the likelihood of error in reaching decisions.[70]

WTO provisions concerning export subsidies could provide flexibility to allow efficient export subsidies in two ways. First, the requirements relating to export subsidies could be flexible. These requirements could take the

[66] Lawrence and Stankard, above n 6, at 30.

[67] Louis Kaplow, 'Rules Versus Standards: An Economic Analysis', 42(3) Duke Law Journal 557 (1992).

[68] See, e.g. in the trade context Horn, Maggi and Staiger, above n 43, at 2–3 (formalizing the costs of contracting and discussing WTO agreements as incomplete contracts) and Schwarz and Sykes, above n 1.

[69] See, e.g. Schwartz and Sykes, above n 1 and Trachtman, above n 1.

[70] Kaplow, above n 67, at 608–11.

form of a rule (where the requirements are specified *ex ante*) or a standard (which is broadly expressed with the details of the requirement to be determined through adjudication).[71] Both rules and standards can be more or less complex. Second, the flexibility could arise through the remedies employed to enforce the requirement. In an attempt to explain the various factors that must be considered in determining the optimal remedy, the next section will discuss three options for addressing export subsidies: a complete ban without any flexibility in the remedy; a flexible rule or standard with a strict (inflexible) remedy; and an inflexible requirement with a flexible remedy.

III. RULES, STANDARDS AND REMEDIES

A. A ban on export subsidies and an inflexible remedy

One option would be to prohibit members from using export subsidies in any circumstances and to back this prohibition with a strong penalty aimed at deterring violations. Such a prohibition would have low *ex ante* costs of promulgation as the *ex ante* information costs would be low. Further, it would likely be relatively clear and therefore cost members little to understand and enforce the rule. There is, of course, a cost to such a simple rule—the efficiency loss from prohibiting efficient uses of the export subsidies (assuming for the moment that it is too expensive for the parties to bargain for a solution after a member challenges an alleged violation).

In form at least, such a ban and strict remedy is what exists under the current provisions. A relatively clear ban on export subsidies would make sense if it is expensive to identify *ex ante* the situations in which such subsidies would be efficient. The lower *ex ante* costs of specifying conditions may then compensate for the loss of flexibility to adapt to changing political or economic circumstances. The ban under the SCM Agreement is relatively clear. There is some ambiguity in the requirement that to be prohibited the subsidy must be 'contingent, in law or fact, . . . upon export performance'. The SCM Agreement attempts to provide some specificity through the Annex to the SCM Agreement which contains a list of examples of export subsidies. This list is non-exclusive, however, and there remains flexibility as to the definition of impermissible subsidies, despite the absolute ban.[72] The Appellate Body has retained this flexibility by interpreting the term 'contingency' broadly.[73] However, this flexibility relates to whether the subsidy is in fact 'contingent' on export leaving room for governments to develop programs that may have a legitimate domestic subsidy aspect despite appearing to relate in some form to exports. What the

[71] On the difference between rules and standards, and the overlap between them, see Kaplow, above n 67, at 559–66.

[72] Green, Trebilcock and Milat, above n 10, at 22–25 (discussing the Annex).

[73] See Green, Trebilcock and Milat, above n 10, at 26–27.

flexibility does not do is allow members to use subsidies that are contingent on exports—i.e. if the subsidy is contingent under the definition on exports, they are prohibited (whether or not they are otherwise efficient because, e.g. the goods are experience goods).

The rhetoric concerning the remedy for breach of the ban on export subsidies is that it is focused on deterrence.[74] However, two aspects of how the remedy has been interpreted point to both its under-inclusiveness and over-inclusiveness.[75] First, the requirement to withdraw the subsidy 'without delay' has been interpreted, with one exception, as being prospective in nature, rather than retrospective.[76] This interpretation means that the subsidizing government cannot make any more payments under the impugned programme but does not have to seek repayment of export subsidies it has already paid out. As a result, there is complete flexibility concerning short-term export subsidies, which makes the provision under-inclusive as these short-term subsidies may be inefficient. Still assuming high transaction costs of bargaining around the prohibition, this prospective application reduces the costs in political terms of banning export subsidies as member governments can still use short term, one off subsidies as a political safeguard without any formal sanction.[77] However, this reduced political error cost comes at the expense of increased error costs in welfare terms as members can use inefficient short-term export subsidies without fear of formal penalties. They can, e.g. use strategic trade subsidies to divert production from more efficient sources while complying in the long run with the prohibition. Prospective remedies therefore create potentially greater concerns for export subsidies than for other violations.

If the law required retrospective withdrawal (i.e. required the subsidizing government to obtain repayment of the entire export subsidy), there would be stronger incentives for members not to provide such subsidies as the subsidized firms would have to pay back the funds. Firms would also be less likely to seek such subsidies or rely on government assurances of such subsidies.[78] Members have raised concerns that retrospective repayment of

[74] See, e.g. *US–FSC (arbitration report)*, above n 33, para 5.41.

[75] See Kaplow, above n 67, at 591 (on the under-inclusiveness and over-inclusiveness of simple rules).

[76] The one exception is the panel decision in *Australia—Subsidies Provided to Producers and Exporters of Automotive Leather—Recourse by the United States to Article 21.5 of the DSU (Australia-Leather (21.5))*, WT/DS126/RW, adopted 11 February 2000, para 6.8–17 and 6.50, which has not been followed in subsequent cases.

[77] Schwartz and Sykes, above n 1, argue that the prospective nature of remedies permits flexibility for efficient adjustments as new circumstances arise. The Appellate Body has upheld a panel decision that essentially held that the requirement to withdraw a subsidy includes not making any further payments even under pre-existing commitments (*Brazil—Export Financing Programme for Aircraft—Recourse by Canada to Article 21.5 of the DSU*, WT/DS46/AB/RW (2000), at para 47).

[78] See Green, Trebilcock, and Milat, above n 10.

subsidies may lead to conflicts with domestic law, such as where it constitutes a form of expropriation or breach of contract.[79] However, the WTO has not permitted such domestic considerations to excuse compliance, in accordance with more general international law principles.[80] It may also lead to fewer countries entering into trade agreements if there is no short-term political safeguard as is provided by the prospective nature of the remedy.[81] However, a requirement of retrospective withdrawal prevents inefficient breach and, as will be seen in Section III (C) and (D), channels flexibility into either bargaining or compensation. In either case, the flexibility comes at a price which aids in ensuring the efficiency of any subsidy.

Second, as noted earlier in Section I, arbitrators have set the 'appropriate' level of countermeasures as the amount of the subsidy, with a possible additional penalty where there is deliberate continued non-compliance. The level of subsidy, however, is not necessarily connected to the level of remedy required to induce compliance (which should be at least the level of benefit (political or welfare) obtained by use of the export subsidy, increased to take account of the probability of enforcement).[82] Setting damages at the level of subsidy may be too low, particularly in cases where there are significant spillover effects from the subsidy. This may occur, e.g. in the strategic trade setting for aircraft. In other cases, the level of subsidy may be higher than the level of benefit, although this is less of a concern if the penalty is supporting a property rule (and therefore a high penalty is required to enforce specific performance) and there is a less than certain probability of enforcement.

In rhetoric, therefore, the current provisions are a complete ban backed by remedies aimed at enforcement.[83] Such provisions would be relatively low cost to create, understand and enforce but (assuming high costs of bargaining around the prohibition) would come at the cost of banning efficient uses of export subsidies. What in actual fact prevails in terms of export subsidies is a relatively clear ban (with some flexibility); but an inappropriately flexible remedy which permits short-term inefficient subsidies and is both over-inclusive and under-inclusive in terms of long-term subsidies.

[79] Gavin Goh and Andreas Ziegler, 'Retrospective Remedies in the WTO after Automotive Leather', 6 Journal of International Economic Law 545 (2003) at 556.

[80] Goh and Ziegler, above n 78, at 555–6.

[81] Pauwelyn, above n 1.

[82] Robert Howse and Damien J. Neven, 'United States—Tax treatment for "Foreign Sales Corporations" Recourse to Arbitration by the United States under Article 22.6 of the DSU and Article 4.11 of the SCM Agreement (WT/DS108/ARB) A Comment' in Henrik Horn and Petros C. Mavroidis, (eds) *The WTO Case Law of 2002* (Cambridge: Cambridge University Press, 2005) 36 and Spamann, above n 44.

[83] Howse and Neven, above n 78.

B. A flexible requirement and inflexible remedy

As Kaplow notes, a rule can be either simple (as in the ban discussed earlier) or complex.[84] If there are instances where export subsidies are efficient, one option would be to identify precisely in the SCM Agreement which types of export subsidies are efficient and therefore permissible and which are inefficient and therefore banned. With such a rule, we could be more confident in enforcing the ban with a strong remedy aimed at ensuring compliance. However, as with contracts generally, it is both expensive (and likely impossible) to identify precisely *ex ante* all of the situations in which an export subsidy is efficient.[85] Such a rule would be relatively low cost to enforce since the conditions under which the prohibition applies would be specified.

If the agreement does not specify *ex ante* exactly the conditions in which export subsidy bans are efficient, it may set out a standard such as that members cannot use 'inefficient' export subsidies. Such a standard would have a low *ex ante* cost of promulgation but high costs of enforcement. Panels or the Appellate Body must determine which export subsidies actually are efficient and which are not. These determinations would require considerable information—not just about whether a subsidy diverts trade in a particular instance but also whether the overall efficiency costs of such a diversion are offset by the benefits to consumers in other countries.[86] This difficulty in assessing efficiency can be compared to challenges against actionable subsidies. Actionable subsidies require a determination that the subsidy has caused serious prejudice which involves considerable information and is open to error by panels.

There is then a trade-off between flexibility through a complex rule and a standard in terms of *ex ante* promulgation costs and *ex post* enforcement costs. Kaplow notes that a key determining factor will be the frequency with which the issue arises.[87] The more frequently it arises, the more beneficial it is likely to be to specify the rule with greater complexity *ex ante*. Given that export subsidy complaints constitute a significant share of disputes in the WTO,[88] their frequency would seem to favour a more complex rule

[84] Kaplow, above n 67, at 588–90.

[85] See, e.g. Schwartz and Sykes, above n 1, at 191–2; Pauwelyn, above n 1, at 24; and Horn, Maggi, and Staiger, above n 43 (specifying conditions under which contracting costs and uncertainty may affect the rigidity of the agreement and the discretion it provides for domestic decisions).

[86] See Lawrence and Stankard, above n 6, at 32 (arguing that, in 'strict economic terms', there should be a requirement that the subsidy cause some relatively precisely specified injury prior to its being prohibited 'as well as a weighing of the damage done to producers against the benefits accorded to consumers.')

[87] Kaplow, above n 67, at 585.

[88] Of the 363 disputes that have been filed with the WTO since 1995 (which can be grouped into 270 distinct subject matters), 8.5% cited the Agreement's export subsidy provisions. These data were calculated using the dispute settlement statistics compiled by Simon Lester and Kara Leitner for WorldTradeLaw.net. As noted by the authors, the grouping of disputes

(although the rate of use is somewhat endogenous—i.e. there may be currently greater use of export subsidies because of the existing rule and remedy).

However, there is an additional consideration which is important in determining whether a rule or standard would be preferable—the institutions making the determination. The members of the WTO would have to agree on a specification of the efficient forms of export subsidies. It seems unlikely that the WTO members would have the expertise to make the decision. However, even if they did, the bargaining around the promulgation of the rule would make it unlikely that the resulting rule specified the efficiency conditions correctly. These negotiations would entail high bargaining costs as WTO decisions are made by consensus. A standard, on the other hand, relies on the expertise and judgment of panels or the Appellate Body. As noted earlier, the costs of determining the efficiency of each export subsidy on a case-by-case basis would be very high and would require considerable expertise on the part of the body making the determination.

If there are only a few export subsidies that are efficient and not allowing them creates only small welfare losses, the current rule (prohibiting export subsidies) may be optimal.[89] If, on the other hand, the welfare costs of prohibiting efficient export subsidies are high and the transaction costs of *ex post* bargaining are high, much will depend on the relative competence of the panels/Appellate Body versus the members in determining the efficient policy. Whether the rule or the standard then would be viewed as preferable will depend in large part on the likely error costs of the different institutions (WTO members as a whole or the panels/Appellate Body) mis-specifying the rule.[90] There are two types of error costs that are of concern—the costs of wrongly specifying/determining efficient export subsidies as inefficient and of wrongly specifying/determining inefficient subsidies to be efficient.[91]

---

into matters is subjective, and reflects an assessment of the similarity of separate requests for consultation. Separate consultation requests filed by different countries with respect to the same subsidy, e.g. would be counted as a single subsidy. These data incorporate all material available as of 8 May 2007. For the purposes of the analysis in this article, we have defined an export subsidy dispute as one that either cites Article 3.1(a) of the SCM Agreement, or that cites Article 3 and makes specific reference to export subsidies.

89 The converse would be true if export subsidies were generally efficient and the rule was that all export subsidies were permitted. If transaction costs of bargaining were high, the relative efficiency of this rule would depend on the error (welfare) costs of permitting inefficient export subsidies.

90 Further, countries may be less willing to sign agreements which attempt to specify such instances in advance, as they will not be able to adjust to changing political or economic conditions. Schwartz and Sykes, above n 1, at 184.

91 These errors are analogous to Type I and Type II errors in other contexts. There may be a further difference between rules and standards in that violating a rule may give rise to a greater reputational cost than violating a standard. A country that violates its international agreements may bear reputational costs such as where other countries become less likely to enter into agreements with it in the future (see, e.g. Trachtman, above n 1, at 141–42; Schwartz and Sykes, above n 1, at 196–8 and Pauwelyn, above n 1, at 61–67). This difference

As a result, if the requirement is flexible (such as a complex rule or a standard) but the remedy is not (e.g. where there is a high penalty for non-compliance and the transaction costs of bargaining are high), a rule may be preferable to a standard given the apparent frequency with which export subsidies are used. However, given the few situations in which export subsidies are likely to be efficient, the error costs from the current simple rule (the prohibition on export subsidies) may be low compared to the costs that arise from either the members as a whole or the Appellate Body seeking to establish more complex requirements. The question then becomes whether a simple (inflexible) rule can be combined with a flexible penalty.

C. An inflexible requirement and a flexible remedy

If there is a simple, inflexible requirement, it can be combined in certain circumstances with a remedy that provides flexibility for parties to adjust to or reach efficient outcomes. The simple requirement would result in low *ex ante* promulgation costs and low *ex post* costs of enforcement in the sense of determining whether a violation has actually occurred. However, the flexibility in the remedy creates other costs. There are two main options for flexible remedies: (i) a 'property' rule (a requirement to comply backed by a high penalty aimed at deterrence); and (ii) a 'liability' rule (where the remedy is set according to the harm caused by the violation).[92] This section considers each in turn and their attendant costs.

1. Property rules and transaction costs

The ultimate efficiency of an inflexible rule will be tied to how it is enforced—the remedy that is applied. The Coase Theorem is helpful here. As noted in the last section, if the transaction costs of bargaining after the violation are high, the efficiency of the rule or standard (whichever option is chosen) will depend on relative institutional competence (of the members at large setting the rule or the panel/Appellate Body setting the standard). However, if the transaction costs of bargaining *ex post* are low and the members are permitted to agree on a resolution between themselves, the rule or standard can incorrectly specify the conditions for efficiency and the parties will still be able to reach an efficient outcome through negotiations.[93]

in reputational cost may arise because a respondent may argue that a decision - maker applied a standard incorrectly which may be easier than arguing that a rule was wrongly applied. It would be harder to argue, e.g. that there was no export subsidy (where the rule was a complete prohibition) than that there was an export subsidy but it was efficient. The use of neutral third parties, and in particular the Appellate Body, reduces this ability to argue mistake by the decision maker to some extent (see Schwartz and Sykes, above n 1).

92 See, e.g. Schwartz and Sykes, above n 1, Trachtman, above n 1, and Pauwelyn, above n 1.

93 Schwartz and Sykes, above n 1, at 182–3.

Where transaction costs of bargaining are low, a property rule may be optimal.[94] The property rule would set a high penalty for violating (i.e. a penalty aimed at deterrence) but allow parties to bargain to a mutually acceptable solution. It has the virtue of allowing the parties who likely have better information (the governments involved) to determine efficiency.[95]

The first question to ask is whether the transaction costs of bargaining are high or low in the case of export subsidies? Transaction costs (including the risk of hold outs) will depend on the number of parties to the bargain. In the case of export subsidies, in many cases (such as the strategic trade context), the numbers may be low as the importing countries would not complain (they are benefiting) and there would only need to be a negotiation with the few other countries with relevant industries. However, as the number of countries increases, the transaction costs would increase (as in the case of agricultural subsidies). The risk of strategic export subsidies declines but the risk of hold out increases. Given that a number of countries could claim affected industries or potential industries, the transaction costs of bargaining may be high.

There is an additional factor which may make the transaction costs of bargaining high—who can obtain a remedy. For most violations, any party bringing a challenge can obtain a remedy but the remedy is tied (at least notionally) to the level of impairment.[96] Under the current export subsidies rule, on the other hand, the provisions are not tied to cause harm to the complaining party. Any party can apparently bring a challenge and the remedy is the entire amount of the subsidy—i.e. focused not on harm to a party but the level of damages that can result in compliance.[97] This approach can be seen most clearly in the *US–FSC* case where the European Community (EC) was permitted to retaliate in the full amount of the subsidy even though it was not the only country affected by the subsidy.[98] The export subsidies provisions therefore increase the transaction costs of settling—if a member settles with one party, there is a risk that any other party can bring a complaint for the whole value of the subsidy. These provisions therefore create a hold out problem.

Further, as export subsidies are prohibited and (as noted earlier) Article 4 of the SCM Agreement does not permit agreements as to compensation, the transaction costs of settling may be even higher. Guzman and Simmons term disputes 'lumpy' where they do not admit to a continuous form of solution (such as agreeing to a lower level of subsidy) and find some

[94] See, e.g. Schwartz and Sykes, above n 1.

[95] Pauwelyn, above n 1, at 40–44.

[96] See, e.g. DSU, Article 22.4. See also Trachtman, above n 1.

[97] Green, Trebilcock, and Milat, above n 10, at 51–52; Trachtman, above n 1, at 135–36, and 152, and Lawrence, above n 1, at 57–58.

[98] *US–FSC (arbitration report)*, above n 33, paras 6.19 and 6.28.

empirical evidence that 'lumpy' cases are less likely to settle than 'continuous' cases (such as tariff disputes), at least where the dispute involves a democratic pair of countries.[99] If so, the inability to agree on continuation of any level of export subsidy is an added transaction cost which implies a reduced likelihood of settlement or bargaining around complaints. It may be harder to reach a settlement where the remedy will not be applied in the same sector.[100] The respondent has to balance political capital across sectors. Export subsidies cases (likely more so than other measures) may not arise between countries with substantial trade between themselves and particularly not in the relevant sector (such as where two countries are competing for exports to third-country markets).[101] As a result, the transaction costs of bargaining in the cases of a property rule may be high.

These high transaction costs (in particular, of the current rules) may explain the relatively high rate of escalation among export subsidy disputes. The 363 disputes that have been filed with the WTO since 1995, can be grouped into 270 distinct subject matters.[102] Of these matters, 21% cited the SCM Agreement, and 8.5% cited the Agreement's export subsidy provisions. Of all dispute matters that escalated from a request for consultations to a panel report (or an ongoing panel in the case of recent disputes), SCM matters represented 24.4%, and export subsidy matters represented 10.2%. Settlement therefore seems slightly less likely in export subsidy matters.[103]

However, the contentiousness of export subsidy disputes can be seen more readily in their heightened tendency to generate multiple panel and AB reports. Export subsidy disputes accounted for 13.2% of the total number of panel reports and ongoing panels, significantly higher than their 8.5% of consultation requests. Export subsidies also represented 51.2% of all SCM panel reports and ongoing panels, compared to 40.4% of all SCM

[99] Andrew Guzman and Beth Simmons, 'To Settle or Empanel? An Empirical Analysis of Litigation and Settlement at the World Trade Organization', 31 Journal of Legal Studies S205 (2002), at 222–3.

[100] See Nzelibe, above n 1, at 8 (discussing the importance of tying retaliation to the industry that benefits from the WTO violation). See also Lawrence, above n 1, at 50 (arguing that the ability to retaliate in other sectors, where trade is robust, does little for the industry that has been injured by the WTO violation).

[101] Guzman and Simmons, above n 99, at 224 (finding that for all trade disputes, as the complainant's exports to the respondent increase, the tendency to settle increases which they attribute to the unwillingness of the complainant to harm its export market).

[102] As noted earlier, these data were calculated using the dispute settlement statistics compiled by Simon Lester and Kara Leitner for WorldTradeLaw.net. These data incorporate all material available as of 8 May 2007. Two matters that cited exports subsidies in the consultation stage were not included in the panel count as the requests to establish a panel did not reference export subsidies.

[103] Disputes that produce a panel report have generally reached the point of adjudication without settling, and we consider them to have escalated. But see Guzman and Simmons, above n 99, at 208 (arguing that a dispute has escalated as soon as a panel has been established because the prepanel stage presents the greatest opportunity for settlement).

consultation requests. These higher percentages were maintained for Appellate Body reports, with export subsidies referenced in 12.2% of total reports and 52.6% of SCM reports.[104] The contentiousness of export subsidy disputes is further evidenced by their tendency to result in Article 21.5 proceedings because of disputes over compliance with DSB recommendations. Export subsidies constituted 27% of all Article 21.5 reports, and 71.4% of the Article 21.5 reports relating to the SCM Agreement.[105]

If the transaction costs are high, a property rule combined with an inflexible requirement will only reach an efficient result if the body promulgating the rule or standard creates the optimal rule or standard. In the case of export subsidies, transaction costs seem likely to be high in general. The current rule seems to actually increase the transaction costs of bargaining and therefore make the efficient outcome even less likely. There is, however, another option in the face of high transaction costs—a liability rule—which is discussed in the next section.

2. *Liability rules and valuation costs*

If the transaction costs of bargaining are high, one possibility is not to use a property rule but instead a liability rule which allows the subsidizing party to 'buy' its way out of its obligations. A liability rule avoids the need for bargaining and therefore any error costs that result from an inefficient rule or standard combined with a lack of bargaining.[106] Liability rules reflect an efficient breach approach to the WTO agreements—that the agreements are incomplete in design and that members can violate the agreements provided they are willing to bear the costs. If the penalty is set at the level of harm caused by the violation, members will only violate the agreement (and pay damages) in cases which increase global welfare (or in the case of a political model of the WTO agreements, increase in political welfare of the governments).[107] However, there are error costs associated with liability rules as well. If the penalty is set incorrectly (i.e. it does reflect the actual harm caused), then the members will engage in too much or too little breach depending on whether the penalty is set too low or too high. The party setting the penalty (such as a panel or an arbitrator) may make a mistake in setting the penalty if it is difficult to ascertain

[104] There were no ongoing disputes before the AB at the time of writing.

[105] Where an Article 21.5 panel report was appealed, the initial panel report and the Appellate Body report are counted separately.

[106] See Trachtman, above n 1, at 148–51; Pauwelyn, above n 1, at 21–25; Schwartz and Sykes, above n 1, at 182–3.

[107] Schwartz and Sykes, above n 1, at 182; Trachtman, above n 1, at 151–52. This reasoning stems from Calabresi and Melamed. As noted earlier, there is an on-going debate about whether this is an appropriate positive or normative view of the WTO agreements. For arguments against this view, see Pauwelyn, above n 1, and Jackson, above n 9.

the exact level of harm or if certain harms (such as environmental effects) are not quantified.[108]

There are two separate questions relating to valuation: what should be the measure of the damages and who should make that determination. In terms of the measure of the damages, for efficient breach the damages should be set at the level of harm caused by the breach. How should this harm be measured? If whatever measure is chosen cannot be readily estimated, a property rule may be favoured.[109] As Trachtman notes, a central issue is whether harm should be seen as welfare-based (i.e. related to the losses to the injured member(s)' economic welfare) or politically based (i.e. related to losses to the political officials of the government of the injured member(s)).[110] He argues that, while there may be positive (as opposed to normative) reasons to view the WTO agreements as maximizing joint political welfare, calculating harm based on an estimation of the political harm from another member's policies would be intractable. Schwartz and Sykes, who take a public choice view of the WTO agreements, recognize the difficulty in measuring these harms but, as Trachtman notes, this limits its usefulness as a basis for liability rule remedies.[111] Trachtman argues the WTO should use economic welfare-based remedies and hope that accountability mechanisms will lead governments to follow the incentives created. As a starting point for the DSU remedies, he recommends setting remedies at the level of injury caused by the violation to all members calculated as the amount of the transfer plus consumer deadweight loss (multiplied by the inverse of the probability of enforcement and including the costs of enforcement).[112]

If the WTO's objective is seen as maximizing economic welfare, the damages should be related to the harm caused by the export subsidy to the welfare in all other countries.[113] Under the current system for export subsidies, members challenging export subsidies can take 'appropriate' countermeasures if the subsidizing member does not withdraw the subsidy without delay. As noted earlier, decisions by arbitrators have determined that 'appropriate' in terms of countermeasures requires deterrence and incentives to bring measures into compliance with the Agreement. They have set the 'appropriate' level as the level of subsidy (even where the complainant accounts for much less than all subsidized imports) and have added in one case an extra 20% penalty. Interpreting 'appropriate' measures in this way

[108] Pauwelyn, above n 1, at 32–33, e.g. discusses difficulties in valuation (including a category of cases in international law for which he argues there can be no quantification).

[109] Trachtman, above n 1, at 144. Even where it is difficult to measure harm, however, it may still be necessary to weigh the seriousness of potential valuation errors against the risk of no bargaining with high transaction costs.

[110] Trachtman, above n 1, at 152–55.

[111] Schwartz and Sykes, above n 1, at 187, and Trachtman, above n 1, at 152.

[112] Trachtman, above n 1, at 166–67.

[113] Trachtman, above n 1, at 166–67.

has invoked considerable criticism.[114] From an efficient breach perspective, there is no necessary connection between the level of subsidy and the harm caused to other members. The level of subsidy may be much lower than the harm (such as where from a strategic trade perspective a threat of a subsidy is able to deter the formation of an industry in other countries) or higher than the harm (as may have been the case in the *US–FSC* case).

The DSU currently relates the penalty for breach of other (non-export subsidy) provisions to the harm caused to the member(s) challenging the measure.[115] If harm for export subsidies is measured in this manner, the remedy for breach of export subsidies would in theory be no less readily measurable than for any other violation. One concern is that this level of damages or equivalence in retaliation can underestimate the harm caused, because a liability rule for export subsidies should take account of the harm from export subsidies but net of benefits to consumers in other countries.[116] However, tying the remedy to harm at least brings it closer to the efficient remedy, reducing inefficient incentives.

The other important issue is who sets the level of the remedy. Under the prohibited subsidies provisions of the SCM Agreement (Section I), the complainant proposes countermeasures and the responding party may seek arbitration of these measures to determine whether they are 'appropriate'. Under the pre-WTO structure, the complaining party could impose countervailing duties (i.e. set the price) for general violations of agreements. However, subsidies came under a special regime—specific amendments to GATT and then the 1979 Subsidies Code.[117] Interestingly, the Subsidies Code had specific provisions that prohibited export subsidies on non-primary products and requested that signatories not use export subsidies on primary products to increase their share of world trade beyond what was equitable. The Code set out a procedure where there was a dispute over export subsidies. The procedure involved consultation, adjudication by a Panel and possible authorization of countermeasures by a Committee on Subsidies and Countervailing Measures.

This procedure is interesting, as Schwartz and Sykes argue that one of the reasons for the DSU was to limit penalties for violations of the agreements because under the prior system of unilateral measures there was the potential that complainants would opportunistically impose very high penalties.[118]

[114] Bagwell, above n 1 at 24; Lawrence, above n 1 at 58; Spamann, above n 44, at 75, and Trachtman, above n 1, at 135–7 and 139–40.

[115] DSU, Article 22.4.

[116] Trachtman, above n 1, at 157–8 and 166–67 (discussing the differences in different calculations of harm) and Lawrence and Stankard, above n 6, at 29 and 32.

[117] Michael J. Trebilcock and Robert Howse, *The Regulation of International Trade*, 3rd ed., (London/New York: Routledge, 2005) and John H. Jackson, *The World Trading System* (Cambridge: MIT Press, 1997) 288.

[118] Schwartz and Sykes, above n 1, at 187.

They argue that the new system allows for a limit on penalties which facilitates efficient breach. The SCM Agreement provisions, in effect, do not change the procedures for subsidies. The procedures remain primarily focused on neutral arbitration, leaving them based on what Schwartz and Sykes argue, leads to more limited level of remedies despite the fact that the export subsidies provisions (in rhetoric at least) focus on prohibition and deterrence which should justify larger remedies. The reason may be that the multilateral route is more likely not only (as Schwartz and Sykes argue) to limit scope for excessive penalties but also for retaliation—a neutral third-party setting (or at least authorizing) the countermeasures aids in acceptance and legitimacy by respondents.[119]

As a result, valuation concerns make it difficult to be confident that the remedy for breach of export subsidy provisions could be tailored to the harm caused either on a welfare or political basis. The use of a neutral arbitrator makes the countermeasures much more likely to be acceptable to the parties if the appropriate basis could be determined. However, the error costs from an incorrect valuation seem large. Further, the errors in general appear to be on the undervaluation side.[120] If so, members will engage in too much breach. The effect will then depend again on error costs—are the costs greater from an incorrect liability rule (i.e. an incorrect level for the remedy) or from prohibiting efficient subsidies (which would be the case with a property rule, backed by strong sanctions but with high transaction costs of bargaining). Given the limited nature of efficiency enhancing export subsidies, from a welfare perspective it would appear that the former costs are higher where the current remedy is used (i.e. a remedy based on the level of subsidy). However, if the remedy is tied to the level of harm (in terms of the trade effects), it may be the case that the simple ban tied to a liability rule is preferable because of the flexibility it provides.[121]

[119] See Schwartz and Sykes, above n 1, at 202–04 (discussing the benefits of arbitration of the level of countermeasures as opposed to unilateral determination). But see Eric Reinhardt 'Aggressive Multilateralism: The Determinants of GATT/WTO Dispute Initiation 1948–1998' (1999 Annual Meeting of the International Studies Association, Washington, DC, 17, 20 February), http://userwww.service.emory.edu/~erein/research/initiation.pdf (arguing that the initiation of a WTO dispute makes it significantly more likely that the respondent will retaliate by launching a WTO dispute against the complainant).

[120] Trachtman, above n 1, at 144–45 and Spamann, above n 44, at 45–46. Such undervaluation is exacerbated where the remedy is only applied prospectively. It is further exacerbated if the probability of enforcement is low. However, in terms of the probability of enforcement, there may be some incentive to engage in litigation depending on the remedy which would help overcome some of the potential underdeterrence concerns. Further, reputational costs may increase the penalty from violations, thereby compensating for the lower valuation of the remedy. However, it is difficult to determine how much of a reputational cost may be incurred in any particular case and the reputational cost of a breach of a liability rule is likely lower than for a property rule (and possibly zero). For a discussion of reputation, see Trachtman, above n 1; Pauwelyn, above n 1, and Schwartz and Sykes, above n 1.

[121] There is, of course, one further option—a flexible requirement (complex rule or standard) along with a flexible remedy (such as a liability rule or property rule where transaction costs are low). However, the various factors and error costs of this option are merely a

D. Flexibility and efficiency

In summary, then, the design of the requirement and the remedy involve trade-offs. There are costs of promulgation, information, enforcement, error, and bargaining. The distribution of these costs varies across different combinations of requirements and remedies. In order to allow optimal flexibility (including, possibly in some cases, no flexibility), the trade-offs across these costs must be considered. This trade-off is closely tied to the nature of the institutions which make decisions under each alternative.[122]

In the case of export subsidies, there are inefficiencies that arise from a simple ban on export subsidies such as is currently in place. The flexibility could come from a more complex rule or standard. However, it will be costly (particularly considering information costs and competency) for either the WTO members as a whole to set a sufficiently complex rule or the panels or Appellate Body to set an appropriate standard. The ban may therefore be the best requirement, but there should then be some flexibility through the remedy if this can be achieved at a reasonable cost. This flexibility should not come through a prospective remedy as is currently the place, as a prospective remedy in the case of subsidy permits short-term breach at no cost. Such a requirement increases the use of inefficient subsidies. As the *ex post* costs of bargaining in the case of export subsidies are likely high (particularly under the current rules), a liability rule may be preferable to a property rule. In order to achieve a reasonable valuation cost, the liability rule should be based on trade effects as is the case for other violations. Such a rule would at least be an improvement over the current rule setting the remedy at the level of subsidies which is both over-inclusive and under-inclusive.

IV. FORM OF REMEDY AND PUBLIC CHOICE CONCERNS

The earlier discussion focused on issues that applied to both a welfare and a public choice view of the objective of remedial provisions. It examined whether flexibility for efficient adjustments should arise from the nature of the requirement (including whether the requirement should be a standard or a rule) or of the remedy. In terms of the remedy, the focus was on the level of the remedy (should it be set at a level to ensure deterrence or at

---

combination of those costs for the options discussed, giving rise to a range of error costs—both on the side of promulgating the requirement and enforcing it.

[122] These costs are relevant across all measures. For example, tariffs may also raise trade-offs favouring a ban, although other costs (such as adjustment and political economy costs) may be sufficiently large to support a more flexible rule. Reciprocity in negotiating tariff reductions and gradualism in phasing in the reductions may be a means of moderating these adjustment and politicaleconomy costs.

the level of harm). However, it is important to consider a related question—what form should the actual remedy take? This issue assumes importance in part because of public choice concerns about how damages actually affect the decisions of officials in different states.[123] Public choice concerns incorporate the theory that public officials respond to interest groups with the greatest ability to aid their political or economic aspirations—i.e. to provide revenue for re-election campaigns, to provide future employment or even to provide straight payments. Schwartz and Sykes have argued that such public choice concerns provide a positive explanation for a number of the provisions of the WTO agreements which they view as fostering joint political maximization of member governments.[124]

The public choice view is important for considering the remedies for violation of the export subsidies provisions. First, public choice concerns arise with the level and objective of the remedies imposed upon the violating member. The remedies in the form of countermeasures have been argued to harm the consumers of the complaining state without necessarily harming the protected interests in the violating member and so not leading to any incentive to comply with the WTO agreement.[125] Such a result would occur where the countermeasures by the complaining state hurt other industries than the subsidized industry.[126] In some ways, this difficulty could be seen to be even worse for export subsidies as the disputes may occur with respect to exports to third countries where the disputants may not have a significant trade in the good between themselves or even much trade at all. The result would be countermeasures that may not create much harm to political interests of the governing officials.

Larger penalties based on benefit to the subsidizing member (or its governing officials) or seeking to induce compliance, are more likely to have an effect in such cases as they do not need to be tailored to the specific level of benefit. Nzelibe has argued that such large remedies may not be used in the WTO setting because there is no centralized enforcement and there is a risk of an escalating trade war in the face of stiff countermeasures.[127] However, the risk of such a trade war may be one of the key reasons for channelling export subsidies disputes into neutral arbitration of the level of remedies. As noted earlier, Schwartz and Sykes argue that the use of neutral arbitrators protects respondents from an overly high price for breach. It also has the potential effect of protecting the complaining party from

[123] Nzelibe, above n 1, at 11.

[124] Schwartz and Sykes, above n 1.

[125] Nzelibe, above n 1, at 2–3 (setting out the argument that damages will not affect incentives of political officials).

[126] This concern is related to, though separate from, the concern discussed earlier that the valuation of either harm or benefit on a political economy (as opposed to welfare) basis would be very difficult.

[127] Nzelibe, above n 1, at 10.

retaliation as it is more difficult for the respondent to claim retaliation is justified, if the countermeasure is in accordance with the decision of a neutral arbitrator. The real difficulty with larger penalties is not the retaliation but the lack of flexibility in combination with a simple rule such as a prohibition. The question then becomes whether the form of the remedy can be altered to make it more effective.

A related notion is that some countries will not have the ability to actually enforce the provisions. Developing countries in particular, may not have enough trade with larger countries to effectively use remedies.[128] This concern arises with the general provisions which permit countermeasures 'equivalent' to the nullification and impairment. It is an even greater concern with inducing compliance through property rules backed by even larger penalties (including possibly those tied to the level of subsidy).[129] Further, this system provides no compensation (and in fact causes possible harm) for countries that are small (i.e. cannot affect their own terms of trade).[130]

The ability actually to use the remedies may be one reason for the distribution of complainants in export subsidies matters.[131] As with the use of the dispute settlement system generally, the complainants are mainly industrialized countries. Industrialized countries were the complainants in 75.0% of export subsidy disputes, as compared to 67.3% of all WTO disputes.[132] The distribution among industrialized countries, however,

[128] See, e.g. Nzelibe, above n 1, at 2–3 and 29–35 for a discussion of these developing country issues.

[129] The use of a prohibition may lead to greater reputational harm to a subsidizing country and therefore there may be some further aid to even developing countries from having these provisions, even if they cannot avail themselves fully of the formal penalties. See Pauwelyn, above n 1, at 61–67 and Trachtman, above n 1, at 141–43 discussing the role of reputational penalties and the different effect of reputation in the face of efficient breach as opposed to mandatory compliance approaches.

[130] Lawrence, above n 1, at 95–96; Bagwell, above n 1, at 17; and Trachtman, above n 1, at 128–29.

[131] There may be other reasons such as that developing countries lack the capacity to participate in the dispute settlement system or are fearful of challenging more economically powerful states (see, e.g. Andrew T. Guzman and Beth A. Simmons, 'Power Plays and Capacity Constraints: The Selection of Defendants in World Trade Organization Disputes' (2005) 34 Journal of Legal Studies 557; Horn and Mavroidis, above n 36 (summarizing the empirical literature on participation in disputes), and Chad P. Bown and Bernard M. Hoekman, 'Making Trade Agreements Relevant for Poor Countries: Why Dispute Settlement is Not Enough' Journal of World Trade, forthcoming, http://people.brandeis.edu/~cbown/papers/Bown-Hoekman-Relevance.pdf).

[132] These export subsidy statistics were calculated by applying the methodology described in Henrik Horn and Petros C. Mavroidis, 'The WTO Dispute Settlement System 1995–2004: Some descriptive statistics' (World Bank WTO Dispute Settlement Database, http://go.worldbank.org/X5EZPHXJY0). The general WTO dispute statistics are those calculated by these authors. Horn and Mavroidis count requests for consultation involving several complainants as multiple binary disputes. They classify countries into G2 (US and EC15), IND (all other OECD members and developed nations), LDC (the UN's list of Least Developed Countries), and DEV (all other countries). These data incorporate all material available on 28 February 2005 for disputes begun before 31 July 2004.

is dramatically different. The US and EC 15 are the complainants in 54.2% of export subsidies cases, but only 28.3% of all WTO disputes. All other industrialized countries have a lower rate of being complainants in export subsidies cases (20.8%) than in general WTO disputes (31.8%). Developing countries (including the least-developed countries) also made up a lower share of complainants in export subsidies cases than in all cases combined (25.0% for export subsidies cases as opposed to 32.7% for total cases). Dispute initiation may be less attractive to poor countries because they are unable to take advantage of the full scope of the remedy.[133]

A second public choice concern arises where the trade dispute cannot be easily negotiated in a trade setting—i.e. some aspect of the dispute makes it difficult to resolve through remedies tied to trade. For example, Schwartz and Sykes note that a tariff reduction may not be very well suited to the case of a country seeking to protect the health of its citizens.[134] There is nothing in particular about export subsidies which give rise to such an effect—they seem to be, in Guzman and Simmons' terms, incremental (variable) and open to negotiation. They only become 'lumpy' because the SCM Agreement institutes a ban and does not permit negotiation over compensation. This lumpiness makes it more difficult to bargain or to reach an agreement with various domestic constituents.

One option for addressing these concerns about the form of the remedy is to allow countries to trade or auction their right to countermeasure to other members. This suggestion has the benefit of providing the power to parties which may be able to use it.[135] However, the country which obtains the power may not have the incentive to use the power fully to induce compliance—as its incentive is to benefit its domestic industries to the maximum extent as opposed to induce compliance. This incentive, to aid its domestic industries, may at the same time provide maximum

[133] The data for who are respondents in these cases is difficult to interpret given the transition periods for developing countries. As mentioned earlier, Article 27.2(a) of the SCM agreement allows LDCs to continue to use export subsidies until they reach export competitiveness, and Article 27.2(b) allows other developing countries to maintain their export subsidies for eight years after the entry into force of the WTO agreement, unless they reach export competitiveness before then. However, the US and EC 15 were by far the greatest respondents in both export subsidies cases (54.2% of cases) and total cases (56.2%). All other industrialized countries were much more likely to be respondents in export subsidies disputes (41.7%) than for all disputes combined (17.4%). Developing countries, on the other hand, were much less likely to be respondents in export subsidies cases than for all cases (4.2% in export subsidies cases and 26.3% for all cases).

[134] Schwartz and Sykes, above n 1, at 192.

[135] K. Bagwell, P.C. Mavroidis, and R.W. Staiger, 'The Case for Auctioning Countermeasures in the WTO' (NBER Working Paper Series No. 9920, August 2003), http://www.nber.org/papers/w9920.pdf.

leverage for compliance but it may not given that it may not be aimed at groups with power to force the subsidizing government to change its behaviour.[136]

Another option is monetary compensation or a fine paid by the subsidizing country to the harmed countries. Such monetary payment provides compensation to the harmed countries and provides some incentive for compliance.[137] However, there are concerns about how to enforce this remedy—countermeasures have the benefit of being self-enforcing (i.e. complaining countries can undertake them themselves without any cooperation from the subsidizing country).[138] Further, there is a concern that such payments will not have a significant incentive effect on the subsidizing country where the government can spread the costs of the compensation across less powerful groups (such as taxpayers).[139]

A final alternative that has been proposed has been liberalization of other trade restrictive measures by the subsidizing country. Such liberalization allows for compensation for the harmed countries regardless of their size and provides an incentive to the subsidizing country to comply.[140] It creates concerns about the MFN principle, which would require the liberalization commitment to be extended to all members.[141] In one sense, this may not be problematic in the case of export subsidies. It provides a significant incentive for compliance and reflects the difficulty in determining exactly who is harmed by the subsidy. Lawrence argues for preauthorized contingent compensation—which essentially seems to be liquidated damages whereby a member specifies in advance the concessions it will provide if it breaches the agreement.[142] However, such a result seems unlikely to be effective. Either the actual remedy will not be tied to the harm and so it will not correspond to the efficient level of compensation (and therefore permit efficient breach), or will unlikely be sufficiently punitive to increase the incentive to comply with a property rule (as governments seem unlikely to be able to obtain agreement from powerful domestic industries to hurt them if they wish to benefit some other industry).

As a result, the form of the remedy will be as important as the level. The current form (countermeasures) is potentially ineffective both because it may not harm those with political power in the subsidizing state and because it may not be accessible as a remedy for certain (smaller) countries. The best alternative would appear to be a form of compensating trade concessions.

[136] Nzelibe, above n 1, at 9 and 12–13.
[137] Lawrence, above n 1, at 84 and Bagwell, above n 1, at 11–12 and 15.
[138] Lawrence, above n 1, at 85; Trachtman, above n 1, at 163 and Bagwell, above n 1, at 16.
[139] Nzelibe, above n 1, at 9 and 12.
[140] Lawrence, above n 1, at 87.
[141] Bagwell, above n 1, at 15 and Trachtman, above n 1, at 134.
[142] Lawrence, above n 1, at 86–88 (on contingent liberalization commitments).

While this may run into difficulty with the MFN principle, it would have the virtue of aiding countries which do not have the power to impose countermeasures. Further, for some small countries which have a single form of export (such as a mono-crop) which is affected by export subsidies in another country, compensating trade concessions may be difficult to achieve. Financial compensation may therefore be necessary as an alternative form of remedy.

V. REFORMING ENFORCEMENT

Export subsidies illustrate some interesting issues about reforming remedies for violations of WTO obligations. In order to maximize economic welfare, it is important to consider the remedy in conjunction with the nature of the requirement (including whether it is simple or complex and whether it is a rule or standard). Efficient adjustment to new circumstances requires flexibility. This flexibility can arise in a number of ways, each involving a trade-off among various costs. These costs include the costs of designing an optimal rule or standard, the costs of enforcing the rule or standard, the error costs of creating the wrong rule or standard and the costs of bargaining after a breach has occurred.

In the case of export subsidies, there are error costs from the current simple ban on export subsidies—i.e. there are certain instances in which export subsidies may be efficient. However, designing a requirement and/or a remedy to provide the flexibility to obtain the efficient result is difficult. The difficulty in *ex ante* specifying the efficient situations by the WTO members as a whole or *ex post* by panels or the Appellate Body suggests that it is better to provide the flexibility through the remedy. Further, there seem to be high *ex post* bargaining costs where there has been a violation of a ban on export subsidies (especially under the current rules). Such high transaction costs militate in favour of a liability rule. The error costs of incorrectly specifying the harm from the export subsidy seem not large if trade effects are used as the basis for the remedy as in the general case. Export subsidies also point to the necessity of considering the form of the remedy. Some countries may have difficulty using countermeasures (not to mention the fact that countermeasures create barriers to trade). There is a need to consider new forms of remedies such as compensating trade concessions and monetary compensation.

Export subsidies therefore provide a good example of a range of concerns underlying the remedies debate. One central point is that each type or combination of requirement or remedy gives rise to a trade-off over various types of costs. These costs are closely related to the relative competence of the institutions which are called upon to make choices or decisions for each type of requirement or remedy, whether it be the WTO members as a whole, panels or the Appellate Body, or the members as individual decision makers. A single form of requirement and remedy is unlikely to be efficient for all types of violations of WTO obligations. These costs and institutional considerations are central to the debates over remedies for violations of WTO obligations and must be considered for each type of violation.

THE WTO'S ENVIRONMENTAL PROGRESS

*Steve Charnovitz**

ABSTRACT

The linkage between trade and the environment stands out as an important challenge in global economic governance. Over the past decade, the WTO devoted considerable attention to this issue and included it on the agenda of the Doha Round. In parallel, the jurisprudence on trade and the environment has experienced significant advances. This study provides an overview of the main institutional changes at the WTO and of the developments in the jurisprudence most relevant to the interaction between the environment and trade. Specifically, this study focuses on General Agreement on Tariffs and Trade (GATT) Article XX and takes note of many positive (and a few negative) features of the key Appellate Body decisions.

INTRODUCTION

Over the past decade, an important period of reform has commenced in the interplay of trade and the environment. The debate began about 80 years ago and can be capsulized briefly. The initial debate occurred in the 1920s during the preparatory period for the first multilateral trade law instrument, the Convention for the Abolition of Import and Export Prohibitions and Restrictions. That Convention contained an exception for trade restrictions imposed for the protection of public health and the protection of animals and plants against diseases and against 'extinction'.[1] A generation later, the debate was rekindled in the drafting of the Charter of the International Trade Organization (ITO) and the General Agreement on Tariffs and Trade (GATT). The ITO Charter's Commercial provisions contain a general exception for multilateral environmental agreements (MEAs), in addition to the general exceptions that parallel those in the contemporary GATT Article XX (general exceptions). The MEA exception of 1948 applies to measures 'taken in pursuance of any inter-governmental agreement which relates solely to the conservation of fisheries resources, migratory birds or wild animals', and which meets some

* Faculty of Law, George Washington University, 2000 H Street, Washington, DC 20052. E-mail: scharnovitz@law.gwu.edu.

[1] Convention for the Abolition of Import and Export Prohibitions and Restrictions, 8 November 1927, 97 League of Nation Treaty Series 391, Article 4, Ad Article 4, not in force.

additional conditions.[2] The debate on trade and the environment was revived in the early 1970s, and then became quiescent again. By the late 1980s, the GATT had developed an inward-looking personality, and began to be perceived as being unsympathetic to the challenges of protecting the environment. Emblematic of this environmental insensitivity was the GATT Secretariat Report of 1992 on 'Trade and the Environment' which proclaimed that 'In principle, it is not possible under GATT's rules to make access to one's own market dependent on the domestic environmental policies or practices of the exporting country'.[3] A new era in the trade-environment debate began in 1996–98. This era was fostered by enlightened Appellate Body jurisprudence and boosted by the attention given to the environment by trade negotiators in the waning days of the Uruguay Round.

This article calls the past decade a 'reform' period for the trading system not because of the birth of a new solicitude for the environment, but rather because the earlier green fundamentals of the trading system are now being respected. As will be seen subsequently, the Appellate Body gave little attention to the historic roots, preferring instead to formulate its environment-friendly holdings as an 'evolutionary' approach to interpretation. Nevertheless, in my view, the dramatic change in trade jurisprudence over the past decade is not evolutionary (and not revolutionary), but rather is reformist in orientation.

For this *Journal* to take note of 'trade and the environment' in this anniversary issue is appropriate indeed. Attention to the environment appeared in the first pages[4] of this *Journal*, and over the past ten years, the *Journal* has presented considerable cutting edge scholarship on this linkage.[5] The *Journal* has also run book reviews on this topic.[6]

[2] Havana Charter for an International Trade Organization (ITO Charter), 24 March 1948, http://www.wto.org/english/docs_e/legal_e/prewto_legal_e.htm (visited 10 June 2007), Article 45(1)(a)(x), not in force. The three additional conditions for such an international agreement are: (i) that it is not used to accomplish results inconsistent with the ITO Chapter on Intergovernmental Commodity Control Agreements, (ii) that it is not used to accomplish results inconsistent with the purposes of the ITO Charter, and (iii) that the agreement is given 'full publicity'. Ibid, Articles 60(1)(e), 70(1)(d). Note that GATT Article XXIX:1 calls on parties to 'undertake to observe to the fullest extent of their executive authority the general principles... of the Havana Charter...'

[3] GATT Secretariat, *International Trade 90–91*, Vol. 1, 1992, 19–43 at 23.

[4] John H. Jackson, 'Global Economics and International Economic Law', 1 Journal of International Economic Law 1 (1998), at 3.

[5] For example, Daniel C. Esty, 'An Environmental Perspective on Seattle', 3 Journal of International Economic Law (2000) 176; David Vogel, 'Environmental Regulation and Economic Integration', 3 Journal of International Economic Law (2000) 265; Barbara Eggers and Ruth Mackenzie, 'The Cartagena Protocol on Biosafety', 3 Journal of International Economic Law (2000) 525; Andrew Green, 'Climate Change, Regulatory Policy and the WTO: How Constraining Are Trade Rules?', 8 Journal of International Economic Law (2005) 143; Andrew Green and Tracey Epps, 'The WTO, Science and the Environment', 10 Journal of International Economic Law (2007) 285.

[6] For example, Kevin P. Gallagher, 'Review of Gary P. Sampson, The WTO and Sustainable Development', 9 Journal of International Economic Law (2006) 511.

The purpose of this article is to provide a brief survey of the past decade in the trade and environment debate. The article proceeds in three parts: Part I examines the most significant institutional developments at the WTO on trade and the environment. Part II examines developments in WTO jurisprudence, focusing on GATT Article XX. Part III concludes.

I. INSTITUTIONAL DEVELOPENTS

To fast forward to the conclusion, the environment has now become a mainstream trade issue. That transformation of the world trading system is to be commended. While it is still too early to declare victory on the visionary calls of fourteen years ago for 'greening the GATT',[7] the progress made since 1994 has surely been greater than expected by the governments and non-governmental organizations (NGOs) who, in the early 1990s, called for a more environment-friendly trading system.[8] Today, there is considerable recognition of the public order contributions of the WTO, not just for the world economy, but also for the global economy.

A. WTO treaty provisions on the environment

In retrospect, some of the most important greening occurred in the new world trade constitution, that is, the Marrakesh Agreement Establishing the World Trade Organization (WTO Agreement) and its annexes. Let me briefly review those provisions. The Preamble to the WTO Agreement was based on the Preamble to the GATT, but a small change was made. Whereas the GATT's Preamble recognizes that trade relations should be conducted with a view to listed objectives including 'developing the full use of resources of the world...', the WTO's Preamble modifies this by recognizing among the listed objectives, 'allowing for the optimal use of the world's resources in accordance with the objective of sustainable development, seeking both to protect and preserve the environment and to enhance the means for doing so in a manner consistent with their respective needs and concerns at different levels of development'. At the time this addition was made, few thought that such preambular

[7] This was the title of the leading scholarly analysis: Daniel C. Esty, *Greening the GATT: Trade, Environment, and the Future* (Washington: Institute for International Economics, 1994). An even earlier volume was Kym Anderson and Richard Blackhurst (eds), *The Greening of World Trade Issues* (Hertfordshire: Harvester Wheatsheaf, 1992).

[8] Among those actors: the European Free Trade Association (EFTA) countries, the Talloires Group, the Global Environment & Trade Study, the Foundation for International Environmental Law and Development (FIELD), and World Wildlife Fund (WWF).

language would have any future legal significance. Yet, surprisingly it did; in *US—Shrimp*, the Appellate Body relied upon the WTO Preamble to interpret the General Exceptions in GATT Article XX.[9] In subsequent years, this preambular language has often been referred to by governments, WTO adjudicators, and WTO officials as justification for a stronger environmental dimension to the WTO. For example, in *US—Shrimp*, the Appellate Body stated that the Preamble shows that WTO negotiators 'decided to qualify the original objectives of the GATT 1947', and demonstrates a recognition by WTO negotiators that optimal use of the world's resources should be made in accordance with the objective of sustainable development'.[10] Moreover, the Appellate Body declared that states 'should' protect the environment 'either within the WTO or in other international fora'.[11] In the follow-on *US—Shrimp* litigation in 2001, the compliance panel reached the conclusion that 'sustainable development is one of the objectives of the WTO Agreement'.[12]

All agreements in the WTO system supervise trade-related environmental measures (TREMs),[13] but within these agreements, there are a number of provisions that specifically address the environment. Most of them were not part of the pre-WTO system. A brief catalogue follows: The Agreement on Agriculture provides that certain payments for government environment programs may have a qualified exemption from the Agreement's required subsidy reduction commitments.[14] The Agreement on the Application of Sanitary and Phytosanitary Measures (SPS Agreement) includes 'ecological and environmental conditions' within its criteria for a risk assessment, and requires governments to consider 'ecosystems' as one factor in determining pest or disease free areas.[15] The Agreement on Technical Barriers to Trade (TBT

[9] See John H. Jackson, 'Justice Feliciano and the WTO Environmental Cases: Laying the Foundations of a "Constitutional Jurisprudence" with Implications for Developing Countries', in Steve Charnovitz, Debra P. Steger and Peter van den Bossche (eds), *Law in the Service of Human Dignity. Essays in Honour of Florentino Feliciano* (Cambridge: Cambridge University Press, 2005) 29–43 at 40.

[10] WTO Appellate Body Report, *United States—Import Prohibition of Certain Shrimp and Shrimp Products*, WT/DS58/AB/R, adopted 6 November 1998, paras 152–53.

[11] Appellate Body Report, *US—Shrimp*, above n 10, para 185.

[12] Panel Report, *United States—Import Prohibition of Certain Shrimp and Shrimp Products—Recourse to Article 21.5 of the DSU by Malaysia*, WT/DS58/RW, para 5.54, adopted 21 November 2001, as upheld by Appellate Body Report, WT/DS58/AB/RW. In my view, a WTO commitment to sustainable development is a hollow victory for environmentalists because that term has been stretched in a way so as to make it acceptable to all and meaningful for no one. For a good discussion of 'sustainable development' today, see David G. Victor, 'Recovering Sustainable Development', Foreign Affairs 85 (2006), 91.

[13] For this analysis, I have adopted the TREM acronym invented in the early 1990s by Paul Demaret. As used here, a TREM is an environmental measure that affects trade (e.g. a tax).

[14] Agreement on Agriculture, Article 6.1, Annex II paras 2(a), 8(a), 12.

[15] SPS Agreement, Articles 5.2, 6.2.

Agreement) recognizes the protection of the environment as a legitimate objective.[16] The Agreement on Trade-Related Aspects of Intellectual Property Rights (TRIPS) contains an environmental exception with regard to patents. Members may exclude an invention from patentability when the prevention of domestic commercial exploitation is necessary to protect human, animal, or plant life or health or to avoid serious prejudice to the environment.[17] The Agreement on Subsidies and Countervailing Measures (SCM Agreement) provided non-actionable status for financial assistance from government to industry to promote adaptation to new environmental requirements.[18] Unfortunately, this provision lapsed after five years, and the WTO failed to reinstitute this safe harbour. As a result, TREM subsidies are now potentially outlawed by the WTO, including those which may be called for in other WTO agreements.[19] The General Agreement on Trade in Services (GATS) contains an exception for measures 'necessary to protect human, animal or plant life, or health'.[20]

During the past decade, as the WTO system has matured, some of the environmental omissions in WTO law have become more evident. For example, the GATS, unlike the GATT, does not contain a policy exception for conservation measures.[21] The TBT Agreement lacks an environmental exception to its requirement that measures accord national treatment, accord most-favoured-nation treatment (MFN), and 'not be more trade restrictive than necessary to fulfil a legitimate objective'.[22] Another example is the Understanding on Rules and Procedures Governing the Settlement of Disputes (DSU) which requires that panels adjudicating GATS disputes regarding 'prudential issues and other financial matters' have the necessary expertise to the specific financial service under dispute.[23] Yet, the DSU Article 1.2 and Appendix 2 lacks an analogous requirement for expertise in environmental disputes.

Experience within the WTO system has also pointed to new possibilities for using WTO rules to improve the environment. For example, the TBT Agreement requires the use of international standards as a basis for technical regulations except when such standards would be 'an ineffective or inappropriate means for the fulfillment of the legitimate objectives

[16] TBT Agreement, Article 2.2

[17] TRIPS Agreement, Article 27.2.

[18] SCM Agreement, Article 8.2(c).

[19] For example, Article 66.2 of the TRIPS Agreement directs developed country WTO Members to 'provide incentives to enterprises and institutions in their territories for the purpose of promoting technology transfer to least-developed country Members'.

[20] GATS Article XIV(b).

[21] See Uruguay Round Decision on Trade in Services and the Environment.

[22] TBT Agreement, Articles 2.1, 2.2.

[23] GATS Annex on Financial Services, para 4; DSU Article 1.2 and Appendix 2.

pursued . . .'.[24] In the *EC—Sardines* case, the WTO Appellate Body gave this rule a broad scope by holding that even voluntary, non-consensus standards qualified as 'international standards'.[25] The potentialities of this discipline for upward environmental and health harmonization have barely begun to be explored.[26] The next section in Part I looks at organizational improvements within the WTO.

B. Organizational developments

The Uruguay Round negotiators called for a WTO Committee on Trade and Environment (CTE) which was set up in 1995. The CTE's achievements have been modest,[27] most notably being a symbol of the institutionalization of environment issues into WTO processes.[28] In particular, the Committee has served as a venue where national officials from trade and environment ministries can meet together, and where representatives from some MEAs and the UN Environment Programme can regularly meet with trade officials.[29] The value of such mutual socialization should not be underestimated.

In addition, the CTE has also commissioned from WTO staff a number of very useful background papers which eventually are made publicly available. These background papers have often been written by staff in the WTO Trade and Environment Division. Since the mid-1990s, this Division has

[24] TBT Agreement, Article 2.4.

[25] WTO Appellate Body Report, *European Communities—Trade Description of Sardines*, WT/DS231/AB/R, adopted 23 October 2002, paras 221–22. The term 'international standard' is not defined in TBT. The Appellate Body rejected the EC's contention that Article 2.4 of the TBT Agreement does not apply to non-consensus standards. The Appellate Body's explanation is illogical, in my view, because it seems based on the proposition that a 'standard' in the TBT Agreement can be a non-consensus document. That is obviously correct, but begs the question of what an *international* standard is. The Appellate Body's conclusion has rendered inutile the sentence in the TBT definitions that 'Standards prepared by the international standardization community are based on consensus'.

[26] Note, however, that the TBT Agreement proclaims that 'developing country Members should not be expected to use international standards as a basis for their technical regulations or standards . . . which are not appropriate to their development, financial and trade needs'. TBT Agreement, Article 12.4.

[27] One measure of its meagre output can be seen in the Annual Report of the CTE. In 2006, 2005, 2004, and 2003, the Report for each year ran less than two full pages. The 2002 Report ran three pages. Perhaps the best analysis of the CTE is Gregory C. Shaffer, 'The Nexus of Law and Politics: The WTO's Committee on Trade and Environment', in Richard H. Steinberg (ed.), *The Greening of Trade Law* (Lanham: Rowman and Littlefield Publishers, 2002) 81–114.

[28] The WTO Secretariat describes environment as a 'horizontal' issue. WTO Secretariat, 'Trade and Environment', http://www.wto.org/english/tratop_e/envir_e/envir_e.htm (visited 6 June 2007).

[29] The CTE has not granted observer status to many international environmental organizations, for example, the Montreal Protocol Secretariat, the International Labour Organization, and the IUCN which is a hybrid international organization.

employed a number of talented staff who have made significant internal bureaucratic and external scholarly contributions. In 1999, the WTO Secretariat published a Report on Trade and Environment. That Report had some serious weaknesses,[30] but was warmly greeted and continues to be widely cited. The information disseminated on the WTO website about trade and environment has been useful, especially because it is available to anyone in the world with an internet connection. In some instances, however, the Secretariat continues to disseminate incorrect or at least questionable legal interpretations about TREMs, particularly process-related ones.[31]

From the early years of the WTO, on approximately an annual basis, the WTO Secretariat has sponsored a Public Forum where civil society and private sector participants are invited to attend, and gain an opportunity to interact with government officials and WTO bureaucrats. Environmental concerns have been an important focus of these Forums which have also devoted attention to developmental, trade, and sometimes social issues. Such Public Forums, however, have not significantly made up for the fact that even in its second decade, the WTO continues to resist making arrangements, consistent with those in other major international organizations, for consultation and cooperation with NGOs.

The WTO Secretariat is also responsible for writing reports for the Trade Policy Review (TPR) process. Many TPRs do take note of some ecological factors. For example, the 2005 TPR on Nigeria notes that Nigeria promotes environmentally friendly farming practices, an environmental shrimp fisheries project, and has transport infrastructure policies seeking environmental sustainability.[32] On the other hand, the TPR notes that gas production leads to environmental pollution.[33]

Although it is true that the multilateral trade negotiating process at the WTO has performed poorly since the mid-1990s, one brighter spot has been the 22 successful accession negotiations. So far, these negotiations have not addressed environmental concerns in any significant way. The accession negotiations routinely demand WTO-plus commitments from applicant

[30] Steve Charnovitz, 'World Trade and the Environment: A Review of the New WTO Report', 12 Georgetown International Environmental Law Review (2000) 523.

[31] For example, the Secretariat opines:

> Under existing GATT rules and jurisprudence, 'product' taxes and charges can be adjusted at the border, but 'process' taxes and charges by and large cannot. For example, a domestic tax on fuel can be applied perfectly legitimately to imported fuel, but a tax on the energy consumed in producing a ton of steel cannot be applied to imported steel.

WTO Secretariat, 'Trade and Environment at the WTO', April 2004, at 21. In my view, no legal authority exists for this proposition, and the Secretariat certainly offers no analysis of GATT Articles II, III, or XX that would justify its conclusion.

[32] WTO, 'Trade Policy Review Nigeria', Report by the Secretariat, WT/TPR/S/xx147, 13 April 2005, at 55, 59, 80.

[33] Ibid, at 66.

countries, but the WTO has not used its bargaining leverage to seek improvements in sustainable development.

The trade and environment debate has also had some broader impact. First, environmentalists have influenced the trading system by exporting into it norms in favour of organizational transparency. Although the trading system has always demanded transparency at the national level, the GATT had a blind spot about its own lack of transparency. In my view, criticism by environmentalists, other NGOs, and trade scholars was instrumental in the early 1990s in leading trade bureaucrats to begin to open up the trading system.[34] Today, the WTO website is among the best in international organizations in providing synopses of activities and downloads of documents. It was the environmental and consumer NGOs that first thought to send *amicus curiae* briefs to the WTO, and these once quixotic efforts eventually led the Appellate Body to open the door to amicus briefs. It was also environmentalists who first called for open trade panel hearings, and this was recently tested at the WTO.[35] Second, the trade and environment issue at the GATT/WTO has had some systemic implications for the environment regime. The most important has been an appreciation of the benefits to the trading system of the organizational strengthening that occurred in the 1990s. This led some environmentalists (and some within the WTO) to call for a World Environment Organization. The early 1990s debate on the trade-law status of environmental treaties also led to the use of the acronym MEAs and the greater community identity of those autonomous international entities. Today, MEAs are one issue being considered in the Doha Round.

C. The environmental dimension of trade negotiations

The current round of multilateral trade negotiations, the Doha Development Agenda, was launched in 2001, and the negotiations are ongoing as of June 2007. The Doha Agenda contains several environmental elements which WTO Director-General Pascal Lamy has termed the 'environmental chapter'.[36] It seems very likely that if the Doha Round is successfully brought to conclusion, the results will include new environmental

[34] For example, see John H. Jackson, 'World Trade Rules and Environmental Policies: Congruence or Conflict?', 49 Washington and Lee Law Review (1992) 1227, at 1255 ('Nevertheless, the environmentalists . . . have several legitimate complaints about GATT dispute settlement procedures, among others. First, they note appropriately that the GATT lacks a certain amount of transparency.')

[35] See 'WTO Opens "Hormones" Panel Proceedings to Public', WTO News, 27 September 2006.

[36] 'Lamy Urges Support for Environmental Chapter of the Doha Round', WTO News, 5 February 2007.

provisions. Among them there may be needed disciplines for fishery subsidies.[37]

The Doha Declaration sets out a negotiating agenda and a forward work program for the WTO.[38] Because the negotiations are a work in progress, I will not cover them here. It should be noted, however, that the negotiating process is not being conducted with sufficient transparency, and therefore, the interested public is not always able to appreciate what is going on so that public opinion can be injected. For example, a recent paper by the Secretariat said to contain a reduced list of environmental goods is classified in the JOB series which is not available the public.[39]

D. Competition with preferential trade agreements

The WTO is in competition with other fora in the negotiation of new trade liberalization. In recent years, comparatively greater progress has been made in achieving liberalization in bilateral and regional free trade agreements, also known as preferential trade agreements (PTAs). All PTAs negotiated in the 2000s embrace numerous 'trade-and' issues beyond the rules now in the WTO. Investment is the most common WTO-plus issue in PTAs.

Many PTAs have provisions regarding the environment. For example, the China–Chile Free Trade Agreement states that the parties 'shall enhance their communication and cooperation on labor, social security and environment...'.[40] The Japan–Mexico Agreement devotes an article to Cooperation in the Field of Environment.[41] The PTAs negotiated by the United States all contain a chapter on environment that commits parties to enforce their own environmental laws and provides for dispute settlement should that not occur. These PTAs contain side agreements to effectuate environmental cooperation and capacity building. The most recent development in the United States is that after the 2006 elections, the new majority party (the Democrats) demanded stronger environmental provisions

[37] For example, see Roman Grynberg, 'WTO Fisheries Subsidies Negotiations: Implications for ACP Fisheries Access Arrangements and Sustainable Management', in Roman Grynberg (ed.), *WTO at the Margins* (Cambridge: Cambridge University Press, 2006) 607–32.

[38] These environmental objectives are reiterated in the Hong Kong Ministerial Declaration, WT/MIN(05)DEC, 22 December 2005, paras 30–2.

[39] See 'CTE Update', Bridges, May 2007, 8.

[40] Free Trade Agreement between the Government of the People's Republic of China and the Government of the Republic of Chile, 18 November 2005, Article 108, http://www.sice.oas.org/tradee.asp#CHL_CHN (visited 6 June 2007).

[41] Agreement between Japan and the United Mexican States for the Strengthening of the Economic Partnership, 17 September 2004, Article 147, http://www.sice.oas.org/Trade/JPN_MEXDraftEPA_e/JPN_MEXind_e.asp (visited 6 June 2007).

in pending PTAs (e.g. Panama and Peru). The Bush Administration agreed to such a plan which is now being formalized.[42] Under this agreement, the pending PTAs will require both parties to implement seven listed MEAs; the list was carefully selected to only include MEAs that both parties had already ratified.

The utilization of PTAs was given considerable discussion in the 2005 Report of the Consultative Board to the WTO Director-General (Sutherland Commission).[43] The Report seems to criticize the 'injection of particular "non-trade" objectives into [preferential] trade agreements' such as 'significant labour and environmental protection undertakings'.[44] The Report expresses a concern that such requirements may not only be 'templates' for future PTAs, but also 'forerunners of new demands in the WTO'.[45] In my view, the Board was correct in laying down the marker that provisions used in PTAs are not necessarily appropriate for the WTO. The Board's discussion on this point is a bit cryptic, but I doubt that the Board meant to suggest that environmental provisions should be left out of PTAs because their presence in PTAs could serve as a precedent for inclusion in the WTO. Such a position would be untenable, in my view, because a bilateral or regional level agreement might be an appropriate level for a mutual environmental commitment that would not make as much sense in a multilateral agreement. To be sure, the Board is correct in questioning whether a trade agreement is the optimal instrument for an environmental (or other non-trade) commitment in the first place.[46] Yet, even if a trade agreement is not optimal, there may well be domestic political or institutional reasons why trading partners may find it easier to gain parliamentary approval for trade agreements than for environmental agreements. For example, in the United States, the US Congress periodically makes available a fast track approval process for international agreements on trade that is not available for international agreements on the environment.

[42] Sarah Lueck, John D. McKinnon and Greg Hitt, 'Bush, Congress Agree On Trade Standards', *Wall Street Journal*, 11 May 2007, A2.

[43] See 'Mini-Symposium on the Consultative Board's Report on the Future of the WTO', 8 Journal of International Economic Law (2005) 287.

[44] 'The Future of the WTO, Addressing Institutional Challenges in the New Millennium,' Report by the Consultative Board to the Director-General Supachai Panitchpakdi, January 2005, para 87, http://www.wto.org/english/thewto_e/10anniv_e/future_wto_e.pdf (visited 6 June 2007).

[45] Ibid, para 87.

[46] Ibid, para 33.

II. DEVELOPMENTS IN DISPUTE SETTLEMENT UNDER GATT ARTICLE XX

Only three environmental disputes have been fully adjudicated at the WTO: *US—Gasoline, US—Shrimp,* and *EC—Asbestos*.[47] This caseload is less than what might have been expected given the high-profile concerns of the early 1990s about environmental trade barriers. In the first two of these cases, the challenged measure was found to be a WTO violation. In *Gasoline,* the US regulation found to be a GATT violation was corrected. In *Shrimp,* the US import ban found to be a GATT violation was corrected and then found to be in compliance by the DSU Article 21.5 panel and the Appellate Body. In *Asbestos,* the French regulation was found to be consistent with WTO law. A fourth case, *Brazil—Tyres,* was released as this article was finalized, and so will not be discussed here.[48]

All of these cases pivoted to a large extent on GATT Article XX (general exceptions), and the adjudications turned around the reputation of world trade law as being insensitive to the environment.[49] Despite the fact that violations were found in two of the three cases, the generally well-thought-out Appellate Body decisions inspired confidence in the adjudication process, and convinced many environmentalists that legitimate environmental measures would be permitted by the WTO. In all three original environmental cases, the decisions of the panels were flawed and the Appellate Body had to reverse some of the central holdings. Although space considerations prevent a comprehensive review of the Article XX caselaw, I will highlight the key holdings and related jurisprudence.

An important development for Article XX was that the Appellate Body cast aside some of the GATT and early WTO panel holdings that threatened to render the environmental exceptions unusable. With the ostensible intention of saving the trading system,[50] a series of panels had

[47] In addition, there have been five disputes involving the SPS Agreement. Any SPS case is concerned with threats to human, animal or plant life, and health. If the SPS cases are counted as environmental cases, then the environmental case load is considerably higher and the win/loss ratio much lower. In all five of the SPS cases, the challenged measure was found to be a violation. Two of those five cases had a DSU Article 21.5 panel that found continuing violations. For reasons of space, this article will not discuss the SPS cases comprehensively, but will offer comments on aspects of them.

[48] Daniel Pruzin, 'WTO Panel Backs EU in Ruling Against Brazil's Import Ban on Retreaded Tires', BNA Daily Report for Executives, 13 June 2007, A-1. The panel ruled against Brazil's claim for an Article XX(b) exception.

[49] See Carrie Wofford, 'A Greener Future at the WTO: The Refinement of WTO Jurisprudence on Environmental Exceptions to GATT', 24 Harvard Environmental Law Review (2000) 563; Robert Howse, 'The Appellate Body Rulings in the Shrimp/Turtle Case: A New Legal Baseline for the Trade and Environment Debate', 27 Columbia Journal of Environmental Law (2002) 491.

[50] See, e.g. GATT Panel Report, US—Restrictions on Imports of Tuna, 39S/155, 1991, unadopted, paras 5.25, 5.27, 5.32; GATT Panel Report, *US—Restrictions on Imports of Tuna,* DS29/R, 1994, unadopted, paras 5.26 ('Under such an interpretation the General Agreement could no longer serve as a multilateral framework for trade among contracting parties'), 5.38;

fabricated illogical reasons as to why Article XX could not be used.[51] Far from saving the GATT/WTO, these holdings threatened the trading system by triggering worries as to its hostile attitude toward the broader public interest. By reversing the *US—Gasoline*, *US—Shrimp*, and *EC—Asbestos* panels, the Appellate Body not only corrected errant holdings,[52] but also sent a signal to the public that the era of runaway panels on environmental matters was over.[53] In *EC – Asbestos*, the Appellate Body upheld the panel on Article XX, but reversed the panel's holding regarding the structural relationship between GATT Articles III and XX. The jurisprudence is now clearer that Article III and XX 'are distinct and independent provisions of the GATT 1994 each to be interpreted on its own'.[54] One hopes that this holding lays to rest the Appellate Body's puzzling statement in *US—Gasoline* that Article XX(g) 'may not be read so expansively as seriously to subvert the purpose and object of Article III:4'.[55]

In place of the convoluted Article XX jurisprudence of the past, the Appellate Body resuscitated Article XX[56] by establishing a multistep framework for panels to evaluate Article XX claims. For an Article XX(b) claim, a panel should begin the sequence of analysis by considering whether the challenged measure fits within the scope of a particular paragraph in Article XX, and whether the purported state interest in preventing a risk is genuine.[57] Then, the panel looks for the required 'degree of connection' specified in the paragraph (e.g. 'necessary').[58]

Panel Report, *US—Import Prohibition of Certain Shrimp and Shrimp Products*, WT/DS58/R, adopted 6 November 1998 as modified by the Appellate Body Report, paras 7.44 (holding that Article XX allows governments to derogate from GATT provisions so long as 'they do not undermine the WTO multilateral trading system'), 7.60, 7.61. Perhaps in its most brazen misleading statement, the *Shrimp* panel claims to be basing its holding not only on WTO rules, but also on 'international law', and in that regard, the panel refers to general international law and international environmental law. Ibid, para 7.61.

[51] See Steve Charnovitz, 'GATT and the Environment: Examining the Issues', 4 International Environmental Affairs (1992) 203, at 211 (pointing out that 'increasingly stringent tests are being created by panels on an ad hoc basis').

[52] See, e.g. Appellate Body Report, *US—Shrimp*, above n 10, para 121 (criticizing the panel for an interpretation that would render Article XX exception 'inutile').

[53] The Presiding Member of the Appellate Body division in each of these three cases was Florentino Feliciano, a point well appreciated by Professor Jackson in his contribution to the Feliciano *Festschrift*, above n 9.

[54] See WTO Appellate Body Report, *European Communities—Measures Affecting Asbestos and Asbestos-Containing Products*, WT/DS135/AB/R, adopted 5 April 2001, para 115.

[55] See WTO Appellate Body Report, *United States—Standards for Reformulated and Conventional Gasoline*, WT/DS2/AB/R, adopted 20 May 1996, at 18.

[56] The Appellate Body noted that Article XX contains provisions to permit important state interests 'to find expression'. Appellate Body Report, *US – Gasoline*, above n 55, at 29–30.

[57] See Appellate Body Report, *EC—Asbestos*, above n 54, paras 157, 162.

[58] Appellate Body Report, *US—Gasoline*, above n 55, at 18.

The next step is to further appraise the measure under the chapeau of Article XX, taking into account the particular paragraph that provides a provisional justification. The Appellate Body grasped the internal logic of Article XX that had eluded several panels of putting the chapeau to work to catch illegitimate attempts to misuse an environmental exception.[59]

A. Paragraph (b) of Article XX

The challenge in adjudicating Article XX(b) has not been in identifying measures that actually fit within that paragraph; rather, the challenge has been to show that a contested measure is 'necessary'. As the Appellate Body explained in *US—Gambling*, this test is objective.[60] (The Appellate Body made this statement with reference to the GATS General Exceptions, but in doing so, made clear that it was relying on its GATT Article XX doctrine.[61]) In *EC—Asbestos*, the Appellate Body said that 'it is undisputed that WTO Members have the right to determine the level of protection of health that they consider appropriate in a given situation'.[62] Some scholars have read this statement to mean that the Appellate Body 'rejected categorically the notion that a member's right to determine its level of protection should be subject to considerations of proportionality'.[63]

The method to be used in determining whether the challenged measure is 'necessary' (to achieve its intended purpose) is difficult to outline succinctly because the jurisprudence is confusing. A 'necessary' measure is significantly closer to the pole of being indispensable than to the opposite pole of merely making a contribution to the policy goal. For measures that are *not* indispensable to achieve the Article XX(b) objective,[64] the 'necessary'

[59] See Charnovitz (1992), above n 51, at 218 (noting that the Article XX chapeau had atrophied from inattention and calling on panels to use the Article XX chapeau in environmental cases); Donald M. McRae, 'GATT Article XX and the WTO Appellate Body', in Marco Bronckers and Reinhard Quick (eds), *New Directions in International Economic Law. Essays in Honour of John H. Jackson* (The Hague: Kluwer Law International, 2000) 228–36, at 227 (noting that GATT panels 'had paid little attention to the *chapeau*' and that under the WTO, 'new life has been breathed into the *chapeau*').

[60] See WTO Appellate Body Report, *United States—Measures Affecting the Cross-Border Supply of Gambling and Betting Services*, WT/DS285/AB/R, adopted 20 April 2005, para 304.

[61] Appellate Body Report, *US—Gambling*, ibid, paras 291–92, 305. Given this symmetry, this study will draw on *Gambling* because it provides the most elaborate exposition by the Appellate Body of the General Exceptions.

[62] WTO Appellate Body Report, above n 54, para 168. Relatedly, see WTO Appellate Body Report, *EC Measures Concerning Meat and Meat Products (Hormones)*, WT/DS26/AB/R, WT/DS48/AB, R, adopted 13 February 1998, para 177 (taking cognizance of a right and 'duty' of WTO Members to protect the life and health of their people).

[63] For example, see Robert Howse and Elisabeth Türk, 'The WTO Impact on Internal Regulations', in George A. Bermann and Petros C. Mavroidis (eds), *Trade and Human Health and Safety* (Cambridge: Cambridge University Press, 2006) 77–117 at 113.

[64] When a measure is indispensable to achieve the Article XX(b) goal, then presumably that measure is deemed necessary. See Howse and Türk, ibid, at 114–15. Yet, in their most recent

standard is to be judged in every case through a process of weighing and balancing a series of factors.[65] The factors are open-ended, but should include: (i) the relative importance of the common interests or value pursued by the measure, (ii) the contribution made by the measure to the realization of the ends pursued by it, and (iii) the restrictive impact of the measure on international commerce.[66] The defending government bears the burden of putting forward evidence and arguments that enable a panel to assess the measure in light of the relevant factors to be weighed and balanced in a given case.[67] The defending government does not have to show that its measure is better than all alternatives, in order to establish that its measure is necessary.[68] If the complaining government points to an alternative measure that, in its view, the defendant government could have taken,[69] then the defendant bears an additional burden of showing that the measure it actually used remains necessary even in light of that alternative, or in other words, why the proposed alternative is not, in fact, 'reasonably available.'[70] The determination of whether the proposed alternative is reasonably available is also accomplished through a balancing test by looking at the extent to which the alternative contributes to

---

judgment on Article XX(d), in *Mexico—Taxes on Soft Drinks*, the Appellate Body said nothing about a special category of indispensable measures. WTO Appellate Body Report, *Mexico—Tax Measures on Soft Drinks and Other Beverages*, WT/DS308/AB/R, adopted 24 March 2006, paras 66, 80.

65 WTO Appellate Body Report, *Korea—Measures Affecting Imports of Fresh, Chilled and Frozen Beef*, WT/DS161/AB/R, WT/DS169/AB/R, adopted 10 January 2001, para 164. This test was applied to Article XX(b) in Appellate Body Report, *EC – Asbestos*, para 172. The importation of the Article XX(d) test to Article XX(b) has been criticized by some scholars. For example, see Anupam Goyal, *The WTO and International Environmental Law* (Oxford: Oxford University Press, 2006) 139–140.

66 Appellate Body Report, *US—Gambling*, above n 60, para 306.

67 Appellate Body Report, *US—Gambling*, ibid, paras 309, 310, 323. No case has yet occurred where a measure itself has been judged on its own to fail this balancing test. One reading of the jurisprudence is that the Appellate Body's term 'weighing and balancing' is a misnomer, and what is going on instead is that the measure in place is only weighed against a reasonable alternative measure. This is the interpretation put forward by Don Regan, as I understand it, and he may well be correct that the Appellate Body has not called for weighing adverse trade effects against other values. In other words, in a hypothetical case, the Appellate Body would not demand that an existing measure with 80% effectiveness and significant trade impact be replaced by a reasonable alternative measure with 70% effectiveness and no trade impact. See Michael Trebilcock and Michael Fishbein, 'International Trade: Barriers to Trade', in Andrew T. Guzman and Alan O. Sykes (eds), *Research Handbook in International Economic Law* (Cheltenham: Edward Elgar, 2007) 1–61 at 45 (making a similar point).

68 Appellate Body Report, *US—Gambling*, above n 60, paras 309, 310, 320.

69 The alternative measure has to enable to defendant government to achieve its desired level of protection with respect to the objective pursued. Appellate Body Report, *US – Gambling*, ibid, para 308.

70 Appellate Body Report, *US—Gambling*, ibid, para 311.

the realization of the end pursued.[71] If there is an alternative measure that achieves the same life or health end and is 'less restrictive of trade', then the panel could find that the measure being used is not necessary.[72] In justifying its measure, a government may 'rely in good faith, on scientific sources which, at that time, may represent a divergent, but qualified and respected, opinion'.[73] In that regard, one might note the Appellate Body's statement (given in the context of the SPS Agreement) that a panel determining whether sufficient scientific evidence exists should 'bear in mind that responsible, representative governments commonly act from perspectives of prudence and precaution where risks of irreversible, e.g. life-terminating, damage to human health are concerned'.[74]

B. Paragraph (g) of Article XX

For Article XX(g), three issues have to be addressed: first, is the measure concerned with the conservation of exhaustible natural resources? Second, is the measure one 'relating' to the conservation? And third, is the measure made effective in conjunction with restrictions on domestic production or consumption?

[71] Appellate Body Report, *EC—Asbestos*, above n 54, para 172. An alternative measure is not reasonably available if it is merely theoretical in nature, imposes an undue burden on the regulating government, or the regulating government is not capable of taking it. Appellate Body Report, *US—Gambling*, above n 60, para 311.

[72] See Appellate Body Report, *EC—Asbestos*, above n 54, para 172 (last sentence). The Appellate Body's consideration of a trade restrictiveness factor in connection to a health measure was noteworthy because (despite fifteen years of scholarly commentary to the contrary) this was the first GATT/WTO holding for Article XX(b) to do so. See GATT Panel Report, *Thailand—Restrictions on Importation of Internal Taxes on Cigarettes*, 37S/200, para 75 (no mention of a less trade restrictive test). The *Thai Cigarette* panel explained that Article XX(b) would 'allow contracting parties to impose trade restrictive measures inconsistent with the General Agreement to pursue overriding public policy goals to the extent that such inconsistencies were unavoidable'. Ibid, para 74. The panel further noted that Article XX(b) 'clearly allowed contracting parties to give priority to health over trade liberalization'. Ibid, para 73. In my view, it was unfortunate that the Appellate abandoned these principles and replaced them with a balancing test in which trade can trump health. The Appellate Body does not explain why it did so, but the reason is probably that a trade-restrictiveness test had been incorporated into the SPS Agreement (Article 5.6) and the TBT Agreement (Articles 2.2, 2.3), and it is inevitable (and probably intended by trade negotiators) that such norms would eventually be imported in GATT Article XX. For example, in the first SPS case, the Appellate Body had declared that there is a 'delicate and carefully negotiated balance in the SPS Agreement between the shared, but sometimes competing, interests of promoting international trade and of protecting the life and health of human beings'. Appellate Body Report, *EC—Hormones*, above n 56, para 177.

[73] Appellate Body Report, *EC—Asbestos*, above n 54, para 178.

[74] Appellate Body Report, *EC—Hormones*, above n 62, para 124. See William J. Davey, 'Reflections on the Appellate Body Decision in the *Hormones* Case and the Meaning of the SPS Agreement', in George A. Bermann and Petros C. Mavroidis (eds), *Trade and Human Health and Safety* (Cambridge: Cambridge University Press, 2006) 118–132 at 122–23 (discussing the precautionary principle).

In *US – Shrimp*, the measure to safeguard sea turtles was challenged on the grounds that turtles are not an exhaustible natural resource. Although the Appellate Body could easily have decided this issue based on GATT precedent where fish had been found to fit within Article XX,[75] the Appellate Body instead utilized a teleological approach. Noting that the term 'exhaustible natural resources' in Article XX(g) had been written over fifty years earlier, the Appellate Body proclaimed that these words 'must be read by a treaty interpreter in the light of contemporary concerns of the community of nations about the protection and conservation of the environment', and, furthermore, that the term

> natural resources is not 'static' in its content or reference but is rather 'by definition, evolutionary'.[76]

The Appellate Body then pointed to a number of sources, including the mention of sustainable development and the environment in the WTO's Preamble, the UN Convention on the Law of the Sea, the Convention on Biological Diversity, Agenda 21, and the Resolution of Assistance to Developing Countries adopted in conjunction with the Convention on the Conservation of Migratory Species of Wild Animals.[77] Whether these are cited as sources of law, or facts taken note of (or introduced by) by the Appellate Body, is unclear. Based on this analysis, the Appellate Body concluded that 'it is too late in the day to suppose that Article XX(g) of the GATT 1994 may be read as referring only to the conservation of exhaustible mineral or other non-living natural resources'.[78] This was an important Appellate Body decision both for the result reached and the jurisprudential technique followed.

The Appellate Body did not reach the question of whether the natural resource to be conserved has to be within the physical territory or legal jurisdiction of the country whose government is imposing a challenged import ban. Reaching this issue was not necessary because in *US – Shrimp*, the endangered turtles were highly migratory. Therefore, the Appellate Body saw a 'sufficient nexus' to the United States.[79]

[75] Appellate Body Report, *US—Shrimp*, above n 10, para 131.

[76] Ibid, paras 129–30 (internal footnote omitted).

[77] Ibid.

[78] Ibid, para 131 (internal footnote omitted). The footnote states that the 'drafting history does not demonstrate an intent on the part of the framers of the GATT 1947 *to exclude* "living" natural resources from the scope of application of Article XX(g)'. See para 131, n 114. My own research many years ago of the negotiating history led me to include that the conservation of living resources was not the central purpose of the Article XX(g) exception, but that the drafters had agreed, in a different context, that fisheries and wildlife could be exhaustible natural resources. See Steve Charnovitz, 'Exploring the Environmental Exceptions in GATT Article XX', 25 Journal of World Trade (October 1991) 37, at 45–47.

[79] Appellate Body Report, *US—Shrimp*, above n 10, para 133.

Whether in a future dispute involving land-based biodiversity the Appellate Body would see a sufficient nexus to the country concerned about protecting planetary biodiversity remains to be seen. Textually, Article XX(g) does not contain any language suggesting that its coverage is geographically limited. While it is true that the first tuna–dolphin panel held that Article XX(b) and (g) were not extra-jurisdictional,[80] that report was not adopted. In my view, it was unfortunate that the Appellate Body in *US—Gasoline* chose to take cognizance of this discredited panel report and, even worse, to bring it into WTO jurisprudence.[81] Still, I would be surprised to see a holding that a WTO Member claiming a GATT Article XX(g) exception is compelled to permit imports of products made from a foreign endangered species even when such commerce gives incentives for killing the species. Perhaps, the principle of *in dubio mitius*[82] would be helpful to the adjudicator on the grounds that the governments drafting Article XX did not impose on themselves more onerous requirements than those specifically mentioned in Article XX.

On the 'relating to' prong of the Article XX(g), the Appellate Body in *US – Gasoline* seemed to distance itself from the GATT jurisprudence which had given that term a strict meaning of 'primarily aimed at'.[83] A more nuanced approach was further articulated in *US—Shrimp*, where the Appellate Body examined the relationship between the general structure/design of the measure and the conservation policy goal it purports to serve.[84] Regarding the US import ban on shrimp, the Appellate Body held that the means were 'reasonably related' to the ends.[85]

The last issue to be considered in adjudicating Article XX(g) is whether the measure is made effective in conjunction with restrictions on domestic production or consumption. Here, the Appellate Body made two important holdings: one, this prong requires evenhandedness between regulation of imports and domestic activity.[86] Two, while term 'effective' does not establish

[80] GATT Panel Report, *US—Tuna*, 1991 (unadopted), above n 50, paras 5.26, 5.27, 5.32.

[81] See Appellate Body Report, *US—Gasoline*, above n 55, at footnotes 37 and 38; Aaditya Mattoo and Petros C. Mavroidis, 'Trade, Environment and the WTO: The Dispute Settlement Practice Relating to Article XX of the GATT', in Ernst-Ulrich Petersmann (ed.), *International Trade Law and the GATT/WTO Dispute Settlement System* (London: Kluwer Law International, 1997) 327–43 at 327–32 (criticizing the GATT report in the first tuna–dolphin case).

[82] See Appellate Body Report, *US—Hormones*, above n 62, para 165 and n 154 (explicating the principle).

[83] Appellate Body Report, *US—Gasoline*, above n 55, at 18–19.

[84] Appellate Body Report, *US—Shrimp*, above n 10, paras 136–37.

[85] Ibid, para 141.

[86] Appellate Body Report, *US—Gasoline*, above n 55, at 20–21; Appellate Body Report, *US—Shrimp*, above n 10, para 144.

an empirical effects test, this does not mean that a consideration of 'the predictable effects of a measure is never relevant'.[87] No further exposition of this point has occurred because there have not been any Article XX(g) cases since *US—Shrimp*. In a thoughtful analysis of the *US—Shrimp* compliance Report, Robert Howse and Damien J. Neven suggest that 'in future cases, in considering the fit between a Member's measure and its environmental objective, the adjudicator should take into account the relative efficiency of the various policy instruments that a Member may choose to impose on another Member as a condition of access for its imports'.[88]

C. The chapeau of Article XX

The chapeau of Article XX exists as a further condition for recourse to the General Exceptions. The focus of appraisal by an adjudicator under the standards of the chapeau is how the measure is applied, rather than how the measure is designed.[89] The evaluation is conducted in the context of a provisional justification under a specific paragraph in Article XX.[90] In the first holding on this matter, the Appellate Body assigned to the culprit government the burden of proof for the chapeau.[91] To explicate Article XX's chapeau, the Appellate Body, once again, sought guidance from the Preamble to the WTO Agreement, and also considered the Uruguay Round Decision on Trade and Environment.[92] Even more remarkably, the Appellate Body declared that the chapeau, it could seek 'additional interpretive guidance, as appropriate, from the general principles of international law'.[93] In addition, Body explained that under general principles of law and international law, recourse to Article XX must be exercised 'reasonably'.[94] As WTO law commentators, such as Joost Pauwelyn, have pointed out, the Appellate Body arrogates to itself considerable discretion and adjudicative authority.

[87] Appellate Body Report, *US—Gasoline*, above n 55, at 21.

[88] Robert Howse and Damien J. Neven, '*US—Shrimp*. United States—Import Prohibition of Certain Shrimp and Shrimp Products: Recourse to Article 21.5 of the DSU by Malaysia', in Henrik Horn and Petros C. Mavroidis (eds), *The WTO Case Law of 2001* (Cambridge: Cambridge University Press, 2003) 41–71 at 66.

[89] Appellate Body Report, *US—Gasoline*, above n 55, at 22.

[90] Appellate Body Report, *US—Shrimp*, above n 10, para 120; But see para 146 regarding the necessity of considering XX(b).

[91] Appellate Body Report, *US—Gasoline*, above n 55, at 22–23.

[92] Appellate Body Report, *US—Shrimp*, above n 10, paras 152–55.

[93] Ibid, para 158 (internal footnote omitted that cites to Article 31(c)(3) of the Vienna Convention on the Law of Treaties).

[94] Appellate Body Report, *US—Shrimp*, above n 10, para 158 (internal footnote omitted that cites to two treatises and three cases of the International Court of Justice); see also Appellate Body Report, *US—Gasoline*, above n 55, at 22 ('reasonably').

A puzzling, and I believe unfortunate, feature of the Appellate Body's holdings on the chapeau is the notion that WTO Members have a legal 'right' in WTO law to have their exports accepted by other WTO Members. Given the WTO's indulgences for antidumping measures, its policy space for protectionist tariffs and tariff-rate quotas, and the availability in the DSU of suspension of concessions or other obligations (SCOO) against innocent exporters in the event of governmental non-compliance, surely no practical right to trade exists under WTO law. Yet, for the most sensitive national policy areas, those covered by Article XX exceptions, the Appellate Body in *US—Gasoline* held that Article XX must be applied reasonably with due regard both to the legal duties of the regulating government 'and the legal rights of the other parties concerned'.[95] But other than procedural rights, what right does the exporting government have that can be counterpoised to invocation of an exception? In *US—Shrimp*, the Appellate Body elaborated on this doctrine of WTO rights. For example, the Appellate Body states that an invocation of an Article XX(g) exception, if abused, will 'render naught the substantive treaty rights in, for example, Article XI:1 of other Members'.[96] Still, it is one thing to say that an abusive invocation of Article XX is disallowed, and quite another to say that the Article XI obligation confers an independent right. Given the myriad trade barriers tolerated WTO law, I would have thought that it is too late in the day for the Appellate Body to suppose that US trading partners have a legal right[97] to export shrimp to the US economy.

In any event, the Article XX chapeau forbids 'arbitrary or unjustifiable discrimination between countries where the same conditions prevail, or a disguised restriction on international trade'. In *US—Gasoline*, the Appellate Body held that the impugned measure constituted both unjustifiable discrimination and a disguised restriction. The main problems were that the US regulator had not pursued the possibility of entering into cooperative arrangements with the plaintiff countries to mitigate administrative problems, and had not taken into account foreign costs of compliance.[98]

[95] Appellate Body Report, *US—Gasoline*, above n 55, at 22.

[96] Appellate Body Report, *US—Shrimp*, above n 10, para 156. The point is repeated in para 159.

[97] Ibid, paras 181 ('negation of rights of Members'), 182 ('suspension *pro hac vice* of the treaty rights of other Members'), 186 ('rights of other Members'), 163 ('a right to export shrimp'). At least in its early years, the Appellate Body seemed to have a statist perception of international trade as being 'trade between territorial sovereigns'. Appellate Body Report, *US—Gasoline*, above n 55, at 27.

[98] Appellate Body Report, *US—Gasoline*, above n 55, at 27–28. In a broader Article XX context in a later case, the Appellate Body criticized the regulating government for shifting the costs of enforcement to imported goods instead of evenly distributing such costs between domestic and imported products. Appellate Body Report, *Korea—Beef*, above n 65, para 181.

Arbitrary discrimination has been further elaborated. In *US—Shrimp*, the Appellate Body explained that arbitrary discrimination can occur when a defendant government requires certification of an exporting country, and yet does not give that country a formal opportunity to be heard, to respond to arguments made against it, and to receive a formal, written, reasoned decision, and to have a procedure for appeal. Such a program violates the chapeau because it allows arbitrary discrimination between certified and uncertified countries. An import ban can constitute arbitrary discrimination when it applies 'a rigid and unbending standard' that does not take into consideration 'different conditions' in exporting countries.[99] In the follow-on case, the Appellate Body upheld a revised US shrimp regulation that conditioned importation on whether the foreign regulatory program was comparable in effectiveness to the US program.[100]

Unjustifiable discrimination has been elaborated in three ways by the Appellate Body in *US—Shrimp*. First, the Appellate Body saw such discrimination in the way that the US government had given one group of countries three years (from 1991 to 1994) to adjust to US turtle safety measures, while giving the complaining countries less than four months to adjust in 1995–96.[101] Oddly though, the Appellate Body did not explain why a phase-in period in 1995 had to be as long as one in 1991. Nor did the Appellate Body attempt to reconcile its objection with the post-1997 subsequent practice of WTO Members of not automatically granting countries that join the WTO (through accession) the benefit of the phase-ins prescribed in the WTO Agreement. The second instance of unjustifiable discrimination occurred when US regulators negotiated cooperative agreements on sea turtle conservation with some countries, but did not attempt to do so with the complaining countries.[102] The Appellate Body postulated that the need for such environmental cooperation was recognized internally in the WTO in the Uruguay Round Decision on Trade and Environment and the 1996 Report of the CTE, and in addition was also recognized in Agenda 21, the Convention on Biological Diversity, and the Convention on the Conservation of Migratory Species of Wild Animals. The Appellate Body did not explain exactly the relevance under the Vienna Convention on the Law of Treaties of these two environmental Conventions, particularly in light of the fact that the defendant United States is not a party to

[99] Appellate Body Report, *US—Shrimp*, above n 10, paras 163–64, 177. Such a situation can also be unjustifiable discrimination. Ibid, paras 165, 176.

[100] Appellate Body Report, *US—Shrimp (Article 21.5 – Malaysia)*, above n 12, paras 144, 149.

[101] Appellate Body Report, *US—Shrimp*, above n 10, paras 173–74.

[102] Ibid, paras 167, 171, 172. See also Appellate Body Report, *US—Shrimp (Article 21.5 – Malaysia)*, above n 12, para 124 (explaining that the United States is not required to conclude an international agreement).

either of them.[103] The third instance of discrimination occurred when US regulators devoted less efforts to technology transfer to the complaining countries than to some other countries.[104] This holding is the only one I am aware of in WTO jurisprudence that applies an MFN-like requirement to subsidies.

The Appellate Body did not appear to consider whether the complaining governments in the shrimp–turtle dispute had made any significant efforts to safeguard sea turtles (or to negotiate with the United States). Contrary to what the Appellate Body suggested in calling the US law a 'weapon',[105] one might instead perceive the US import ban as a shield and the practices in the complaining countries that killed endangered sea turtles as the weapon. Although the WTO law appears to lack principles of estoppel, the Appellate Body has suggested that sovereign states 'should' act together within the WTO 'or in other international fora, to protect endangered species or to otherwise protect the environment'.[106] Whether the Appellate Body will someday insist that a complainant government do so remains to be seen.

III. CONCLUSION

An appropriate closing for a contribution to a first-decade anniversary symposium is to make predictions about the next decade. I believe that a new cycle has begun in international governance that will be characterized by greater attention to the environment. These concerns will continue to influence the development of international economic law, and the advances on environment in the WTO wrought by the Appellate Body will not be reversed. The Doha Development Round will eventually be completed in some form, and the new package of WTO amendments will include some

[103] See Joost Pauwelyn, 'Non-Traditional Patterns of Global Regulation: Is the WTO "Missing the Boat"?', in Christian Joerges and Ernst-Ulrich Petersmann (eds), *Constitutionalism, Multilevel Trade Governance and Social Regulation* (Portland: Hart Publishing, 2006) 199–227 at 215 (noting that the Appellate Body's reference to treaties raises questions of legitimacy and state consent). In *EC—Approval and Marketing of Biotech Products*, the panel stated that following Article 31(c)(3) of the Vienna Convention on the Law of Treaties did not require the panel to consider as a rule of international law, treaties that are not applicable between all the parties to the dispute. Panel Report, *European Communities—Measures Affecting the Approval and Marketing of Biotech Products*, WT/DS291/R, WT/DS292/R, WT/DS293/R, adopted 21 November 2006, paras 7.70–7.95. The panel used that holding to justify not making use of the Convention on Biological Diversity and its Biosafety Protocol. This holding has implications for the longtime debate on MEAs as to what would happen if a defendant government cited an MEA for justification that had not been ratified by the complaining government.

[104] See Appellate Body Report, *US—Shrimp*, above n 10, para 175.

[105] Ibid, para 171.

[106] Ibid, para 185. The Appellate Body has also suggested that the good faith notion applies to all Members, not just a plaintiff. Appellate Body Report, *US—Shrimp (Article 21.5 – Malaysia)*, above n 12, para 134, n 97.

significant environmental provisions. The next decade may also bring more trade disputes regarding the environment on knotty issues such as government-created marketable rights to address climate change, biofuels production on deforested land, and genetically modified agriculture. One hopes that the WTO will be up to these challenges, and that it will get better at working with other international institutions to achieve more effective global governance.

COMPETITION LAW AND THE WTO: RETHINKING THE RELATIONSHIP

*David J. Gerber**

ABSTRACT

This essay identifies obstacles to the inclusion of a competition law regime in the WTO and suggests changes that are likely to be necessary if competition law is to become an effective part of the WTO. Two obstacles have impeded inclusion of competition law in the WTO's legal regime and are likely to continue to do so. They are (i) a lack of confidence that the norms, practices and procedures of the WTO rest on a robust conception of community and (ii) uncertainty and concern about what form of competition law might be included and what its role in the WTO would be. In order to reduce the first of these obstacles, the institutions and members of the WTO will need to develop a conception of community that engenders widespread confidence in the WTO's basic modes of operation. Eliminating the second obstacle would require clarification of the kind of competition law that would be acceptable within the WTO, and this, in turn, is likely to require development of a form of competition law that is specifically designed for the WTO and that can elicit the long-term support of all categories of members. The essay suggests that the competition law issue is intricately interwoven with the future of the WTO. The changes that would be necessary to introduce and successfully implement competition law in the WTO are to a large extent the same as those that the institution will need to make if it is to enrich its role as an institution.

INTRODUCTION

Prior to the creation of the WTO there were two serious attempts to create a comprehensive normative framework for international economic relations – one at the Geneva International Economic Conference in 1927 and another following the Second World War. In both, competition (or 'antitrust') law was often portrayed as an important part of the proposed framework. If such a framework were to be effective, so the argument went, it would have to include

* Distinguished Professor of Law in Chicago-Kent College of Law, Chicago, Illinois. Email: Dgerber@kentlaw.edu. The author would like to thank Sungjoon Cho for his comments on an earlier draft of this article and for his many insights into the issues treated here.

not only norms governing the conduct of states, but also norms governing the conduct of private institutions that had sufficient power to impede international trade and competition. Private institutions were seen as posing threats to international competition that were potentially as serious as those posed by governments. Despite this history and the logic of the policy argument, competition law was not included in the WTO, and efforts to place it on the WTO's negotiating agenda have failed. Why the changed perspective and what does the change suggest about the WTO's path ahead? What obstacles stand in the way of including competition law in the WTO and making it effective? And how might competition law contribute to developing the effectiveness of the WTO? This essay addresses those questions.

The pre-WTO efforts at economic norm-making on a global scale were based on a conception of the international economy as a shared resource in which norms could be expected to enhance the value of that resource for all participants. In this sense, conceptions of community were the basis for the normative plans. To be sure, these visions of community were aspirational. In 1927, they were based more on hopes for the future than on existing realities, and post-Second World War efforts were driven by US visions of the future that were not always shared by others. Nevertheless, competition law was considered important in both efforts.[1]

In the context of the WTO, a narrower vision of international economic relations has prevailed. In it, the focus is on the actions of states that impede trade and competition, while the actions of private institutions that may have similar effects have been curiously privileged. From this perspective, the WTO's mission appears unbalanced, treating that part of the problem whose treatment best serves US and European interests, but neglecting the issues whose treatment would weigh most heavily on US and European companies, given that they are most likely to have the economic power necessary to engage in global-level anticompetitive conduct.

The WTO's tenth anniversary presents a valuable and timely opportunity to reflect on the relationship between competition law and the WTO. Although there has been much discussion of the issue of competition law in the WTO, most writing on the subject was done several years ago and thus does not reflect recent experience. Moreover, competition law raises fundamental issues about the operation and role of the WTO that have marred its successes during its first decade and that are thus at the forefront of current discussions.

This essay makes three basic claims. The first is that two main obstacles have impeded inclusion of competition law in the WTO's legal regime and

[1] For the Geneva conference, see Wallace McClure, 'National Economic Independence in the Light of the International Economic Conference', 27 American Journal of International Law 668 (1927). The Havana charter episode is discussed in Susan Ariel Aaronson, *Trade and the American Dream* (Lexington: Kentucky UP, 1996) and William Diebold, Jr., 'The End of the I.T.O.', *Essays in International Finance*, 16, (1952) Princeton: Princeton University.

that these are likely to continue to inhibit establishment of an effective competition law in the WTO. They are (i) a lack of confidence that the norms, practices and procedures of the WTO rest on a robust conception of community and (ii) uncertainty and concern about what form of competition law might be included and what its role in the WTO would be.

A second claim is that competition law could become an effective part of the WTO, but only if and to the extent that the above-mentioned obstacles can be eliminated or significantly reduced. In order to reduce the first of these obstacles, the institutions and members of the WTO will need to develop a conception of community that engenders widespread confidence in the WTO's basic modes of operation. There has long been talk about a 'community of nations', but few would argue that the current operations of the WTO rest on a robust concept of community.[2] In its current form, the WTO operates primarily as a venue for negotiating and transferring access rights to the markets of member countries,[3] but introducing competition law into the WTO would require a different or at least additional conception of the WTO's goals and operations. Eliminating the second obstacle would require clarification of the kind of competition law that would be acceptable within the WTO, and this, in turn, is likely to require development of a form of competition law that is specifically designed for the WTO and that can elicit the long-term support of all categories of members.

The third basic claim is that the competition law issue is intricately interwoven with the future of the WTO. It points, for example, to obstacles and opportunities that face the WTO as an institution. It can also serve as a metric of the WTO's progress toward a more compelling conception of community. The changes that would be necessary to introduce and successfully implement competition law in the WTO are to a large extent the same as those that the institution will need to make if it is to enrich its role as an institution. Finally, competition law can also serve as an incentive for WTO members to work toward those changes.

I. COMPETITION LAW IN THE WTO: IDENTIFYING THE OBSTACLES

One way of assessing a future role for competition law in the WTO is to examine the obstacles that have impeded its inclusion so far. I will here focus on the most recent rejection of competition law – i.e. the failed attempt to

[2] Sungjoon Cho has elaborated the concept of 'community' in relation to the WTO concept very effectively and with excellent insights, and I am indebted to him for discussing the topic with me and enriching my understanding of the issue. See Sungjoon Cho, 'The WTO's Gemeinschaft', 56 Alabama Law Review 483 (2004).

[3] The canonical treatment of the WTO's creation, objectives and intended roles is discussed in John H. Jackson, *The World Trading System: Law and Policy of International Economic Relations*, 2nd ed. (Cambridge, MIT Press, 1997). For detailed discussion of current patterns of operation, see Sungjoon Cho, 'Doha's Development', 24 Berkeley Journal of International Law (forthcoming, 2007).

include it on the negotiating agenda for the Doha round of negotiations.[4] The story has many dimensions, including, in particular, political ones, but my concern here is only with the basic outlines of legal and institutional development.

The effort to include competition law in the WTO began to take shape in the mid-1990s under the leadership of the European Union. Arguing that competition law belonged in the WTO because private distortions of competition were a significant problem, key leaders in the European Commission sought to put it on the agenda for the impending negotiations. In preparation for this possibility, the WTO appointed Frederic Jenny, a well-known French economist and vice president of the French Competition Council, to conduct studies of its feasibility. Jenny gathered support for such a move and became relatively confident that significant support existed.[5] Nevertheless, the effort to put competition law on the agenda failed, when both the United States and a large group of developing countries declined to support it.

Although many factors were involved in this failure, lack of confidence in the norms and procedures of the WTO was a central theme. Each resistant group doubted that the WTO would make decisions on the basis of adequate respect for that group's interests. In the United States, there was fear that a competition law in the WTO might be directed primarily at large multinational firms, many of which are US-based. US government officials were not prepared to accept such a threat to US interests.[6] Developing countries also generally showed little confidence that a competition law regime in the WTO would be implemented in ways that reflected a broad set of Member State interests.[7] Many feared that its main effect would be to assist US, European and Japanese firms in getting access to their markets and raw materials. The suspicion was not without foundation. The US had aggressively used antitrust for this purpose in the not too distant past (e.g. Japan in the early 1990s) and market access was a focus of much US and European energy in the WTO. Growing disenchantment with the results of the TRIPS agreement undoubtedly played a significant role in engendering distrust of competition law, because developing countries often believed

[4] Philip Marsden describes the sequence of events in Philip Marsden, *A Competition Policy for the WTO*, (London: Cameron May, 2003) 55–66.

[5] For Jenny's view of these issues, see, e.g. Frederic Jenny, 'Cartels and Collusion in Developing Countries: Lessons from Empirical Evidence', 29 World Competition Law Review 109 (2006). Rob Anderson, a WTO official with experience in the Canadian competition authority, also played an important role in this process.

[6] See, e.g. Joel L. Klein, 'Anticipating the Millenium: International Antitrust Enforcement at the End of the Twentieth Century' (Speech presented at the Fordham Corporate Law Institute, 24th Annual Conference on International Law and Policy on 9 November 2000).

[7] For a recent discussion of the positions of developing countries in this debate, see Aditya Bhattacharjea, 'The Case for a Multilateral Agreement on Competition Policy: A Developing Country Perspective', 9 Journal of International Economic Law 293 (2006).

that the seemingly neutral provisions of that agreement had been applied in ways that gave undue and unanticipated advantages to developed country interests at the expense of developing countries.

The common thread linking these two rejections was a lack of confidence in the processes that create, shape and implement norms in the WTO. For different reasons, the two groups were unwilling to entrust their interests to the WTO in the context of competition law, because they did not believe that those interests would be adequately protected. In effect, neither group had confidence that the WTO was likely to operate on the basis of a robust conception of community.

Confusion and uncertainty about the kind of competition law that might be included in the WTO added to this distrust. Developing countries have generally had little, if any, experience with competition law, and this in itself made them uncertain and cautious about what such a law might contain. Moreover, there was little doubt that the US would demand an antitrust law modeled on its own antitrust thinking and that this model was likely to dominate any discussion of what form competition law should take. For many developing countries, however, this US model remained suspect.[8] There were fears, for example, that it might not only coerce access to markets, as noted above, but also inhibit cooperative responses from domestic companies. The US conception of antitrust law (and increasingly also the EUs conception of competition law) seemed more likely to affect agreements among producers in developing countries than the unilateral conduct of multinationals, and this seemed to many to represent an imbalance designed to favor developed country interests.

For American observers and officials, on the other hand, there was fear that whatever form competition law might take in the WTO, it might be implemented in ways that harmed US interests. For example, one concern was that it would be ineffective and thereby 'water down' the more rigorous treatment of competition law in the US and Europe.[9] Others feared a different result – that competition law might be used to target US multinational corporations. Finally, there is widespread confidence in US antitrust circles that US antitrust is simply the 'right' form for competition law, not only for the US, but generally.[10] As a result, there is significant resistance to deviating from that form. The current US antitrust orthodoxy relies heavily on economic analysis, specifically neo-classical economics, to provide its norms and to apply them. It emphasizes the harms that result

[8] Ibid at 316–23.

[9] See e.g. Diane P. Wood, 'The Internationalization of Antitrust Law: Options for the Future', 44 DePaul Law Review 1289 (1995), at 1294.

[10] See, e.g. Ky P. Ewing, *Competition Rules for the 21st Century: Principles from America's Experience* (The Hague: Kluwer Law International, 2003). For discussion of this view of the 'correctness' of US antitrust law, see David J. Gerber, 'Competition', in Peter Cane and Mark Tushnet (eds), *The Oxford Handbook of Legal Studies* (Oxford: Oxford UP, 2004) 510.

from agreements among competitors, but pays significantly less attention to potential harms from unilateral conduct.

II. COMMUNITY AND THE POTENTIAL ROLE OF COMPETITION LAW IN THE WTO

The failure of these efforts to include competition law within the WTO signals the need to reassess and reconceive the relationship between the WTO and competition law. The two obstacles identified above are likely to prevent effective inclusion of competition law in the WTO, unless there is serious rethinking of fundamental issues in that relationship. This section outlines some of the elements that may be of value in such an effort.

In this rethinking, it is important to identify three components of current thinking that impede development of an effective relationship between competition law and the WTO. One is the 'eternal failure' image. Some commentators have claimed that the failure of previous attempts to achieve a transnational competition law means that it cannot succeed now (or, perhaps, ever). Such a claim is at best unpersuasive. Past failures of efforts to develop a transnational competition law may highlight the difficulties faced by current attempts in the WTO, but they can do no more than that. The current situation differs in often extensive ways from the situations in which prior attempts have been made, and thus there is no basis for assuming that the difficulties and outcomes of prior efforts will be repeated in the future. Moreover, the kinds of changes suggested in this essay are feasible and would, if pursued, further distinguish future situations from past failures. That such 'doomed to failure' claims are made by serious scholars suggests the degree of mystification surrounding the issue and underscores the need for rigorous rethinking of the issues involved.

A second image that may constrain rethinking on this issue assumes that competition law must *serve* 'trade' interests. Discussions of competition law in the WTO often assume that the WTO's objective is to protect international trade and that competition law must, therefore, serve trade objectives. Framed this way, the existing obstacles to effective inclusion of competition law are likely to remain. It is precisely this image of competition law as a trade tool of developed countries that concerns developing countries. The fear that competition law would serve primarily to increase access by US, European and Japanese firms to developing country markets has fueled resistance to the competition law project. If competition law were seen not as subservient to trade law, but rather as coequal with trade law, the path forward would be more inviting, and progress would be more promising. In this view, competition law and trade law operate as equally legitimate and institutionally supported legal regimes, each with its own objectives and institutional and intellectual tools. They are related to each other by the objective of protecting the competitive process on the transnational level. Trade law treats the constraints placed on global competition by governments, while competition law treats the impediments created by private firms. They operate in tandem.

Third, and related, is the assumption that competition law would have to be conceived and implemented in the same way that current WTO law is conceived and implemented – i.e. that it must operate in the same ways as the existing trade law regime operates. This assumption tends to block points of entry for competition law into the WTO. With certain exceptions,[11] the current WTO system is concerned with rights, basically market access rights. In it, states bargain with other states over the degree to which individual states will relinquish their rights to exclude particular products or business activities from their territory. Rights to exclude are the fulcrum, and the enforcement mechanism is based on the denial of access rights by one state against another for its failure to honor obligations regarding its use of such access rights.

Competition law represents a fundamentally different kind of legal regime. In it, the issue is conduct standards. These may be shaped by a variety of goals, but they must be generally applicable in order for a competition law regime to achieve legitimacy and political support. In contrast to the current regime of market access negotiations, a competition law regime is not amenable to bargaining over specific benefits and costs to individual members. The assumption that competition law would have to 'fit' into the current trade law regime easily leads, therefore, to the conclusion that a competition law project must be rejected as inappropriate for the WTO. There is, however, no necessary basis for assuming that competition law must operate according to the same principles as those on which the WTO currently operates.

Identifying these constraints on current thinking underscores the need to rethink the relationship between competition law and the WTO. It highlights the differences between competition law and the traditional concerns of the WTO and suggests that inclusion and operation of a competition law regime in the WTO calls for a revised perspective on the modes of operation of that organization.

III. TAKING COMMUNITY SERIOUSLY

A full analysis of the many issues involved in creating the conditions for an effective competition law in the WTO is beyond the scope of this brief essay. Here I merely identify two factors that are likely to be critical to the success of such an enterprise. The first involves the WTO's mode of operation, and

[11] For insightful discussion of recent developments in this area, see, e.g. Thomas Cottier, 'From Progressive Liberalization to Progressive Regulation', 9 Journal of International Economic Law 779 (2006).

the second involves the form of competition law that might be considered for inclusion in the WTO.

If, as I argue above, lack of confidence in the basic mode of operation of the WTO has been an obstacle to introducing competition law into the WTO, then changing the perceptions that underlie that lack of confidence is likely to be a necessary condition for including competition law in the WTO. Accordingly, a primary objective must be to develop norms and procedures that are perceived as consistent with a 'community-based' image of the WTO. The issue is whether the WTO can take the idea of community seriously and give it operational force.

A. Decisional factors

In considering that issue, it is necessary to take into account the context in which decisions about competition law will be made.[12] Curiously, discussions about introducing competition law into the WTO often overlook the basic fact that the introduction of such a law will depend on voluntary, political decisions by the Member States acting in their own interests. There is no current institutional mechanism for obligating members to accept such provisions or for pressuring or shaping their decisions on this issue. Competition law can be expected to affect many interests in most, if not all, Member States, and thus the introduction of a competition law regime will require high-level political support. The issue is far too large and too sensitive to be entrusted to 'experts' or to be pushed through 'under the radar'.

This decisional context means that the issue has to be located at the systemic level. It necessarily involves perceptions of how the WTO's institutions operate and cannot be framed as a narrow and technical issue. It requires persuading Member States to support a rather vague normative project that could have very broad ranging consequences. A focus on the basic modes of operation of the WTO is thus politically imperative for framing a conception of community that could support the introduction of competition law into the WTO. It is not only a conceptual and perceptual issue, but also a highly practical one that requires convincing skeptical political leaders to accept a controversial project that is likely to have consequences that are not only significant and potentially menacing, but also difficult to predict.

Some have suggested that there is little point in thinking about 'community' in the context of the WTO until and unless members routinely adhere to the commitments they have already made. In this view, 'community' must be seen as a distant ideal because there is insufficient cooperation with existing WTO obligations to justify expecting higher levels of commitment.

[12] For discussion of related issues, see Mitsuo Matsushita, 'Basic Principles of the WTO and the Role of Competition Policy', 3 Washington University Global Studies Law Review 363 (2004).

The degree to which a member fulfills current WTO obligations may indicate its willingness to accept additional obligations, but its relevance for moving toward a greater degree of 'community' should not be overstated. Willingness to fulfill obligations is associated with the perceived legitimacy of the processes by which the obligations are incurred. A deeper and broader conception of community is likely, therefore, to increase the willingness of states to fulfill their obligations. Viewed from this perspective, the argument that a deeper conception of community is not yet 'ripe' is inapposite and should not block the path of competition law development.

B. Competition law and a WTO-based concept of community

In considering the development of a more 'community-based' conception of the WTO that could support an effective competition law regime, three factors seem likely to be central.[13] All relate to interests and incentives. This conception of 'community' is more objective than some commentators have proposed. It casts 'community' as a dynamic process rooted in and driven by the interplay of interests and incentives. Although major writers consider factors such as empathy to be an important element in building a more community-based WTO,[14] this largely subjective conception has limitations under current conditions. It can be of value in many cases, but a more objective conception of community that is based on interests and incentives aligns more closely with the current realities of the WTO and thus may be more persuasive for those skeptical of including competition law in the WTO.

1. Respecting interests

One dimension of an enriched version of community calls for increased opportunities for members to influence WTO decisions. It would require that members be heard in all situations where their interests may be affected, and it would require that with regard to any decision, WTO decision makers give significant weight to the interests of all categories of members that might be significantly effected by that decision. The experience of developing countries in recent years has led many to question whether their views and interests are given this type of respect in the current operations of the WTO.[15] Disparities in power and influence within the WTO tend to increase sensitivity on this issue among those with less power. If members believe that

[13] This discussion is directed specifically to the concept of community as it relates to the competition law issue. A fuller elaboration of the concept is beyond the scope of this article. In addition to Sungjoon Cho's valuable work, see Steven Brint, '*Gemeinschaft* Revisited: A Critique and Reconstruction of the Community Concept', 19 Sociological Theory 1 (2001).

[14] See, e.g. Cho, above n 2, at 519–23 (advocating a conception of community in which empathy plays an important role).

[15] For in-depth discussion of these kinds of 'global balance' issues, see Ethan B. Kapstein, *Economic Justice in an Unfair World* (Princeton: Princeton UP, 2006) and Frank J. Garcia, *Trade, Inequality, and Justice: Toward a Liberal Theory of Just Trade* (Ardsley, NY: Transnational Publishers, 2003).

their interests will be taken into account and given weight in the decision-making process, they are more likely to accept the potential costs that may be involved in the operation of a competition law regime.

Meeting this objective will require modification of some WTO decision-making procedures and patterns of operation. In the context of competition law, however, such modifications are critical because, in contrast to the current trade-based regime, competition law involves conduct standards and procedures that are intended to be *the same for all participants* and *to apply equally to all participants*.[16] Members are not likely to support such a normative regime unless they are convinced that they have the opportunity, singly or with others, to play significant roles in developing and applying these kinds of general conduct norms.

2. Aligning interests and incentives

A second component of this enriched image of 'community' involves the alignment of interests. Members must be convinced that their interests are generally aligned with the interests of other members over the range of decisions affecting them. This does not mean, of course, that the interests must be identical or even always similar. It does mean that non-transitory conflicts among significant and stable groups of members over major issues are likely to make a competition law regime unacceptable and unworkable. For example, as long as members perceive major and non-transitory conflicts between the interests and objectives of developed and developing country members, many developing countries will find it difficult to accept a competition law regime, not least because developed countries are markedly better equipped to use institutional rules and procedures to their advantage.

In the current WTO regime, such long-standing and well-entrenched conflicts have become a significant impediment to effective development of the WTO's institutions. Developing country disappointment over the implementation of the TRIPS agreement has been a central motif in discussions of the WTO for several years.[17] Such conflicts can be expected to be even greater in the competition law context, however, because, as noted, competition law involves the development and application of generalized conduct standards, and thus it depends for its legitimacy on confidence in the processes by which decisions are made. Major and non-transitory conflicts, especially those involving significant power disparities, would generate distrust in those decision making processes.

[16] Joseph Weiler discusses related issues of legitimacy with penetrating insight in Joseph H.H.Weiler, 'The Rule of Lawyers and the Ethos of Diplomats: Some Reflections on the Internal and External Legitimacy of WTO Dispute Settlement', 35 Journal of World Trade 191 (2001).

[17] See, e.g. Tomer Broude, 'The Rule(s) of Trade and the Rhetos of Development: Reflections on the Functional and Aspirational Legitimacy of the WTO', 45 Columbia Journal of Transnational Law 221 (2006).

3. Shared interests

Although attainment of the goals noted above—i.e. generalized respect for the interests of all groups and reasonable alignment of interest-based incentives – is likely to be a necessary condition for the establishment of an effective competition law regime in the WTO, it will probably not be a sufficient condition. This is likely to require, in addition, a widespread perception that the WTO is operating and will continue to operate on the basis of 'shared interests'. This means that members must perceive their interests to be associated and interwoven with goals, projects or processes that they share with the other members. Where interests are shared in this sense, each participant expects to derive benefits for itself from the combined actions or decisions of the others in the group. Those decisions and actions may involve, for example, the success of a set of development goals or the creation of better decision-making processes. The interests are shared in the sense that each participant derives benefit from the same source as the other participants, and thus the costs of participation of each are tied to the incentives and benefits of the others. This form of shared interests can generate confidence in decision making processes, support for institutional decisions and impetus for contributions to shared projects.

Two main types of shared interests are likely to be prominent. One is political and institutional. The perception that the interests of all members are closely associated with the stability, effectiveness and development of particular WTO procedures such as the dispute resolution process may, for example, provide incentives for firms to factor this shared institutional interest into their own decisions. Another category of shared interests is economic.[18] For example, to the extent that members identify their interests with the goal of reducing obstacles to economic development in developing countries, this provides incentives for them to incur costs in the operation of a competition law regime in the expectation that such a regime would help reduce such obstacles and thus provide (shared) benefits for each that exceed those costs.

If members of the WTO were confident that the WTO would operate in ways that would respect, promote and develop the interests just outlined, this would provide a solid basis for introducing competition law into the WTO framework. It would reduce or eliminate most of the current obstacles to the competition law project. There is, however, one additional obstacle that stands in the way of introducing competition law and making it effective. I refer to uncertainty about the concept of competition law itself and expectations about the consequences of introducing whatever form of competition law might be proposed.

[18] For discussion of some of the economic and political issues involved, see, e.g. Bernard M. Hoekman, 'Economic Development, Competition Policy and the World Trade Organization', 37 Journal of World Trade 1 (2003).

IV. COMPETITION LAW: PERCEPTION AND ILLUSIONS

Discussions of the potential role of competition law in the WTO often proceed as if the meaning of 'competition law' were self-evident. They often imply that there is only one kind of competition law and that everyone knows what the term means. Few address the question 'what kind of competition law would be introduced and what would the probable consequences of its operation be?' For those who wish to include competition law in the WTO, this strategy is attractive, not least because it projects a relatively straightforward and low-cost path of negotiation. If there is no need to talk about the content of competition law, then many fewer decisions need to be negotiated. Many assume that the best path is, therefore, to get the abstract idea accepted and to discuss later what it represents in practice. In this context, some go further and refer to European Union experience, claiming that competition law was initially introduced there without any developed sense of what was involved, leaving not only its details, but also its basic form for later development.[19]

Although this strategy is often used in multilateral negotiations, it may not be appropriate in the case of competition law at the WTO. It assumes that keeping the project vague will allow all participants to agree to support it because they will imagine the introduction of a form of competition law that they support or at least could accept. Here that assumption is highly questionable. The parties may well imagine the opposite. The assumption can be expected to hold only where at least one of two conditions is met. Either the parties must believe that the project will have no significant consequences for their interests or they must be confident that they can predict roughly what the potential consequences of introducing a competition law would be for them. Neither of these conditions is met here. First, the potential for competition law to affect a wide range of interests among members is high, so each member must expect potentially significant consequences from the introduction of such a regime. Second, the differences in forms of competition law and the potential consequences of choosing and implementing them are poorly known and understood, so there is little basis for a member to have confidence in predictions about what such a regime would mean for its interests. Moreover, it is precisely the lack of confidence in the current WTO decision making processes that is a cause for concern by many members, and thus they are unlikely to have confidence

[19] This claim is misleading. The introduction of competition law ideas into the Treaty of Rome was based on well-developed ideas of the basic form such a competition law could be expected to take. These ideas derived primarily from US and German thought and experience and thus were not widely known in some countries. It was clear, however, that Germans would initially be entrusted by the other signatory states with taking the lead in developing competition law within the then 'common market,' and this is what occurred. For discussion, see David J. Gerber, *Law and Competition in Twentieth Century Europe: Protecting Prometheus* (New York and Oxford, England: Clarendon Press, 1998, 2001) 232–65; 346–84.

that they could significantly influence decisions regarding implementation of the idea. As a result, in the absence of greater clarity about the forms, possibilities and variations of competition law, each member is likely to project a concept of competition law that would cause the greatest harm to its interests. Its representatives are virtually impelled to do so as a means of minimizing damage to the interests they represent.

A. Differing conceptions of competition law

Under these circumstances, it is difficult to expect the WTO's membership to support inclusion of a competition law regime. Even if it were included, it is difficult to imagine it becoming effective. In order to make such a project both possible and effective, it is important to identify the range of conceptions of competition law and on that basis to develop a concept of competition law that is appropriate for inclusion in the WTO.[20]

Identifying the range of meanings of 'competition law' minimizes misunderstandings about the nature of the project and is likely to increase the alignment of expectations regarding it. The objective is to provide a minimum degree of content about what the project of including competition law in the WTO might entail. I do not suggest, of course, that the details need to be worked out in advance, but the basic conception – the basic outlines of goals and methods – should be clarified so that decision makers at least know what they are being asked to support and, perhaps later, implement.

The first step in clarifying the picture is to distinguish 'competition law' from 'unfair competition law', because inconsistencies in use of the terms and their analogues in languages other than English often cause confusion even at this basic level. In the context of some national legal regimes, the term 'competition law' (or its cognates) includes two distinct legal regimes. One protects competitors against *unfair* competition; the other protects the process of competition from restraints. Unfair competition law regimes contain principles and procedures that entitle a private party to take legal action against an economic actor who has engaged in conduct that is deemed 'unfair' and thereby harmed the economic interests of the plaintiff. Unfair competition law is often understood as part of or closely related to tort law, and it is specifically intended to protect private economic interests. This is NOT what is contemplated in the context of the WTO.

'Competition law' in the narrower sense is a fundamentally different conception, and it is this use of the term that is relevant in the context of

[20] For discussion of the range of differences among existing systems and the issues involved in comparing and relating them to each other, see David J. Gerber, 'Comparative Antitrust Law', in Mathias Reimann and Reinhold Zimmerman (eds), *Oxford Handbook of Comparative Law* (Oxford: Oxford UP, 2006) 1193. For further discussion of how competition laws can relate to each other in the context of globalization, see David J. Gerber, 'Competition', above n 10.

the WTO. At its most basic, 'competition law' involves protection of the process of competition. In the US and increasingly in other parts of the world, the term 'antitrust law' is applied to such regimes. Here the objective is to protect the competitive process against *restraints* on the process. It seeks to eliminate obstacles to the effective functioning of markets in order to allow the competitive process to provide to the fullest extent possible the economic benefits that effectively functioning markets can provide. The primary beneficiary of such a regime is the public. In some national regimes, private parties may be entitled to sue for violations of competition law and thus pursue their own private interest, but the goal of the legal regime is to provide a public good.

Even within this form of competition law, however, there is significant variation in goals, perspectives, methods, institutions and operative concepts.[21] In short, there is no single model of competition law. I will here note only two fields of difference among many.

One area of difference involves the goals of competition law. The narrowest view of competition law's goals is currently found in US antitrust law, where the generally accepted goal is 'consumer welfare'. As used in this context, this is a technical term derived from economic science, specifically, from neo-classical economics. The basic standard for applying the law is whether conduct has increased price above a competitive level or is likely to have that effect. This goal requires for its application significant reliance on economists and economic science. It has been developed over the last three decades, primarily in the United States, where it has now become the orthodox understanding of what competition law's goals should be.[22]

Competition law can also have other goals. In the United States, for example, the current narrow view of antitrust's goals is relatively new. For decades before the 1970s the courts developed the goals of antitrust on an ad hoc basis. They included, for example, economic goals defined in terms of the structure of markets. Here the concern was that particular market structures, especially those dominated by small numbers of firms with large shares of the market, were in themselves a restraint on competition, and antitrust law should be used to prevent the creation and strengthening of those positions. Antitrust was also seen at times as a tool for preventing dominant firms from using their economic power to harm or eliminate small and medium-sized enterprises. It was believed that such practices were indirectly harming society itself by eliminating the opportunities for smaller firms to compete and for local firms to remain independent. The courts also considered political goals. Here competition was protected in order to

[21] See, e.g. Juergen Basedow (ed.), *Limits and Control of Competition with a View to Harmonization* (The Hague: Kluwer Law International, 2002) and Roger Zaech (ed.), *Towards WTO Competition Rules* (The Hague: Kluwer Law International, 1999).

[22] For discussion of this evolution, see Gerber, 'Competition', above n 10, at 512–22.

protect the political process from the undue influence of very large corporations. This mixture of goals was not always internally consistent, and dissatisfaction with this inconsistency is one of the factors that have led to a radical narrowing of antitrust's goals during the last three decades.

In Europe and elsewhere, the goals of competition law often also exhibit extensive variety. For example, concern with the power of large firms to distort competition has been a major focus of competition law in Europe. This has supported the idea that dominant firms are subject to special scrutiny and owe a 'special duty' not to use their power to distort competition. In addition, the European Union's competition law goals have included the integration of national markets. Here the idea is that in order to achieve a single and undistorted market, it is necessary to prevent powerful firms or groups of firms from impeding the process of economic integration. In developing countries, an objective of competition law is sometimes to protect domestic firms by seeking to prevent powerful foreign firms from using their power or size in ways that impede the development of domestic firms. In some countries, there are also special features of competition laws based on unique circumstances. In South Africa, for example, competition law has included special provisions to protect firms owned and managed by those who suffered from apartheid.

A second range of difference relates to competition law methods – i.e. the means of implementing normative goals. There are two basic approaches. In the United States, private enforcement has always played an important role in implementing antitrust law, and in many ways the development of US antitrust law has been colored and shaped by this heavy reliance on private litigation. In most of the rest of the world, however, enforcement relies predominantly or exclusively on administrative decision making. This reliance influences all aspects of thinking about competition law, including, *inter alia*, procedures, the forms of information available to decision makers, the political incentives to take enforcement action and the norms of competition law themselves.

B. Toward a WTO-compatible competition law

Given this level of variation in the aims and methods of competition law, it will be necessary to make choices about the general characteristics of a competition law that might be considered for introduction into the WTO. Broad-based support for choices of this kind is likely to require development of a form of competition law that is specifically designed to fit the needs and objectives of the WTO. Here conceptions of 'community' can be expected to play a major role. In order for all categories of members to support a competition law project for the WTO, the project should be consistent with the more community-oriented conception of the WTO outlined above.

Many factors may be involved in developing such a conception of competition law. I here suggest several elements that would support such a conception and facilitate its introduction and implementation. They are intended to be consistent with and to foster an enriched form of community within the WTO.

One involves the general conception of competition law. Critical to success of the project will be establishing the perception that the regime is a 'shared resource' in whose success all members have a stake and from which each expects to derive significant net benefits for itself.[23] This assumes that all members view improved efficiency on global markets as beneficial to their own interests. Most, if not all, members can be expected to see *some* benefits in such improved efficiency, but their view of the *net* benefits is likely to depend on the expected costs to them. If a Member State expects the operation of the system to lead to forms and patterns of economic development that it considers politically unacceptable, those costs will weigh heavily in that member's assessment of the net value of the project.

On a more general level, willingness to support a competition law regime will depend on how the expected benefits of the system are likely to be distributed. If such a regime is expected systematically to favor one group or set of interests over others, competition law will for many members appear not be a shared resource, but rather a tool for the attainment or maintenance of advantages by the favored groups. The success of a competition law project at the WTO will depend, therefore, on creating justified expectations that the net benefits to members will be widely and relatively evenly distributed. A form of competition law that serves primarily to achieve market access for developed country companies is not likely to be acceptable.[24]

A second factor involves the goals of a WTO competition law regime. Given the significant variations among goals in existing and past competition law systems, the choice of goals to guide decision making is of central importance. The relatively narrow economic efficiency goal of the current US system has much to commend it for many purposes and in many contexts, but the diversity of needs within the WTO may call for a degree of flexibility in the goal structure that would include developmental goals. This will require serious and creative thought in defining the relationships among the goals themselves and relating them to the objectives of the WTO as an institution.

[23] For discussion of related issues involving competition law and the WTO as a 'public good,' see Josef Drexl, 'International Competition Policy after Cancun: Placing a Singapore Issue on the WTO Development Agenda', 27 World Competition 419 (2004).

[24] For discussion of the relationship between market access issues and competition law, see gen. Eleanor Fox, 'Toward World Antitrust and Market Access', 91 American Journal of International Law 1 (1997) and Daniel K. Tarullo, 'Norms and Institutions in Global Competition Policy', 94 American Journal of International Law 478 (2000).

An important element here is likely to be the temporal perspective of the goals. The WTO context is likely to require a longer-term, developmental dimension. The goal of competition law at the WTO level would enhance the economic welfare of national economies at significantly different stages of economic development, and thus an effective competition law would have to take that longer-term perspective into account. A goal structure that focuses exclusively on the short-run and immediate effects of anticompetitive conduct may have limited attractiveness.

At least as important as defining the goals of such a competition law regime is the task of developing its methods. This third factor is institutional and procedural. Among existing competition law systems, differences in the way decisions are made and goals implemented are in many ways more important than differences in the goals and articulated norms themselves. In order for competition law to be an effective part of the WTO, the institutional framework must generate confidence that an enriched form of community, as discussed above, would actually be built into the fundamental decision-making processes that implement competition law.

In shaping a competition law regime that would be appropriate for this context, several factors are likely to play key roles. First, the decisional structure should assure a high degree of independence for the decision-makers. The history of competition law everywhere highlights the risks of interference from both public and private actors and repeatedly shows that if such independence is not provided, competition law is unlikely to flourish. Second, the decision-making institutions must include and interrelate solid expertise in several areas, including national and regional competition law experience, economics, including, in particular, international development economics, and international relations. Without such a foundation of expertise, decisions are not likely to achieve the status and consistency that will be necessary for the success of a competition law project.[25] And, third, the institutions and procedures should not be dominated by individuals, thought patterns or modes of operation from one country or group of countries. While there will be much benefit in using experience accumulated at the national and regional levels, competition law institutions that do not reflect the interests, values and problems of all categories of WTO members are not likely to engender trust on the part of those whose interests and concerns are not represented. In short, for them such a competition law would have little to do with 'community'.

The process of designing a competition law regime for the WTO should draw on existing models and experience at the national and European levels, but it is unlikely that any single current competition law system could be

[25] For in-depth analysis of current issues in WTO decision making, see William J. Davey, *Enforcing World Trade Rules: Essays on WTO Dispute Settlement and GATT Obligations* (London: Cameron May, 2006).

transplanted effectively to the WTO context. The needs and political situation of the organization differ greatly from anything that has yet been tried. It is thus necessary to think afresh about competition law rather than merely assume that some existing form would be appropriate for the WTO.

Fortunately, some foundations for pursuing such a goal are already present within the institutions of the WTO. The Working Group on Trade and Competition that was established in the late 1990s in preparation for the Doha Round brought together specialists and gathered information from many sources. This information and experience could be used as a base for developing a WTO-specific conception of competition law. Moreover, the Trade Policy Review Mechanism has a broad mandate for developing policies that might relate to trade, and it is well-positioned to contribute to the development of an appropriate form of competition law.

V. CONCLUDING COMMENTS

This brief essay has identified two main obstacles to the inclusion of competition law in the WTO—(i) a perceived lack of 'community' in the norms and operations of the WTO and (ii) uncertainty about the form and potential consequences of the competition law that might be introduced. The inclusion of competition law as an effective part of the WTO is likely to require that substantial progress be made in eliminating both obstacles.

The obstacles are imposing. They relate to basic perceptions and conceptions of the WTO and the processes by which decisions are made within it. Reducing such obstacles will, therefore, require reconceiving and re-imagining the relationship between competition law and the WTO. A WTO that operates primarily as a forum for negotiating market access rights is likely to require modification if it is to support an effective competition law regime. It is likely that the success of such a modification will depend on its capacity to generate trust among all categories of WTO members. It is likely also to include development of a conception of competition law that treats global competition as a resource to be shared by all.

The image of 'community' within the WTO context may long—or even permanently – remain a vague ideal to which reference is occasionally made, but which has no operative role in WTO decision making. If it is to be more than that, competition law may serve as both a metric of progress and a mechanism of support, and the benefits are likely to reach far beyond the institutions of the WTO.

THE PRESENT AND FUTURE OF THE INVESTOR-STATE DISPUTE SETTLEMENT PARADIGM

*Won-Mog Choi**

ABSTRACT

While the World Trade Organization (WTO) system remains faithful to the long-standing traditional paradigm of state-to-state dispute resolution, dispute resolution mechanisms in the area of international investment are undergoing a radical change. Traditionally, the paradigm of 'diplomatic protection' has served as a basis for the settlement of investment disputes among states. In earlier commercial agreements, including the Friendship, Commerce, and Navigation Treaties (FCNs) concluded from 1940s to 1960s, the resolution of international investment disputes took the form of state-to-state dispute resolution. This paradigm shifted in the 1970s when direct investor claims, modelled on treaties that European countries had been putting forward since 1959, were allowed under a series of bilateral investment treaties initiated by the United States. This shift has been reflected in subsequent efforts to reach a multilateral agreement on investment (MAI) and in many free trade agreements (FTAs). Also, in the area of international human rights law, it is an increasing trend to allow an individual to have direct recourse to international human rights protection bodies, such as the Human Rights Committee established under the International Covenant on Civil and Political Rights, after the exhaustion of domestic remedies. The allowance of direct claims has helped to make up for the typical shortcomings of the diplomatic protection mechanism where, the espousing state has frequently exercised excessive discretion in deciding whether to advance claims due to considerations of a political nature, unrelated to the particular case, so that this mechanism can increase international friction. On the other hand, the strong point of diplomatic protection has been its capacity to screen out frivolous or dishonest claims by individuals. The question whether various international dispute settlement mechanisms may eventually converge into an effective system based on a direct claim procedure is a vexing one. It is uncertain whether the model of

* Professor of Law, Ewha Womans University, Seoul; S.J.D. and Attorney-at-law. E-mail: wmchoi@ewha.ac.kr.

investor-state dispute settlement (ISDS) can play a pioneering role in this ongoing process. Any pertinent answers to such questions require a thorough comparison of the benefits and drawbacks of such a development. Lessons from the experiences under the ISDS system and its modification efforts should be fully taken into account so the newly emerging dispute resolution system will not lead to tension between nations in an area where precedent is scant, but the need is great.

I. TRADITIONAL PARADIGM OF DIPLOMATIC PROTECTION: WHERE THE STORY BEGAN

As the most important means of obtaining reparation for the treatment of aliens which runs counter to international law, over the last century, diplomatic protection[1] has come to be a procedural corollary to the legal responsibility. As early as 1924, in the first judgment on the *Mavrommatis Concessions Case*, the Permanent Court of International Justice (PCIJ) deemed the right of a state to protect its subjects injured by the acts of another state to be 'an elementary principle of international law'.[2] In this light, the right to grant diplomatic protection has been included as a fundamental diplomatic or consular function in two treaties aimed towards worldwide participation, namely the Vienna Convention on Diplomatic Relations and the Vienna Convention on Consular Relations.[3]

In general, a state may exercise diplomatic protection only after the injured private party, making the complaint, has tried and failed to obtain relief through 'ordinary channels'[4]—i.e., through the domestic courts of the state ostensibly responsible for the injury. According to the International Court of Justice (ICJ), 'the rule that local remedies must be exhausted before international proceedings may be instituted is a well-established rule of customary international law'.[5] Before resorting to an international court, it has been considered necessary that the state where the violation occurred should have an opportunity for redress within the framework of its own domestic legal system.[6] Once the private party has exhausted local remedies

[1] International Law Commission (ILC), *Draft Articles on Diplomatic Protection*, Article 1, UN Doc. A/CN.4/L.647 (2004) ('Diplomatic protection consists of resort to diplomatic action or other means of peaceful settlement by a State adopting in its own right the cause of its national in respect of an injury to that national arising from an internationally wrongful act of another State.')

[2] PCIJ, *Mavrommatis Palestine Concessions* (*Greece v United Kingdom*), 1924 P.C.I.J., ser. A, No. 2, at 11–12.

[3] Article 3.1(b), Vienna Convention on Diplomatic Relations ('protecting in the receiving State the interests of... its nationals'); Article 5(a) and (e), Vienna Convention on Consular Relations ('protecting in the receiving State the interests... of its nationals, both individuals and bodies corporate...' and 'helping and assisting nationals...').

[4] Above n 2.

[5] ICJ, *Interhandel* Case (*Switzerland v United States*), 1959 I.C.J. 5, 27 (21 March).

[6] Ibid at 27.

and its state advances the claim, the dispute undergoes a sort of theoretical 'transformation'.[7] The state is now 'asserting its own rights—its right to ensure, in the person of its subjects, respect for the rules of international law'.[8] The origination of the claim of an injury to a private interest becomes 'irrelevant', and the espousing state is now the 'sole claimant'.[9] This rule requiring exhaustion of local remedies has become customary international law and can also be found in numerous relevant treaties. A considerable number of decisions based either on the customary law or on those treaty provisions mention this rule.[10]

It is generally accepted that the institution of diplomatic protection has brought a remarkable stability to international relations. In a rapidly changing and sometimes volatile international setting, diplomatic protection grants a natural or legal person engaged in international business or similar activities, the opportunity to rely on assistance from the strongest possible institutional supporter of these activities, i.e. his or her home state. Therefore, diplomatic protection has facilitated a burgeoning movement of people, goods, capital, and services across state boundaries. At a minimum, the right of states to protect their nationals can serve as a warning signal to states inclined to ignore treaty or customary law obligations. In this way, diplomatic protection has played a key role in promoting international economic relations.

II. FLAWS OF DIPLOMATIC PROTECTION AND SHIFT OF PARADIGM

Yet for all the advantages ascribed to diplomatic protection, it turns out that the paradigm has some serious flaws. The nationality rule leaves millions of stateless persons without any protection. The notion of the state as claimant against another state has had important consequences, for it tends to politicize disputes, increasing international friction.[11] The espousal of a claim by one state against another may give rise to political controversy if it is viewed as the institution of an 'unfriendly' action.[12] Indeed, equating the interests of powerful individuals with the interests of an entire country has been described as the greatest threat to peace in the modern world.[13]

[7] ILC, *Preliminary Report on Diplomatic Protection*, 5, UN Doc. A/CN.4/484(1998) (prepared by Mohamed Bennouna).

[8] Above n 2.

[9] Ibid.

[10] See PCIJ, *Mavrommatis Concessions Cases*, PCIJ, ser. A, No. 2 (1939), at 12 of the 1924 judgment; PCIJ, *Panevezys–Saldutiskis Railway Case*. PCIJ, ser. A/B, No. 76 (1939), at 18; PCIJ, *Electricity Company of Sofia Case*, PCIJ, ser. A/B, No. 77 (1939), at 78; ICJ, *Interhandel Case*, above n 5, at 27.

[11] See Hersch Lauterpacht, 'The Subjects of the Law of Nations', 63 Law Quarterly Review (1947), 438, 454.

[12] See Ibid.

[13] J.L. Brierly, 'La Fondement du Charactère Obligatoire du Droit International', 23 Recueil Des Courts 468, 531 (1928).

The political nature of diplomatic protection also means that power differences inevitably affect the resolution of international disputes in which this protection is invoked. Diplomatic protection, it has been said, 'came to be seen by developing nations, particularly in Latin America, as a discriminatory exercise of power rather than as a method of protecting human rights'.[14]

Even for nationals from powerful states, diplomatic protection has had its drawbacks, for the espousing state has complete discretion over the claim. The espousing state acts as the sole judge to decide whether and to what extent such protection will be granted, and also if and when the grant of protection will cease. Any exercise of this discretion may be determined by considerations of a political nature, unrelated to the particular case.[15] Moreover, whether or not such discretion is in fact determined by considerations of a political nature in a controversial case, there is still the problem that it will be perceived to have been thus determined.

These shortcomings of the traditional paradigm have led several prominent international law scholars to argue for a reform that would allow individuals access in their own right to adjudication by international tribunals, including the ICJ.[16]

A. GATT/WTO

Notwithstanding these suggestions for direct claims by individuals, the World Trade Organization (WTO) (and GATT 1947) dispute settlement system remained with the form of the state-to-state dispute resolution based on the diplomatic protection paradigm. However, it opted for one significant

[14] ILC, *First Report on Diplomatic Protection*, 15, UN Doc. A/CN.4/506 (2000) (prepared by John R. Dugard), at 5; see also ILC, *Preliminary Report on Diplomatic Protection*, 5, UN Doc. A/CN.4/484 (1998) (prepared by Mohamed Bennouna), at 3 (noting that 'one of the main criticisms of this institution' has been 'that it is in essence discriminatory because only powerful States are able to use it against weaker States'). In response, Latin American countries developed the Drago Doctrine (prohibiting the use of force to recover debts) and the Calvo Doctrine (maintaining that States owed aliens no duties beyond national treatment). See generally Amos S. Hershey, 'The Calvo and Drago Doctrines', 1 *American Journal of International Law* (1907) 26 (explaining the background of the doctrines).

[15] ICJ, *Barcelona Traction, Light and Power Company, Ltd*, 1970 I.C.J. 3, 44 (5 February) ('[I]t is clear that by international law there is no legal duty incumbent upon the state to extend diplomatic protection. Whether such a duty exists towards the citizen is a matter of municipal law of his own country, the general rule being that even under municipal law the state is under no legal duty to extend diplomatic protection.').
Restatement (Third) of Foreign Relations Law section 902, cmt. l (1987) ('The President may refuse to present a claim, settle it by negotiation, abandon it, or join it with other claims for *en bloc* resolution.').

[16] Lauterpacht, above n 11, at 453–58; see also Philip C. Jessup, 'Responsibility of States for Injuries to Individuals', 46 Columbia Law Review (1946) 903 at 910 (favouring 'procedural developments in international relations such as the establishment of special claims commissions to which the individual would have the right of direct access'); J.L. Brierly, *The Law of Nations* 277 (Humphrey Waldock 6th edn, New York: Oxford University Press, 1963) (suggesting that 'allowing individuals access in their own right to some form of international tribunal... is a possible reform which deserves to be considered').

procedural reform: removal of the crucial requirement of 'exhaustion of local remedy'.

According to Article XXIII of GATT, 'if any benefit accruing to [any contracting party] directly or indirectly under this Agreement is being nullified or impaired...as the result of...the application by another contracting party of any measure ...', the contracting party may bring a WTO complaint. In other words, if a GATT benefit accruing to *a national* of one WTO member is impaired by another member's actions, such a case constitutes the situation where 'any benefit accruing to any contracting party *indirectly* under this Agreement is being nullified or impaired'.[17] Therefore, home states may bring a WTO complaint on behalf of a national whose benefit has been impaired, regardless of whether he or she has exhausted local remedies. This interpretation is confirmed by state practice: GATT dispute settlement proceedings are repeatedly pursued in parallel with domestic court proceedings over the same issues of antidumping, countervailing duty or other trade measures.[18] The same procedural reform is also in effect under the GATS and TRIPS Agreements.[19]

Turning away from the time-consuming constraint of 'exhaustion of local remedies', the WTO indicated an intention to facilitate the flow of trade and dispute resolution among states for the greater benefit of the global trading system. Other than this procedural facilitation, however, all the other drawbacks under the traditional state-to-state dispute settlement mechanism still persist.

B. Human rights conventions and development of the EU

A fundamental departure from the paradigm of diplomatic protection has materialized in a number of human rights conventions. Despite considerable differences in detail, the European Convention for the Protection of Human Rights and Fundamental Freedoms (1950),[20] the American Convention on Human Rights (1969),[21] and the United Nations Human Rights Covenants (1966)[22] recognize the 'inherent dignity' and 'the equal and inalienable

[17] This may be called an 'indirect injury' case. In comparison, in a direct injury case, injury occurs upon a state itself: a typical example is an armed attack against foreign warship or diplomatic mission.

[18] See Ernst-Ulrich Petersmann, ed. *International Trade Law and the GATT/WTO Dispute Settlement System* (London: Kluwer Law International, 1997), at 117.

[19] See Article XXIII of GATS, and Article 64 of TRIPs Agreement.

[20] Convention for the Protection of Human Rights and Fundamental Freedoms, Council of Europe, European Treaties ETS No.5 (concluded at Rome on 4 November 1950, as amended by Protocol No. 11).

[21] American Convention on Human Rights, O.A.S.Treaty Series No. 36, 1144 U.N.T.S. 123, entered into force on 18 July 1978, reprinted in Basic Documents Pertaining to Human Rights in the Inter-American System, OEA/Ser.L.V/II.82 doc.6 rev.1 at 25 (1992).

[22] International Covenant on Civil and Political Rights, 999 U.N.T.S. 171 (16 December 1966); International Covenant on Economic, Social and Cultural Rights, 993 U.N.T.S. 3 (16 December 1966).

rights of all members of the human family [as] . . . the foundation of freedom, justice and peace in the world'.[23] Treaty rights under these agreements directly accrue to individuals within the jurisdiction of the signatory parties regardless of their nationality.[24] The emancipation of the individual from the exclusive jurisdictional protection of his home state under human rights conventions is obvious given that individuals may even institute proceedings against their own state under certain conditions of rights' violation and accession to optional protocols.[25] The Vienna Convention on the Law of Treaties supports the opinion that 'treaties of a humanitarian character' protect individuals *qua* individuals and not merely as nationals.[26]

In fact, the very formation of the European Union is based on the basic tenet that individuals in Europe transcend the status of mere nationals of a state. They are viewed as citizens of the Union.[27] Under Union, rather than national, law, individuals are legal subjects with their own rights and duties. It is a fundamental principle of EU law that such law be applied generally and equally within the entire Union. It is very doubtful whether the home state of an individual injured by another EU member may go further, especially by using reprisals in reliance on its customary right to grant diplomatic protection. Diplomatic protection exercised by an individual member state is becoming something of a historic relic in Europe.

However, efforts to introduce such a direct claim system into the human rights conventions fell short of completely eliminating the exhaustion of local remedy rule. The European Court of Human Rights may only deal with private petitions 'after all domestic remedies have been exhausted'.[28] Individuals who have 'exhausted all available domestic remedies' may

[23] See the Preambles of the 1966 Covenant on Civil and Political Rights and of Covenant on Economic, Social and Cultural Rights.

[24] See Article 1 of the European Convention for the Protection of Human Rights and Fundamental Freedoms (giving protection to 'everyone within their jurisdiction'); Preamble and Article 1 of American Convention on Human Rights (recognizing that 'the essential rights of man are not derived from one's being a national of a certain state, but are based upon attributes of the human personality', and ensuring to 'all persons subject to their jurisdiction' the freedom and rights). See also, e.g. Article 2 of the International Covenant on Civil and Political Rights (ensuring to 'all individuals within its territory and subject to its jurisdiction' certain freedoms and rights).

[25] See Article 34 of the European Convention for the Protection of Human Rights and Fundamental Freedoms, and provisions of the Optional Protocol to the International Covenant on Civil and Political Rights.

[26] See Article 60.5, Vienna Convention on the Law of Treaties (prescribing that 'provisions relating to the protection of the human person contained in treaties of a humanitarian character' are not affected by any termination or suspension of the operation of the treaties as a consequence of their breach).

[27] See Preamble ('. . .resolved to establish a citizenship common to nationals of their countries . . .') and Article 2('. . . to strengthen the protection of the rights and interests of the nationals of its Member States through the introduction of a citizenship of the Union. . .') of the Treaty on European Union, C 321 E/7.

[28] Article 35 of the European Convention for the Protection of Human Rights and Fundamental Freedoms.

submit a written communication to the Human Right Committee for consideration under the Optional Protocol to the International Covenant on Civil and Political Rights.[29] Any submission of a petition to the Inter-American Commission on Human Rights is also subject to the local remedy exhaustion rule under the American Convention on Human Rights.[30]

C. International investment treaties

More radical change has taken place in dispute resolution mechanisms in the international investment field. Originally, traditional diplomatic protection governed the field in settling investment disputes among states. Between 1923 and 1938, the United States negotiated a series of Friendship, Commerce, and Consular Relations Treaties (FCCRs) containing explicit protections for foreign investors.[31] Subsequently, from 1946 to 1966, the United States concluded a set of Friendship, Commerce, and Navigation Treaties (FCNs).[32] Many of the FCNs, like the FCCRs and earlier commercial agreements, were concluded with developed countries, including Belgium, Denmark, Germany, Italy, France, the Netherlands, and Japan.[33] Although the FCNs displayed a good deal of continuity with their predecessors,[34] one important difference was the appearance in the FCNs of a provision for the resolution of disputes, which the United States had previously resisted.[35] Almost all of the FCNs provided for state-to-state dispute resolution by the ICJ.[36] In practice, however, state-to-state dispute

[29] Article 2 of the Optional Protocol to the International Covenant on Civil and Political Rights.

[30] See Article 46 of the American Convention on Human Rights.

[31] See William S. Dodge, 'Investor-State Dispute Settlement Between Developed Countries: Reflections on the Australia-United States Free Trade Agreement', Vanderbilt Journal of Transnational Law, 39 1 (January 2006), at 12–13. See also Kenneth J. Vandevelde, 'The Bilateral Investment Treaty Program of the United States', 21 Cornell International Law Journal 201, at 205–08 (1988); Robert Renbert Wilson, *United States Commercial Treaties and International Law* (New Orleans: The Hauser Press, 1960), at 113–16.

[32] See Vandevelde, above n 31. See also Wilson, above n 31, at 116–22.

[33] See Wilson, above n 31, at 333–34. It seems that the United States has difficulty in concluding FCN treaties with third world states, although it successfully negotiated them with major developed countries. See Vandevelde, above n 31, at 207.

[34] See Herman Walker, Jr, 'Modern Treaties of Friendship, Commerce, and Navigation', 42 Minnesota Law Review 805, at 807 (1958) (noting that the pattern of FCNs was 'of a kind with its predecessors, and in the same direct line of evolution, having the same broad design and covering generally the same subject-matter').

[35] See Dodge, above n 31. See also Wilson, above n 31, at 23 ('Prior to World War II, there had been suggestion of inserting in a commercial treaty a clause binding the parties to adjudicate disputes concerning interpretation or application, but the United States did not agree with the suggestion.').

[36] One exception was the treaty with Muscat. Wilson, above n 31, at 24. In fact, efforts to create multilateral investment rules were made in the course of drafting the Charter for an International Trade Organization (ITO), which was sort of a precursor agreement of the WTO Agreement. See Article 12, Havana Charter for International Trade Organization (ITO), Report of Committees and Principle Sub-Committee of the United Nations Conference on Trade and Employment, Final Act and Related Documents, UN Doc. E/Conf.2/78 (1948). However, in the aftermath of the failure of the ITO project, GATT was

resolution under these treaties was exceptionally rare, and only in the single incident of the ELSI case did the United States in fact take a claim against another developed country to the ICJ.[37]

This situation shifted in the 1970s when direct investor claims were introduced in a series of bilateral investment treaties (BITs) initiated by the United States. Modelled on treaties that European countries had been putting forward since 1959,[38] these BITs differed from earlier commercial treaties, including the FCCRs and FCNs, in that BITs focused exclusively on investment issues and were targeted at the less developed countries.[39] One of the most striking difference was that BITs allowed direct investor claims without requiring the exhaustion of local remedies. The first BIT, the United States signed in 1982 provided for the International Center for the Settlement of Investment Disputes (ICSID) arbitration.[40] The recently revised US model BIT offers a menu of alternatives, including arbitrations under the ICSID Convention, ICSID Additional Facility Rules, UNCITRAL Rules or other, mutually agreed upon arbitration rules.[41] Recently, this menu seems to be referred to by European countries.[42]

BITs offered foreign investors the benefits of avoiding domestic courts in the less developed countries, which were considered to entail oftentimes risky and burdensome proceedings. In addition, foreign investors preferred the use of a comparatively depoliticized process in which they could press their own claims without the need for intermediation by their home states.[43] On the

---

the only body left standing. As the GATT made no attempt to deal with foreign investment issues, the institutional separation of trade from investment issues in the multilateral arena continued until the Uruguay Round in the 1980s. By the late 1960s, bilateral treaties had become the primary instruments for dealing with investment issues.

[37] See Dodge, above n 31. See also ICJ, *Elettronica Sicula S.p.A. (ELSI)* (*United States v Italy*), 1989 I.C.J. 15 (20 July).

[38] Rudolf Dolzer and Margrete Stevens, *Bilateral Investment Treaties* 1 (The Hague, Boston, London, Martinus Nijhoff Publishers 1995) ('The modern BIT is European in origin.').

[39] Dodge, above n 31; Vandevelde, above n 31, at 206–09.

[40] Article VII.3, Treaty Concerning the Reciprocal Encouragement and Protection of Investments, US–Egypt, as modified on 11 March, 1986 (originally signed on 29 September, 1982). See also the earliest BITs led by the United States, e.g. Article VI.3, Treaty Concerning the Encouragement and Reciprocal Protection of Investment, US–Morocco, 22 July, 1985; Article VII.3, Treaty Concerning the Encouragement and Reciprocal Protection of Investment, US–Bangladesh, 12 March 1986, http://www.unctad.org/sections/dite/iia/docs/bits/us_egypt.pdf.

[41] See United States 2004 Model BIT, Article 24(3), http://www.state.gov/documents/organization/38710.pdf.

[42] For example, the Italy–Bangladesh BIT, signed in 1990, offers three options regarding the investor-state arbitration: an arbitration at a Party's national court having territorial jurisdiction, under UNCITRAL Rules, or under ICSID Convention. See Article 9 of the Italy–Bangladesh BIT, at http://www.unctad.org/sections/dite/iia/docs/bits/italy_bangladesh.pdf. However, the Germany-China BIT, concluded in 2003, offers the same menu as that under the US model BIT. See Article of the Germany–China BIT, at http://www.unctad.org/sections/dite/iia/docs/bits/china_germany.pdf.

[43] See Dodge, above n 31, at 14.

part of the less developed countries that signed these agreements, BITs were affordable means to encourage investment flow in an increasingly competitive world.[44] The debt crisis of the 1980s had limited the supply of financial loans to excessively indebted developing states and thus made foreign direct investment (FDI) a more desirable, and in some cases desperately needed, source of foreign capital.[45] In addition, the process by which developing states acquire control over their indigenous natural resources had progressed since the immediate post-war period and was no longer the same urgent priority.[46] Thus, the interests of developing countries have markedly shifted from an attitude of various degrees of hostility against foreign investors towards a recognized need to attract and retain FDI.

D. MAI, FTAs, and others

Such a shift has been reflected in subsequent efforts to reach a multilateral agreement on investment (MAI) in the 1990s and many free trade agreements (FTAs). MAI negotiations in the OECD would have allowed direct claims had they proven successful, but they ended without result.[47] Historically, developing countries, largely serving as recipient countries of foreign investment, have resisted initiatives to develop investment rules at the multilateral level. Indeed, the choice of the OECD (composed mainly of developed states) as the negotiating forum for the MAI was specifically driven by a desire to exclude developing countries from negotiations due to the concern that the developing states' demands would dilute the MAI commitments.[48]

In the aftermath of the failure of the MAI negotiations, FTAs became the primary channel to incorporate the direct claim model into the investment area. Therefore, the 1990s were characterized by a strong push to conclude

[44] See generally Andrew T. Guzman, 'Why LDCs Sign Treaties That Hurt Them: Explaining the Popularity of Bilateral Investment Treaties', 38 Virginia Journal of International Law 639 (1998). BITs with the following countries have entered in force with the United States: Albania, Argentina, Armenia, Azerbaijan, Bahrain, Bangladesh, Bolivia, Bulgaria, Cameroon, Congo (Kinshasa), Congo (Brazzaville), Croatia, Czech Republic, Ecuador, Egypt, Estonia, Georgia, Grenada, Honduras, Jamaica, Jordan, Kazakhstan, Kyrgyzstan, Latvia, Lithuania, Moldova, Mongolia, Morocco, Mozambique, Panama, Poland, Romania, Senegal, Slovakia, Sri Lanka, Trinidad and Tobago, Tunisia, Turkey, Ukraine. See Bilateral Investment Treaties Currently In Force (from the Trade Compliance Center), http://www.ustr.gov/Trade_Agreements/BIT/Section_Index.html.

[45] See Jurgen Kurtz, 'A General Investment Agreement in the WTO?—Lessons from Chapter 11 of NAFTA and the OECD Multilateral Agreement on Investment', 23 (4) University of Pennsylvania Journal of International Economic Law (Winter 2002), at 720.

[46] Ibid.

[47] See The MAI Negotiating Text 70–6 (as of 24 April 1998), http://www.oecd.org/dataoecd/46/40/1895712.pdf. For a discussion of the failure of these negotiations, see generally Peter T. Muchlinski, 'The Rise and Fall of the Multilateral Agreement on Investment: Where Now?', 34 International Law 1033 (1999).

[48] See Kurtz, above n 45, at 173–6.

regional rules to liberalize investment flows.[49] Of these various regional initiatives, NAFTA Chapter 11 is notable for setting high standards for investment liberalization, investment protection, and dispute settlement including direct claims by individuals.[50] Many of the US FTAs concluded after NAFTA also came to include the investor-state dispute settlement (ISDS) system based on the new paradigm of direct claims by individuals.[51] In investment disputes, this system has now become a common feature.

In addition, there are other international agreements which enable private persons to make direct claims to international dispute settlement bodies. Examples include the International Labour Organization (ILO) system of complaints;[52] the dispute settlement mechanisms provided for in the Convention Establishing the Multilateral Investment Guarantee Agency (MIGA);[53] and the 1982 Law of the Sea Convention.[54] Certain other treaties, including the WTO Agreement on Pre-Shipment Inspection,[55] and Agreement on Government Procurement,[56] prescribe direct claims by individuals as a fundamental mechanism for domestic dispute settlement procedures.

III. THE PARADIGM OF INVESTOR-STATE DISPUTE SETTLEMENT ("ISDS")

A. Why is ISDS necessary?

In the absence of other specified arrangements, a dispute between a host state and a foreign investor will normally be settled by the domestic courts of the host state. From the investor's perspective, this type of dispute settlement

[49] See ibid.

[50] Ibid.

[51] Most FTAs initiated by the US have the ISDS system, but one important exception is the FTA between the US and Australia. In general, FTAs initiated by EU do not include the ISDS mechanism. The primary reason seems to be because the Commission does not have authority to be a defending party (on behalf of the member state that is the host of investment) against investors in ISDS claims. Therefore, the ISDS system is included in BITs to which each EC member state is party. See e.g. Article 8, UK–Argentina BIT, at http://www.unctadxi.org/templates/DocSearch.aspx?id=779; Article 9, Italy–Bangladesh BIT, at http://www.unctad.org/sections/dite/iia/docs/bits/italy_bangladesh.pdf; Article 9, Germany–China BIT, http://www.unctad.org/sections/dite/iia/docs/bits/china_germany.pdf.

[52] Article 24 of the ILO Charter (petition procedure by enterprises or labour associations to ILO Secretariat against Members' failure to ensure an effective observance of treaties).

[53] Article 57(b) of the Convention Establishing the Multilateral Investment Guarantee Agency (arbitration procedure for settling disputes between the Agency as subrogee of an investor and a member state).

[54] Article 187(c) of the UN Law of the Sea Convention (Sea-Bed Dispute Chamber procedure for disputes between parties to a contract, being States Parties, the Authority or the Enterprise, state enterprises and natural or juridical persons).

[55] Article 2.21 of the Agreement on Pre-shipment Inspection (user Members' duty to establish procedures to receive, consider, render decisions concerning grievances raised by exporters).

[56] Article XX of Agreement on Government Procurement (Members' duty to enabling procurement suppliers to challenge alleged breaches of the Agreement by a Member arising in the context of procurements).

carries important disadvantages. Rightly or wrongly, host state courts are not perceived to be sufficiently impartial in this type of situation. In addition, domestic courts are formally bound to apply domestic law even if that law should fail to protect the investor's rights under international law.[57] This amounts to an institutionalized bias towards host state law and over against other legal commitments and obligations. In addition, regular domestic courts as might be expected, often lack the technical expertise required to resolve complex international investment disputes which necessitate a consideration of multiple contexts.[58]

Domestic courts of other states appointed in their stead in an attempt to secure fairness are usually not a realistically workable alternative. In most cases, such courts lack effective territorial jurisdiction over investment operations taking place in another country. Even if a host state were to agree to a choice of forum clause pointing to the courts of the investor's home state or of a third state, sovereign immunity or other contravening judicial doctrines typically render such proceedings moot.[59]

Furthermore, even if diplomatic protection is available, it can only be brought to bear after the exhaustion of the possible local remedies, which is precisely where all of the earlier problems are encountered.

Given the earlier considerations, direct arbitration between the host state and the foreign investor provides one potentially attractive alternative. Arbitration is usually both less costly and more efficient than litigation in domestic courts.[60] It furthermore offers the parties the vital opportunity to select arbitrators who are more neutral and reliable, and who have the oftentimes crucially necessary expertise in the field. Thus, the advantage for the investor is obvious: direct access to an effective international forum is available, should a dispute arise.[61] The possibility of going to arbitration is an important element of building confidence in the legal security required for a sound investment decision.[62] The advantage for the host state is twofold. First, the investment climate is improved and so does the likelihood of attracting additional international investment funds. In addition, by consenting to an investor-state arbitration, the host state in fact is able to protect itself against other forums for foreign or international litigation.[63] Finally, the host state also is able to effectively shield itself against the problem of diplomatic protection extended by the home state of the investor in question.[64]

[57] See UNCTAD, Overview–Course on Dispute Settlement, ICSID, UNCTAD/EDM/Misc.232, p 7.

[58] See ibid.

[59] See ibid.

[60] Ibid.

[61] Ibid at 12.

[62] Ibid.

[63] See ibid. See Article 26 of the ICSID Convention; Article 1121 of NAFTA.

[64] See ibid. See Article 27 of the ICSID Convention; Article 1121 of NAFTA.

Overall, one of the biggest benefits of the ISDS system is that it brings a much needed 'depoliticization' of investment disputes between parties to the treaty at issue. Equating the private investment interests with those of the entire nation could ultimately lead to tensions that threaten the peace in the modern world. The ISDS prevents this threat by substituting direct claims by individuals for the mechanism of diplomatic protection; it reduces unnecessary diplomatic friction in the area of investment between disputant countries by broadening the legal context into a wider arena of global economic interest, not merely the particular two national entities involved in a given case.

After all, legal obligations that exist but cannot be fully enforced are rather like ghosts that may be seen in the code of the law but are elusive to the grasp and hence for practical purposes exert little power. It is of fundamental importance that the substantive rules of investment treaties do not fade into this sort of ghostly apparition. If they were to do so, their entire purpose would have been lost and confidence would erode, defeating the very impetus which gave rise to the treaty negotiation in the first place. Fully efficient and enforceable investment dispute settlement rules under the ISDS system will promote investments to the greatest extent, while upgrading the investment environment between the signatory parties to a globalized standard, a stated major goal of both the investment treaties and FTAs. Notwithstanding this basic necessity of ISDS system, there arise several practical problems, particularly, in regard to the matter of proceedings of ISDS.

B. Proceedings

The US model BIT and the investment sections of many US FTAs offer a menu of alternatives, including (i) arbitration under the ICSID Convention if both the host state and the investor's home state are parties to the Convention; (ii) arbitration under the ICSID Additional Facility Rules if either the host state or the investor's home state are parties to the Convention; (iii) arbitration under the UNCITRAL Arbitration Rules; or (iv) arbitration under any other rules to which both the investor and the host state agree.[65]

According to the ICSID Convention, the host state (a contracting state) or the investor (of a contracting state) may initiate ISDS proceedings.[66] Under the BITs and investment sections of FTAs, however, only an investor (either national or an enterprise of a contracting state) may bring claim against the other state.[67] This investor must not be a national of the

[65] See Article 24(3) of 2004 US Model BIT, above n 43. See also Article 1120 of NAFTA.
[66] Article 36.1, ICSID Convention.
[67] See e.g. Articles 1116 and 1117, NAFTA and Article VII.3, BIT between the US and Cameroon, http://tcc.export.gov/Trade_Agreements/Bilateral_Investment_Treaties/index.asp.

host state.[68] However, if a foreign investor operates through a company that is registered in the host state, it is possible for the investor and the host state to agree that the company will be treated as a foreign investor because of the foreign control of the business entity.[69] By the same token, NAFTA prescribes that an investor 'on behalf of an enterprise of another party that is a juridical person that the investor owns or controls directly or indirectly' may submit to arbitration.[70]

Participation in the ICSID Convention does not, by itself, constitute a submission to the ICSID Centre's jurisdiction. For jurisdiction to exist, the Convention requires separate consent in writing by both parties.[71] In BITs and FTAs, such consent by contracting states is made upon the coming into force of the agreements.[72] This is tantamount to the WTO's compulsory jurisdiction system, according to which accession to the WTO brings automatic jurisdiction of the WTO dispute settlement procedure as a part of the package.[73] Given that it is precisely the lack of such compulsory jurisdiction which has resulted in the small number of cases brought under the ICJ and enforcement mechanisms of human rights conventions, the automatic consent clause in the BITs and FTAs is noteworthy and likely to be of significant impact.

Therefore, what is needed after the formal agreement on BITs or FTAs is the taking of action by the investor who makes claim. In giving its own consent to such action, the investor must 'waive its right to initiate or continue before any administrative tribunal or court under the law of any Party, or other dispute settlement procedures'.[74] In other words, such consent is 'deemed consent to such arbitration to the exclusion of any other remedy'.[75] This means that BITs and FTAs do not require the exhaustion of local remedies before the making of the ISDS claim.[76] As in GATT/WTO dispute settlement proceedings, the removal of the requirement for exhausting local remedies does greatly facilitate the establishment of an investment dispute resolution process, which in turn builds investor confidence and thus contributes to faster and greater investment flow.

The proceedings under the ICSID Convention are independently self-contained. This means that they are free of the intervention of any

[68] Article 25(2)(a) of the ICSID Convention; Article 1117.4 of NAFTA ('An investment may not make a claim under this section.').
[69] Article 25(2)(b) of the ICSID Convention.
[70] Article 1117 of NAFTA.
[71] Article 25(a) of the ICSID Convention.
[72] Article VI.4 of BIT between the US and Ukraine, http://tcc.export.gov/Trade_Agreements/Bilateral_Investment_Treaties/index.asp; Article 1122.1 of NAFTA.
[73] Article XXIII of GATT and Understanding on Rules and Procedures Governing the Settlement of Disputes (DSU).
[74] Article 1121.1 of NAFTA.
[75] Article 26 of the ICSID Convention.
[76] In comparison, in arbitration under ICSID Convention a contracting state 'may require' the exhaustion as a condition of its consent to arbitration. Article 26 of the ICSID Convention.

outside bodies.[77] In particular, domestic courts have no power to stay, to compel or to otherwise influence ICSID proceedings.[78] Domestic courts have the power to order provisional measures only in the unlikely case that the disputant parties agree to such action.[79] An ICSID tribunal is also able to obtain evidence by its own direct investigation as well as through expert reports. An *ad hoc* Committee may annul ICSID tribunals' award determinations if (i) the tribunal was found to have not been properly constituted, (ii) it manifestly exceeded its powers, (iii) there was evidence of corruption or serious departure from fundamental rules of procedure, or (iv) the award inadequately states the rationale for its determination.[80] Furthermore, the ISDS provides a system essentially impervious to any attempt at frustration of the proceedings by a recalcitrant party. Arbitrators not appointed by the parties are appointed by the Centre.[81] The decision on whether there is jurisdiction in a particular case is with the tribunal.[82] Non-submission of memorials or non-appearance at hearings by a party does not delay the proceedings.[83] All of these procedural rules guard against efforts to prolong or interfere with litigation by a recalcitrant participant in the proceedings. Such rules thus facilitate an effective dispute resolution process and increase the confidence of those who would agree to submit to such procedures.

Given the complex nature of a claim that can be initiated by a private person against a sovereign state, the possibilities of an abuse of the system or frivolous claims are always of concern. There are procedural rules that prevent abuses of ISDS claims. First, the disputing parties must first attempt to settle any claim through consultation or negotiation.[84] Note that in BITs and FTAs, a claim may be generally made only after six months have elapsed since the events giving rise to a claim.[85] This means that at least a six month period for consultation and/or negotiation is guaranteed. Second, the disputing investor must deliver written notice of intention to submit a claim to arbitration at least ninety days before the claim is submitted.[86] This prior notification will give the defending state some degree of predictability

[77] See above n 57, at 17–18.

[78] Ibid.

[79] See Article 47 of the ICSID Convention (A tribunal has the power to recommend provisional measure.) See also Article 1121.1 of NAFTA (the investor is not required to waive his right to initiate or continue 'proceedings for injunctive, declaratory or other extraordinary relief, not involving the payment of damages …').

[80] Article 52(1) of the ICSID Convention.

[81] Article 38 of the ICSID Convention; Article 1124.2 of NAFTA; Article VII.2 of BIT between US and Ulraine, at http://tcc.export.gov/Trade_Agreements/Bilateral_Investment_Treaties/index.asp.

[82] Article 41 of the ICSID Convention.

[83] Article 45 of the ICSID Convention.

[84] Article 1118 of NAFTA; Art. VI.2 of US–Ukraine BIT, above n 81.

[85] Article 1120.1 of NAFTA; Art. VI.3 of US–Ukraine BIT, above n 81.

[86] Article 1119 of NAFTA.

and time to prepare for the defence. Third, there exists a certain period of statute of limitation. In NAFTA, an investor may not bring an ISDS claim if more than three years have elapsed from the date of the alleged breach or damage.[87] Therefore, investors may not take action on a long-standing grudge against a host state by acting 'from the closet', so to speak. Claims are required to be brought with 'good faith' and very importantly, a transparency that allows the claim to be considered on its formal merits. Fourth, an investment company that is registered in the host state, by itself, may not make an ISDS claim.[88] Fifth, once ISDS proceedings have started, they must proceed to the exclusion of any other remedies, again, upping the ante for participants to only bring claims for which they authentically want an actual adjudication. No 'forum shopping' between domestic courts and arbitration proceedings is permitted to the complaining investor.

Under these procedural rules, ISDS cases continue to grow unabated, with virtually none of them initiated by governments.[89] If the cases that were settled or undisclosed and other cases where a party signalled its intention to submit a claim are included, the total number of these treaty-based investment arbitrations is impossible to measure.

Although this dramatic growth of ISDS cases by itself does not necessarily signal the frequency of frivolous claims, it has given rise to concerns about

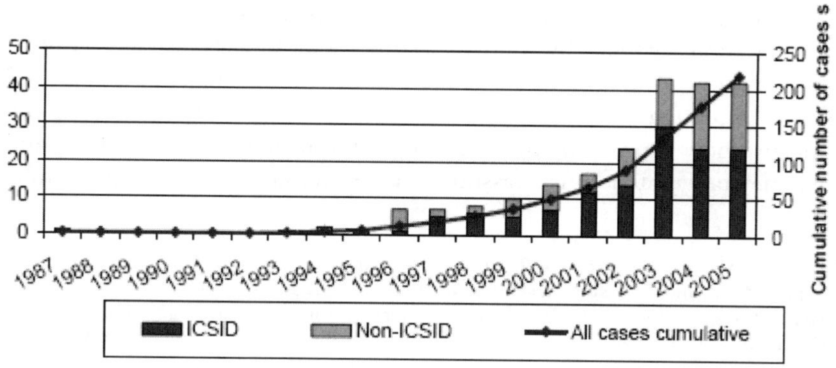

Figure 1. Known investment treaty arbitrations (cumulative and newly instituted cases, by year). *Source: UNCTAD.*[90]

[87] Article 1116.2 of NAFTA.

[88] See above notes 68/69.

[89] The cumulative number of known treaty-based cases is 219 by November 2005. 132 of them have been brought before the ICSID. Almost two-thirds (69%) of the 219 known claims were filed since the beginning of 2002. See UNCTAD, Latest Developments in Investor-State Dispute Settlement (UNCTAD/WEB/ITE/IIT/2005/2), at 1, http://www.unctad.org/en/docs// webiteiit20052_en.pdf. Under US FTAs, only investors may generally make ISDS claims, whereas arbitration cases submitted under the ICSID Convention may be initiated by 'any Contracting State or any national of a Contracting State'. See Article 36, ICSID Convention.

[90] See UNCTAD, above n 89.

such claims. In several instances, there have been a multitude of claims lodged in relation to a single investment or against a particular government action.[91] In the Argentine emergency measure cases, a series of financial emergency actions taken by Argentina gave occasion to claims from several dozen companies,[92] and in a beef case against the United States, more than 100 individual claimants in the beef industry have brought claims with regard to the same facts.[93] This phenomenon triggered several reactions on part of governments. For example, the United States—Uruguay BIT provides for a special state-state binding arbitration procedure[94] available at an early stage of the dispute settlement process aimed at preventing frivolous claims or seeking interim injunctive relief. In addition, the treaty provides that certain public policy measures including a 'negotiated restructuring of a debt instrument issued by Uruguay' are not subject to ISDS.[95] In the recently concluded US–Korea FTA negotiation, a special provision was inserted to exclude 'real estate price stabilization' policy measures from the scope of ISDS[96] on top of the exclusion of 'health, safety, and environment' policy measures.[97]

Certainly, this new trend of carving out specific public policy fields from ISDS's jurisdiction will give a solution to the frivolous claim problem in the designated fields, while maintaining a balance between the purpose of protecting investment and preserving legitimate public policies.

It has long been considered to be a serious drawback that views or recommendations issued by human rights bodies such as the Human Rights Committee lack binding effects and enforcement power.[98] ICJ decisions, although binding on the parties to the specific dispute, are mostly not supported by adequate enforcement mechanisms, and hence inevitably tend to assume a symbolic rather than fully

[91] Ibid, at 3.

[92] See e.g. *CMS Gas v The Argentine Republic* (more than 30 investors challenging a series of *de facto* peso devaluation measures taken by Argentina to halt an economic crisis).

[93] *Canadian Cattlemen for Fair Trade v the United States* (complaint filed on 12 August 2004 in NAFTA ISDS) (Canadian cattle producers challenging the US ban on imports of Canadian live cattle following the discovery of a BSE-infected cow from an Alberta herd).

[94] See Article 37, section C, Treaty between the United States of America and The Oriental Republic of Uruguay Concerning the Encouragement and Reciprocal Protection of Investment, http://www.ustr.gov/assets/Trade_Agreements/BIT/Uruguay/asset_upload_file748_9005.pdf.

[95] Ibid Annex G.

[96] See Annex 11-B, Negotiation Text of Free Trade Agreement between the Republic of Korea and the United States of America, http://www.mofat.go.kr/mofat/fta/eng/eng_list.htm.

[97] According to most US FTAs signed since 2002, public welfare policy measures to protect 'health, safety, and environment' are not subject to ISDS. See Annex 10-D, US-Chile FTA; Exchange of Letters on Expropriation, US–Singapore FTA; Annex 10-B, US–Morocco FTA; Annex 10-B, US–Peru FTA; Annex 10-C, US-CAFTA-DR FTA; Negotiation Text of Free Trade Agreement between the Republic of Korea and the United States of America, at http://www.ustr.gov/Trade_Agreements/Bilateral.

[98] See Article 5.4 of the Optional Protocol to the International Covenant on Civil and Political Rights: there is stated no binding enforcement mechanism.

enforceable authority.[99] In comparison, ISDS arbitral awards are ultimately binding, and non compliance with an award by a state would result in a breach of the ICSID Convention and culminate in a reversion to the right of diplomatic protection by the investor's state of home nationality.[100] The Convention thus provides a singularly effective system of enforcement: awards are recognized as final in all state parties to the Convention, and the pecuniary obligations arising from such awards are to be enforced in the same manner as final judgments of the local courts in all state parties to the Convention.[101] Domestic courts have no power to review ICSID awards in the course of their enforcement. However, in the case of an award against a state the normal rules of immunity from execution will apply; in actual practice this will usually mean that execution of an award is not possible against assets that serve the public function of a state.[102]

ISDS awards are not subject to further review except under certain highly constrained conditions provided by the ICSID Convention itself.[103] Although this finality has generally been seen as an advantage over judicial settlement—for the savings it brings in costs and time – it may sometimes come at the risk of having to live with flawed or inconsistent awards on the same or very similar questions or facts. Some discussions on the possible introduction of an appeal system for investment disputes have been undergone,[104] and as a result, a provision requiring parties to consider the issue of establishing an appellate body was inserted in recently concluded US FTAs and the 2004 US Model BIT.[105]

Given this trend, an appeal mechanism under the ISDS system is likely to appear in the near future. Future decisions by the parties to such agreements to establish an appellate body would mean in practice the creation of an

[99] Article 94 of the UN Charter (recourse to the Security Council is only available option in noncompliance situations).

[100] See Article 27 of the ICSID Convention. In case of FTAs, such non-compliance is subject to a state-to-state dispute settlement procedure under FTAs. See e.g. Article 1136.5 of NAFTA.

[101] Article 54 of the ICSID Convention; Article 1136 of NAFTA.

[102] See Article 55 of the ICSID Convention.

[103] See Articles 49–53 of the ICSID Convention. Article 1136 of NAFTA.

[104] See e.g. E. Lauterpacht 'Aspects of the Administration of International Justice' 1991; S. Schwebel 'The Creation and Operation of an International Court of Arbitral Awards', in Hunter, M. Mariott and A., Veeder, V.V. (eds) *The Internationalisation of International Arbitration*, 115 (London: Martinus Nijhoff Publishers, 1995). For debates in MAI negotiations, see 'Selected Issues on Dispute Settlement'(Note by the Chairman) DAFFE/MAI(98)12, 13 March 1998.

[105] See Annex 10-H, US–Chile FTA; Letter exchange, US Trade Representative R. Zoellick to Singapore Minister of Trade and Industry G. Yeo on 6 May 2003, US–Singapore FTA; Annex 10-D, US–Morocco FTA. See also Annex D, 2004 US Model BIT, above n 41. ('Within three years after the date of entry into force of this Agreement, the Parties shall consider whether to establish a bilateral appellate body or similar mechanism to review awards rendered under Article . . . in arbitrations commenced after they establish the appellate body or similar mechanism'.). More recently, the US-CAFTA-DR FTA sets out a specific schedule for establishing a negotiating group to develop an appellate body. See Annex 10-F, US-CAFTA-DR FTA.

ad hoc appeal tribunal under each treaty. However, given a risk of fragmentation of the dispute settlement system that could ensue through *ad hoc* tribunals, a universal and standing body specialized in appellate investigations—as is the case of WTO Appellate Body—should be established. In this regard, ideas on the creation of an optional ICSID Appeals Facility established and operated under a set of Appeals Facility Rules deserve exploration.[106] Introduction of such appellate mechanism will increase global support for the ISDS system at a time of growing number of cases. Coherent investment decisions rendered through its screening process will increase predictability under, and enhance legitimacy of, the ISDS system. Increased possibility of rectification of legal errors by the process is important because it can allay public concerns that otherwise arbitral awards, affecting important public policy issues, could be enforced despite serious errors.

Given that the WTO Appellate Body has created a sound jurisprudence having precedential value in a relatively short period of time, introduction of an appeal mechanism into ISDS is recommendable in order to foster a more consistent and rigorous application of international law in arbitral awards. The potential problem of additional delays and costs could be limited by setting specific time limits in the appellate process as in the case of WTO appellate process.[107]

C. Remedial actions

First, the general principles of possible remedies need to be mentioned. According to a general principle of international law, the breach of an obligation entails the responsibility of the defaulting state, and should give rise to remedial options for the injured state. The traditional means used for diplomatic protection could take the form of 'consular action, negotiation, mediation, judicial and arbitral proceedings, reprisals, retorsion, severance of diplomatic relations, economic pressure and, as a final resort, the use of force'.[108] This means that an ultimate remedy may take the form of an exercise of purely retaliatory force against the defaulting state. However, the use of force as a retaliatory means is generally prohibited under the current United Nation system.[109] In this light, the Draft Articles on Responsibility of States for Internationally Wrongful Acts states that countermeasures against a state which is responsible for an internationally wrongful act are limited to

[106] For detailed discussions in this regard, see ICSID, 'Possible Improvements of the Framework for ICSID Arbitration' (ICSID, 22 October 2004), http://www.iisd.org.

[107] Article 17 of DSU (setting a sixty day time limit from the notification of the decision to appeal with a possibility of extension to ninety days).

[108] See International Law Commission, First Report on Diplomatic Protection, 15, UN Doc. A/CN.4/506 (2000) (prepared by John R. Dugard). But see Draft Articles, above n 2 (limiting diplomatic protection to means of 'peaceful settlement').

[109] See Articles 2.3 and 2.4, Charter of the United Nations.

the non-performance, for the time being, of the usual international obligations.[110]

Remedies recognized under the Draft Articles include the cessation of illegal acts, restitution in kind, reparation by equivalent means, satisfaction and guarantees of non-repetition. First of all, the state responsible for the internationally wrongful act is under an obligation to promptly cease that action and to offer appropriately assurances and guarantees of non-repetition if circumstances so require.[111] Full reparation for the injury caused by the wrongful act is also required under the Draft Articles. Such reparation is, if possible, 'restitution, that is, to re-establish the situation which existed before the wrongful act was committed'.[112] 'Insofar as such injury is not made good by restitution', the responsible state must 'compensate for the damage caused thereby'.[113] The compensation must cover any financially assessable damage, including loss of profits, insofar as such damage may be clearly established.[114] Interest on any principal sum of compensation due must also be paid as needed in order to ensure full reparation over time.[115]

If the injury cannot be made good by restitution or compensation, satisfaction for the injury must be given in the form of 'an acknowledgement of the breach, an expression of regret, a formal apology or another appropriate modality'.[116]

Basically these remedies, which come under the general principles of international law, have a retroactive (re-establishment of past situation and/or compensation for the damage caused) as well as prospective (cessation of illegal acts and guarantees of non-repetition) nature.

The remedies described in GATT/WTO are strictly prospective. In GATT/WTO dispute settlement proceedings, the claimant states have regularly requested only withdrawal of the illegal act without demanding reestablishment of the *status quo ante* or of the situation that would have existed in the absence of the illegal act. This practice is currently codified in DSU as follows:

> 'The first objective of the dispute settlement mechanism is usually to secure the withdrawal of the measures concerned if these are found to be inconsistent with the provisions of any of the covered agreements.[117] The provision of compensation should be resorted to only if the immediate withdrawal of the measure is impracticable and as a temporary measure

[110] Article 49, Draft Articles on Responsibility of States for Internationally Wrongful Acts, Report of the ILC on the Work of its Fifty-third Session, UN GAOR, 56th Session, Supp No 10, p 43, UN Doc A/56/10 (2001).
[111] Ibid, Article 30.
[112] Ibid, Article 35.
[113] Ibid, Article 36.
[114] Ibid.
[115] Ibid, Article 38.
[116] Ibid, Article 37.
[117] Article 3.7 of DSU.

> pending the withdrawal of the measure ...[118]. Compensation and the suspension of concessions or other obligations are temporary measures available in the event that the recommendations and rulings are not implemented within a reasonable period of time'.[119]

Under the WTO system, any compensation or retaliation can thus only be taken to induce future compliance.

The reason for this prospective remedy is that GATT/WTO rules prescribe minimum standards for the non-discriminatory treatment of traded goods and, in GATT jurisprudence, are construed to protect 'expectations on the competitive relationship between imported and domestic products' rather than 'expectations on export volumes'.[120] Moreover, it is often impossible to recreate retroactively the 'lost trade opportunities' or to calculate, and make good for, 'lost trade volumes'.[121] Even the reimbursement of illegal customs duties or illegal internal taxes has never been requested in GATT dispute settlement practice since, *inter alia*, their repayment to individual importers would not re-establish the competitive conditions to which exporting countries had been entitled in the past under GATT law.[122] Therefore, it is no wonder that the WTO Agreement turns a well-known deaf ear to requests for retroactive remedies.

In contrast, the ISDS mechanism is based on the retroactive remedy rule. For example, NAFTA stipulates that arbitral tribunals may award only 'monetary damages and any applicable interest', 'restitution of property', and/or 'costs'.[123] If restitution is awarded, 'the disputing party may pay monetary damages and any applicable interest in lieu of restitution'.[124] Such retroactive remedies in the ISDS system are indispensable because the primary purpose of investment rules is to give an ex post reparation of damage illegally inflicted upon a private investor.

However, retroactive remedies alone are not sufficient. It must be noted that many investment rules, including provisions on national treatment, most-favoured-nation treatment, and minimum standard of protection, also play a role in protecting 'expectations on the competitive relationship'

[118] Ibid.

[119] Ibid, Article 22.1.

[120] See e.g. *US Taxes on Petroleum and Certain Imported Substances*, Panel Report adopted on 17 June, 1987, in BISD 34 S/136, at 158. See also Ernst-Ulrich Petersmann, 'International Trade Law and the GATT/WTO Dispute Settlement System 1948-1996: An Introduction', in Ernst-Ulrich Petersmann (ed), *International Trade Law and the GATT/WTO Dispute Settlement System* (London: Kluwer Law International, 1997), at 42.

[121] See Petersmann, ibid.

[122] Ibid. However, in the field of antidumping and countervailing duty law several panel reports have recommended not only the revocation of illegal antidumping or countervailing duties but also their reimbursement, including *New Zealand's Anti-dumping Duties on Imports of Electrical Transformers from Finland* (BISD 32S/55, July 1985), and *US Anti-dumping Duties on Cement Clinker from Mexico* (BISD 39 S/391 and GATT document ADP/82). See ibid.

[123] Article 1135 of NAFTA.

[124] Ibid.

Table 1. Comparisons among various International Dispute Settlement Mechanisms

	Traditional treaties	GATT/WTO	Human rights conventions (modern)	BITs/MAI/FTAs (modern)
State-to-state	O	O	O	O
Exhaustion of local remedies	O	X	O	X
Direct claim	X	X	O	O
Remedies	Restitution/ Compensation/ Satisfaction	Withdrawal	Withdrawal Commitment to no similar future violations	Monetary damages

O = existent; X = absent.

between investors. Although one particular investor's interest is usually at issue, an arbitral panel's award is keenly watched by many current or potential investors. In this light, prospective remedies announced by an arbitral panel can greatly contribute to bringing about both stabilization and predictability in shaping future investment decisions. In this sense, the cessation of illegal acts and guarantees of non-repetition in addition to any retroactive damage awards may be effectively introduced into the ISDS remedy system.

In this light, the remedies prescribed in human rights conventions are noteworthy. They are mostly retroactive as well as less frequently prospective. For instance, in *Lee Eun-Jeong v Korea*, the Human Rights Committee issued a view recommending appropriate compensation and amendment of the law in violation of the Covenant.[125] In addition, it determined the state party to be under an obligation to ensure that similar violations not be allowed to occur in the future.[126] In *Shin Hak-Chul v Korea*, declaring that Korea's confiscation of a picture painted by the petitioner, as well as a criminal conviction brought against in connection to this confiscation, violated his right to freedom of expression under the Covenant, the Committee recommended that the state party should compensate him for his wrongful conviction, annul his conviction, pay for legal costs, return the painting, and avoid any and all similar violations in the future.[127] These combined remedies will not only compensate for past damage, but also affect the future of human rights protection.

[125] Paras 9–10, Views of the Human Rights Committee under the Optional Protocol to the International Covenant on Civil and Political Rights in the case of *Lee Eun-Jeong v Korea*, Communication No. 1119/2002 (CCPR/C/84/D/1119/2002).

[126] See ibid.

[127] Paras 7–10, Views of the Human Rights Committee under the Optional Protocol to the International Covenant on Civil and Political Rights in the case of *Shin Hak-Chul v Korea*, Communication No. 926/2000 (CCPR/C/80/D/926/2000).

IV. CONCLUSIONS

While the WTO system continues to respect the traditional paradigm of state-to-state dispute resolution, the dispute resolution mechanism in the international investment area has undergone a radical change.

Parts of the strong provisions included in the investment dispute settlement procedures in current FTAs have their basis in similar BIT language developed in response to threats of discrimination and/or expropriation in the 1950s and 1960s. In the last few decades, most developing countries have moved away from hostility against foreign investment and have, unilaterally or through making treaties with developed states, begun to actively liberalize their national investment policies within international developmental parameters. Hence, the direct claim precedent of the ISDS system is becoming something of a worldwide trend in the investment field.

Furthermore, in the area of international human right law, it is becoming an increasing trend to allow an individual to have direct recourse to international human rights protection bodies after the exhaustion of domestic remedies.

The evolution of a system of direct claims makes up for the shortcomings of the traditional diplomatic protection mechanism. In particular, it overcomes the problem which is entailed by the complete discretion over the claim by the espousing state, which has frequently exercised its discretionary power on the basis of political or similar considerations, unrelated to the facts of a particular case, an exercise in power which has been shown to have the capacity to greatly exacerbate international friction.

On the other side of the ledger, diplomatic protection does have the strong point of being able to screen out frivolous or dishonest claims by individuals of bad intent. In addition, the perception still persists that direct claims through the ISDS mechanism combined with the removal of exhaustion of domestic remedy rule may eventuate in an excessive restriction of state sovereignty.[128]

[128] This perception is commonly shared by NGOs and among civil society activists, and it provided one of the major reasons of MAI failure. In February 1998, more than 600 organizations from 67 countries released a joint statement calling for the suspension of MAI negotiations until substantive and procedural concerns are met. According to the statement, the draft MAI 'elevates the rights of investors far above those of governments, local communities, citizens, workers and the environment', handcuffing their democracies. These groups called MAI 'a dagger through the heart of democracy'. See generally, Public Citizen, 'National and International Opposition to the MAI', http://www.citizen.org/trade/issues/mai/Opposition. In addition, this concern was heavily raised during NAFTA negotiations and Korea–US FTA negotiations. See e.g. Public Citizen, 'North American Free Trade Agreement (NAFTA)', at http://www.citizen.org/trade/nafta, and Korean Alliance against KorUS FTA, 'Let's Stop Importing Speculative Investment Flow by Stopping Korea-US FTA', at http://nofta.or.kr/webbs/view.php?board=nofta_24&id=88&page=4.

The question of whether various international dispute settlement mechanisms may eventually converge on a system based on direct claims is both complex and vexing. It is highly uncertain whether the model of direct claims under ISDS can play a pioneering role in efforts to develop such a process. Yet, about all that can be accurately said at this juncture is that the ISDS is indeed marching toward a new system of dispute settlement across the flawed terrain of the traditional paradigm with its base procedure of diplomatic protection, and that it meets a balancing of a variety of interests in taking account of investors' rights to protection of their assets and host states' need to ensure confident investment flow. The compulsory jurisdiction, quasi-judicial arbitral panel procedures, and large number of cases suggest that the ISDS system has potential to serve these purposes. With appropriate modifications of the system through on-going efforts to carve out legitimate public policy fields from the jurisdiction of ISDS, to establish a widely accepted appellate mechanism, and to increase consistency of decisions, the ISDS paradigm could serve quite well in many respects as a model for the improvement of dispute resolution in other worldwide organizations.

One would hope that, in the course of exerting the considerable effort required to bring about a convergence of various dispute settlement systems, the full impact of the cause and effect of the evolution of the ISDS system will be adequately assimilated, and the different perceptions on the value of direct claim procedures will be taken into account when determining how to fairly deal with each other as world citizens to attain a better outcome, meaning a more peaceful and prosperous world.

Index